i

ii

Church Planting Movements In North America

Editor,
Daniel R. Sanchez, Ph. D.

Forward by Dr. Henry Blackaby

Preface by Dr. Kenneth Hemphill

Church Starting Network
2006

CHURCH PLANTING MOVEMENTS IN NORTH AMERICA

Library of Congress Cataloging- in-Publication Data

Sanchez, Daniel R. 196—

   Church Planting Movements in North America
   Includes chapters by various authors

ISBN

1. Church Planting Movements 2. Title

Dedicated to all those who are
engaged in the exciting ministries
that seek to enhance the development of church
multiplication movements in North America

CONTENTS

Unit I.
Need for Church Planting Movements

Unit II
Theological and Historical Foundations
for Church Planting Movements

Unit III
Case Studies of Church
Planting Movements

Unit IV
Crucial Factors in Church
Planting Movements

Unit V
Contextualized Strategies for
Church Planting Movements

ix

Unit VI
Implementing Church
Planting Movements

Forward

Henry Blackaby

Being instrumental in helping to spark church planting movements in North America can be one of the most exciting, fulfilling, and significant ministries in which a servant of God can participate. I had the privilege of being in the midst of the activity of God as a pastor when He used a small church to see 38 new congregations come into being in 12 years. In one way, this came as a surprise to me as a pastor. I had not purposed to do this when I became the pastor of this church. But everything that I had read in the Scriptures, especially the New Testament and the Book of Acts alerted me to what God would be doing in and through our church family.

I knew that God "was not wiling that any should perish but that all should come to repentance..." (2 Pet. 3:9). This Truth, from the heart of God, became a guide to me as a pastor of a small struggling church of 10 people who wanted to 'disband', they were so discouraged! I was in the midst of a city of 135,000 people, and a Province in Canada of one million. Further, I was a part of a nation that had few born again believers. My heart cried out, *"How, LORD, will you be working where I am to bring all people to the knowledge of the Truth?"* I found that if you seriously ask God such a question, He will answer clearly. But when He does, He will expect an obedient response from me (us).

I had to first "see what God Himself was doing" to see that none was neglected in hearing of God's great salvation (Heb. 2:1-3). Second, I would have to alert God's people to the activity of God, and teach them from the Scriptures what this

xi

meant to us. And third, I had to be ready to "follow Christ our LORD" as He guided us to be on a mission with Him where we were, according to the scriptures.

It didn't take long, for the day I arrived to pastor this church, I found a group of men waiting in a car to talk with me, from the city of Prince Albert, 90 miles to the north of us. They simply said: "We have been wanting a church in our city for a number of years. As we have prayed God assured us that He would guide us. Then we heard that you were coming to pastor this church, and after weeks of praying, we were assured that you were to be our pastor, too, and help us become a New Testament church. So we have come to tell you what God has been doing with us, and what He is saying to us!"

I had decisions to make immediately. Since God was speaking to them, I must both listen and ask God how I was to obey Him. HE was "at work", and let me see where HE was working. He had already convicted me of what Jesus said to others: "...if anyone serve Me, let him follow Me and where I am there the servant will be also. If anyone serves Me, him the Father will honor..." (John 12:26). Now it was my turn! This would mean a second congregation. But I had never started another church before, and the church I was pastoring had never either. But God reminded me that it was not I who would be starting a new congregation, but HE. I had to decide whether I would be obedient to HIM, and let HIM build His church(es) through me (us). My answer was, "Yes, LORD!" Then is when I knew HE would show me (us) one step at a time how to obey Him, and be a part of His building churches. Little did I know that another biblical Truth also underway: if we were faithful in a little, He would give us more!

But I faced another challenge: I must teach His discouraged people about God and His faithfulness to any of His people would know Him and obey Him as their LORD. So I taught and taught this small group of people what to expect from God, and how to know it was Him. Later I put what I taught them, and how they responded, in two booklets: *What The Spirit Is Saying To The Churches*, and *Experiencing God*, both of which have been used of God as a "witness unto Him" to encourage His people in other churches to let God begin other churches through them, so that none would perish.

I did not start out to "DO a church planting movement"! I started out to be obedient to Him who was at work in us, and through us, according to a pattern of activity revealed already in the New Testament, especially the book of Acts. As I read carefully what God had eternally planned to do once His great salvation was accomplished, His pattern of activity was clear. First, I saw that Acts 1:8, was not a *"command"*, it was a Divine *"announcement"* of what God was about to do. The believers in Jerusalem needed to "follow Him" and then they saw Him doing what He had promised. However, they would have to "receive power when the Holy Spirit comes upon you" (Acts 1:8), and then "be witnesses to Me" (NOTE: not witnesses *for* Him, but as He was working, and where He was working, they were to be witnesses *unto* Him). This would be seen in Samaria, where God would be working, but where those being saved needed someone to tell them more completely about Jesus – who He was, what He had done, and the implication for their lives. This is seen is Acts 8. God was the One *"on mission"*! They were to *"join Him in His activity"*. This seems to be the witness of Acts throughout. Acts 8:4 – "...therefore those who were scattered went everywhere preaching the work..." This did not include the Apostles, for they stayed in Jerusalem (Acts

8:1). Then we read: "…then the *churches* throughout all Judea, Galilee and Samaria had peace and were edified. And walking in the fear of the LORD and in the comfort of the Holy Spirit, *they were multiplied…*" (Acts 10:30). Then, to complete the Divine "announcement" about what God would be doing, Acts 11:19 records: "…now those who were scattered after the persecution that arose over Stephen's death traveled as far as Phoenicia, Cyprus, and Antioch preaching the word…"

The 'revelation' from the Book of Acts guided us as to what we could be expecting from God to be doing where we were – in our city, our province and in our nation. And this is exactly what we experienced Him doing. We were to "follow Him, and serve "Him". And this we did, and God established churches everywhere. He led us to "grid off" the province, and to watch to see whom He would bring to our attention that He had been working with to establish a church. When God showed us where HE was working, we did join Him, and taught those people to expect God to use them also in "Taking the Gospel to every person in their area", and that God would be starting new churches all along the highways, etc. until every person had the opportunity to hear. Each new congregation heard, and did what they now knew was GOD's strategy. This eternal purpose of God through the planting of churches turned the Roman Empire upside down, and was still His eternal purpose for our cities, our nations and the world. We were given the privilege of experiencing Him at work where we were, and as obediently joined Him, we would experience a "church planting movement of God", too.

As we faced the need for "laborers" (i.e. pastor or leader for each new congregation) we again went to the scriptures and obeyed God by PRAYING, as He told His disciples in Matt.

9:35-38. God provided! We suddenly began to reach university students, who when they were saved, had an incredible burden to serve Him. We saw over 100 respond to the call into ministry/missions – and go "on mission with God to start new churches". We had financial needs, and God again led us to Scriptures: Phil. 4:19 – "...and my God shall supply all your needs according to His riches in glory by Christ Jesus..." We had to TEACH these Truths to God's people, and they received them with joy and anticipation, and were not disappointed as God met every need by His Grace.

So Acts 1-11, and other Scriptures, became our "church planting manual." It was not 'methods', but RELATIONSHIP with God! We did not write a booklet on methods, for others to use. He *was* our 'method'! It is still true that He is not willing that ANY should perish, but that all should come to repentance. And His eternal plan to do this is still in place. He is looking for those "whose hearts are loyal to him, so He can prove Himself strong on their behalf...." (2 Chron. 16:9). As we know Him, love and trust Him, see Him and obey Him – He accomplishes His eternal purposes though us. This is the witness that I share, and this is the witness of this book!

Church Planting Movements in North America is a compilation of the experiences of others who also bear witness to the God we serve and who yearn to see a mighty movement of the Spirit of God sweep across our land resulting in the establishment of thousands of churches reaching every people group and population segment. God Who is at work around every church – small and large – will be with those who are working where He is working, taking His Good News to every person. HE will begin where you are and work out from there to the ends of the earth, just like He did in the Book of Acts. It is now "our turn to be obedient and faithful!" But the people of God must be taught from the Scriptures of God and His purposes and His ways, so that when they see Him "*at work*" where they are, they can be obedient and experience Him fully. Each church will have a *unique* experience with God! He rarely does the same thing twice, so that God's people will not look to "methods," but to Him.

I commend the authors of this volume for seeking to put into one resource book, valuable information and witness concerning church planting movements. My prayer is that every serious-minded pastor or church leader would find in this work vital assistance and encouragement in their own obedience to Christ in His desire that "none should perish, but that all should come to repentance."

Preface

A Divine Encounter and a Kingdom Lesson

Kenneth Hemphill

Those who know me well are quite aware that I am always on the look out for a good coffee shop. To say that I enjoy a good cappuccino is a vast understatement. It is not just the coffee; however, I love the ambience of a good coffee shop. I was recently in Hendersonville, North Carolina. I soon discovered that there is a wonderful coffee shop in the downtown area of this lovely mountain town. The Black Bear Coffee Shop was the destination for the afternoon.

I made my pilgrimage to the coffee shop with two friends. One worked for the North Carolina state convention and the other was a young man who was considering youth ministry. As I sipped my skinny wet cappuccino at a table in the front of the shop, I noticed a large gathering of youth on the outside porch. I asked the aspiring youth pastor where he would go to reach young people in Hendersonville if he were to work in a local church. After noticing his puzzled expression, I nodded toward the crowd on the front porch. I then quite sagely suggested that he should spend the afternoons there among the youth. I was quite pleased with myself for dispensing such critical kingdom information.

As I gazed around the coffee shop, I appreciated the collection of local water color painting. I actually enjoy collecting original art by unknown local artists. It was then that

I noticed the comfortable looking overstuffed furniture in the rear of the shop. Sitting on the sofa was a middle-aged guy with the longest teased dreadlocks that I had ever seen. These dreads didn't stream down his head like those of Ricky Williams; they careened and pointed at every direction on the compass. He was a large man dressed in cut off jeans and Birkenstocks. Beside him sat a somewhat younger man with hair cascading across his shoulders.

I made a quick and cursory assessment and concluded that they were left over hippies who didn't know Woodstock was over. I nearly glanced outside to see if their ancient Volkswagen bus with flower power symbols was parked near by. I know now that I shouldn't have, but I made quick value judgments about this pair by "looking at the cover."

My wandering thoughts were disrupted when the guy with the "dreads" got up and ambled out of the room. It was at this point that I noticed that this guy was big and the teased dreads made him seem rather daunting. For some reason unknown to me, I chose this moment to amble about the coffee shop to look at the paintings. When I arrived in the section where the gentleman had just vacated, I looked down and noticed to my utter surprise an open, well-worn, underlined Bible. It was at this point that the Holy Spirit began my kingdom lesson for the day.

I looked at the young man still remaining on the couch and noticed that he too had his Bible open. I paused to ask him if he knew the author of the book. With tenderness he replied that indeed he did. Then to my utter surprise he told me that the gentleman who had just left the shop was his pastor. They met in the coffee shop weekly so that the pastor could mentor this young man. I explained to the young man what I did for a living and that I was in the area to speak on the kingdom at Fruitland, a local Bible college.

If I had any illusion that the Holy Spirit had finished His kingdom lesson for the day, it was quickly dissipated. At this point that Mr. Dreads came back into the room. The young disciple excitedly introduced me to the pastor of his house church. Without pausing the pastor embraced me like a long lost brother. I am sure we must have created quite a scene.

We discussed several issues in the next minutes including the nature of love which comes instinctively from the heart when we accept Christ. He then explained how God had given him a love for his parishioners, most of who had dropped out of the new age movement so prominent in Asheville. He acknowledged that many of them had a colorful past but that God had given him a love for them. The Holy Spirit kept nudging me about my judgmental attitude and lack of love or concern for those who are so different from me on the surface. But the lesson wasn't over yet.

My new found pastor friend looked at me and tenderly stated, "Dr. Hemphill, most of us went to your church first and you didn't want us." I knew, in an instant that he was correct. If he had walked into many of our churches and taken a seat, he would not only have raised eyebrows, he would have prompted folks to shuffle seats and ensure that their children were well-protected from such strange looking folks. I stood convicted.

Then with absolute kindness he said, "That's okay. We understand that we look a little different. All we're asking is that you pull for us Dr. Hemphill." I was profoundly impacted by his simple plea. I decided then and there that I would not waste another breath debating styles and methodologies. I am not going to argue about cells or Sunday school, contemporary or traditional worship, I am going to pull for anyone who doesn't compromise the truth of God's word and is committed to reaching people with the gospel. For us to be a kingdom people and reach the world it will take a variety of styles of church.

This tale is not quite finished. Soon after this kingdom encounter, I had the privilege of speaking to a group of pastors in Tennessee. I told the story of my coffee house encounter and then I noted that if this gentleman had come to their area to plant a church designed to reach the new-age drop outs his greatest critics would probably be some of us in this very room. Heads were bowed in agreement. I indicated that we need to repent of this attitude and begin to pull for each other. I then noted that if we didn't care who got the credit, we could accomplish a great deal for the kingdom. I thought revival was going to break out in the room as there was a hearty chorus of "amens."

If we are going to be a kingdom people we are going to have to pull for each other and work together. We must be of one mind in the essentials of the faith, but we must allow for diversity in our quest to reach every tribe, tongue, and nation. In the coffee shop I discovered an important truth. Rev. "Dread" (my nickname for my new friend) was reaching a distinct people group we had overlooked.

Overview of this Book

Church Planting Movements in North America investigates the possibility that such movements not only *can* happen in North America but actually *are being experienced.* These authors share insights and experiences about these church-type groups that are participating in efforts that are reaching the plane of church multiplication. The book divides into five units.

Unit I
Need for Church Planting Movements

Chapter 1   **Mike Steele**

Church Planting Movements
in North America

Mike Steele reports on movements happening in many countries and describes emerging church planting movements in North America. Mike Steele is the Director of the North American division of Disciple A Whole Nation (DAWN), the Spontaneously Multiplying Simple/Organic Church Planting Movements in North America. His extensive opportunity to observe church planting movements and his leadership for the initiation of simple church networks in North America makes his contribution important.

Chapter 2   **Daniel R. Sanchez**

Crucial Issues in North American
Church Planting Movements

Dr. Daniel R. Sanchez focuses on crucial issues that we must address if we are to experience church planting movements in North America. Sanchez served as a missionary in Central America, an Associate Director at the Home Mission Board, as Director of Missions for the Baptist Convention of New York., and for the last twenty years, as professor for church planting classes at Southwestern Baptist Theological Seminary. As Director of the Scarborough Institute for Church Planting and Growth, he has conducted church planting seminars in many states and in numerous countries. His passion is learning what God is doing through church planting movements throughout the world and a yearning to see this happen in North America.

Unit II

Theological and Historical Foundations for Church Planting Movements

Chapter 3   **Dan Morgan and Mike Barnett**

Biblical and Historical Foundations for Church Planting Movements

Drs, Dan Morgan and Mike Barnett investigate the biblical and historical foundations for church planting movements. Dr. Morgan currently serves as the Nehemiah professor of the North American Mission Board assigned to Southwestern Baptist Theological Seminary. He has had extensive experience as a church planter, as a church planter strategist, and as a professor focusing on church planting models.

Dr. Mike Barnett and his wife Cindy served twelve years with the International Mission Board of the Southern Baptist Convention working in the 10/40 Window. His business background allows him to work in international business development. Formerly at Southwestern Theological Seminary in Fort Worth, Texas, he currently teaches from the Elmer V. Thompson Chair of Missionary Church Planting at Columbia Bible Seminary and School of Missions, Columbia, South Carolina.

Chapter 4   **Brent Ray**

A Theological Foundation for Church Planting Movements

Dr. Brent Ray outlines the basic theology that under girds movements that lead to church multiplication. Dr. Ray is Executive Director of Hope for the Heart Ministries. He served as a missionary and later as an Associate to the Regional Leader in the Republic of Brazil. His missionary experience includes leading in evangelistic efforts, training the laity, teaching in seminaries, and assisting in the development of contextualized strategies on the mission field. He holds a B.A. degree from Baylor University, the Masters of Divinity degree and a Doctor of Ministry Degree from Southwestern Baptist Theological Seminary.

Unit III
Case Studies of Church Planting Movements

In this unit, the authors present case studies from a variety of settings in other countries as well as in North America. While North America is the focus of this book, there is much that we can learn from what the Lord is doing in other parts of the world. These case studies share the principles and practices that have contributed to their growth. Some of these case studies are full-blown while others are in their initial stages.

Chapter 5   Bill Fudge

The Fastest Growing Church Planting Movements to Date

Dr. Bill Fudge served for many years as a missionary in South Korea where he mastered the language as well as the culture of that country. For the past four years, Fudge has been a Regional Leader in East Asia. He presents a case study of the most rapidly multiplying church planting movement currently taking place anywhere in the world.

Chapter 6   Neil Cole

Organic Churches and Church Planting Movements

Neil Cole is the Executive Director for Church Multiplication Associates and the founding leader of Awakening Chapels. He is the author of *Cultivating a Life for God: Multiplying Disciples Through Life-Transformation Groups* and co-author of *Raising Leaders for the Harvest*. Along with Paul Kaak, he has produced the training manual entitled *Organic Church Planter's Greenhouse*. He has also contributed articles to *House 2 House Magazine*.

Chapter 7   Harold Bullock

From Cell-Based Churches to
Church Planting Movements

Harold Bullock serves as the senior pastor of Hope Community Church in Fort Worth Texas. Having planted one of the pioneer cell-based churches in Southern Baptist life, Bullock shares valuable insights he has learned. For many years his congregation was not considered "a church" because it did not own a building, use traditional methods for discipleship, or have a traditional church staff. Much of what he has learned can be applied to current church planting movement efforts. In addition to reaching many people for Christ, this church has been instrumental in starting more than 80 churches in the United States and Abroad. Pastor Bullock is the author of *Sharper Strokes – Living Smarter Not Harder* and *The Battle For The Worlds.*

Chapter 8   Ebbie C. Smith

GlocalNet and NorthWood Church:
A Church Planting Movement

During his studies at Fuller Theological Seminary, Dr. Ebbie Smith became a disciple of Dr. Donald Mc Gavran. His knowledge of the modern Church Growth Movement as well as his personal experience in teaching church starting and supervising students in this task give Dr. Smith an excellent vantage point from which to analyze and write about this growing Church that has been instrumental in starting many congregations in the United States and in other nations. As a part of his 15 years of service in Indonesia, Smith led an evangelistic and church starting ministry with seminary students that eventuated in over 30 churches. Smith has written *Balanced Church Growth: Church Growth on the Model of Servanthood; Healthy Church Growth: New Directions for Church Growth in the 21st Century; Spiritual Warfare for 21st Century Christians;* and others. He was one of the editors and contributors to *Missiology: An Introduction to the Foundations, History, and Strategies of World Missions.*

Unit IV
Crucial Factors in Church Planting Movements

The authors analyze and discuss vital issues that either contribute to the exponential growth of church planting movements or hinder their progress. Among the crucial factors are those related to oral learners, ethnolinguistic dimensions of church planting movements, means of assessing church planting movements, and some imperative changes that are needed for the development of church planting movements.

Chapter 9   **Jim Slack**

*Church Planting Movements
among Oral Learners*

Dr. Jim Slack is Research Director with the International Mission Board. In addition to the numerous strategies that he has researched, he focused on the concept of Chronological Bible Storying in connection with his Doctor of Ministry Professional Project. Along with Dr. Grant Lovejoy, Dr. Jim Slack has conducted workshops in many seminaries in North America as well as in many countries. This strategy opens the door for the communication of the Gospel to vast pockets of population in North America as well as throughout the world.

Chapter 10   **Daniel R. Sanchez**

*Ethnolinguistic Dimensions of
Church Planting Movements*

The fact that Dr. Daniel Sanchez grew up in a bi-cultural, bi-lingual environment along with his extensive study in the area of cultural anthropology give him a rich background from which to write on subject. His concern is that often very sincere and dedicated people make serious mistakes in their church planting strategies because they are not aware of the ethnolinguistic dimensions of the church planting task. In this chapter he offers principles as well as practical tools for effective intercultural church planting.

Chapter 11   Jim Slack

Constructing Worldviews for Church Planting Movements

From the time that Dr. Jim Slack served as a missionary in the Philippines he has worked with distinguished anthropologists in the development of processes and instruments that assist Christian workers in the task of constructing worldviews the people groups they want to reach with the gospel. This chapter provides valuable insights on how to accomplish this task. Appendix Eight contains a practical description of the process and a valuable instrument for constructing a worldview.

Chapter 12   Jim Slack

Assessment of Church Planting Movements

Dr. Jim Slack, Research Specialist for the International Mission Board and co-author of *To The Edge: Planning Process for People Group Specific Strategy Development*, has conducted assessments of church planting movements in many different parts of the world. The criteria that he has developed and field tested provide an excellent tool to ascertain if a church planting movement is taking place and what the strengths and weaknesses might be.

Chapter 13   J. D. Payne

Suggested Shifts for Church Planting Movements

Dr. J.D. Payne is Assistant Professor of Church Planting and Evangelism in the Billy Graham School of Missions, Evangelism and Church Growth and Director of the Church Planting Center at The Southern Baptist Theological Seminary in Louisville, Kentucky. Dr. Payne has earned degrees at the University of Kentucky (B.A. Sociology, Southern Seminary (M.Div. Missions, Evangelism, and Church Growth) and a Ph. D. (Evangelism and Church Growth). He has served in church planting and pastoral roles in Kentucky and Indiana. He has written several articles and reviews for academic periodicals in the areas of church planting and church growth. This chapter appeared in the Journal of The American Society for Church Growth (Volume 14, 2003) under the title of "Suggested Shifts in Preparation for the Spontaneous Expansion of the North American Church."

Unit V
Contextualized Strategies for Church Planting Movements

This unit discusses the development of contextualized strategies in a variety of settings including local churches, associations of churches (judicatories), and state conventions as well as specialized groups such as urban dwellers, multi-housing residents and non-literates.

Chapter 14   Kenny Moore

Church Planting Movements
in Urban Areas

Kenny Moore is the State Director of Mission for the Colorado Baptist Convention. Prior to coming to this position he served as Urban/Ethnic Church Planter Strategist for the Denver Baptist Association. Having served as a Minister of Mission in Dallas at the Calvary Baptist Church of Oak Cliff, along with the other ministry roles that he has played give him valuable knowledge and experience in the area of church planting.

Chapter 15   Tom Billings

Associational Strategy for
Church Planting Movements

Dr. Tom Billings, the Director of Missions for the Union Baptist Association speaks about the emerging Church Planting Movement paradigm in Houston, the fourth largest city in the United States. His plan to develop co-existing, cooperating church models connecting traditional churches with people groups (local and global), offers hope and guidance for contexts in which the traditional church model has been utilized for many decades. Dr. Billings has encouraged the utilization of simple church models to reach unchurched and dechurched segments of the population in this large metropolitan area.

Chapter 16   Barbara Oden

Church Planting Movements in
Multi-housing Settings

Barbara Oden is Multi-Housing Church Planter Catalyst for the Dallas Baptist Association assigned through the Church Planting Group of the North American Mission Board. She started her ministry in multihousing communities in Houston where she worked as an apartment community manager. She utilized that experience when she served for four years as a Multihousing Coordinator for the Union Baptist Association. She also served as Director of Church Extension for the Southern Nevada Baptist Association. Perhaps her greatest challenge came when she served as the Multihousing Church Planter for the Metropolitan New York Baptist Association. She co-authored *Multihousing Congregations* with David Bunch and Harvey Kneisel.

Unit VI
Implementing Church Planting Movements

This unit shares valuable principles, practices, and insights related to the implementation of church planting movements. Persons who have first hand acquaintance with church planting movements share valuable insights related prayer, training,, laity involvement, and disciple multiplication.

Chapter 17   Joe Hernandez

Training Leaders for Church
Planting Movements

Jose A. (Joe) Hernandez, Ph.D. is Vice President of North American Church Planting CityTeam Ministries. Prior to accepting this position, he served as the Director of the Equipping Team, Church Planting Group of the North American Mission Board. He has led in the development and implementation of the components of the Church Planting Process which provides for the nurture and equipping of the church planting teams and those who work with them. In addition to this, he has received Strategy Coordinator training from the International Mission Board. He utilizes the wealth of knowledge and experience in compiling information for this chapter on training leaders for church planting movements.

Chapter 18   Billie Hanks

Disciple-Making In Church
Planting Movements

Dr. Billie Hanks is the Executive Director of the International Evangelism Association. A true pioneer in the area of one-on-one discipleship, Billie has contributed to the development of many leaders who in turn are touching the lives of thousands of persons. Through this Association, Billie is impacting many states and many countries around the world with his emphasis on the multiplication of disciples. Billie and his Association have published excellent discipleship materials. Among these are: *A Call to Joy: Encouraging the Growing Believer, A Call to Growth: Establishing the Growing Believer, The Spiritual Journal: Quarterly Devotional System,* and *Operation Multiplication: Discipler Equipping Guide.* In this chapter, Billie shares biblically centered insights on the most effective ways to make disciples in Church Planting Movements.

Chapter 19   Van Kicklighter

The Role of the Laity in Church
Planting Movements

Van Kicklighter is an Associate Director of the Mentoring Team, Church Planting Group of the North American Mission Board. Throughout his ministry, Van has been convinced that the laity plays a vital role in the implementation of the Great Commission at home and abroad. He specializes in enabling leaders to discover, train, and empower lay church planters across North America.

Chapter 20   Neil Cole

Starting Organic Congregations in
Church Planting Movements

In his previous chapter in this book, Neil Cole is the Executive Director for Church Multiplication Associates and the founding leader of Awakening Chapels, discussed the emergence of organic church networks. In this chapter, he shares valuable insights on how to start and nurture organic churches.

Chapter 21   W. Mark Snowden

The Use of Media in Church
Planting Movements

Mark Snowden serves as a communication specialist at the North American Mission Board. He has served as the communications director for the Oversees Operations Office of the International Mission board, Southern Baptist Convention. He ministered with the IMB 18 years and also worked for the Kentucky Baptist Convention and the Radio & TV Commission. He holds a Masters of Science in Communications Management form Virginia Commonwealth University in Richmond, Virginia, and has studied at Southern Baptist Theological Seminary.

Chapter 22   Daniel R. Sanchez

What Will It Really Take to Have
Church Planting Movements
in North America?

After dialoguing with numerous effective and committed leaders of church planting movements and after reading the informative and inspiring chapters in this book, Dr. Daniel Sanchez addresses the bottom line, what will it really take to have full-blown church planting movements in North America? He has written this chapter with the deep desire that we acknowledge what needs to happen and that we make the commitment to be instruments in God's hands so that there will be a biblically based church within walking distance of every person in North America.

Introduction

Daniel R. Sanchez

"Could it possibly happen here in North America?" This is one of the most piercing questions people ask when they hear about the absolutely astounding church planting movements that are occurring in highly strategic areas of the globe such as China, India, Africa, Latin America, and the Muslim World.

In a recent meeting, the leaders of twelve house church networks in China estimated a total of 58 million members in their groups alone without counting other networks.[1] Some experts estimate that 30 thousand Chinese persons are coming to Christ every day, which amounts to more than 10 million new believers annually.[2]

Mike Steele reports that DAWN Philippines celebrated the attainment of its goal of growing from 5,000 congregations in 1974 to 50,000 by the end of AD 2000.[3] He adds that in Zimbabwe, evangelical churches grew from 10,000 to 20,000 in a ten-year period. Steele explains that in one year (2001), a newly emerging church planting movement yielded 48,000 new believers and 1,700 new churches.[4] Steele also states that fourteen nations in Latin America planted a total of 87,500 new churches in the last decade.[5]

Rad Zdero reports that "Ethiopia's Kristos Church, founded in the 1950's and numbering 5,000 members in 1982, grew to 50,000 members by 1990 using home groups after nearly a decade of Marxist repression which included the confiscation of all church buildings."[6]

1

In his book, *Church Planting Movements: How God is Redeeming a Lost world*, David Garrison reports that a missionary strategist assigned to a North Indian people group found just 28 churches among them in 1989. By the year 2000, a church planting movement had erupted, catapulting the number of churches to more than 4,500 with an estimated 300,000 believers.[7] "Each month," David Garrison asserts, "an estimated 1,200 new churches are started in Africa."[8]

During the past decade in a Latin American country, despite relentless government persecution, Baptists grew from 235 churches to more than 4,000 churches with more than 30,000 converts awaiting baptism.[9] Even among "the last of the giants" (the Muslim World), amazing things are happening. Garrison reports that in an Asian Muslim country, more than 150,000 have embraced Jesus and gather in more than 3,000 locally led Jesus Groups.[10] He explains that "more Muslims have come to Christ in the past two decades than at any other time in history."[11]

As we can see from these reports, thousands are coming to Christ every day around the world as a result of the amazing church planting movements that are taking place. Sadly, however, the opposite is occurring in North America. While a few evangelical denominations are making heroic efforts to reach people through traditional and some innovative church planting strategies, the fact remains that we are losing ground every day.

In the decade of the 90's there was a loss of more than 50,000 churches (or 10,000 a year) in the major denominations alone.[12] Overall, the number of evangelical churches dropped from 383,000 in 1993 to around 325,000 churches by the year

2000.[13] American churches lose an estimated 2,765,000 people a year to nominalism and secularism.[14] America loses 72.11 churches per week or 10.27 per day.[15] "During the last ten years, the combined communicant membership of all Protestant denominations has declined by 9.5% (4,498,242), while the national population increased by 11% (24,153,000)."[16] In 1900, there were 27 churches for every 10,000 persons. Today, there are 11 churches for every 10,000 persons.[17]

Half of all the churches last year did not add one new member through conversion growth. Evangelical churches have failed to gain an additional two percent of the American population in the past fifty years.[18] In other words, we are not even reaching our own children. With an unchurched population of between 180 million and 190 million, the U.S. ranks third behind China and India in the number of unsaved people.[19]

Even though there was a surge in religious activities (especially church attendance) immediately following the terrorist attack on September 11, 2001, the sad truth is that many Americans soon returned to their irreligious lifestyles. A survey taken by *USA Today* on the first anniversary of the attack reveals that weekly attendance to religious services had actually dropped one percentage point from the pre-attack level to the post-attack level (26% March 2001 to 25% March 2002).[20] This survey also revealed that immediately following the attack, 74 percent of those surveyed stated that they "pray more than they usually do." A year later however, only 41 percent said that they "pray more than they usually do."[21] This led Paul Hampson, author of the article based on this survey, to conclude that: "Americans' attitudes changed, but not their actions."

3

What will it take for church planting movements to sweep across North America, reach millions of unchurched people for Christ, and transform our society with the values of the Kingdom of God? This question has been burning in the minds of numerous church planting strategists in North America and motivated us to enlist the help of extraordinarily committed people who have been used mightily of God in church planting movements abroad and others who are working devotedly to spark church planting movements in North America to share their experiences, reflections, and vision in the chapters of this book.

The purpose of this book, therefore, is to examine current best practices and understanding of church planting at home and abroad and look forward to full-blown Church Planting Movements in North America. Due to the fact that house church networks represent the predominant model being employed today in church planting movements, special attention will be given to this approach. [22] At the same time, since the North American context has its own unique characteristics, other church multiplication models will be explored. The models that emerge in North America may very likely be different from those that are currently being used in other parts of the world. [23] We agree with Wolfgang Simson when he states that many North Americans who have grown up in denominational structures or work in areas with an existing church history. They cannot turn back the wheel of history. A mixed forest of denominational and traditional churches, as well as house churches, will continue because each church group can perform particular roles and tasks. [24]

4

Larry Krieder resonates with this idea when he states that the Lord is using diversified types of structures to build His church today. He explains:

> From the traditional church to the emerging house church networks, God's spirit is being poured out on His people. Our God is a God of infinite variety; you see it in His creation, from the long-necked giraffe to the multicolored butterfly. You see His variety in the skin color of His people and the multitude of talents and gifts He gives. God had no interest in producing clones when He created our world. It is my conviction that He continues to bless variety and creativity in His church today by the many different structures and methods He uses to accomplish His purposes. Although I sincerely believe that the new house church networks are tailor-made for today's generation and will be a force in returning to the New Testament model of church life, I believe God is using conventional structures – what I call community and mega churches – to play their part in God's future plan. God will build His kingdom regardless of our models, structures or plans. Both those churches that operate within a more traditional setting and those that operate outside of the traditional structures are needed. It is a big job to equip the saints for ministry and bring the gospel to a lost and dying world. We need everyone to work together, allowing the new and the old to coexist and complement each other. [25]

In their book, *Getting Started,* Tony and Felicity Dale make a similar point when they state that:

Throughout the world God is blessing in traditional and cell churches of every description, as well as house church movements. Within many of the traditional and cell-based models of church, we see the Holy Spirit nudging people towards something more organic, based on smaller groups. All three models of church need to be working together to advance the Kingdom of God in any way that they can.[26]

We are mindful of the fact that significant segments of the population in North America can best be reached through traditional church models. Because of their religious upbringing or their cultural perceptions of what churches should be like, many Americans will not respond to outreach models that do not feel "like church" to them. It is obvious, however, that there are also large segments of the population that are not being reached through traditional or even some of the more innovative congregational models. Since we are seeing evidence of the effectiveness of basic church networks around the world, how willing are we to consider similar approaches in North America in order to reach these large unchurched segments of our population?

While we are not aware at this time of any full-blown church planting movements in North America on the scale of what is taking place in other parts of the world, we are beginning to see the emergence of some of these movements in a number of places.[27] An example of this is the basic church networks that are emerging throughout America. In her New York Times article, "Search for the Right Church Ends at Home," Laurie Goldstein states that over 1,660 house churches can be found in Web pages in this country.[28]

In his book, *House Church Networks: A Church for a New Generation*, Larry Kreider describes what is beginning to take place:

It is happening again. A new species of church is emerging throughout North America. In major cities as well as rural areas, a unique kind of church life is peeking through like fresh growth of new crops through the surface of the soil. Hungry for community and relationships, people are learning the values of the kingdom by first-hand participation... Within the next ten to fifteen years, I believe these new house church networks will dot the landscape of North America just as they already do in other nations of the world.[29]

In his forward to Kreider's book, C. Peter Wagner enthusiastically affirms the emergence of new house church networks when he states:

House churches aren't exactly new because for the first couple hundred years of the Christian movement, all churches were house churches. However, they have not been the most common form of churches in our generation (with the exception of China), so it is very important for us to understand what they look like and how they operate. They are in the process of becoming a permanent and very visible feature on the landscape of faith these days... For growing numbers of the new generation, house churches, not the traditional church, will most likely draw them to God.[30]

Many North American church leaders are praying passionately and asking God's Spirit to move in a mighty way across our land. One of these is Jim Montgomery, founder of Disciple A Whole Nation (DAWN) ministries. He describes a meeting that he had with leaders who came from every section of the nation and represented denominations, local churches, parachurch ministries and house church networks:

> This group's vision is to see the presence of the risen, incarnate Christ available within walking distance of every person of every class, kind and condition in America. This group affirms mega churches, community churches, and churches of every kind. Their passion is to utilize all forms of churches that honor Christ to bring healing to our nation. Their dream is the vast multiplication of converts, gathered together primarily in house churches blanketing the land.[31]

From a Canadian perspective, Rad Zdero reports on the house church movements that are emerging:

> The Free Methodist Church in Canada (FMCiC) is officially supporting house church planting efforts both in British Columbia and Ontario, in which the current writer is involved. Recently at the 2002 Canadian General Conference of the FMCiC held in Toronto, my cohorts and I ran a workshop entitled "Initiating House Church Movements" which was very positively received. The latest official FMCiC magazine also included a feature article on the topic...[32] Dove Christian Fellowship, known mostly for its cell-based churches, is now embracing and supporting the house church movement as a genuine work of God.[33] Mission organizations such as Campus Crusade for Christ (CCC) have been planting 'home fellowship groups' for years in various

parts of the world.[34] All of these efforts will put added resources into and a positive light on house churches.[35]

Tony and Felicity Dale are among the pioneer house church planters in America. Medical Doctors by profession, they left England, their native land, where they had been a part of a house church network, to relocate in Austin, Texas. In addition to starting a house church network in Austin, they have started a new magazine entitled *House2House* that ministers to believers who have a heart for house churches and house church networks.[36]

Another pioneer in basic church strategies in North America is Neil Cole, who has been instrumental in starting numerous Life Transformation Groups on the West Coast. He reports: "During our first year, we started 10 churches. In our second year, we started 18 churches. The next year 52 new starts were added. In 2002, we averaged two churches a week being started and had 106 starts. Last year (2003) we saw around 200 starts in a single year. Today, there are probably more than 400 churches in 16 states and 12 nations around the world."[37] Through their Greenhouse Intensive Training Events, Neil Cole, Paul Kaak, and their team members are equipping many to start similar groups in many parts of the country. Neil Cole's book, *Cultivating a Life for God,* provides valuable insights on the formation and development of life transformation groups[38]

Many others are being led by the Lord to utilize basic church strategies to reach those who require innovative approaches if they are going to respond to the Gospel. It is inspiring and challenging to learn about couples such as Jim and Betty Herrington who were willing to sell their suburban home

9

and move with two teenage children to Houston's Montrose area, a neighborhood with more than 600 homeless children and many drug addicts, to plant house churches. [39] Herrington explains that God stirred in him a deep conviction that somebody needed to go to these difficult places, stake the land, and declare that the church will not surrender these people to the enemy. Herrington and his fellow workers indicate that almost everyone they reach comes out of the drug, sex, or alcohol culture that is in Montrose. The people in this community are troubled by radical ignorance of Christian doctrine combined with deeply embedded cynicism toward organized religion.

These realizations convinced the workers that a network of house churches was the most effective way to reach Montrose. They started with just one house church, but the number quickly began to multiply as they began to connect with people in the community. They went from one to two and two to three and then four and now have five. Two congregations target those in recovery from drugs and alcohol. One targets unwed mothers who are a part of the street kid population. The fifth one targets the families of those whose father is incarcerated. Each of these has specialized ministries that grow out of the house church initiative. [40]

A new model of church multiplication is now emerging and has excellent potential. John Worcester is developing the prototype of a "radically missional church" that exists to plant other churches. In its first year and a half, TEAM CHURCH has been able to start six churches. It has a goal to start four reproducing churches a year. TEAM CHURCH has already grown from a handful of people to over 1000 regular attendees in what it calls its orchard of churches. TEAM CHURCH meets on Sunday evenings for its main worship service and sends its members out in teams to do mini-mission trips on Sunday morning (and other times) to help its church plants all around the Dallas-Fort Worth Metroplex. These teams help planters by conducting evangelistic block parties, doing community listening surveys, and helping with other outreach activities. They send music, children's, and teaching teams of 20-30 workers to help launch services of the new churches.[41]

Mike Steele shares the vision of seeing basic churches in every neighborhood in this country. He reports in 2003 that as many as 75 networks in 18 states that have simple church gatherings. All of this has been birthed in the last three years.[42] By 2005, Steele sees the strong possibility of over 150 networks functioning in the United States.[43]

The task of reaching North Americans for Christ and discipling them through biblically sound, spiritually vibrant, and culturally relevant congregations is an awesome one. In this book, therefore, we are going to explore what the Lord is already doing in the emerging basic church networks in strategic places in North America. Some of these emerging networks appear to have some of the characteristics that have contributed to church planting movements abroad. Other networks are exhibiting characteristics of a hybrid approach, which emphasizes individual house churches that get together periodically for celebration services. Additional networks may emphasize the utilization of strong, established churches that have a vision for starting a vide variety of churches at home and abroad. Still other networks may end up being church multiplication efforts but not church planting movements. To help readers gain a clearer understanding of what is occurring, the authors in this book analyze the issues, examine obstacles, and explore paradigm shifts that might be needed to facilitate church planting movements in North America.

The important thing from the perspective of this book is what can be learned from these case studies and applied to future church starting efforts. Through the writing of these chapters, we want to *examine prayerfully what the Lord is doing and explore ways in which we might be instrumental in sparking church planting movements that sweep across our land and result in churches that are within reach of every people group and population segment in North America.*

Endnotes

[1] Paul Hattaway, Brother Yun, Peter Xu Yongze, and Enoch Wang, *Back to Jerusalem*, Waynesboro, GA: Gabriel Publishing, 2003, 2.

[2] Ibid.

[3] See Mike Steele's chapter in this book entitled, "An Emerging Church Planting Movement in America."

[4] Ibid., 49.

[5] Ibid.

[6] Gateway Films, "Against Great Odds" (video), 1992, See also, Rad Zdero, *The Global House Church Movement*, Pasadena: William Carey Library, 2004, 69-76.

[7] David Garrison, *Church Planting Movements: How God is Redeeming a Lost World,* Richmond: WIG Take Resources, 2004, 17

[8] Ibid.,

[9] Ibid.,

[10] Ibid.,

[11] Ibid.,

[12] Patrick Johnstone, *Operation World*, 1993.

[13] Dudley, *Faith Communities Today*, March 2001,(www,hirr.hartsem.edu)

[14] American Society for Church Growth (ASCG), "Enlarging Our Borders," Report presented to the Executive Presbytery, January 1999, cited in Larry Kreider, *House Church Networks: A church for a new generation*, Epharata, PA: House To House Publications, 67.

[15] Ibid.

[16] Charles Arn, Institute for American Church Growth, "Enlarging Our Borders," Report presented to the Executive Presbytery, January, 1999.

[17] Glenn Smith, "A New Kind of Church: Glocal," unpublished paper, 2002, 1.

[18] Arden Adamson, secretary-treasurer, Wisconsin-Northern Michigan District, "Enlarging Our Borders," Report presented to the Executive Presbytery, January, 1999,cited in Larry Kreider, *House Church Networks: A church for a new generation*, Epharata, PA: House To House Publications, 67.

[19] Arden Adamson, secretary-treasurer, Wisconsin-Northern Michigan District, "Enlarging Our Borders," Report presented to the Executive Presbytery, January, 1999,

[20] Rick Hampson, USA TODAY/CNN/GALLOP POLL, Wednesday, September, 11, 2002, 12A.

[21] Ibid., 2A.

[22] The term *"Basic Church"* instead of *"House Church"* is used for two reasons. First, the word "basic" stresses the plain, uncomplicated, fundamental, and reproducible make up of the groups. Second, while it is true that most of the groups in church planting movements meet in houses, many groups meet in warehouses, boardrooms, restaurants, coffee shops, construction sites, classrooms, apartments, mobile homes, or whatever space is available to them. By not confining their strategy to a specific building structure, those who employ the *"Basic Church"* approach have an endless number of possibilities regarding meeting places. The term *"church"* is used to convey the idea that these groups carry out the basic functions of a New Testament church as described in Acts 2:40-47. The term *"Network"* is used to make the point that these are not isolated, separatist, and antagonistic groups but cooperating, interdependent, and vitally linked groups that find encouragement and strength in mutual accountability and ministry. See Larry Krieder, *House Church Networks: A church for a new generation*, Ephrata, PA: House to House Publications, 2001, 1.

[23] For a discussion of church planting models see, Daniel R. Sanchez, Ebbie C. Smith, Curtis E Watke, *Starting Reproducing Congregations*, Church Starting Network, www.churchstarting.net

[24] Wolfgang Simson, *Houses That Change The World*, Carslile, UK: OM Publishing, 1998, xxxi.

[25] Larry Krieder, House Church Networks: A church for a new generation, Ephrata, PA: House to House Publications, 2001, 17.

[26] Felicity Dale, editor, *Getting Started*, Austin: House 2 House Ministries, 2003, 26.

[27] Ibid, 126.

[28] Laurie Goldstein, New York Times, "Search for the Right Church Ends at Home," April 2001.

[29] Larry Krieder, *House Church Networks: A church for a new generation*, Ephrata, PA: House to House Publications, 2001, 2.

[30] C Peter Wagner, "Forward" in Larry Krieder, *House Church Networks: A church for a new generation*, Ephrata, PA: House to House Publications, 2001.

[31] Jim Montgomery" The Healing of the Nation," *House 2 House*, Special Issue, 5, Austin: www house2house.tv

[32] Rad Zdero, "The House Church Movement", *The Free Methodist Herald*, vol.80, no.3, May/June 2002, www.fmc-canada.org

[33] Dove Christian Fellowship, www.dcfi.org

[34] Robert Fitts, *Saturation Church Planting*, Last Days Ministries, 1994, 71-78.

[35] Rad Zdero, "The House Church Movement", *The Free Methodist Herald*, vol.80, no.3, May/June 2002, www.fmc-canada.org

[36] Larry Krieder, *House Church Networks: A church for a new generation*, Ephrata, PA: House to House Publications, 2001, 32. The Dale's Web site is: www.house2house.tv.

[37] See, Organic "Churches and Church Planting Movements," a chapter in this book.

[38] Neil Cole, *Cultivating a Life for God*, Carol Stream, Ill: Church Smart Resources, 1999.

[39] David Roach, "House Churches and City Transformation," Baptist Press, April, 2003.

[40] Felicity Dale, editor, *Getting Started*, Austin: House 2 House Ministries, 2003, 126.

[41] For more information see www.TeamChurchDFW.com.

[42] Mike Steele, chapter 1 in this book.

[43] Letter to Author, May 2005.

14

Chapter 1

Emerging Church Planting Movements in North America

Mike Steele

A Worldwide Perspective

Some things become painfully obvious when seen in the light of solid information. For years the Church in the United States has been in a constant state of decline with no end in sight. Our neighbors to the north, Canada, have seen an increase in church starts beginning in 1997.[44] Gatherings of believers are multiplying around the world at an unprecedented rate. While Church planting movements flourished in other countries, here in the United States we continued to see a precipitous decline in church starts in spite of the fact that a few evangelical denominations are making determined efforts at church starting.

I have been privileged to work with Disciple A Whole Nation (DAWN) ministries for a decade. I had become acquainted with DAWN through a worldwide survey I had been commissioned to do for the AD2000 and Beyond Movement. Getting a picture of what God was doing around the world, seeing the massive growth of the church worldwide, led me to give my life fully to the idea of seeing a gathering of believers (a church) within easy access of every person of every class, kind, and condition of mankind. That led ultimately to being invited to join DAWN Ministries. Early assignments with DAWN took me to ministry in parts of Africa, Asia, Europe, the Caribbean, and Latin America before I began facilitating the

15

work of DAWN in North America. Through this opportunity, I have been able to see church planting movements happening on several continents.

The DAWN strategy for mobilizing the whole Body of Christ in whole nations to work most directly at completing the Great Commission is now being implemented in about 150 nations around the world. DAWN suggests an approach that begins in prayer, utilizes information, and works continually in process toward the filling of the nation with gatherings of believers. It leads the Church to pursue a prophetic message from the Lord for the peoples of the land toward filling that land with disciples and disciple-making communities.

DAWN Philippines, where it all began in 1974, has celebrated the fulfillment of its goal to increase from about 5,000 congregations in 1975 to 50,000 by the end of AD 2000.[45] Likewise, the Church in Zimbabwe has completed its project of doubling their 10,000 churches to 20,000 in a ten-year period. In the process, they saw 1.6 million come to Christ and into church membership. This represents fully 20 percent of the whole population coming into the Kingdom in this very brief period![46]

Fourteen nations in Latin America have witnessed the planting of a total of 87,500 new churches since 1992, the result of direct planning among the churches. Five of these Churches reached their goals ahead of time. Venezuela, for example, previously had the lowest growth rate in the whole region. In 1992 the church leaders in Venezuela established a goal to increase from 4,900 congregations to 12,000 by AD 2002. They reached their goal in 1998 and set a new goal of 25,000 total churches by AD 2005. Meeting in Miami in 1999, the combined national Churches of the whole Latin region set a goal to plant 500,000 more churches in the ten years to follow.[47]

Similarly, amazing things have been happening in both China and India with projections of new churches growing by leaps and bounds. In just one small province in one of these countries, application of the DAWN strategy resulted in the number of churches increasing from three to 550 and the number of believers from 100 to 55,000 in just five years. That exploded again in the next two years to 1,250 churches and 225,000 members.[48]

Vibrant young leaders in another far eastern country were half way into their project of planting 30,000 new churches among an unreached people group, previously the largest unreached people group in the world. Across the Middle East— where, until recently, getting a convert or two on occasion was possible but where starting new churches was hardly ever mentioned—actual church planting projects were underway.

As of October 2003, the DAWN vision has been a factor in over 1,050,000 churches being planted in more than 100 nations in the last ten years.[49] In the first three years of the new century, plans have been laid in over 110 countries for the planting of more than 12 million new congregations in the next decade. Hundreds of volunteer DAWN associates carry a heart for the completion of the Great Commission and a burden to see their nations saturated with the presence of Christ in the form of local gatherings of believers. Yet, in this country, most have never heard of DAWN, nor of such movements as those I mentioned above, nor others popping up in many places around the world.

America – The Exception to the Trend

Five years ago, I began to crisscross the nation, following the Holy Spirit, in search of answers for mobilizing a church planting movement in the Church in America. In the process, I talked with thousands of pastors, read dozens of books, and prayed.

The facts spoke loudly. Hundreds of thousands of churches were half full each Sunday with little prospect of dynamic new growth. Well-known researchers are speaking of at least 80 percent of the churches being stagnant or declining in growth. Yet few church leaders would entertain the notion of a fresh move of God in our land. It is no wonder that a high percentage of pastors in a poll indicated they would get out of the ministry if they could.

America – Last of the Giants

Jim Montgomery of DAWN Ministries had used this phrase to describe the United States as the one place where it would take a miracle of God to see a DAWN-type saturation church planting project. Imagine trying to get the Church of America to join in what would appear to be yet another campaign to evangelize the nation. Had not every local church at some point thrown its energies and resources into a cooperative effort that in the long run, produced little or no new growth for their congregation?

There are at least two instances where Jim and others made an effort to share the concepts of a church planting movement in the United States to no avail. DAWN's work in the US had proven to be hopeful at best. Many attempts to cast vision to pastors and church leaders across the land had been met with a cold reception. Jim often spoke of America as being the last place to see a DAWN-type project occur.

Misperceptions

American Christians tend to believe we are the most churched country in the world. The reality, however, is that the United States is the fourth largest unchurched population in the world. It also became obvious that much of what we had identified as Church in the United States had very little chance of multiplying and filling the nation with the glory of God. I observed that of the perhaps 3,000 mega-churches, some had excellent discipleship strategies, yet in many others those attending were little more than spectators. Most neighborhood churches see gatherings between 40 and 80 people. Most of these churches haven't baptized a new member in years.

Something in the structure of Church that had worked so well for our parents had lost its glimmer in this post-modern world. It wasn't reproducing disciples who walked in the love of the Lord and set their world on fire. It just wasn't authentic or real anymore, to many in this "emerging" generation. It was viewed by many as a system of do's and don'ts, as legalistic and controlling. While it is reaching some, its ability to transform culture and reach two hundred million people is seriously in question.

It seemed to me that the culture in North America had changed dramatically over the past century, but the Church had not caught up. In fact, much of the church now looked and acted in large measure, just like the culture. To a large extent, our measure of success and our system of validation and affirmation matches the business models of our day. True life in Christ and the joy of community in Christ have faded on many fronts. The tremendous move of God around the world is being thwarted in the U.S. by what had become "Standard American Churchianity."

My persistent prayer was, "Lord, how can we impact the millions of people who have either left the Church or won't go to it?" In response, the Lord began to paint a picture of "church" that was new, refreshing, able to multiply by becoming "all things to all men" in order to reach the masses that wanted a relationship with Jesus but needed a new door through which to enter. It wasn't so much about structure as it was about a way of life.

Then the Lord reminded me of the old saying, "All roads lead home." Jesus summed up all that was written when *He encouraged us to fall in love with His Father and let that love flow through our families and spheres of influence.* I realized that the problem in the American Church was centered on the decline in true intimacy with the Father and in the understanding of nurturing communities where life and love is shared and freely expressed among the beloved. Our hearts are broken and only the love of the Father can heal them.

Ultimately, the Lord began to connect me with a network of men and women similarly passionate about the health of the church and the re-discipling of our nation. We had the strong impression the Lord was leading us to some answers. We began seeing glimpses of what he was doing in out-of-the way places here and there. Could it be these scattered, unconnected oases in the desert held the answers to what we were looking for?

Emerging Movements

In this process of observing the overall church culture in America that seemed inadequate at best to move up to another level of growth and impact, we began to bump into little movements that appeared to be making an impact in their spheres. While a few were in rebellion against the status quo, a new growing group of believers had begun to model biblical community, earnestly seeking the mind of the Lord for his people.

These small networks in various parts of the country had been developing a thought process revolving around the idea of church planting movements. They were not all using the same terminology, but there seemed to be a common DNA. The three main strands of their DNA were: 1) **D**ivine Truth; 2) **N**urturing Relationships in Communities; and 3) **A**postolic Mission of the Kingdom.

The idea of living every day with Jesus and each other was a common thread. Their belief in a 24/7 relationship with God and His people led them to see structure as a secondary issue. "Church" IS the people and happened in the midst of the people. Several of these networks became acquainted and began to share together their ideas of relational community. They are investing in a discipleship process much in the style of Jesus' model of discipleship. They are living relationally with each other. And they are growing!

While still in its infancy, the last three years have yielded a growth rate that is off the charts. In 2000, we were aware of about five such networks of three to five gatherings each that exhibited "Simple Church" concepts. By 2003 there were over 75 such networks that we knew of, with the number of gatherings well exceeding 1,000. Every week people are calling or emailing us to say they have caught the idea and are starting their own gatherings and networks.

One Body, One Bride, One Family

These new expressions of "church' believe there is but one Body in many expressions. Larry Kreider in his book, *House Church Networks* states:

> House churches, and churches of any kind, should never be exclusive entities cut off from the rest of the body of Christ. The healthy house church will focus on loving the Lord, loving each other, reaching the lost and loving the rest of the body of Christ anywhere and everywhere. Healthy believers will want to relate closely to the rest of the body of Christ because they want to be "one with the Father and each other.[50]

Rather than living in isolation they see themselves as another extension of all that God is doing in the world. Furthermore, they see the opportunity to partner with more traditional models of "church" to saturate a city or state with the presence of Christ.

These new "Simple Church Networks" were looking for a way of "being" the church that could be embraced by multitudes of pastors, denomination leaders, and the average man and woman in the pew. They were praying for a paradigm that would be perceived as a prophetic word from the Lord that would be immediately seized by the early adopters and carried into the bulk of the Body of Christ in America. This way of life can be lived out in any grouping of the Body of Christ and bring everyone closer to God and each other.

What do they look like?

Some of these small movements seemed quite exotic in nature. As told in the DAWN REPORT Magazine, for example, I had recently met with a wonderful group of young people in their twenties who had begun multiplying house churches in Las Vegas, Nevada. In the heart of "sin city," they were gathering bar waitresses, card dealers, and hotel employees in their homes. Finding a place of acceptance and healing, many would come and participate even before they had come to know the Lord.[51]

In a short period of time, they were already meeting in 15 different locations. Later I learned that one of their team had planted six new gatherings in just three weeks. They had developed their mission statement to read *"We exist to see a church within walking distance of every person in Las Vegas and we exist to see a church planting movement in every major city of the United States."*

In nearby Los Angeles, likewise not noted for its piety, I met with a similar group of leaders. They have developed a training program they call "Greenhouse." They also developed the DNA model now expressed across this nationwide relational network. They reminded people that healthy time with Jesus and each other would lead to natural reproduction (evangelism). Many who are responding to this approach are in their 20's and come from fractured backgrounds. One young man I met was

23

an ex-drug dealer who is now planting a house church in the very neighborhood where he used to make his illicit living. Others are planting churches in various alternate lifestyle communities.

One of their approaches is to multiply "Life Transformation Groups." Each LTG is made up of three people who: 1) read 30 chapters of Scripture a week, 2) confess their sins for cleansing and healing, and 3) pray for a friend to join them. When a new friend joins the group of three, it now becomes two groups of two asking the Lord to bring a third to each. Using this model, they have planted over 200 gatherings in the last few years

While these networks were joining together relationally, another expression of the movement was emerging. God brought Tony and Felicity Dale from England some 5 years ago. They had been a part of a growing movement in England in the 70's and 80's. God led them to produce a magazine to catalyze what many were thinking and thousands responded. Last years final issue reached 50,000 copies. It became a point of connection and validation for many to see God at work. They also spawned a network in their hometown. They have raised leaders to give facilitation to this network and are now engaged in sharing the vision across the nation and the world.

One pioneer had been pursuing a multiplying model state by state across the whole country. Robert Fitts had already been planting house churches for over 12 years. Robert has faithfully shared the message of "simple life" in Christ with thousands. In the last year, Robert has developed a relational network, Outreach Fellowship International (OFI), in 16 states, which has over 100 gatherings.

In cities such as Dallas, Cincinnati, Seattle, Portland, Denver, and Colorado Springs and in states, such as parts of New Hampshire, Maryland and in other states, these networks are springing up sharing a simple message of love in Christ and love with each other.

Growth of the Simple Church Movement

The year 2003 brought with it a pleasant surprise. Many who had long been in traditional denominations began to ask what it would look like to see these simple expressions of "church" emerged through their denominational channels. It seems that the Holy Spirit is speaking these truths into multiple spheres of influence all at once. We like to say this is a sign that the Holy Spirit is the initiator. Some had been doing serious study of the Church in America and rethinking biblical models of church. Their desire was to touch the perceived needs of American believers and unbelievers alike. Furthermore, they were implementing models of church that fit the above criteria and were beginning to see multiplication through discipleship and nurturing community life.

None of these networks, of course, has yet achieved the kind of growth I have described from nations overseas. Still, I see a new wind blowing across the land. To the glory of God, this simple-church movement appears to be a cloud the size of a man's fist that promises a deluge of a new discipleship and church planting thrust in our troubled land.

What is Simple Church?

We at DAWN Ministries believe the evidence is there that God is raising a movement which will bring a whole new vitality, empowerment and expansion to the Church in North America. Though referred to by such terms as "organic church," New Testament church, house church, redemptive community, *oikos*, lighthouse or other terms, an umbrella name we use is "simple church."

A basic definition of simple church could be, *"Simple church is a small group of people seeking intimate relationship with God and each other through hearing from God and living the Kingdom lifestyle."* From such a kernel definition, we see God developing many different models and expressions of the Body. We are aware of a number of different models that are all built on this core expression of simple church. Others seem to pop up quite regularly.

Since this new paradigm for doing church in America is spontaneously springing up in many forms, in many places and developed by many different leaders, there is naturally a plethora of names by which it is identified. We have searched for a common phrase for all such gatherings and have come up with "simple church." Simple in the sense that any believer, emphasizing the priesthood of all believers, could say, "I could do that."

As Neil Cole writes, "Simplicity is the key to fulfilling the Great Commission in this generation. If the process is complex it will break down early in the transference to the next generation of disciples. The more complex the process the greater the giftedness needed to keep it going. The simpler the process the more available it is to the Christian population. . . . We must keep the message simple and unencumbered by complex methodologies or structures."[52]

Webster's Dictionary helps define simple. It mentions the term, simplicity, that is, something simple. The dictionary goes on to discuss the term, simple, indicating that this is a matter that consists of few parts or is without any or much ornamentation, sophistication or complexity. Finally, the dictionary explains the word essential, showing that this word carries the idea of necessary or something that one cannot do without it. Simple has the idea of being of the utmost importance or relating to or arising from the real nature of a thing or person. Simple means a commodity contains all that is best or most important in a thing. It is as perfect as the mind can conceive. Simple is the basic or fundamental part of a thing.

A simple church is church in its most natural and simplest state of being.

What about Structures?

God wants every one of His people, I believe, to be vehicles, channels of His blessing. We have to understand what is essential for church, so that every one of us can do it and be an integral part of it. For years, the Body of Christ in Western Culture has assumed that Church is a major event requiring great expertise to lead. Often we have missed the essential truth of the role of extended families in starting new churches. In earlier times, people were linked together in community. Extended family was always present. It included aunts and uncles, cousins and next of kin. It ALSO included neighbors, friends, co-workers, and employees. Singles who hear the word "family" often feel excluded because our current model of family is nuclear in definition. Simple church uses the broadest sense of the term to join people together from every walk of life.

Simple church is infinitely flexible. You can do it any place, any time, any where with anybody. You don't necessarily need a "church" building. In England they meet in pubs. In Africa, meetings may be under the trees.

One significant question most people ask has to do with family structure. The idea of the church as an extended family often gets tangled in our culture's expression of a nuclear family model. In Bible times, an extended family was, simply put, all those in your sphere of influence. Therefore, simple churches can flow out of relationships in any grouping of people. Simple church can be started with a group of singles committed to follow the Father and care for each other. It can start with a small "group" and move up from there to gatherings of nuclear families, households, extended families, people within a sphere of influence, groups of families, *oikos*, *ethne*, clan, or tribe affinity group. It is people loving God and each other.

Another structural question has to do with our current forms of church. Most people think of the church as a place and event at a certain time. Since simple church is about people, where they meet is secondary. The important idea does not revolve around a building or a meeting place but a lifestyle. When they do gather they could be in cells, house churches, neighborhood churches, mega-churches and so on. Simple church is at the core of life in Christ, no matter the structure used for the gathering of the saints together. Simple church is about being "church" not going to "church."

What's Ahead

A relational network of simple church gatherings is exploding all around the country. Though it takes many forms, shapes and sizes, at a heart level, simple church is a way to experience Kingdom life lived out in relational intimacy with God and with fellow believers. Simple church can be experienced in an extended family, a neighborhood gathering, the cell of a larger congregation, an affinity group or other small gathering. It is characterized by outreach to the unsaved, by reproducing every time the group reaches about 15, with participation by all in the gathering. Imagine what a mega-church would look like with all their families living out a simple church lifestyle? You would see hundreds of families incarnating the love and presence of Christ in their neighborhoods daily. The Kingdom alive and incarnating the presence of Christ in the midst of the people in a community would be a tremendous example of the love of Christ touching every part of life.

The essentials of Simple Church affect real life! It's going to be a source of life for you, for your family, for your neighbors and for your whole neighborhood! Church happens 24/7, all week long! If you set out to start a church, it is common to put the church in front of family. But, if you start out to be God's people as a family, and bless each other, (and you can do that), then other people will just naturally be drawn in, and it won't take a toll on your family.

At the start of this chapter I shared that God has been moving through His Body around the world for at least the last 15-20 years in a new and pervasive way. It may just be the season for the Church in the United States to join this work of the Holy Spirit around the world and enjoy the life of the Kingdom in this country. Preliminary informal research shows there are now over 75 networks in 18 states that have simple church gatherings. All this has been birthed in the last three years. We hope and pray that 2005 will be a year that diverse groups within the Body of Christ see this new expression as a forerunner of the changes the Holy Spirit would like to bring in this land. It is our sincere belief that we are on the verge of a significant movement of God in North America that will spawn healthy, multiplying "extended families" all across our nation.[53]

While researching his soon to be published book **'Apostolic Genius'**, Alan Hirsch, author of **'The Shaping of Things to Come'** "stumbled upon some extremely notable, even astonishing, discoveries by important observers of the global Christian scene." Barrett highlights particularly the development of the so-called **'Neo-Apostolic' networks and movements**, of which there are already over 20,000 around the world, numbering around 394 million Christians.

According to Barrett, *these Christians reject historical denominationalism and all restrictive central authority, and attempt to lead a life of following Jesus, seeking a more effective missionary lifestyle.* They are **the fastest-growing Christian movements in the world**. Barrett estimates that by the year 2025, these movements will have around 581 million members, 120 million more than all Protestant movements together. Hirsh, who has invited all of Australia's missionary movements to a conference in Victoria (Forge National Summit,

1-3 July 2005), confirms the trend from his own experience, and believes that **these new Christian movements "are simply under the radar of traditional Christianity," at least as long as it holds on to the classical Constantine church structure (pastor + building + programme = church).**[54]

---

[44] Jacqueline Dugas, et al, *Transforming our Nation*, Richmond, BC: Church Leadership Library.

[45] *DAWN Report*, Issue No. 45, October 2001, 1-3.

[46] Ted Olsen, DAWN Report, Issue No. 46, March 2002, 1-2.

[47] Jim Montgomery, *DAWN 2000: 7 Million Churches To Go*, Pasadena: William Carey Library,   1989.

[48] Ibid.

[49] Jim Montgomery, I'm Gonna Let it Shine, Pasadena: William Carey Library, 2001.

[50] Larry Krieder, House Church Networks: A Church for a New Generation (Ephrata, PA: House to House Publications, 2001), 30l

[51] Mike Steele, DAWN Report/House 2 House, Issue No. 49, 1-2.

[52] Neil Cole, *Cultivating a Life for God*, Church Smart Resources. This book takes an in-depth look at a tool called "Transformation Groups" and explains how this tool can release the awesome power of multiplication in a church, Field Tested in his own church, the author has found that this simple and reproducible system has numerous advantages.

[53] For more information on this fledgling church planting movement, visit our website at   www.DAWNministries.org/regions/nam/index.html

[54] Alan Hirsch, www.forge.org.au

Chapter 2

Crucial Issues In North American Church Planting Movements

Daniel R. Sanchez

Initiating Church Planting Movements in North America is a challenging task. One of the reasons for this is that Christian churches have been in existence in this continent since the colonial period. Over the years, traditional church planting strategies and structures have become the *modus operandi* for most denominations. While church planting movement strategies have given genuine promise of effective fruit, legitimate theological and methodological issues have surfaced. Because of the crucial nature of these issues, those who would promote church planting movements in North America must address them prayerfully, studiously, and objectively. It needs to be pointed out at the outset, however, that the overall objective must be kept in mind while analyzing these issues.

Workers involved in Church Planting Movements, for instance, are committed to the multiplication principle which they consider essential to the implementation of the Great Commission (reaching all people groups). When Paul articulated his strategy of adapting the presentation of the Gospel to each ministry focus group (being all things to all people 1 Cor. 9:19-21) he defined his objective clearly: "that I might win the more" (v. 19). Similarly, when Donald McGavran advocates using house churches, developing of unpaid lay leaders, multiplying tribe, caste, and language churches, and surmounting of the property barrier, he does it in the context of the urban strategy he had previously articulated.

33

This strategy had had the objective of reaching the largest number of lost people possible.[55] A discussion of issues related to church planting movements, therefore, needs to keep the overriding objective in mind: to reach all of the people groups and population segments in North America with the Gospel and to disciple them in the context of biblically sound, culturally relevant congregations.

Some of the vital issues center on:
- an adequate definition of church;
- an adequate concept of saturation church starting;
- a clear understanding of church planting movements;
- the spiritual conditions that must be met;
- how church authority is exercised;
- how converts are incorporated into the church;
- what types of leadership are needed;
- the focus on people group and population segments;
- recognition of new churches;
- interrelationship of churches;
- maintaining doctrinal integrity;
- the importance of a meeting place;
- financial support;
- the focus of evangelism;
- the way the ordinances are administered;
- the ways in which discipleship is contextualized;
- and the significance of relevant worship.

The fact that these issues are posed as questions indicates that no easy answers for them exist. The nature of the questions also indicate that further dialogue is essential if church planting movements are to take place on a broad scale in North America.

Definition of Church

One of the most crucial issues pertaining to church planting movements in North America has to do with the definition of church that is employed. Many express serious concerns about the way some writers who are involved in church planting movements define church. These understandable concerns demand that church leaders address the question, "What is a church?"

This basic question spawns other related queries: Is a church defined in terms of its membership? If so, how many members does it take to make a church? Does a congregation need to have its own building in order to be considered a church? How much financial strength does a group need in order to be considered a church? Does a congregation need to have a full-time formally trained pastor and staff in order to be a church? Is there a minimal number of organizations that a group needs to have to qualify for church status? Is there a standard number of elected officers that is needed? Is a church determined by the number of functions it carries out? If so what are they? Are there other criteria that need to be employed to ascertain if a group is truly a church?

An additional set of questions relates to the terminology used for these congregations. For example, many ask what to call small churches. Some are calling them "simple churches," others "organic churches," others "house churches" and still others "basic churches." Each of these conveys a specialized type of meaning that needs to be evaluated. While there are several definitions for the term "simple church," in this chapter, I prefer the term "basic church." I define a "basic church," as one that carries out the basic functions of a New Testament church as described in Acts 2:40-47. This coincides with Stan Norman's statement that "In most New Testament passages, the church is depicted as a local assembly of Christians who meet, worship and minister in the name of Jesus Christ.[56]

Answers to these questions rest on the response to the query, "Is the church perceived as an *organization* or an *organism?*" The critical concern remains biblical. What does the Bible say about the nature of the church? If church planting movements are to flourish in North America, a biblically informed definition for the church is imperative. In his chapter, "A Theology of Church," Dr. Brent Ray addresses this question.

Definition of Church Planting Movement

In addition to a definition of church, a definition of a church planting movement is needed. In his book, *Church Planting Movements,* David Garrison defines a church planting movement as "a *rapid exponential increase of indigenous church planting churches within a people group or population segment.*"[57] In order to understand it better, we can parse this definition and then derive some observations about its implication for church planting in North America.

The phrase, *"Rapid exponential increase,"* refers to rapid growth in new church starts. Rapid growth must be seen in juxtaposition with incremental growth. Incremental growth takes place through the process of addition. New churches are started one by one. Perhaps one of the features that characterize church planting in North America is that the vast majority of churches that are planted do not reproduce themselves. This failing marks one of the primary reasons why we are not keeping up with our population growth let alone making gains in our church to population ratios.

Exponential growth, on the other hand, means that two churches become four; four become sixteen; and so on. Some of the leaders of church planting movements from the International Mission Board of the Southern Baptist Convention, based on their experience, define "exponential" as "doubling every 12 to 18 months." A comparative analysis regarding growth rates of church planting movements in the various countries and cultures, however, is needed. What is considered rapid in one area may not apply in another area. In addition, a distinction between the incubation stage and the full-blown stage of church planting movements will increase the knowledge of these God-given efforts.

The phrase *"exponential increase"* in church planting movements in North America reveals several imperative factors. First, the case studies reviewed by Garrison consider movements that are already in progress. A careful study of these examples reveals that in most cases it took some time to get these movements started. These movements do not happen over night. A great deal of prayer, study, training, and seed sowing precedes the beginning of a movement.

Second, even exponential growth begins small. It starts with reaching one group, helping it to reproduce itself, and enabling the growth to continue. For example, Curtis Sergeant observes that ethnic Chinese church planters with a small team of local believers planted six churches in 1994. The following year, 17 more were begun. The next year 50 more were started. By 1997, just three years after the starting, the number of churches had risen to 195 and had spread throughout the region taking root in each of five people groups. At this point the movement was spreading so rapidly that the strategy coordinator felt he could safely exit the work without diminishing its momentum. The next year, in his absence, the movement nearly tripled as the total number of churches grew to 550 with more than 55,000 believers.[58]

Third, all church planting movements do not grow at the same rate. The goal is, however, for them to double as quickly as possible. Leaders should not become discouraged if the rate of growth of a church planting movement is different from those of other movements in other parts of the world.

The phrase, *"Indigenous churches planting churches,"* points to the fact that the churches are generated from within the cultural group. The churches that are planted utilize local means and indigenous leadership from the very beginning. This procedure ensures that the fellowship, teaching, worship, and leadership patterns that are employed are compatible with that to which the culture is already accustomed. An inquirer asked a missionary involved in a church planting movement, "When do you pass the baton to the leaders of the house churches?" He replied, "We never pick it up to start with." The missionary was one of the church planter strategy coordinators who popularized the term *"shadow pasturing."*

The strategy of enabling indigenous churches to plant churches is facilitated by the fact that reproduction is built into the genetic code (DNA) of every new church that is formed.

This strategy makes it possible for churches to start new churches instead of depending on professional church planters and church planting agencies to implement the plans. As Garrison explains, "The initiative and drive of the movement comes from within the people group rather than from outsiders."[59]

A related issue that must be explored has to do with the stage at which an emerging congregation is considered a "church" and therefore has the authority to reproduce itself. In areas where traditional approaches require that congregations go through prescribed stages before they can constitute into churches, are parallel patterns going to be needed to foster the rapid reproduction of indigenous churches? If so, what safeguards will need to be in place to address the concerns of those who have become accustomed to the more traditional approaches?

An imperative question that we must address as we think of church planting movements in North America is "how can we encourage the reproduction of indigenous churches with indigenous leadership?" Perhaps some observations will be helpful. First, "indigenous" means "native," so we need to ask ourselves, what is indigenous or natural in our target communities? Do we need to develop indigenous approaches that are unique to various groups within North America cultures? Second, since large numbers of indigenous leaders are needed, what is the best way to find them, train them, and empower them? Third, since we already have a significant number of formally trained pastors and strategists, how can we help them to undergo the paradigm shift that is needed? This question is addressed by Dr. J. D. Payne in his chapter,

"Suggested Shifts in Preparation for Church Planting Movements."

The phrase "*within a people group or population segment*" points to the fact that church planting movement strategies take into account the associational and relational patterns of the target group. For many of these groups the glue that binds them together is their cultural identity. The fact that they have a common cultural heritage, language, and historical pilgrimage makes it possible for them to associate with one another easily and naturally. The term "population segment" applies to sub-cultural groups within a people group, affinity groups (based on common vocation and/or lifestyle), and groups with common residential patterns (such as urbanized segments).

In light of the fact that large numbers of ethnic groups and affinity groups exist in North America, what do we need to do to ascertain their receptivity to the gospel and to house-centered, basic church-type strategies? Even if we were to grant that some segments of the population are not receptive to non-traditional approaches of church planting, the urgent need to reach and disciple North America compels us to ask, "For the sake of the Kingdom, what segments are responsive to church planting movement strategies and what should these strategies be if they are to be relevant to the North American scene"?

Recently we have adopted the term church multiplication movements rather than continuing the terminology church planting movements. Our intent is not to separate from the simple or organic church movement but to complement these efforts by pointing to strategies that seek to produce churches in multiples. The meaning is basically the same as church planting movements with additional stress on the fact that these churches seek to reproduce in multiples rather than one-by-one. Hence, readers should recognize that when we speak of church planting movements we mean church multiplication movements.

Those considering the church planting movement strategy need to take into account an observation Garrison makes concerning such efforts. He states that church planters must not lose sight of the fact that "it will take a *movement* of churches planting churches to reach an entire nation of people." He cautions that "a church planting movement *is not an end in itself.* ***"The end of all our efforts is for God to be glorified.***"[60] This observation compels us to ask the question, "What would we do differently if the selection of our goals, strategies, resources, and partners in our church planting efforts were guided by the overriding principle that the end of all our efforts is for **God to be glorified**"?

Spiritual Conditions

When we read about the astounding church planting movements taking place in other countries, especially in some that have been resistant to the gospel, we are compelled to conclude that they are truly works of God. Such miracles of multiplication simply could not happen apart from special divine intervention. This leads us to ask several questions.

First, was a spiritual revival already taking place in that setting before the church planting movement began? Many are acquainted with the Great Awakenings that have taken place in Europe and North America in previous centuries. These awakenings witnessed massive numbers of people miraculously turning to God and becoming followers of Jesus Christ. Names such as Jonathan Edwards, George Whitefield, and John Wesley come to mind in relation to these awakenings.[61] In the case of Wesley, large numbers of churches were started as a result of this movement. Has anything like this occurred in connection with recent church planting movements?

Second, have these modern church planting movements been preceded by extensive and sustained intercession on the part of people either outside or inside the people groups in which these movements have taken place? We know that prayer has been listed as one of the universal elements of church planting movements abroad.[62] Some misconceptions about the role of prayer and spiritual factors in these movements could arise. Some might say that these movements are of such supernatural nature that our only option is to wait until they occur. In other words, there is nothing we can do to prepare for these manifestations of God's power.

Others say that these movements occur only when massive numbers of people both inside and outside the people group engage in sustained intercessory prayer. The role of prayer is a given. What we need to know is, are there instances in which initially there was no evidence of a spiritual revival yet as people began to pray, they were guided by the Lord in such a way as to begin to experience a church planting movement? In short, is a spiritual revival or awakening a prerequisite for church planting movements? Dr. Curtis Sergeant addresses the issue of the role of prayer in his chapter, "Prayer Strategy for Church Planting Movements."

Authority in the Church

Another issue related to church planting movements concerns the question of authority in the various congregational models. Where is the authority to make decisions located? This involves decisions related to such matters as the enlistment of church leaders, the selection of a congregational model, and the utilization of financial resources. Is authority located in the central congregation? Is it delegated? Does authority reside with the local group? Or is there another strategy for dealing with the issue of authority?

An additional factor that needs to be considered is the significance of congregational authority for the contextualization in church planting movements. The farther authority to make decisions rests from the local situation the more time it will take the congregations to achieve any measure of contextualization. Further, separating church authority and the new congregations produces a greater likelihood that the churches and the movement will not be contextualized. What would be the impact of this for church planting movements if churches fail to achieve contextualization?

Incorporation of Converts

An issue that closely relates to the previous question is the manner in which new believers are incorporated into the church. If a church is a part of a church planting movement in North America, are converts received into the fellowship in the local setting when they make a decision for Christ or do they have to join a central congregation at a later date? In areas where house churches are considered extensions of central congregations converts are required to attend the worship services, indicate their decision to join the church, and then be voted in by the members of the central congregation. While this is viewed by some as an effective way to monitor house churches, it has created enormous backlogs of people who live far from the central congregation, whose work schedules do not allow them to attend at the appropriate hours, or who have not been able to attend training sessions prescribed by the central congregation at their meeting place.

Two issues need to be considered: One is that the farther away from the local setting the more impersonal the incorporation of the new believer is going to be. The other is that the longer it takes to incorporate new believers the greater the bottleneck that is created. Again the question needs to be asked, what is the impact of this for church planting movements?

Adequate Leadership

Who are the leaders of the churches in church planting movements? In the vast majority of the churches in North America, the pastors are in a special category as "clergy." These leaders, in many cases, have received years of formal training and have the ministry and leadership skills that are needed to administer the work of their congregations. Even in the case of bi-vocational ministers, many church leaders have received the type of training that encourages congregations to consider them officially as their pastors.

In church planting movements, however, neither the resources nor the personnel to institute formal training programs for the house church leaders exist. The house church leaders in these movements have by and large been lay persons who have

44

had a marvelous conversion experience, have opened their homes to reach their extended families and close friends, and have committed to on-going, "just-in-time" training that enables them to continue to learn and grow as they lead their small groups. The chapter on, "The Role of the Laity in Church Planting Movements" provides valuable information on this subject.

Regarding the issue of credentials for church leaders, perhaps the two categories that have been most usually employed have been "ordination" and "licensing" for Christian ministry. Typically ordained persons have received formal training. Often granting a license for ministry has preceded the ordination phase for many. These two methods have been established with the purpose of ensuring that those who serve as leaders have the needed qualifications for their ministry functions.

In light of the fact that church planting movement strategies typically do not initially include formal training and evaluation, the question regarding the type of credentials needed for the house church leaders needs to be addressed. A corollary question relates to the qualifications that are needed to be house church leaders. Are there some biblical guidelines that can be utilized to ensure that people not just declare themselves leaders without any kind of observation and training on the part of church planting leaders?

If house churches are to have effective leaders, it is necessary to involve these in effective leadership training. In order to accomplish this, several questions need to be addressed. Is the training to be formal or informal? If it is to be formal in a centralized training center, how far will it be from the place of ministry of the trainees? Will it require that the trainees leave their jobs and families in order to train full time? What are the implications of this for church planting movements? If it is to be informal, what can be done to ensure that the trainees learn the basics of the Christian life and ministry? Is it to be training *for ministry* or training *in ministry* (while serving in house church ministry)? Is this training to be occasional or on-going? What will be the skill requirements? Will these be high or professional or will the training rest in basic areas? Is the focus going to be to *train leaders* (to carry out expected functions) or to *train trainers* (to train others who will in turn train others? The chapter on, "Training Leaders for Church Planting Movements," provides an excellent model for this type of training.

People Group and Population Segments

When people say that church planting movements will not work in North America, it is fair to ask, among what groups will they not work? It is reasonable to believe that people who are currently churched (that is, members of a church) and some who were previously churched in traditional churches may be predisposed to the more traditional types of churches. Even if this possibility is granted, millions of people in North America are presently not involved in traditional churches. How many of these would be more open to being involved in a house-centered type of group?

As we look at the numerous people groups in North America, we need to ask ourselves, what is the glue that brings them together? Are they centered on extended families? Do they have strong social networks? Do they belong to a particular socio-economic level? Do they have a common ethno-linguistic heritage? Are they bound together by a common type of employment? Do they have a church background but are currently turned off by traditional churches? Do they have a secular background? Answers to these questions can provide valuable clues as to the type of approaches that should be employed in reaching them with the gospel. An extensive discussion on this is provided in the chapter on "Ethnolinguistic Factors in Church Planting Movements."

Recognition of Churches

How can and how should house churches be recognized in highly traditional settings? Many denominations have established procedures for the formal recognition of new churches. For some the process demands a sponsoring church to start a daughter congregation. Generally after a number of years the new congregation is constituted into a church that has both legal status and denominational recognition. In the case of congregations that have been started without a sponsoring church, there have been waiting periods in which the congregations come under the "watch care" of the fellowship of churches (association or judicatory) before they are voted in as cooperating, full-fledged churches.

Church planting movements typically have not followed these processes. Often the congregations have been seen as churches from the very beginning. This procedure has contributed to the rapid multiplication of house churches. A question that needs to be addressed in many settings in North America is, "How can house churches be validated and recognized in such a way as to foster their rapid multiplication without ignoring the basic qualifications of a biblically-centered church?" Is the on-going training of house church leaders a possible way to accomplish this?

Interrelationship of Churches

How can traditional and house churches relate to one another in such a way as to ensure mutual help and encouragement? In many traditional areas, denominations have fellowships or associations (judicatories) of churches that work together to have a unified witness in their communities and to participate in joint missionary endeavors. Typically these associations have mechanisms whereby established churches are accepted into their membership.

Due to its unique characteristics the house church would not generally qualify as a member church in some of these associations. The question that needs to be addressed is, "What changes need to take place in these associations to make room for house churches?" Does a new paradigm need to be developed involving a separate track for house churches? Do house churches need to form networks that relate to existing structures?[63] Is a combination of approaches needed that allows for traditional churches to follow the established track while creating a new track for house churches? Is a combination of these approaches needed? The ultimate question is, how can house churches be a part of the association of churches without employing a process that slows down their rate of growth? This issue is addressed by Dr. Tom Billings in his chapter, "Associational Strategies for Church Planting Movements."

Doctrinal Integrity

Doctrinal integrity constitutes one of the most crucial and perhaps the most emotional issues regarding congregations that arise from church planting movements? Some people ask: "How can we avert heresy in settings where house churches are growing so rapidly that we can hardly keep up with them?" This is indeed a valid question!

A part of this question that also must be examined relates to the area of discipleship. What kind of discipleship will keep new converts from going astray doctrinally? Is it a discipleship that places a significant amount of emphasis on cognitive learning and traditional or cultural practices or is it one focuses primarily on studying the Bible and putting into practice what is being learned (i.e., obedience discipleship)? Is the discipleship that is being employed intensive initially and almost non-existent subsequently or is it on-going throughout the ministry of the house church leaders? Is there the type of vitality in daily Bible study and ministry involvement that serves as an antidote to ward off heresy?

Concerned about doctrinal integrity, some church leaders stress the fact that there is the need to imbed in the soul of new converts the *"Doctrinal DNA"* (genetic code) that will ensure that they understand and observe the basic doctrines of the Bible. This, they feel, will make them immune to doctrinal heresy. From a biblical standpoint, a strong case can be made for the importance of communicating "the faith which was once for all delivered to the saints" (Jude 3). If they are to remain firm in their beliefs, new converts to Christ must be solidly grounded on the doctrines of the Word of God.

Other church leaders call for the inculcation of a *"Denominational DNA"* that will ensure that new converts and new churches understand and adopt the unique characteristics of their denomination. This is motivated by a strong desire to communicate core values that are held in high esteem by the members and leaders of a given denomination.

Perhaps one of the greatest challenges of this task is that of distinguishing between the *biblical* and the *cultural* dimensions of a *"Denominational DNA"*. This differentiation will facilitate the transculturation of denominational distinctives and prevent the imposition of organizational structures and practices that have served the denomination well in its native setting but may become obstacles to the communication of the gospel and the reproduction of churches in another cultural setting. Making this distinction is not an easy task. Propagating practices that are truly biblical will enhance the spreading of the Christian message. Conversely, seeking to impose a *cultural DNA* on other cultural groups could well have the opposite effect. Additional dialogue regarding this issue constitutes one of the most urgently needed efforts in this discussion.

Meeting Place

The place where people meet to worship is also an issue that needs to be addressed. As can be expected, some people who are accustomed to traditional churches quite naturally conclude that churches need to meet in church buildings. Conversely, those who are using house church strategies are open to meeting anywhere that a small group can gather. While many people meet primarily in homes (especially in areas where church buildings are prohibited) others meet in offices, conference rooms, coffee houses, apartments, and whatever space is available to them.

Equating church with buildings limits any church planting effort to the number of church buildings that can be provided. Typically, as Wolfgang Simson points out, the "cathedral concept of church" carries with it a number of assumptions. These include having church on a special day (Sunday), depending exclusively on professional leadership, and finding a way to maintain itself (tithes and offerings).[64] While these types of churches have their place among many groups, there are numerous population segments that will not be reached unless additional church planting models are used. A church building with traditional architecture may constitute an actual hindrance to reaching some groups of people today. These issues are addressed in Dr. J.D. Payne's chapter, "Suggested Shifts in Preparation for Church Planting Movements."

The principle is that the people are the church and they meet wherever they can. The question before us is, "How flexible are we with regard to the place in which a church meets?" Can we overcome the bias that a congregation that does not own a building is not a church or is a second class church? A most harmful regulation is that of requiring the ownership of property before a congregation can be recognized as a church.[65]

Financial Support

Another issue that church planting movements in North America must address relates to the financial support of new congregations. Many national, state, and local mission organizations have financial packages for church planters. The ultimate goal is for the churches to become self-supporting through phase-down financial subsidy plans. Church planters expect that many of their financial needs are going to be provided for the initial period of the church planting process. This type of plan has enabled some denominations to continue to plant significant numbers of churches while other denominations continue to decline.

In most cases, denominations have become "maxed out" in the allocation of their church planting funds and are left with the option of gradual incremental growth in areas where exponential growth is sorely needed. What is the answer? Should current church planting strategies continue while parallel plans are developed for house churches? Is financial subsidy incompatible with church planting movements? *To my knowledge, there is not a single rapidly growing, sustained church planting movement currently occurring in which there is an infusion of foreign (or outside) funds for the support of house church leaders.*

If specialized strategies are developed for church planting movements, church planting catalysts will of necessity refrain from serving as the leaders of the local congregations. To allow the new churches to rely on their own resources from the very beginning will strengthen these congregations in the long run. Turning from subsidy and financial support patterns can become one of the factors that will allow denominations to experience exponential growth through the establishment of new churches. This is the approach that the apostle Paul used and that pioneer missionary thinkers, such John Nevius, Rufus Anderson and Henry Venn recommended.[66] It is consistent with Jim Slack's definition of a church planting movement as "a rapid and multiplicative increase of indigenous New Testament churches planting other churches within a given people group or population segment who can and are evangelizing their people *without significant outside assistance*." (italics mine)[67]

Evangelism Focus

What type of evangelistic focus will contribute most assuredly toward the sparking of church planting movements in North America? Is it the type of evangelism that focuses on reaching individuals, discipling them in the context of existing churches, and eventually trains them to witness to others? Or is it the type of evangelism that reaches individuals, immediately trains them to reach their families and friends, encourages them to start meeting in their homes, and guides them to replicate the process by reaching the unchurched and teaching them to do likewise? It is obvious that reproductive evangelism contributes to the initiation and expansion of church planting movements.

The Ordinances

It must be stated at the outset that observing the ordinances of Baptism and the Lord's Supper are vital functions of New Testament-type churches (Acts 2:40-47). As church planting movements are initiated, this becomes a vital issue. Most evangelical groups are quick to point out that the ordinances are symbolic in nature. The truth remains, however, that some groups believe that only ordained professional clergy can officiate in the observance of these. Many churches license or commission carefully selected and trained persons to officiate in the observance of the ordinances in the worship services that are held in homes and other meeting places.

As we explore the possibility of initiating additional church planting movements, we need to examine the Scriptures more closely to learn how the Early Church observed the ordinances. Finding ways to select, train, and empower local lay ministers to officiate in the observance of the ordinances will contribute toward the multiplication of new congregations.

Contextualized Discipleship

Organizational approaches stand at the zenith of most efforts as discipleship in North American churches. One of the organizational approaches that has served many North American churches well throughout the years and continues to be a powerful instrument for discipling millions of people every year is Sunday School. Many churches have exceedingly well organized graded Sunday Schools and excellent educational buildings in which to house the pupils.

The question arises, however in communities where church buildings and educational buildings are not available or not allowed, is it possible to disciple people? The mandate in Scripture is to "make disciples" (Matt 28:20). This mandate can be carried out in a wide variety of ways. Historically, Sunday School has been one of the best methods, but home Bible studies and cell groups are examples of other methods that can be used very effectively to make disciples. Some of these methods are life-transformation groups in which people encourage each other and hold each other accountable before the Lord. Church planting movements must find many avenues to disciple people. This issue is addressed by Dr. Billie Hanks in his chapter, "Disciple-Making in Church Planting Movements."

Relevant Worship

We thank the Lord for the marvelous churches that have well-planned and inspiring worship services every week in which many highly-trained persons are involved. This is not an effort to argue against the validity of these types of worship services. Instead, it is a challenge to examine what is absolutely essential in developing the type of churches that will spawn church planting movements in North America.

Do home-based groups need to strive to replicate the elaborate worship services held in large churches? Their goal is to bring people together to experience intimate fellowship, to teach each other how to obey the teachings of Christ, to share material and spiritual blessings, to pray together, to share the good news of salvation with others, and train them to repeat the process (Acts 2:40-47). Will having the formal worship service of a large church as a model be a limiting factor in house-centered strategies for church planting movements? These potential limitations to church planting movements can be overcome through sustained prayer, open-minded study of the Word of God, careful analysis of what the Lord is already doing to spark church planting movements, and the patient yet focused training of those who have not yet caught a vision or who need to experience a paradigm shift.

Conclusion

The questions raised above underline some of the crucial issues that we must address if we are to experience more church planting movements in North America. The chapter authors surface additional issues that they have encountered in their local settings. There will also be some diversity between the authors in addressing some of these issues.

Because church planting movements in North America are a work in progress, a significant amount of work is needed related to the clarification of terms and the evaluation and improvement of church planting models that are being employed. It is the hope of the authors that we will continue to work, research, share, and learn as a result of the dialogue that has been initiated in this book. The task of reaching North America with all of its complexity and diversity is a daunting one. We should take comfort in the fact today we have the same source of power and guidance that the Early Church had. Let us continue to explore church planting movement strategies in a spirit of prayer, openness, and expectation.

Endnotes

[55] Donald Mc Gavran, Understanding Church Growth, Grand Rapids: William Eerdmans Publishing Company, 1970, 285-295.

[56] Stan Norman, "Ecclesiastical Guidelines to Inform Southern Baptist Church Planters," un published paper, New Orleans Baptist Theological Seminary, September 28, 2004.

[57] David Garrison, *Church Planting Movements*, Richmond: International Mission Board, 1999, 8.

[58] Ibid., 11.

[59] Ibid., 8.

[60] Ibid., 8,9.

[61] See, Malcolm Mc Dow and Alvin L Reid, *Firefall*, Nashville: Broadman & Holman Publishers, 1997.

[62] David Garrison, *Church Planting Movements*, Richmond: International Mission Board, 1999.

[63] The term "network" is used here to mean a group of house churches that work cooperatively to assist one another and accomplish that which they could not accomplish separately.

[64] Wolfgang Simson, *Houses That Change The World*, Carslile, UK: OM Publishing, 1998, 29.

[65] For a number of years, an Association of churches in an urban area, wishing to protect itself from the emergence of sect-type groups, established a rule that a group could not be considered a church unless it owned a building. Years later, a study indicated that during that time the population doubled in that urban area but the number of churches remained virtually the same.

[66] John L. Nevius *Planting and Development of Missionary Churches* (n.p.: The Presbyterian and Reformed Publishing Company, n.d.). , William A. Smalley, "Cultural Implications of an Indigenous Church," in *Readings in Dynamic Indigeneity*, ed. Charles H. Kraft and Tom N. Wisley (Pasadena, CA: William Carey Library, 1979), The Lausanne Committee for World Evangelization in Ralph Winter, *Perspectives On The World Christian Movement*, Pasadena: William Carey, 1992, 181.

[67] Jim Slack, "Church Planting Movement Assessments: the CPM Assessment Team's Task," (prepared for Southern Baptist Seminaries Related to the Seminary Consortium, Richmond, Va., 17 April 2003), 1.

Chapter 3

Biblical and Historical Foundations for Church Planting Movements

Mike Barnett and Dan Morgan

Church Planting Movement (CPM) is a term of recent coinage. The simultaneous movement into the Christian faith of groups of people sharing common culture and/or ancestry seems, however, to have been an underlying phenomenon of ancient heritage. This phenomenon, labeled "people movements" by western missiologists of the last century [68] reflects the saving working of the Holy Spirit in groups of individuals. Examples of this type of conversion experience exist as early as the Pentecost after Christ's resurrection. Clearly, the Holy Spirit has used the preaching of the gospel to bring groups of people into Christ's kingdom since the very first moment He came to indwell the church.

Before we look at people movements, and their formal expressions through CPMs, we should consider the propriety of such movements from a biblical and theological viewpoint. We can comfortably claim that CPMs are parts of a strategy that is congruent with the work of God in the world, are connected with a Spirit-driven phenomenon evident from Pentecost forward, and are producing remarkable results in many locations around the world. Evidence exists that people movements, initiated and fostered by CPM-style strategies, are indeed occurring in Africa, Asia, South, and Central America.

It must also be noted, however, that not all apparent movements of groups of people to biblical faith represent genuine conversion. Even when the majority of those confessing Christ demonstrate life change consistent with the indwelling of the Spirit, it would be difficult to prove that everyone in the group had an adequate understanding of what they espoused as their new belief. There have been times when the expression of a faith-change is obviously for unworthy motives. Some have come to Christianity from motives of material advantage (e.g., rice Christians). Many undoubtedly thought that Simon (the Sorcerer) had undergone a genuine conversion experience when he "believed and was baptized" (Acts 8:12). His real motive came out when he offered Peter money for the power to cause the Holy Spirit to come upon the lives of people (vv. 18, 19). Peter's response reveals that Simon was still in spiritual darkness (vv. 20-23). There have also been times when the groups of people had no choice and exercised no volition. Constantine's marching of his troops through a river while priests sprinkled them with water in "baptism" is one glaring historical example.

Because CPMs are a formal strategy that is of recent vintage, this chapter will trace the history of the phenomena of people movements, and refer to them as such. Only at the point where CPMs are introduced will we switch terminology in this brief history. For clarity, this point of change took place when Southern Baptist missiologists began to attempt the formulation of intentional strategies to foster people movements, and to conserve the fruit of these people movements by the rapid planting of New Testament churches.

People Movements in the Bible

Constraining this brief history to the New Testament and after, the first recorded people movement must be credited to the events of Acts 2. The salient features, which become a standard for evaluating more modern movements, are: (1) The Holy Spirit uses *means* (the phenomena of people praising God in foreign languages) *to gain* the *attention* of a group of people. (2) These people have a *shared heritage and culture* (Jews of the Diaspora on Pilgrimage to Jerusalem for the festival of Pentecost). (3) There is *proclamation* of Christ and his death, burial, and resurrection with a call for repentance and faith, publicly acknowledged through baptism. (4) There is an *extraordinary response* as large numbers of hearers accept the message and demonstrate this acceptance by being publicly baptized.

The very next chapter in Acts records a second instance of this multi-individual response to the preaching of the gospel. This time the Holy Spirit uses the *means* of the miraculous healing of the well-known beggar at the temple gates. The crowd gathers in response to the electrifying news, and Peter *preaches* Christ; crucified, buried, and rising the third day. He calls for repentance and faith and, though interrupted by the temple guards who arrest them, Acts 4:4 records that *several thousand responded* and were added to the believers. From this point on, the numbers continue to grow, but are noted in more general terms.

The next instance of a "people movement" deals, not with Jews who were related by ancestry and heritage, but a household where people shared a common life, and relational history. This is the "household" version of group conversion. This household was that of Cornelius, a Roman centurion who was at the same time a God-fearer. His story is recorded in Acts 10. There are several notable aspects of this story, which reinforce the pattern noted earlier.

1) The *messenger* (Peter) needed to be persuaded that God really could do whatever He pleased, even if it meant throwing out a cherished tradition of the messenger (do we hear the echo, "We've never done it that way before.") In passing we must note that much of the opposition to CPMs comes from a seemingly similar sentiment.

2) The Holy Spirit, in common with the previous accounts, used *means* to get the messenger and the listeners together, in this case Cornelius' vision of a man telling him to send to Joppa for Peter.

(3) Again in common with earlier occurrences Peter *preaches* a straightforward gospel message. The *entire household* turns to Christ. One must note that after thousands of conversions with no notation of a dramatic outward movement of the Spirit, here that same Spirit comes upon the hearers in power and they speak in tongues, praising God.

The next instance of a large movement to Christ occurs in Antioch among Gentiles who are not recorded as having any prior contact with Judaism, and therefore constitute another distinct people group. Acts 11 records that when Jewish believers from Cyprus and Cyrene preached to Greeks, "a great number of people believed and turned to the Lord" (vs.21). Barnabas was sent by the authorities in Jerusalem to inspect this movement of Gentiles to Christ. Not only did he realize that this was a work of God, but he joined the work and "a great number of people were brought to the Lord" (vs.24). Barnabas then went to Tarsus and brought back Saul. Together they spent a year discipling "great numbers of people" (vs.26). It is noteworthy in passing to realize that until the arrival of

Barnabas the task of beginning the church and discipling the converts was in the hands of ordinary believers with no formal training. It is not clear that Barnabas had formal training. Not until Barnabas retrieved Saul from Tarsus was there a formally trained teacher, in this case discipled by the famous rabbi, Gamaliel.

More examples of large numbers of people coming to Christ as a result of Paul's missionary journeys emerge in the New Testament records. Examples of both regional movements to Christ and household conversion are recorded. We will close this section with one example of each.

The first missions journey of Barnabas and Saul is recorded beginning in Acts 13. At first the two missionaries itinerated throughout the island of Cyprus. However, when they preached for an extended time in Pisidian Antioch, there were dramatic results. This shift in strategy apparently had both a negative and a positive effect. The negative effect was that Jews turned from open debate to hardened, and ultimately violent, resistance to Paul's teaching. The positive effects, however, far outweighed them. Many of both Jews and gentiles believed the message. There was time to develop influential friends so that the gospel permeated all levels of the local society. Most important, however, is the notation of verse 49, "the word of the Lord spread through the whole region." By evangelizing and planting a church in a regional trading center, Paul saw the message carried throughout the region. This is a lesson he seems to have applied from then on.

Our last biblical example comes from events during Paul's second missionary journey, traveling with Silas as a companion. The Holy Spirit directed them by vision to enter

Macedonia, and so they arrived at Philippi. Note that this is a Roman colony and a chief trading center for the region. The account in Acts 16 records first that the trader Lydia and her household converted to Christianity and were all baptized. Later, as a result of a dramatic night in jail, the jailer and his household were converted and baptized. In each case, the decision of the head of the household to convert was immediately followed by the accession of the rest of their household. These are clear examples of multi-individual decisions with no hesitance on the part of Paul to baptize all of them.

This swift review of the biblical record should convince us that where the gospel is preached to crowds having some common relationship, common heritage, or close ties to an influential leader, the Holy Spirit may choose to move in the hearts of people in groups. He may even use the means of a miraculous occurrence or the decision of an influential leader to prompt this people movement to Christ. We will look for these two precipitating factors in other apparent movements to Christ. Now we shift away from biblical history to the post-biblical history of the church.

People Movements in Church History

Space does not allow an exhaustive review of people movements, but we will note some of the better known instances that were recorded by missionaries when they occurred. These examples underline the possibility that God will work through people movements and church multiplication movements in all the world, including North America.

The spread of Christianity in Europe

The appearance of people movements in pre-modern times is well-noted in the journals and writings of missionaries such as Patrick of Ireland, Columba in the north of England, and of his disciples in Gaul. The norm was the movement to Christ of whole tribes of pagan peoples. The methodology differed under God's direction, but the result was similar. Where the missionary brought the good news without insisting on particular forms, the gospel often became indigenized and contextualized to the point that it was seen as *the* answer to the spiritual struggles of that people group and adopted "en masse."

During the third century there is a well-documented instance, the first such, in which the conversion of a king, in this case Tiridates, the king of Armenia, led to the conversion of the noblemen, and then to the spread of the gospel among the common people. The missionary preached in Armenian, not Latin, and the form of Christianity that emerged was indigenous to an extraordinary degree.[69] While we note the common element of an influential leader's conversion leading to many others, we also must note this emerging factor that was not an issue for the biblical setting, *preaching in the local language* rather than Latin. Preaching in the local language is almost universally present where people movements emerge. People respond in greater numbers when they hear the gospel preached in their heart language.

In the next century the Goths were evangelized primarily by the missionary Ulfilas (c.311-383 A.D.). He was of mixed Cappadocian & Goth ethnicity; the Cappadocians had already been evangelized, while the Goths had not. He labored forty years among the Goths, firmly planted Christianity among them, and is remembered best for two achievements: reducing the Gothic language to writing and translating much of the Bible into Gothic literary form.

Christianity took hold in the British Isles in the third century, but was set back with the invasion of the Angles and Saxons. At the end of the sixth century, however, Pope Gregory sent Augustine to the court at Canterbury and the re-conquest of the British Isles by Christianity began. The first year they baptized some 10,000 Saxons into the faith. In the area now Scotland, Celtic Christianity was active. From the training center at Iona, Celtic monks traveled throughout the northern area. Besides preaching in the heart language, they were known for ranging throughout the remote villages of the land, not just the cities and towns. With the conversion of King Oswald of Northumbria in the mid-seventh century, the work expanded greatly. So with the conflux of British, Celtic and Roman Christianity during this time, the British Isles were basically evangelized by the end of the seventh century, and the missionaries from these islands were going to the Continent.[70] Was this a people movement? Not in the most dramatic sense, but nevertheless, through many witnesses several people groups were brought into the Church in a period of just over a hundred years.

Much has been written of the conversion of the different people groups of Europe. The general pattern was one or two people groups at a time, evangelized in their heart language by one or more groups of preaching monks, sometimes with a notable leader, like Boniface. The people group sometimes came into the fold village by village, and sometimes a ruler would convert and the battle for allegiance to Christ was essentially over. Out of the many groups converted, only some would be characterized as people movements. The task took centuries, but was almost complete by the dawn of the 15th century. The overwhelming impression from the stories of the conversion of Europe is that people movements were the norm not the exception.

On other continents the pattern of conversion has been similar, even if less extensive, or less well-documented. Progress has continued through the succeeding centuries up to the present time, when so many are coming to Christ in China. Two examples from this period must suffice before we look at the "Great Century" of evangelical mission effort (1792 – 1910) for a few additional instances of people movements.

Our first example of early people movements comes out of the work of the Jesuits in the Far East. The first missionary of this group was Francis Xavier. He was the close personal friend of Ignatius Loyola, founder of the Jesuits, and was sent out by them even before the Pope had approved their charter. He traveled from Rome to Lisbon, then around Africa and east to India, landing in Goa (a Portuguese trade enclave) in 1542. His first action was to begin the discipling of a whole caste of fishermen and their families who had converted to Christianity en masse. This represented 10,000 souls. The work of discipling, which he began and ordered, continued for the next fifty years, resulting in a strong Christian community of sixteen large villages, prosperous and faithful. Xavier, himself, could not sit still that long. He continued to travel in South India, and found several groups of people of similar heritage to the fisher folk won before he arrived. In each case he led the whole people group to Christ and made arrangements for them to be taught in their native language.[71]

December, 1547 marked a major turning point in Xavier's career. He encountered an exiled Samurai from Japan and began to dream of traveling to that land to establish a church. After several false starts, he arrived on one of the Japanese islands in 1549 to begin work. He prepared the ground for later workers. Over the next 50 years the number of Japanese believers increased to as many as 500,000, with Christian congregants on all the islands. Christianity ultimately became the predominant religion in some prefects in the West and South. One documented case records that in 1571 there were 5600 believers in the Sumitada lordship but by 1577 the whole population of some 50,000 had converted to Christianity, albeit some were pressured to convert by the lord Sumitada.[72] The Jesuits established the church using *preaching in the heart language* and *indigenous principles*, and were well on the way to establishing a truly Japanese form of Christianity. It is unfortunate to end this narrative with the note that once the Japanese islands were politically united, the new Shogun made Christianity illegal and persecuted the Christian community into oblivion. When Commodore Perry landed two hundred years later, however, he found a few small groups who still clung secretly to beliefs and practices of the former Christian community.

A second noteworthy instance of people movements is found in the history of the Russian Orthodox Church. In the eighteenth century they accomplished the evangelization of Siberia and the Russian East. The mission that stands out during this effort is the work of Luke Konashavich, sent to the area of the Volga River. His mission recorded 430,000 baptisms in twenty years. This included three entire people groups and all who resided there who were not Muslims. Though this was atypically rapid progress, the Russian

Orthodox Church established a significant presence in most of this vast land area in just one hundred years. They even extended missions into present day Alaska, where 10,000 believers were reached between 1794 and 1796.[73]

People Movements during
"The Great Century" (1792-1911)

Now we turn to the 19th century and the great push of Protestant missions into the unevangelized parts of the world. Consistent with the history of the expansion of the church, people movements emerged in Southern Asia. Most countries were entered by missionaries during this time, but only a few people movements occurred. Of note is the large number of conversions in the northern part of the island of Celebes, part of Indonesia. By 1900, almost the whole population had converted to Christianity.[74] Another people movement was that of Javanese Muslims to Christ. They were folk Muslims who retained much of their animistic heritage.

We also must mention Burma, where the Karin servant of Adoniram Judson led many of his brethren to Christ while Judson preached to the wealthier Burmese with little success. Two later missionaries, George Dana and Sara Boardman, targeted the Karin with great success. Many indigenous Karin evangelists spread the gospel among the whole group. By 1851 there were possibly as many as 30,000 believers in Burma, and today almost the whole people group has become believers.

Some believe that the case of the Karin movement illustrates how God sometimes plants in a people's history factors that predispose them to respond to the gospel. The Karin believed that long ago they angered the creator God, and since then their punishment was to hold the lowest place of servitude in Burmese society. Some say that the Karin once had a sacred book but lost it long ago. When a Christian preacher spoke of the creator God and brought a sacred book, this aligned with Karin hopes and aspirations. They thus listened more closely than the Burmese to the gospel message.

Without attempting to catalog any more instances of mass turnings to Christ, the point is still made, throughout Christian history, people movements to Christ have been the rule rather than the exception. Even if the reaching of a people began slowly, there is often a tipping point where the whole group turns to Christ in a very short time. Often a key seems to be the provision of the Bible and preaching in the heart language of the group. Another frequent factor seems to be the conversion of *influential leaders*. At other times it is the very fact that they can change their belief system together and still retain the mutual support that is crucial to their survival and well-being. In all these factors we see the overarching activity of the Holy Spirit drawing people to himself. Perhaps the most amazing thing about people movements is that it took so long for western missionaries to recognize that God was at work in ways at variance with their accepted methodology. The shift in missionary understanding of how peoples come to Christ began to take shape in the early decades of the twentieth century.

People Movement Strategies in the Twentieth Century

It is not surprising that the seedbeds for people movement thinking in the early twentieth century were the very same soils that are producing church planting movements today. If the nineteenth century is the "Great Century"[75] of missionary activity, then perhaps the twentieth century should be known as the "Strategic Century." A new generation of missions strategists emerged in the twentieth century.

People Movement Thinkers

These people movement thinkers constructed philosophies of missions built upon the shoulders of their Great-Century predecessors. They were inspired by the successes and failures of pioneers like Robert Morrison, the Hudson Taylors, Lottie Moon, and John L. Nevius. They were informed by missions theorists like Henry Venn, and Rufus Anderson. Much of the best missionary thinking flowed from China and India. A common theme was people movement thinking.

Roland Allen

An Anglican missionary to China, 1895-1903, Roland Allen was one of these critical thinkers. Ahead of his time, Allen returned from the tragic fields of the Boxer Rebellion in China to a pastoral ministry in England. His parish posting provided a platform for four decades of missiological thinking and writing. Like most innovators he was ridiculed and somewhat ignored by his contemporaries. His bold warnings against standard missionary practices of his day fell on deaf ears. His call was to return to the methods of the apostle Paul and strive for the kind of expansion of the gospel witnessed in the first century.

Two major themes preoccupied Allen: the absolute necessity of planting *indigenous* churches, and the expectation that these indigenous churches naturally and expansively *reproduce themselves.* Allen envisioned New Testament-like movements of reproducing indigenous churches planting churches, sweeping across the globe. For him it was a simple process: "If the church is to be indigenous it must spring up in the soil from the very first seeds planted. One or two little groups of Christians organized as churches, with their bishops and priests, could spread all over an empire."[76]

His book, *Missionary Methods: St. Paul's or Ours?,* outlines the Apostle's methods for planting home grown, reproducible churches. *The Spontaneous Expansion of the Church*, explains how indigenous churches naturally reproduce themselves if we stay out of their way. Both volumes were reprinted in the 1960s and remain in print today. They hold a prominent place in the toolboxes of 21st-century cross-cultural missionaries.

J. Waskom Pickett

While Allen was documenting insights gleaned from his missionary service in China, an American Methodist missionary to India was investigating the phenomenon of mass movements of Christian converts in India. In 1933, upon the request of the India National Christian Council, J. Waskom Pickett published the results of his research on people movements in India. His book—*Mass Movements in India*—identified three observations concerning mass movements of converts: (1) more people came to Christ via mass conversion than individual conversion; (2) the quality of mass movements depended heavily on post-baptismal care; (3) the belief that church planting must be a long, difficult process is not correct.[77]

Pickett's case studies reflect the best in critical thinking from a missiological standpoint. For example, his analysis of the expansion of the gospel among the Gara people of Orrisa in India observes that the movement is comprised of indigenous churches, extensively integrated with the lives of their communities and therefore, "understood by the surrounding peoples." Pickett concludes that "one element in the rapid growth of all such churches is that the essential message of the Church is better understood, or is less misunderstood, than it is in the churches which are the result of 'Christianization by extraction.'"[78]

Pickett served as a bishop in India until 1956, was a nationally known figure, promoted evangelism, and led in the establishment of institutional ministries (schools and hospitals) in India and Nepal. Yet biographer Gerald H. Anderson suggests that his greatest contribution was the research and documentation on group movements.[79] Perhaps his greatest legacy is the influence he had on another young missionary to India.

Donald Anderson McGavran

This young missionary was Donald Anderson McGavran, a Disciples of Christ missionary neighbor of Pickett. McGavran was perplexed by the reality that after decades of missionary work in his part of India there were only two or three dozen small stagnant churches.[80] McGavran joined Pickett's research project in search of answers. His goal was to discover the processes for most effectively communicating the gospel so that its expansion would fulfill the commission of Christ to disciple all nations. The first-fruit of this partnership with Pickett and his thirty-one years of missionary service in

India was his classic book, *The Bridges of God: A Study in the Strategy of Missions*. In his introduction McGavran clearly defined his purpose:

> How do peoples become Christian? Here is a question to which not speculation but knowledge must urgently be applied. The question is, in a manner true to the Bible, can a Christian movement be established in some caste, tribe or clan which will, over a period of years, so bring groups of its related families to Christian faith that the whole people is Christianized in a few decades? It is of utmost importance that the Church should understand how peoples, and not merely individuals, become Christian.[81]

The book discarded conventional missionary wisdom and boldly introduced the concept of group thinking so common in Asian culture but so foreign to the individualistic West. He tweaked Pickett's term "mass movements" into "people movements" and cited New Testament and historical examples of people movements as they crossed cultural bridges and swept across Palestine, into the Mediterranean world of the Roman Empire and beyond.[82]

McGavran calculated over 100,000 "God-given" people movement congregations in 1955.[83] He declared that people movements had the advantages of: (1) permanent churches, firmly planted; (2) naturally indigenous churches; (3) spontaneous expansion (referring to Roland Allen's thinking); (4) enormous growth potential; (5) a sound pattern of becoming a Christian.[84]

His charge for the church was to focus resources and energies on strategically facilitating existing people movements to reach the remaining unreached nations.[85]

The Bridges of God was just the beginning. For another forty-five years, McGavran developed and lead the "Church Growth Movement"—undoubtedly the most influential school of missions thought and practice in the twentieth century. As founding Dean of the School of World Mission of Fuller Theological Seminary in Pasadena, California, he wrote dozens of books and influenced hundreds of missionary students. Though he may be most remembered for the Church Growth Institute and its sometimes controversial scientific approach to missions research, McGavran was driven by the desire to understand and advocate for the spread of people movements of churches planting churches.

McGavran and others like him were catalysts for the development of missionary strategy think tanks and practical alliances that literally changed the face of world evangelization. By the early 1970s these concepts were ripe for the picking. It was time for another global conference on world missions.

The Lausanne/Fuller/Southern Baptist Connection!

Since the first evangelism conference in Jerusalem, described in Acts 15, churches have gathered together to discuss strategies and challenges in the Great Commission task. The twentieth century was characterized by numerous international missionary congresses. The topic of people movements was never far from the podium.

The Lausanne movement

The most significant conference for world missions in the last century was undoubtedly the Lausanne Committee for World Evangelization (LCWE), first convened in 1974. Lausanne's role in people group and eventually church planting movement thinking must be recognized. Just as the Student Volunteer Movement (SVM) of the late nineteenth and early twentieth century fueled the fires of missions interest and involvement, the Lausanne movement provided the forum and venue for late 20th-century missiological theory and practice.

American evangelist Billy Graham initiated the call for a multi-denominational and international congress to address issues regarding world evangelization. Sometimes seen as an evangelical counterpart to the struggling World Council of Churches, Lausanne focused not on unity of faith and liturgy but on partnership in the formidable but attainable task of global evangelization. Lausanne was the catalyst for the founding of hundreds of missions agencies, alliances, partnerships, training institutes, missiological publications, and networks in world missions. Practical trends which emerged from this watershed meeting included the specialization of missions agencies, the increased role of the non-western churches, and a shift from geopolitical thinking to strategies focused on reaching distinct people groups.[86]

So, where is the connection with church planting movements? From the first meeting in Switzerland the themes of people movements and the priority of unreached people groups were evident. McGavran's controversial address on people movements and Ralph Winter's article on "hidden" or "frontier" peoples stimulated dialogue in the years to follow.[87]

"The Willowbank Report" of the 1978 LCWE consultation on "Gospel and Culture," asked missionaries to recognize the biblical basis for "family and group conversions," and the theological and sociological advantages of people movement thinking.[88]

Fuller Theological Seminary

Meanwhile the missiological or academic side of missions was equally inspired by Lausanne and kept pace with its developments. The mutually beneficial relationship between the Lausanne movement and the new School of Frontier Missions at Fuller Theological Seminary in Pasadena, California, cannot be overstated. Fuller's imprint on the thinking and actions of missions agencies, schools, training programs, and faculties around the world is undeniable. Students of McGavran became leaders in the world of missions.

Ralph Winter founded the U.S. Center for World Missions in Pasadena—a network hub and incubator for pioneer missions practitioners, with its two journals, theological seminary, publishing arm, and Perspectives on the World Christian Movement courses. Peter Wagner influenced thousands of student missionaries from his Fuller classroom and his dozens of books. The faculties of denominational seminaries and missions agencies were beneficiaries of the Lausanne movement and the Fuller school.

The A.D. 2000 and Beyond organization, led by Luis Bush, came out of the Lausanne II conference in Manila in 1989. Characterized by Peter Wagner as "the most massive catalytic agency for world evangelism known,"[89] it was yet another product of the influence of Lausanne and Fuller. This movement has focused the eyes of contemporary missions on the Unreached Peoples of the World.

The Southern Baptist Connection

Though this connection has mostly gone unnoticed, there is no doubt that the people movement thinking of McGavran and the pioneer focus of Fuller as well as the Lausanne movement in general had a tremendous influence on Southern Baptist missionaries. A glimpse at this flow of influence at just one Southern Baptist institution makes the point.

Cal Guy, a missions professor at Southwestern Baptist Theological Seminary, Fort Worth, Texas, met Donald McGavran in Latin America in 1954. A quick bond formed and a lasting relationship took root. Guy, a philosophy professor by training, was in the enviable position of teaching the basic missions courses for the largest seminary in this largest of denominations. In the years that followed, Guy was joined by faculty members who caught the vision and taught much of what was coming out of Pasadena. Daniel R Sanchez and Ebbie C. Smith were both recipients of missions degrees from Fuller Theological Seminary. Smith retired recently and Sanchez is still at Southwestern.

Even the head of the missions department throughout the late 1980s and 90s, Justice Anderson, though he was not a professed follower of McGavran, planted the basic seeds of pioneer missions thinking flowing from Lausanne, Fuller, and beyond. Two of the primary church planting movement strategists of the Southern Baptist International Mission Board in the 1990s received Doctorate of Ministry degrees under the tutelage of Southwestern Missions faculties.

In the wake of the colonial exploits of the Great Century of missions, people movement thinkers such as Roland Allen, J Waskom Pickett, and Donald McGavran began to lay the groundwork for the second half of the twentieth century of missions. A turning point came in 1974 when the Lausanne conference first met. Lausanne became the forum, the incubator, the procreator for creative missions thinking and actions. Hundreds of missions agencies, networks, and partnerships sprang from the Lausanne movement. The predominant theme of the day was the remaining task of reaching all peoples on earth with the gospel. McGavran's influence through Fuller Theological Seminary and the produce of his students such as Winter and Wagner, impacted the entire missions world. Southern Baptists faculties and missions practitioners joined the flow of unreached people group thinking that preoccupied the Lausanne and Fuller communities. Though Southern Baptists arrived somewhat late on the scene of unreached peoples and people movement thinking, they were to play a pivotal role in the discovery and facilitation of church planting movements.

The Role of Southern Baptists in Church Planting Movements

From its beginnings in 1845, Southern Baptist missions focused on planting churches. R. Keith Parks, the ninth president of the International Mission Board (IMB),[90] expressed the essence of this church planting theme with his slogan, "evangelism that results in churches." Southern Baptist missionaries around the world knew they were to be on task to evangelize the lost in a way that resulted in new churches. The record shows that throughout their over 150 year history IMB missionaries witnessed numerous people movements to Christ and in some cases led in the establishment of thriving conventions of Baptist churches.[91] But a new movement that began in the late 1970s took our understanding about people movements to a new level. This emphasis became a definitive moment in the history of missions and in what is now referred to as church planting movements.[92]

Bold Mission Thrust

Like many denominations, Southern Baptists began to look to the end of the millennium sometime around the mid-1970s. Church leaders were asking the question," What will we do for the Lord in this last quarter century of the second millennium?" In 1976 the Southern Baptist Convention endorsed a plan that challenged the churches and agencies of this powerful denomination to a "Bold Mission Thrust." Specific goals for evangelism and church planting were rolled out over the next few years. The final push for growth at home and abroad was in the last years of the century—1995-2000. IMB goals followed a pattern of ten-fold increase and included: (1) International missionaries serving in 125 countries (up from 82 in 1975); (2) A total of 5,600 international missionaries (up from 2667 in 1975); (3) 10,000 international volunteers per year (an increase from 1200 in 1975); (4) relationships with 75,840 overseas churches (up from 7584 in 1975); (5) overseas church memberships of 8,960,630 (up from 896,063 in 1975); (6) 807,470 baptisms annually (up from 80,747 in 1975).[93]

Just as Southern Baptists were casting a huge vision of growth and expansion for the church around the world, a new leader was rising to the top of the International Mission Board.

International Mission Board

From the beginning of his administration in January of 1980, R. Keith Parks led his staff, at the International Mission Board, to begin to focus more fully on the best way to communicate the gospel in a biblical way so that many more souls could be saved and new indigenous churches could be planted.[94] Parks was known for asking the hard questions and charting new courses[95] He was willing to do "whatever God was asking."[96] He and his staff questioned the high lifestyle of the missionaries, their failure to equip and empower locals to lead, and their imposition of western forms of worship and church on the nationals. They constantly worked to transform traditional democratic missions structures, decentralize strategy decisions, streamline bureaucracies, and overcome the "bricks and mortar" mentality of institutionalized missions. This began to lay a foundation for what would take place later.

The Lausanne connection

About the same time that Bold Mission Thrust was emerging in Southern Baptist life, a larger movement of missions thinking and acting was developing. The previously mentioned Lausanne Congress on World Evangelization (LCWE) convened in 1974 and began to bring together missions leaders from various streams of influence.

In the spirit of Lausanne, Dr. David B. Barrett, missions researcher, editor and author of the *World Christian Encyclopedia* was hired as a consultant by the International Mission Board to develop a global database of the unreached peoples on earth for the purpose of developing an awareness and strategy for reaching them with the gospel.[97]

The changing world

Meanwhile, the world was changing. By the time Southern Baptists began to focus on reaching the least reached, the Iron and Bamboo curtains of communism were becoming porous. Since the mid-1970s China had gradually opened its ideological borders to the West. The process of the devolution of Soviet communism went through phases of *détente* (easing of tensions), *glasnost* (openness) and *perestroika* (reconstruction), and culminated in November of 1989 with the fall of the Berlin wall. Twentieth-century barriers to the communication of the gospel were literally crumbling before the eyes of a highly motivated, post-Jesus movement, Lausanne community of missions workers. The stage was set for a new approach to missions.

Cooperative Services International:
An Experiment in Missiology

In 1984, while preparing for a staff retreat, the issues converged on a prayerful Keith Parks. Like the rest of the Lausanne community, Park's burden for evangelizing the remaining unreached peoples was becoming unbearable. As he evaluated the goals of Bold Mission Thrust, he realized that even if the IMB were able to meet these goals, the task of reaching all peoples on earth would not be finished. As he looked at the remaining task in light of current structures, methods, and practices of the IMB, at least one thing became certain. If Southern Baptists were to fulfill their role in completing the task of the Great Commission, they would have to drastically change how they went about the task of international missions. Over the next three years, a small IMB think tank brain-stormed various ways to embark on a new journey in missions which would allow the IMB to play a significant role in reaching all peoples on earth with the gospel.

The radical shift in strategy evolved through a pilot project initiated by Parks between 1985-88. This project involved field operations through an agency known as Cooperative Services International. CSI carried out experimental missions efforts to more effectively penetrate under evangelized areas of the world, especially those closed to more traditional missions approaches. What started out as a micro-strategy for sending a few English teachers into East Asia developed into an innovative, dynamic, fast-growing mobilization movement of a new generation of IMB missionaries and missionary strategies. In less than ten years CSI grew from a handful of somewhat non-conforming veteran missionaries to the second largest area of the IMB with over 500 missionary workers. Looking back on the development of CSI, their missiological journey followed a path that illustrates the primary principles or "pillars" of strategic thinking and planning that became their template for missionary training: (1) Prayer—comprehensive, global, strategic prayer for each people group engaged; (2) The Word—availability of God's Word in the heart language of the people group; (3) Evangelism— effective and contextualized communication of the gospel in a way that transforms lives and results in new disciples of Jesus; (4) Church planting—effectively planting indigenous, reproducing churches that plant churches; (5) Mobilization— connecting God's people with the Great Commission task among all peoples on earth.

The development of the strategy pillars evolved over a period of years based on the bold, risk-taking, trial-and-error approach taken by the team. In July, 1997, IMB President Jerry Rankin implemented a major reorganization of the entire field office of the board. CSI ceased to exist but the "New Directions" initiated by Rankin bear the signature of the CSI experiment. The paradigm shift was incredible. It changed how missionaries were organized on the field—from basically "mission stations" to people group teams. It streamlined how resources were allocated and managed. It de-centralized specific strategy decisions. It changed the focal point from geopolitical countries to people groups or population segments. It thrust the IMB into the world of other evangelical missions agencies and teams—the Great Commission Christian community. CSI broke through outdated and traditional denominational structures which resulted in the personalization of missions in thousands of IMB churches in the United States. CSI's aggressive use of two-year missionaries resulted in a full pipeline of candidates for career missionary service. These and more influences beyond the scope of this paper are a part of the legacy of this short experiment in Missiology called CSI.

The Cooperative Services International Legacy: Church Planting Movements

Without a doubt, the lasting legacy of the CSI years will be its discovery of church planting movements.[98] Few, if any, CSI veterans would assert that they knew what they were looking for in 1988. They were focused on reaching the least reached peoples on earth. They partnered with other like-minded evangelicals and somewhere along the way they encountered God's miraculous CPMs! It was just that, an encounter with God, a discovery of how He works to accomplish His mission. CSIers will not take credit for a CPM. But CSI and the IMB deserve credit for being willing to let God use them in new and innovative ways as they watched God was working and began to advocate for the CPM model.

Early case studies

One of the early innovators and directors of CSI, David Garrison, began a study in the late 1980s of apparent people movements to Christ, which resulted in the rapid establishment of churches that multiplied themselves into other communities of faith. He drew from the experiences of CSI and Great Commission Christian missions workers throughout the 10/40 Window.

By the early 1990s some IMB missionaries were beginning to propose a shift in methodology that would allow the intentional fostering of CPMs in the settings where missionaries were already deployed. One of these missionaries chose a self-contained people group of Chinese ancestry for a pilot project. They numbered about 4 million souls and lived in a political setting that forced the church to remain underground. His initial entry to the field occurred in 1990. He surveyed the entire geographic area and identified three evangelical churches. Approaching them, he began to dialogue about the need to reach their people and the means to do that. By 1991 the three churches were committed to evangelism and starting new house churches. This missionary partnered with other agencies and developed a strategy that initially relied on "near-culture," native-language-speakers as evangelists and disciplers. They built into the genetic nature of the new churches the expectation and ability to multiply. As new groups multiplied, the near-culture missionaries turned over their roles to the new indigenous leaders. The movement reproduced second and third generation churches and continued to multiply throughout the region and even into other people groups. When the missionary was convinced that the granddaughter house churches were holding to a biblical pattern of doctrine and ecclesiology, he physically withdrew from the area and began to coach the indigenous leaders through letters, email, and occasional visits. Table 1 shows the results of his work through 2001.

Table 1

Year	1993	1994	1995	1996	1997	1998	2001
Churches	3	9	26	76	195	550	900

Another IMB missionary experimented with a slightly different CPM strategy. This was in a country of SE Asia. He began with five believers and trained them to plant churches. Each of them planted at least one church, but with a view to lead that church in multiplying itself rapidly through evangelism. The results of this CPM experiment are in Table 2.

Table 2

Year	1989	1993	1994	1995	1996	1997	1998	2000
Churches	28	36	78	220	547	1200	2000	4300

Garrison published a summary of results such as those discussed above in a little booklet in 1999. In 2004 he published the complete study in his *Church Planting Movements: How God Is Redeeming a Lost World.* The study defines a CPM as "a rapid multiplication of indigenous churches planting churches that sweeps through a people group or population segment.[99] More than just evangelism that results in converts and a single church or even multiple churches, Garrison argued that a CPM must demonstrate the possibility of reaching a whole people group, nation, or population segment within a nation in a way that compels the church to take the gospel to other people groups.

Drawing from these earliest case studies, Garrison and other IMB strategists gleaned the following "ten universal elements" which almost always seemed to accompany CPMs: (1) Prayer; (2) Abundant gospel sowing; (3) Intentional church planting – someone in the early days must intentionally choose to plant new churches; (4) Scriptural authority – The Bible is THE authority for faith and practice; (5) Local leadership – outside "experts" mentor local leaders rather than do the work themselves; (6) Lay leadership – and they make up the majority of workers who are planting new congregations; (7) Cell and/or house churches are present – both can occur in one movement; (8) Churches plant churches – this is when exponential grow occurs; (9) Rapid reproduction; (10) Healthy churches – carry out the five basic purposes of a church.

There were other characteristics which Garrison found present in many or even most CPMs as he defined them, but the ten characteristics above were universally present. It is important to note that this is not a theoretical list, but is based on analysis of actual observations by experts in the field.

New Directions at the IMB

We have already noted the influence of CSI on "New Directions." The practical effects on the field of this change in thinking were enormous. When "New Directions" was implemented in 1998, part of the change was a commitment to involve more missionaries in direct church planting with a focus on the implementation of CPM strategies.

This new initiative was imposed across the board and proved traumatic for many missionaries who were used to working in specialties that didn't involve church planting. Some missionaries resigned, others soldiered along, though without a sense that they were working areas of strength. Many, however, welcomed this refocusing and have thrived in the new environment. Five years into the initiative to focus on church planting movements, an honest evaluation would say that a few have begun. The learning curve has been severe and the early training content has been modified to see if a higher number of missionaries can see these movements fostered.

A related initiative within the IMB has been the continued study of purported CPMs to see if they meet the ten criteria listed in Garrison's booklet. Jim Slack has headed this initiative. This willingness to look critically at results is one of the most encouraging aspects of New Directions. Jim and his team are looking at several fields each year, and have found some additional movements, fostered both by IMB personnel and by indigenous workers who have little contact with outsiders.

"All over the world this gospel is bearing fruit and growing" (Col 1:6). Today reports are confirming that God is empowering CPMs in all corners of the earth. Like the Apostle Paul, in his letter to the Colossians, missionaries simply report what they have seen and heard. Garrison's most recent survey includes the following CPM highlights:

1. India—4000 new churches and some 300,000 believers in less than seven years among Bhojpuri-speaking peoples of Madhya Pradesh State.

2. China—500 new churches and 20,000 believers in a northern Chinese province in less than five years; from 1 million to 5 million believers in Henan Province in only eight years; 236 new churches in one county of Heilongjiang Province in one month; 1700 new churches and 48,000 believers in one year in another area; 920 house churches and 90,000 baptized believers in a southern China province in eight years; more than 30,000 believers baptized every day in China.

3. Africa—681 new Ethiopian believers and 63 new churches in eight months; some 90,000 followers of Jesus Christ among the Maasai of Kenya; 1200 new churches in Africa each month.

4. The Muslim World—16,000 North African Berbers come to Christ in a twenty year period; 13,000 Kazakhs come to over a fifteen year period in Central Asia; 12,000 new Kashmiri believers; more than 150,000 Muslims embrace Jesus in more than 3000 Isa Jamaats (Jesus Groups) in an Asian Mulsim country.

5. Latin America—18,000 youth gather in Bogota, Columbia every Saturday night from some 8,000 youth cell groups; the number of Kekchi believers in Guatemala grows from 20,000 to 60,000 in thirty years; more than 3700 new churches and 40,000 new converts in one Latin American country in the decade of the 1990s.

6. Europe—45 new churches among refugees in a single year in the Netherlands; 30-40,000 Gypsy church members and 150,000 attending worship by 1979;

growth of a cell church in Switzerland to more than 3000 members in just two years.

7. North America—in 17 years a North Carolina congregation becomes the mother of 42 new churches spanning three generations of church plants; in 20 years Dove Christian Fellowship grows from three cells and 25 members to 80 cells and 20,000 members on five continents; one church planting ministry sees a new church planted every week; Saddleback Community Church and Willow Creek Community Church shepherd a combined membership of 40,000 members in 4,000 home cell groups.

These are the highlights of over fifty CPM case studies currently being tracked by the IMB. No one agency, team, or missionary takes credit for these movements of churches planting churches. In a gathering of CPM facilitators, apostolic humility abounds. They all realize that these are God-given movements of peoples to Jesus Christ. He gets the credit. He gets the glory.

Conclusion

How, then do we apply the insights from this brief history to the effort of fostering CPMs in North America. One fact to note is that none of these movements occurred in areas where the gospel had already been extensively preached and the church established in previous generations. This is not encouraging as we consider the post-Christian atmosphere of North America. The other side of the North American context is more encouraging. Many areas of North America are several generations away from a vibrant local Christian witness and in these areas there are encouraging signs. One pioneer in California has established a network of house churches that have multiplied into the dozens and established new networks in other cities of North America. Another worker in Colorado responded to the request of a believer to learn how to read the Bible out loud. The group established to do this began to multiply, and in many of these reading groups people came to saving faith through reading God's Word. The network of these groups has now exceeded 200 in just a couple of years.

Several insights can be gained from this study that may show part of the way forward toward fostering successful CPMs in North America. First, the phenomena of multi-individual conversion, is a common pattern where the Holy Spirit is at work through the preaching of His Word. We can assume that our openness to this phenomenon is congruent with God's Word and God's ways. We should therefore expect Him to work in this way among at least some of the least-evangelized sub-cultures of our continent.

Second, there is no lack of God's Word in the heart language (English) of our many subcultures. This is true whether you need the Word written or in oral, or even in multi-media format. Third, there are enough workers to foster indigenous CPMs in all the venues we find in North America, if we will focus their efforts on training trainers rather than eking out only those results that come from their direct ministry. Fourth, we have an ever-increasing body of international research to study for clues on how to address the sub-cultures of North America – if we will just recognize that we don't live, nor minister any longer in Christendom, nor in a monoculture, but in the most ethnically and culturally diverse country in the world.

Fifth, if we are willing to change the paradigms that have for so long separated domestic from international missions, there are trained workers by the thousands from international settings who could coach and guide domestic mission workers along the path to greater fruitfulness using CPM strategies. In summary, the way forward to seeing CPMs in large number in North America involves the holistic integration of mission thinking from international settings and North American settings into a united effort to reach all the sub-cultures of this planet, including those of North America.

ENDNOTES

[68] J.W. Pickett, A.L. Warnshuis, G.H. Singh, and D.A. McGavran, *Church Growth and Group Conversion* (Pasadena, California: William Carey Library, 1973), ix.

[69] Stephen Neill, *A History of Christian Missions,*(New York: Penguin Books, 1964-77), 54.

[70] Kenneth Scott Lautourette, *A History of Christianity Volume 1: to A.D. 1500, Revised Edition*, (San Francisco: HarperSanFrancisco, 1953, 1975), 347.

[71] Andrew Ross, *A Vision Betrayed: The Jesuits in Japan and China, 1542-1742*, (Maryknoll: Orbis Books, 2000), 17.

[72] Ibid, 53

[73] Neill, 216

[74] Ibid, 291.

[75] Kenneth Scott Latourette, *A History of the Expansion of Christianity*, 7 volumes. (New York and London: Harper and Brothers Publishers, 1937).

[76] Roland Allen, *The Spontaneous Expansion of the Church: and the Causes which Hinder It* (Grand Rapids:Wm. B. Eerdmans Publishing, 1962), 2.

[77] A. Scott Moreau, "Church Growth Movement," http://www.wheaton.edu/Missions/Moreau/courses/545/notes/edtart.pdf, 12/30/03, 2.

[78] Pickett, Warnshuis, Singh, and McGavran, *Church Growth and Group Conversion*, 24-25.

[79] *Biographical Dictionary of Christian Missions*, Gerald H. Anderson, ed. (Grand Rapids: William B. Eerdmans Publishing Company, 1998), 535, s.v. "Pickett, J(arrell) Waskom" by John T. Seamands.

[80] Moreau, "Church Growth Movement," 1.

[81] Donald Anderson McGavran, *The Bridges of God: A Study in the Strategy of Missions* (New York: Friendship Press, 1955), 7.

[82] Ibid., 34-35.

[83] Ibid., 77.

[84] Ibid., 88-93.

[85] Ibid., 110.

[86] Ralph D. Winter, "Four Men, Three Eras, Two Transitions" in *Perspectives on the World Christian Movement*, 3rd ed., eds. Ralph D. Winter and Steven C. Hawthorne (Pasadena, CA: William Carey Library, 1999), 259.

[87] *Evangelical Dictionary of World Missions*, A. Scott Moreau, ed. (Grand Rapids: Baker Books and Paternoster Press, 2000) 745, s.v. "Peoples, People Groups" by Samuel Wilson.

[88] *Perspectives on the World Christian Movement*, 3rd ed., Ralph D. Winter and Stephen C. Hawthorne, eds. (Pasadena, CA: William Carey Library, 1999) 496-97, s.v. "The Willowbank Report" by the Lausanne Committee for World Evangelization, 1978.

[89] Luis Bush and Beverly Pegues, The Move of the Holy Spirit in the 10/40 Window (Seattle: YWAM Publishing, 1999), 17.

[90] Formerly the Foreign Mission Board, the Southern Baptist missions agency changed its name to International Mission Board in 1997. IMB website http://archives.imb.org/FAQ/IMB%20Events.pdf , 12/24/04.

[91] For a comprehensive history of the IMB from 1845-1995, see William R. Estep, *Whole Gospel—Whole World: the Foreign Mission Board of the Southern Baptist Convention: 1845-1995* (Nashville: Broadman & Holman Publishers, 1994).

[92] For the detailed account, see David Garrison, *Church Planting Movements: How God Is Redeeming a Lost World* (Midlothian, VA: WigTake Resources, 2004).

[93] Mark Wingfield, "Success or failure of Bold Mission Thrust difficult to discern through labyrinth of goals," *Baptist Standard*, 18 June, 2001. http://www.baptiststandard.com/2001/6_18/pages/sbc_bold.html, 12/24/03.

[94] Estep, *Whole Gospel—Whole World*, 331.

[95] R. Keith Parks, interview by author, written notes, Richardson, TX, 22 July, 2003.

[96] Gary Baldridge, *Keith Parks: Breaking Barriers and Opening Frontiers* (Macon, GA: Smyth & Helwys Publishing, 1999), 15.

[97] Baldridge, *Keith Parks*, 3.

[98] R. Keith Parks, interview by author, written notes, Richardson, TX, 22 July, 2003.

[99] Garrison, *Church Planting Movements*, 21.

Chapter 4

Biblical and Theological Foundation for Basic Churches

Brent Ray

Oftentimes, when the subject of basic churches or house churches arises, the discussion focuses upon the question of the propriety of calling these small groups *churches*. After all, these groups often own no buildings, do not have full time leaders, have limited budgets, and have no long-standing traditions. The question that begs an answer is, *are these small groups actually churches?*

The Biblical Meaning of Church

This study makes no attempt to present a systematic discussion of the doctrine of the Church. That study has been done effectively by others. [100] This study, rather, seeks to answer a series of crucial questions: Are basic churches actually churches? Can congregations growing out of church-planting movements, churches that meet in houses, cell-group churches, and churches in multihousing communities actually be considered churches? Do these congregations reach the standards of biblical teachings in regard to being churches? Can Bible-believing groups opt for, promote, or even allow these expressions of an "assembly" of Christians to flourish and remain true to biblical standards? What biblical requirements determine what kind of fellowships can be called by the name "church?"

95

We not only answer all of these questions affirmatively, but we will strive to establish the conviction that these expressions of Christianity are *at least* as congruent with the biblical teachings about churches as are some of the organized congregations that have buildings, professional staff, involved programs, and proprietary traditions. We maintain that these basic groups are biblical churches in every sense of the word. We further contend that, in many instances, these small gatherings present greater possibilities for reaching a deeper level of congregational life and service than some of the more traditional approaches. Basic churches are not to be viewed as a "movement apart from the church," or as a method for simply "building up the church," but as the church itself, in what Robert Banks refers to as the church-like character of base communities.[101]

We propose that the only mandates that are necessary for the acceptance of these fellowships as churches are the *biblical* requirements of church. And whereas we recognize that basic churches *are not the only method* of being biblical or effective in Kingdom service, we contend that these small, organic congregations or basic churches tend to incarnate the Gospel more readily than do some of the more traditional Episcopal forms of church. This is not to say that more traditional churches lose their authenticity, fail in their service to larger groups of people, or fail to merit the on-going support of Christians. Rather, the emphasis in this presentation is simply that we can allow for and promote *both* traditional churches and basic churches, and that we champion and embrace both approaches. The biblical concept of Church is a sufficiently large vessel that can contain many approaches to becoming the meaning of the term.

Discovering the actual meaning of church in the Scriptures brings the Christian movement to a decisive step. Much of what the Christian movement has thought, taught, and insisted upon has sprung from ecclesiological tradition rather than biblical sources. Frank Viola alarmingly points to the non-biblical origin of many contemporary church practices.[102] To understand biblically what a church is and should be we need to: (1) Study the biblical requirements for church *and* require nothing more than these; (2) Seek the basic meanings of the biblical metaphors for church *and* embody and incorporate these meanings; (3) Follow the biblical examples of churches in action *and* incorporate these findings in our thinking; (4) Follow the examples of present-day churches in action as they promote *and* express the realities of church planting movements and basic churches; (5) Answer questions about and objections to basic churches; (6) Recognize and respond to the advantages that reside within the nature of basic churches, including those dangers from which such congregations guard the Christian movement.

We believe that following these guides to the meaning of church will allow us to fully accept and implement the concept of basic churches such as congregations that grow out of church planting movements, house churches, cell-group churches, and other expressions of indigenous Christianity.

Biblical Requirements of Church

The Christian movement should follow the pattern of mandating only the biblical requirements of church rather than maintaining man-made lists of extra-biblical prerequisites. To express clearly the biblical pattern of "church" groups need incorporate only the following characteristics as seen in biblical descriptions of churches. The requirements for being a church are:

- Gatherings or fellowships of born-again, baptized believers, patterned after the Triune Nature of Jehovah (more about this in a moment);
- Meeting together for worship, prayer, Bible study, mutual support, and service under the leadership of the Holy Spirit;
- Following God-given leaders who may be either professional or non-professional;
- Observing the ordinances of baptism and the Lord's Supper;
- Reflecting fully and faithfully the meaning of being the Body of Christ through continued Kingdom expansion by means of Holy Spirit-empowered evangelism and missionary efforts.[103]

Congregations that demonstrate these characteristics are totally, completely, biblically, and authentically churches of the Lord Jesus Christ. Churches should be mandated only to conform to these biblical requirements of church. They may have neither special facilities nor professional staffs. They may follow various patterns of worship and service that differ from other congregations. They may set aside some traditional practices and incorporate some non-traditional ways. They may follow unique patterns for spreading the Word of God. *Yet, in the light of Scripture, congregations should be known by the name "church" based upon what they are and what they do!*

The most important requirement for a church is that it lives in accordance with its nature as a creation of God and a reflection of His love. Some have suggested that a church is what it does. A better statement is that a church does what it is—*it responds to its inner nature, its own unique DNA* (which is derived from Spirit of Christ Himself and not from a writ of traditions and extra-biblical prerequisites). While some groups hold denominational principles very dear the primary focus should be that the churches live out the mission of God that Jesus gave them. *In short, a church need not be large, powerful, influential, wealthy, or well-known but it must be missional – reflecting His mission – else it is no church at all!* Once again, we do not intend to suggest that larger congregations with their own facilities, professional staffs, involved programs, expensive equipment, and large budgets are not biblical churches. Rather, we only entreat that same recognition be given to the small fellowships of believers who meet in simple facilities (such as homes, business, schools, etc.) and perhaps follow non-professional leaders, yet also fulfill the aforementioned criteria for biblical churches. It is our co conviction that, the small, basic groups or fellowships that fulfill the characteristics of a biblical church are, in fact, churches in every sense of the word.[104]

But, how do we know what a church "patterned after the Triune Nature of Jehovah" would be? I suggest we go to the Bible and find what Jesus indicated his church would be! Ordinarily this means to look at those passages in Matthew's Gospel (Matt. 16:16-20; 18:15-20). These are important words about the church. We are, however, constrained to believe we should begin before these verses—at that seminal revelation from Jesus as to his ministry.

As the body of Christ, the church is to reflect the missionary nature of Jesus and His ministry as expressed clearly in Luke 4:14-21. After defeating the temptations of Satan, Jesus returned to Galilee, received acclaim in the land, and entered the synagogue in Nazareth. The New Testament declares that:

> *He went to Nazareth, where he had been brought up, and on the Sabbath day he went into the synagogue, as was his custom. And he stood up to read. The scroll of the prophet Isaiah was handed to him. Unrolling it, he found the place where it is written: "The Spirit of the Lord is on me, because he has anointed me to preach good news to the poor. He has sent me to proclaim freedom for the prisoners and recovery of sight for the blind, to release the oppressed, to proclaim the year of the Lord's favor." Then he rolled up the scroll, gave it back to the attendant and sat down. The eyes of everyone in the synagogue were fastened on him, and he began by saying to them, "Today this Scripture is fulfilled in your hearing"* (Luke 4:16-21 NIV).

We need require no more of a group to be called by the name of church today than that they engage in the mission that God gave the Son. What was that mission?

Preaching the Gospel to the poor (Luke 4:14-21) involves far more than simply announcing orally the content of the Message. In fact, to limit the Lord's teaching to announcing the facts of the Gospel is a clear misinterpretation of the Lord's teaching. To proclaim means to express, to make clear, to incarnate, and to share personally the whole meaning of the Gospel with all people including the disadvantaged.

A Christian or a church proclaims the Gospel to the needy only as that Christian or church bonds personally with the poor (disadvantaged spiritually and not just physically), relates to them in their need, and shares in their situation. This proclamation cannot be fulfilled by simply sending relief supplies—though this ministry should never be neglected. Proclaiming the Gospel to disadvantaged people demands personal involvement. The example of proclaiming the Gospel to the poor is the ministry of Jesus who became involved to the extent that he "became *human and dwelled among us*." Biblical churches seek to become "incarnational" and communicate through the pattern that Jesus exampled.

The biblical requirement of being church is that of participating personally and incarnationally in the ministry of God through Jesus Christ as inspired and empowered by the Holy Spirit. A fellowship of believers that is so engaged should be given the name church. A gathering of people that is not proclaiming the Gospel to humanity in this incarnational way is failing to express the meaning of church in the biblical sense. Congregations of any size, who meet in any facility, who follow God-called leaders of any educational level, and who proclaim by word and by deed the Gospel of Christ conform to the biblical requirements for church.

Beginning our study of the nature of the church with the revelation of Luke 4:16-21 does not mean that we overlook the important words of Jesus in Matthew 16:13-20. The fullest meaning of this seminal passage can not be approached in only a few words. For our purposes here, we note only that Jesus announced that his "church" would be built on the foundation of the faith confession that God had given to Peter. Peter's faith in Christ as the Messiah, the Promised Savior, came not from any human source but from the Father in heaven (v. 17). Jesus explained that on the foundation of such faith he would raise his assembly, or church (v.18).

The church Jesus envisioned would stand firm in the world, never to be overpowered by the powers of the underworld, the agents of Satan (v. 18). Furthermore, the church of Jesus is empowered by the gift of the "keys of the kingdom of heaven," the Gospel in all its strength. This empowering of the church allows the church to "loose and bind," as the Lord entrusts to His church the dynamic and redemptive presence of God that is at work in and through His church.[105] Thus, a prerequisite for any group to be a "church" is clearly made visible in that the group actively participates in the Spirit-empowered mission of announcing the entire content of the Gospel. Congregations who serve in this fashion must be granted the designation of church.

Biblical Metaphors of Church

Basic churches also conform to the biblical metaphors of church as seen in Scripture. Further insight into the meaning of church can be gleaned from consideration of the biblical metaphors of church. This suggestion is not to place further requirements on a group before that fellowship can be given the name church. It only suggests that additional light on the nature of these fellowships can be understood from the metaphors. The New Testament suggests that churches follow the metaphors of church. Please note the sentences in italics at the conclusion of the discussion of each metaphor as these sentences suggest some ways churches can insure that they are in line with biblical principles.

The Body of Christ

The metaphor "The Body of Christ" emphasizes the unity of the church as an assembly or group that shares the bread and wine of the Lord's Supper (1 Cor. 10:16-17). As the Body of Christ, the church is to live as a unified community in sacrificial love and fellowship—in a spirit of interdependence among all members. As the Body of Christ, the church is a full participant in the power encounter between God's reign and the forces of evil (Eph. 1:22-23).[106]

A church lives in line with its God-intended nature only as it reflects this unity of interdependence and reflects the diversity of the gifts of the Spirit in its community life and service.

The Family of God

The image for the new people of God which Jesus called into being is the *familia Dei* or family of God (1 Pet. 4:17). In this family, God is the father (Matt. 23:9), Jesus the head of the household, and his followers are members of the household (Matt. 10:25). The older women serve as mothers, the men as brothers, and the group together all serves as joint members of the household.[107] The Apostle Paul often used language that picked up the metaphor of family relations in his view of church teaching that those incorporated into the congregations should view themselves as members of a common family. Their relationships should be based on love and common care. They serve each other in the household (*oikos*). Church is well represented in the language that points out the inter working of a family.[108]

The centrality of the metaphor of the family of God in relation to the subject of basic churches can be easily comprehended by noting Paul's qualifications for church leaders. The Apostle noted that leaders should be persons who managed their own families well (1 Tim. 3:5). This quality was important because the church closely resembles the characteristics of the family. Church leaders need the abilities to manage a household.

The metaphor of the church as the family of God seems to reside in the very method of the early church. The group demonstrated the living reality of life in the Father. The houses in which the groups met served as the foundation points from which outreach began. The elders in the house churches assumed exactly the house-father role.[109] Enlargement through the extended family illustrates a main method of the spread of the Gospel in the first century. The mission of the Lord's early followers followed the house-to-house procedures (Lk. 10:1-12).[110]

To the degree that a church that reflects the nature of the extended family of God in its participants and worship is giving indication that it has the DNA of an authentic church.

The Congregation of Saints

Church is a fellowship of redeemed, regenerate people. It is new type of community (1 Cor. 1:9). As William Beckham puts it, "Jesus established the church as community during the first century—built around a personal relationship with Himself."[111] The fellowship in the church is not something we bring about by activity but is rather an expression of the church's nature. The congregation is a joint life of those gathered in the name of Jesus.

A group lives in line with its God-intended nature only as it lives out this fellowship of saved people.

The People of God

The church is identified along faith lines rather than kinship lines. Life in the church transcends all political, racial, ethnic, and party relationships (Gal. 3:28). Only the church can bring genuine peace to people in the fragmented world (1 Pet. 2:9; Rom. 9:25-26). The church is a worldwide community that reaches to all peoples (Matt. 18:19; Rev. 5:9-10).

A group lives in line with its God-intended nature only as it transcends human divisions and tensions.

The Creation of the Spirit

Church comes into existence not by any human activity or power but only by the activity of the Holy Spirit. Prior to the coming of the Holy Spirit at Pentecost, and His subsequent, abiding presence in the lives of those that are and make up His temple (Eph. 2:21-22), it is difficult to speak of church in any terms other than antecedent. It was in the fulfillment of the promised gift of the Holy Spirit that the term church took on a completely new meaning (John 14:25-26). Church comes from the corporate nature of God's salvation (1 Cor. 2:16; Eph. 2:19; 1 Pet. 2:5).

A group lives in line with its God-intended nature only as it grows out of the salvation experiences of its members and by the direct power of the Spirit.

The Priests of God

The church exists to represent God to humans and humans to God. The church (and the individual members of that assembly) is God's royal priesthood (1 Pet. 2:9). Church exists to inform people of God's love, reflect this love in service, and bring these people into God's Kingdom by witness through the power of the Spirit.

A group lives in line with its God-intended nature only as it serves as God's royal priesthood in ministering to others.

The Worshipping Flock

Church exists to praise and worship the God who created it by His Spirit. Early Christians demonstrated their corporate nature by their corporate love, praise, and service (Acts 2 and Acts 4). Viola observed, "Before we can truly understand anything meaningful about the church, we must first be captured by a consuming revelation of the Person for whom it exists" (Present Testimony Ministry, 2005). The church must worship Him!

A group lives in line with its God-intended nature only as it actively and passionately praises and follows God.

The Confessing Followers

Another metaphor of church relates to the church's confessional nature—church acknowledges or confesses as the fulfillment of God's promises (Messiah) and the seat of all ministry. It was Peter's confession that brought forth Jesus' statement about the establishment of His church (little flock—see Matt. 16:13-20). The Twelve represented the foundation upon which Jesus built his church (Matt. 12:22-40).

A group lives in line with its God-intended nature only as it confesses by word and deed its belief in and allegiance to Jesus Christ as its Lord.

A Living Organism

A church, in the biblical sense, lives, works, functions, and serves, as an organism. Paul taught the Corinthian Christians that, in regard to spiritual gifts, a church resembles a human body with each part dependent upon the others and no part independent of the rest (1 Cor. 12:12-31). An organism first is alive. It has that quality of life that separates it from all else that does not have life. As an organism, the church also is a system of coordinated parts each of which has its distinctive and imperative function. Each part joyfully carries out its necessary function with thanks to God for allowing the service.

The image of the church as organism leads us to understand the tragedy of disunity or lack of commonality among the members of a church. A "church fight" is among the most disturbing misnomers of life. Churches, as organism, should live and serve from an integrated position of each part contributing for the benefit and the welfare of the whole.

A group lives in line with its God-intended nature only as it lives and serves through parts that mutually contribute according to the plan for each part and continues to demonstrate the qualities of life.

The Sharing Fellowship

A church corresponds to the biblical pattern as it shares all that it has with those in need. It shares the new life in Christ. It shares the fellowship of its people. It shares of its material possessions. A church does this, not because it is forced to but because its nature, its DNA, dictates this practice.

A group lives in line with its God-intended nature only as it willingly, joyfully, and sacrificially shares all that it has with others (Acts 2:42-47).

A church in biblical teachings is a fellowship that conforms to the meaning and the spirit of the metaphors of church in the New Testament. The ministry of the church flows naturally out of the nature of the church. The church's nature reflects the mission of God in the world, exists (is possible) because of the redemptive work of Christ, and has the purpose of relating God's redemption to all of life. Church exists as a social community that is both spiritual and human as it becomes a full demonstration of the new humanity and society in the world. [112] Small churches that meet in simple facilities under local leadership meet every aspect of the necessities to be accepted as churches on these criteria.

In describing interaction within the local church, Dr. Keith Eitel offers the following attitudes that characterize biblically sound congregations: [113] (1) Love for one another: Rom. 13:8; 1 Thess. 3:11,12; 4:9,10; 2 Thess. 1:3; 1 Peter 1:22; (2) Forbearance or relaxed tolerance toward others: Eph. 4:2; Col. 3:13;(3) Acceptance or willingness to receive others into assembly: Rom. 15:7; (4) An attitude which is neither judgmental or condemning: Rom. 14:13; 1 Cor. 4:5; James

4:11,12; (5) Willingness to subordinate one's own desires to the needs and interests of others: Phil. 2:3,4; 1 Pet. 5:5,6; Rom. 12:10; (6) Genuine devotion toward one another as Family of God: Rom. 12:10 (7) Harmony or rapport that transcends social barriers: Rom. 12:16-18; 14:19; James 2:1-4 (8) Priority of unity within the congregations: Eph. 4:3, 13; Col. 3:14; (9) Forgiveness: Eph. 4:32; (10) Encouraging one another: Heb. 3:12, 13; 10:24; 1 Thess. 5:11; Rom. 15:4, 5.

Biblical Examples of Churches in Action

Basic churches conform to the patterns exemplified by the churches in the New Testament accounts of the Early Christian movement. Attention to the examples of churches mentioned in Scripture provides great insight into the types of actions, practices, and ministries of churches. In the following paragraphs we summarize a selection of these passages, dealing with the lives and the ministries of churches described in the Bible, revealing several important facets of the teachings concerning the natures of those groups that should be called "churches."

- *These congregations were composed of persons who were saved by the grace of God and the ministry of the Holy Spirit.* They were "called out" from the rest of society to be the people of God (the meaning of the word, ἐκκησία, is "called out"). The Jerusalem believers "gladly received the words of God" through Peter (Acts 2:40-41). Paul referred to the church members in Corinth as "the church of God that is in Corinth" and then described these believers as "those who are sanctified in Christ Jesus, called to be saints," and as those who call upon the name of Jesus Christ, our Lord" (1 Cor. 1:2).

- *These congregations continued without pause the Spirit-led activities of worship, prayer, joint-life (fellowship), ministry, discipleship, and witness.* (Acts 2:41-46). The Jerusalem Fellowship had purpose from which it did not turn. A church, in the biblical sense, centers on these purposes and not on keeping any tradition or set of traditions, not on any particular program or event or programs or events, and not on maintaining a building.[114]

- *These congregations fully proclaimed the Gospel of Jesus even in the face of threats and persecution* (Acts 4:23-37). In the face of prohibition to proclaim Jesus and threat if they did, these disciples prayed only for "*boldness to speak Your word*" (Acts 4: 29). Nothing—be it threat or danger can ever dissuade a biblical church from fully and faithfully proclaiming, by word and deed, the total Gospel of Jesus Christ.

- *These congregations faithfully maintained the true teachings and continuously sought God's will in the Scriptures* (Acts 2:41-42). The doctrines of biblical churches come from Scripture and the leading of the Holy Spirit. No pressure from outside sources ever dictates to the biblical church what it must believe and do. This leadership comes only from the Scripture and the Spirit.

- *These congregations remained faithful in caring for their members in physical and spiritual ways as expressions of their joint-life in Christ* (Acts 2:44-47; 4:32-37; 2 Cor. 8:1-5). No person in a biblical church had an unmet need. Christians in biblical churches gave sacrificially, without holding back, of their goods, to meet the needs of others in the fellowships. Christians in biblical churches gave not from their overflow but of their own goods to meet these needs.

- *These congregations existed in many places as local gatherings of God's people. Paul wrote to the church of God which is at Corinth (1 Cor. 1:2) and the church of the Thessalonians* (1 Thess. 1:1). The local nature of these churches mentioned in Scripture is further seen in the probability that the Christians in Rome met in many small congregations each likely composed of believers from specific parts of the Roman Empire.[115] It is entirely possible that Paul's letter to the Ephesians was sent as a circular epistle to the many congregations in and around the central city of Ephesus.[116]

- *These congregations gathered in many types of meeting places---in synagogues (Acts 18:4), in homes (Acts 18:7; Philemon 2; Rom 16:5), in schools (Acts 19:9), and other places.* The fact is that church buildings were unknown among the Christians until many years after the New Testament.[117] To make facilities a requirement for calling a congregation a church is much like

- *These congregations adjusted creatively with the cultures to which they ministered.* Paul was careful to change the Jewish factors in the message to adjust more adequately to the Greek and Roman cultures of the churches in the Greek and Roman areas (Acts 15). He

111

used Greek words such as "redemption" to express the true meaning of the Christian message. The Apostle John, writing for a non-Jewish group, employed the Greek concept of "*logos*" to express the message. Importantly, the Apostles in adjusting the expression of the message never compromised the meaning of the message.

- *These congregations followed the lead of local leaders, many of whom were not apostles (Acts 14:21-26; Titus 1:5-7; 1 Tim. 3:1-13).* Restricting leadership to those who have been ordained places an unbiblical requirement and excludes those who can serve in a wide variety of ministries in the church.

- *These congregations freely participated in the special services of baptism and the Lord's Supper.* Paul declared that he had not baptized all the believers in Corinth (1 Cor. 1:15-16) and instructed the Corinthians concerning certain ill regularities in the way they were practicing the Lord's Supper (1 Cor. 11:17-34). These facts at least bend our thinking to the possibility that local leaders were presiding over both these church functions. We see no indication that the churches waited until apostles came to observe either baptism or the Lord's Supper. Biblical churches follow their own leaders in observing the special services of the Christian faith.

- *These congregations practiced pastoral care and church discipline over their own members.* (Acts 2:41-42; 1 Pet. 5:1-5; 1 Cor. 5:1-13). Biblical churches practice church discipline on their local level with the goal of reclaiming fallen members not in order to exclude persons from the fellowship. Pastoral care in biblical churches seeks to meet needs, correct behaviors, and stimulate faithful living and service.

- *These congregations were committed to missional ministry that included sending the Gospel to others as well as sharing with the needs of others* (Acts 13:1-4; 2 Cor. 8:1-24). The churches of the New Testament engaged in an enormous ministry of missional outreach through evangelizing the lost, discipling new believers, and starting churches. Reproduction should be written into the DNA of every church. Biblical churches constantly seek ways to reproduce themselves. The goal of healthy church life and growth is bringing responsible, reproducing believers into responsible, reproducing congregations.[118]

Keith Eitel provides an excellent summary of the biblical precepts that must be taken into account in establishing a New Testament church:[119]

- Absolute authority of God's Word. 2 Tim. 3:16-17
- Salvation by faith alone in the finished work of Christ upon the cross—regenerate church membership. Jn. 3:16, Rom. 10:9-10.
- Right grouping of people. (baptized, immersed, adult believers meeting regularly for worship & observance of the two Church ordinances prescribed in the NT, namely Baptism & the Lord's supper). 1 Cor. 11:17-34; Acts 2:42-46; Rom. 6:1-11
- Right Structure (view themselves as a church, choosing for themselves a pastor & deacons) I Tim. 3:1-10.

113

- Right Activities (engaging the attitudes & activities of the church itemized in Scripture. Most are indicated in this document).
- Congregational autonomy of the local church. Indications of local church authority derived from form or function descriptions of NT churches in a sequence of passages. Mt. 18:15-20; Acts 6:3; 13:2-3; 15:2; I Cor. 5:2; & II Cor. 2:6.

These teachings are not exhaustive. However, they suffice to indicate that churches in the biblical period did not possess facilities or requirements other than spiritual necessities for leaders. These small congregations actively practiced evangelism among the lost, development among the believers, worship for the saints, church symbolic services for the congregations, pastoral care for each other, church discipline when it was needed, and corporate life among the members.

What we see in the biblical teachings on the nature of churches, the metaphors of churches in the New Testament, and the examples of churches in the biblical period in no way mitigates against what is now being called "basic churches." Basic churches, as described by the contributors to this book, easily correspond to the nature and examples of the churches of the New Testament period.

Basic churches exist and minister in the world today. The examples of these churches further indicate the necessity of the Christian movement being open to these expressions of gathered Christianity.[120] Other chapters in this book fully describe the present-day existence and ministry of basic churches and church multiplication movements.

Advantages of Biblical Churches

Some question the propriety of designating as "church" smaller congregations that meet in simple facilities, are led by bi-vocational leaders, and employ contextual approaches to worship, ministry, and missions. Some are concerned that such churches will open the door to false teachings and that these teachings cannot be controlled because of the non-traditional natures of the congregations. While it is important to be careful to avoid beliefs and practices that may lead to doctrinal deviation, the fact is that basic churches (e.g., congregations growing out of church-planting movements, cell-group churches, house church patterns, and efforts in multi-housing settings), provide significant safeguards *against* some of the most damaging tendencies within the Christian movement. The very structure of these groups requires an accountability that serves as a safeguard against heresy. By allowing and promoting small groups to be known as and fully function as churches as they conform to the biblical requirements for church, the Christian movement can avoid some of the more devastating "unbiblical" patterns that have emerged in Christian history.

Avoiding the Error of the One Hierarchical, Controlling Church

The pattern of requiring only the biblical elements in allowing congregations to be known as churches avoids the danger of the heresy of the hierarchical, controlling Church. One of the damaging heresies of Christian history is "The Hierarchical Church" The Hierarchical Church has assumed power over salvation and taken the right to dispense, withhold, or withdraw eternal life.[121]

This situation would not have arisen if the emphasis had remained on the local congregations. The hierarchical Church that has coercive power opens the door to endless errors. Christian history demonstrates that the rise of a universal, hierarchical, controlling, and all-powerful Church leads to a pattern of errors that include: [122] (1) Moving away from salvation by Grace to salvation through the Church; (2) Placing works, often in the guise of Church rituals, in the way of genuine salvation; (3) Enabling leadership to exert coercive power and domination that is totally foreign to the leadership plan of Jesus (Matt. 20:24-28); (4) Opening the door for religious persecution and oppression; (5) Weakening the major strength of the Body by allowing the professional staff to perform and thereby failing to equip and engage the entire Body; (6) Denying the creativity of newer forms of Christian expression by demanding conformity to the Church standard beliefs and practices.

Avoiding the Universal, Hierarchical, Central Church pattern must receive a high priority from those concerned with a biblical expression of Christianity.

Avoiding the Limitation of Only An Ordained Professional Ministry

The pattern of requiring only the biblical elements in allowing congregations to be known as churches also avoids a second major error that has arisen in the Christian movement— that of an ordained, professional leadership that stands different and apart from the rest of the Body. The biblical way

116

is for church leadership to be servant leaders who equip the Body (the entire membership) to employ their particular spiritual gifts in the ministry of the Lord. Church leaders should not perform; they should equip others to do the task.[123]

The above pattern clearly follows the biblical way as outlined in Paul's epistle to the Ephesians (Eph. 4:11-16). This passage indicates that the leaders are given by the Lord to the church. The Lord then commissions these leaders to equip or prepare the body of Christ, that is, the members, so that they (*purpose*) can perform the works of ministry. It is by these works that the body itself will be built up, reach unity, and attain maturity. The body will never mature properly if the leadership does the work on behalf of the body. Ministry by proxy is not the NT model for church.

Clearly the biblical pattern calls for God-called leaders to equip the entire body *for the performance of the Holy Spirit-empowered services.* Restricting any ministry in the church to those who have some denominational entitlement or credentials is heresy. Speaking biblically, every church should have within its membership persons who can, are expected, and are allowed to carry out every function the church needs to promote. Churches growing out of church-planting movements, house churches (cell groups), and multi-housing ministries provide a safeguard against the development of such restrictions that place power and service only in the hands of the "ordained ministry."

Avoiding the Danger of
Self-centeredness in the Church

Accepting and establishing that only the biblical patterns are required to be "church" also avoids the self-centeredness that has so often conflicted with groups reaching the biblical nature of church. Churches that do not feel the need to enhance their facilities, their statuses, and their positions do not so easily develop unbiblical patterns of spending all of their resources on themselves rather than on others. Such churches that look toward extensive reproduction are willing to place their energies and possessions into missions of reproduction.

Avoiding the Danger of Loss of Focus

Mandating only the biblical requirements of church also avoids the error of losing focus on the main task. When only the biblical requirements are demanded, the churches can focus on evangelism and Christian maturity rather than any artificial mandates. Facilities, constitutions, vested leaders, patterns of contribution, and mandated actions often eventuate from losing focus on the main task.

In the 1500s, focus on building St. Peter's Basilica eventuated in offering salvation for money in the form of indulgences. When church is simply the biblical church such loss of focus is less likely. Some Christian leaders in England in the 1790s allowed their belief in the doctrine of election to hinder them from accepting the responsibilities of attempting to evangelize the peoples in other lands. Church leaders in the 1930s lost the concept of missions as calling people to salvation and substituted good deeds and loving service, both good in themselves, for seeking conversion. The effect in all three cases was a loss of focus on the main task and a hindrance to the spread of the Gospel.

Avoiding the Danger of
Restricting Multiplication

Mandating only the biblical requirements of church also avoids the danger of restricting church multiplication. The danger of restricting church multiplication flows from several streams. One of these arguments is the idea that a new church cannot, or at least should not, be started without a sponsoring church or mother church. While the pattern of having a church sponsor the new start is often an effective plan, to restrict church starts to this one pattern can often hinder spontaneous outreach. The mother church concept is actually not a biblical teaching but a human invention. Throughout the NT it was primarily *Christians* that started new churches, not other or even mother churches.

A second danger that can hinder church multiplication is that of demanding trained, often ordained leadership for every new church and limiting church starts by the availability of such leaders. As seen, the New Testament does not demand trained, ordained leaders for every congregation that is considered a church. Leadership truly lies in the harvest. God will raise up leaders for his churches. We must refuse to limit church multiplication to the availability of trained, ordained, and certainly full-time leaders.

A third danger that sometimes hinders church multiplication is that of requiring facilities and equipment before a group can be accepted as a church. Some associations of churches receive only congregations that own property as churches. Some groups think a church can not actually be a church until a building is available. These misguided and unbiblical prerequisites often lead churches to fail to plant new churches because they do not have the funds for a new church building.

What Shall We Do in Regard
To Basic Churches

The biblical and theological implications of the meaning and requirements for "church" naturally lead to the questions of what the contemporary Christian movement should do about these groups. The Christian movement *should return to the New Testament of pattern of mandating nothing more that the biblical requirements for fellowship to be called church. Those fellowships that are composed of born-again, baptized believers, who congregate for the purposes of worship, prayer, Bible study, mutual support, and service under the leadership of the Holy Spirit, following God-given leaders, observing the ordinances of baptism and the Lord's Supper, reflecting fully and faithfully the meaning of being the Body of Christ through Spirit-empowered evangelism and missionary efforts must be accepted as churches without consideration for other factors.* Mandating only the biblical requirements for "church" avoids many errors in our ecclesiology. But more importantly, defining church in accordance with biblical precepts brings to the surface many of the unique opportunities of becoming "church" in the fullest and most biblical meaning of the term.

Endnotes

120

[100] Among many volumes, both older and more recent, are: H. E. Dana, *A Manual of Ecclesiology,* 2d edition with L.M. Sipes (Kansas City, KS: Central Seminary Press, 1944); Paul S. Minear,, *Images of the Church in the New Testament* (Philadelphia: Westminister, 1960); Paul S. Minear, *The Obedience of Faith* (London: SCM, 1970); Jophannes Blauw, *The Missionary Nature of the Church* (Grand Rapids: Eerdmans, 1962); Del Birkey, *The House Church: A Model for Renewing the* Church (Scottdale, Pa: Herald Press); Darrell L. Guder, ed. *Missional Church: A Theological Vision for the Sending of the Church in North America* (Grand Rapids: Eerdmans, 1998); Craig Van Gelder, "Missional Challenge: Understanding the Church in North America,: in *Missional Church: A Theological Vision for the Sending of the Church in North* America, ed. Darrell L. Guder (Grand Rapids: Eerdmans, 1998); James Emery White, *Rethinking the Church:A Challenge to Creative Redesign in an Age of Transition,* Rev. and Expanded (Grand Rapids: Baker Books, 2003 [original publication 1997]; Craig Van Gelder, *The Essence of the Church: A Community Created by the Spirit* (Grand Rapids: Baker Books, 2000).

[101] Robert Banks, *The Home Church* (Sutherland, Australia: Albatross Books, 1986).

[102] Frank Viola, *Pagan Christianity: The Origins of Our Modern Church Practices,* Present Testimony Ministry, 2002.

[103] See Acts 2:40-47. Throughout the NT, the most fundamental definition of church is a local assembly of Christians who gather for worship, prayer, teaching, Bible study, ministry and missions.

[104] We define "basic church" as a congregation of believers in Christ who carry out the functions of a church as described in Acts 2:40-47.

[105] Craig Van Gelder, *The Essence of the Church: A Community Created by the Spirit* (Grand Rapids: Baker Books, 2000), 85-86.

[106]*Ibid.,* 110-111.

[107] Gehring, *House Church and Mission,* 46-47.

[108] Robert Banks, *Paul's Idea of Community: The Early House Churches in their Cultural Setting,* rev. ed. (Peabody, MS: Hendrickson Publishers, 1994 (original publishing date 1979), 47-55.

[109] Wolfgang Simson, *Houses the Change the World: The Return of the House Church,* 157.

[110] Ibid., 47-48.

[111] William A. Beckham, *The Second Revolution: Reshaping the Church for the Twenty-First Century* (Houston, TX: Touch Publications, 1995), 136.

[112]Simson, 128.

[113] Keith Eitel, unpublished paper, "The Baptist Character of a Local Congregation, 2006.

[114] James Emery White, *Rethinking the Church: A Challenge to Creative Redesign in an Age of Transition,* Rev. and Engl. (Grand Rapids: Baker Books, 2003), 31.

[115] Paul Minear, *The Obedience of Faith* (London: SCM, 1970), 8.

[116] Pheme Perkins, "The Letter to the Ephesians." In *The New Interpreter's Bible,* ed. Leander Keck, 12 vols. (Nashville, TN: Abingdon Press, 2000), XI: 352-53.

[117] H. E. Dana (second edition with L. M. Sipes, *A Manual of Ecclesiology* (Kansas City, MO: Central Seminary Press, 1944), 13-21.

[118] Ebbie C. Smith, *Growing Healthy Churches: New Directions for Church Growth in the 21st Century* (Ft. Worth, TX: Church Starting Network, 2003): 61.

[119] Keith Eitel, unpublished paper, "The Baptist Character of a Local Congregation," 2006. This segment was adapted from Waren Doud: URL:http://www.realtime.net/~wdoud/

[120] Keith Eitel offers a similar list in describing the activities in the local church: 1) Evangelizing, discipling, and baptizing the lost: Matthew 28:16-20; Acts 2:40-47; 2) Edifying one another: Eph. 4:29; 1 Thess. 5:11; Rom. 14:18-20; 15:1,2; 3) Serving one another: Gal. 5:13; 4) Being kind to one another: Eph. 4:32; 1 Peter 3:8,9; 5) Showing hospitality: 1 Peter 4:9; 3 John 5-8; 6) Partaking of the Communion: 1 Cor. 11:17-34; Acts 2:42-46; 7) Admonishing one another: Rom. 15:14; 1 Cor. 4:14; 1 Thess. 5:14; 8) Restoring carnal believers: Gal. 6:1; 9) Praying for one another: James 5:16, op. cit.

[121] See Austin Flannery, "The Hierarchical Church," *Vatican II* (NY: Costello Publishing Co. 1975), 369-87

[122] See James McCarty, *The Gospel According to Rome* (Eugene: Harvest House. 1995).

[123] See Flannery, *Vatican II.*

Chapter 5

The Fastest Growing Church Planting Movements

Bill Fudge

In looking at Church Planting Movements, I want to highlight the most robust CPM that I have seen. The movements are still in the initial stages time wise, but have developed more rapidly and extensively than I have seen before. I will describe some of these particular movements.

Characteristics of the Areas

One particular church planting movement occurred in an industrial area where many foreign and domestic factories are operating. It is also in an urban environment where there are several cities of one million or more in population. Rural communities as well as suburban areas separate those cities. All kinds of housing from landed dwellings, high-rise complexes, factory dormitories, and farming communities function in the area.

Extensive immigration from other parts of the country marks the nature of this community. Because of the large number of factories, workers have immigrated to this part of the country for employment. Factory work, though very long hours, and often in a harsh environment, is still much sought after as an area of employment.

The area is one of great commerce. Entire businesses have grown up to supply the materials needed in the factories, and to supply the needs of the factory laborers in terms of recreation, clothing, food, and transportation. These facts have made for a diverse population.

Description of Growth

The Church Planting movement has progressed in the last two years from inception in November 2000, to reporting over 1,000 churches planted in the month of January 2003. These new churches could be described as typically being a group of 10-20 baptized believers, meeting in domestic living facilities, and led by one or more unpaid lay persons who have been trained to witness to their friends and family. These leaders guide participative Bible studies train those in the church to also share their testimonies with their family and friends, and then repeat what the founders of the group have done in witness, leading Bibles studies, and training others. Each of these "groups" recognizes that it is an autonomous church with the responsibility of carrying out the functions of the Body of Christ in fellowship, mutual encouragement, outreach to the lost, discipling the believers and administering baptism and the Lord's Supper.

Another picture of this is that a person who becomes a Christian and is a part of a group is also trained to witness to their friends and begin their own group. Often, therefore, a person has double accountability. He may be accountable TO the group that he originally was a part of WHILE he is also accountable FOR a group that has been evangelized and is meeting separately.

124

Key to Growth: Training of Trainers

One of the keys to this Church Planting Movement is that leadership training focuses not on "training of leaders" but upon *'training of trainers.'* The leader associated with this movement states that "trained leaders expect to care for their congregation and lead it," whereas *trainers are expected to start and lead a congregation, AND train those in that congregation to also BE TRAINERS, thus start and lead a group of new believers while training those in turn to do the same.* The word description of that simple change in concept from "leaders" to "trainers" is a bit convoluted, and the outworking of it looks at first glance as "chaotic," but the end result is often VERY fruitful as those saved realize their part in sharing the gospel of Jesus. The *"training of trainers"* approach is actually a fulfillment of the great commission words of Jesus to "teach them to obey all that I have commanded you."

This Church Planting Movement has been termed by one as actually a "training of trainers Movement." I think that is an accurate statement. The dynamic of this movement is found in the number of trainers trained, and the planning for those trainers in turn to train other trainers.

One story out of this CPM illustrates the point. In an interview with a country farmer who had received this *training of trainers*, he told of his experiences by saying:

> I have been a Christian for 30 years, and a pastor of this church for 20 years. I did not really know how to lead people to accept the gospel and I did not know I should start other churches. But I went through the 'training of trainers' and became a trainer. I then understood the importance and had the desire to train others

to also start churches and to be trainers themselves. My goal is to train each of my church members to start their own church and to train their church members in turn to start their own churches.

This country pastor, who had served as pastor of a country church as an unpaid, lay pastor for 20 years, had a part in starting, either directly or indirectly, 121 churches. He participated in eight months by training his church members, who in turn trained those in the churches that they started. This is a record of church multiplication and leadership training.

Basic Assumptions Followed
By the Worker in this CPM

1. A CPM can start anywhere people are responding to the gospel

The assumption is that a CPM is a natural spiritual outworking of the Holy Spirit in the lives of believers as they share their faith, gather together to worship the Lord, rehearse the doctrine of the Apostles and praise Him for what he has done in them and in their midst. CPM is no mystery of grace, it is in fact the very grace that brings people to salvation, and the dynamic of the Holy Spirit working in their lives. Hence a CPM is possible wherever people are responding to the gospel of Jesus by coming to Him for salvation.

2. Any believer can and should be witnessing to friends, family and colleagues

Any believer can tell what he knows and has experienced in his faith in Christ. With this as an assumption, all who come to be trained are trained first and foremost in sharing their personal testimony. Believers may not be able to give a reasoned discourse on a particular scripture, or doctrine, but they can share their own experience of faith, and what the Lord continues to do for them as they walk with Him.

3. Lay people can start and lead a church as they win friends, family and colleagues

The assumption is that the body of Christ does not have to have a highly trained or professional person or people to lead it. The body of baptized believers can gather to worship together, read and discuss God's word together, pray together, sing praises together, and encourage one another and reach out to the lost around them without training. It was done in the early days after Pentecost, as they gathered in houses "breaking bread, praising the Lord, and rehearsing the teachings of the Apostles." It was done in those churches the Apostle Paul left as he traveled across Asia Minor preaching the gospel and starting churches. It continues to happen in places across the world where people lead others to join together in His name as the body of Christ.

4. People are trained better if they serve during the training rather than completing training before serving

The assumption in this CPM is that people are more effectively trained when their training is JIT (just in time). The modeling of Jesus is strong in this as He trains the 70 in one area and asks them to immediately use what they have heard and apply (obey) what they were trained to do. Those who immediately applied (obeyed) the training they are given, come back with practical, real life questions born from the experience of obedience.

5. Training is to train 'trainers', not 'leaders'---hence multiplication

The assumption is that people trained to be 'trainers' will do more than just lead a group, but will also train others to start other groups and lead that group to start others and train others in turn. Those trained to lead a church that they start do lead, but the impetus or seed for multiplication is most often missing as the 'leaders' focus upon growing, strengthening, guiding and teaching the group for which they are responsible. Moving from the concept of training 'leaders' to training 'trainers' has pushed this CPM forward in rapid multiplication as each obedient trainer in turns trains others, etc.

6. A church can meet anywhere, but a rented/purchased meeting place is a detriment to multiplication

The assumption is that people who love the Lord can find a place to meet. The meeting place is even easier to solve when those meeting together are not strangers, but are mutual acquaintances, or family. While nothing is wrong with a group deciding to rent or purchase a meeting place, it does set a pattern that makes rapid multiplication of churches more difficult, and it pushes the group to focus upon itself and its facilities.

7. Large groups are OK, but small, replicating groups and replicating trainers (leaders) are better

Small groups of 10-20 in which all are provided training to be trainers and where all are encouraged to share their faith have shown the most rapid growth. There is nothing wrong with larger groups. In fact, some groups will grow larger, but those groups become focused on growth of the group rather than multiplication of churches. Small groups require less natural leadership ability thus expanding the pool of potential leaders.

8. *A rapid pace of multiplication is not necessarily dangerous*

The urgency of sharing the gospel does call for a rapid pace of multiplication. An important facet of training trainers is built in accountability to a group of fellow workers. Often concern is expressed that rapid multiplication will make the groups more subject to cults and aberrations, but there is no evidence to show that is the case as long as good accountability groups are in place and basic tools of understanding God's word exist. *Anecdotal evidence seems to show that cults do not come into actively expanding movements*, but do center their attention more on churches that have quit growing and starting new churches.

Characteristics of This
Church Planting Movement

1. *Willing Christians*

The work began in an area where there were already significant Christian people. The worker found willing Christians, ready to be trained to see rapid and ongoing growth take place. But the real growth came when new believers were challenged and trained immediately to share their faith in Jesus with friends, family, and colleagues. Those new believers were

Christians willing and ready to be trained to share what they had just experienced.

2. *Training Trainers*

The worker decided early on that he must not focus on training leadership to lead the churches, but **TRAINERS**, who would start and lead churches, while training those within the fellowship to also start and lead churches, and to teach those to also train others within their fellowship to do likewise.(Matt 28:20)

3. *Simple, Reproducible Training*

The training process that has evolved is simple enough for most people to easily be trained, and used to train others. It emphasizes the authority of the Scriptures, preparing, practicing and using one's personal testimony, witnessing and winning those in one's relationship chain, and beginning immediately to incorporate the new believers in a new worshipping group (church) while training them to also reproduce subsequently.

3. *JIT Training*

Training is done while people carry it out. It is *Just-in-Time training* in which the trainees learn 'today' what they apply, obey, and teach to others 'tomorrow'. This *Just-in-Time training* contributes greatly to people learning and applying what they are taught. They are asked to apply what they have learned, and to teach it to at least 2 other people before the next meeting.

4. *Anyone Can Be Trained*

No believer who desires to be trained is excluded from training who wants to be trained. The leadership bar is quite low, thus the pool of potential trainees is much larger. Many who receive the training do not carry through into application, so it is important to train as many as are willing. Some of the most unlikely seem to catch the idea and spirit of the responsibility the best. To see a massive movement develop, the goal should be to train tens and hundreds, rather than just a few.   All the while, accountability must be built into the ongoing format of teaching and training.

5. *Obedience and Accountability*

Obedience to the Word, and regular accountability to each other to "do" what they are trained to do are VERY IMPORTANT, even imperative. Regular meetings with those being trained are imperative. The meetings should not be just for training, but to rehearse and review the previous training, and to see how it is being applied, deal with questions, issues, doubts, failures and victories. Personal issues will also surface in this time that needs to be prayerfully dealt with. This gives an opportunity for the overseer to mentor, show concern and love for the Trainee, and to model the reliance upon the Word of God in finding answers for life's problems.

5. *Spiritual Growth of the Trainers*

While it does not take a person of vast or great experience to be a Trainer, it does require someone who is GROWING as a follower of Christ, Growing in Obedience to His word. Maturity is not marked by the length of one's Christian experience, but by the obedience and growth in one's experience. (In our experiences, we have all met new believers (from the standpoint of time from conversion), who were far more mature in Christ than older believers (time wise). Trainers must continue to grow in the Lord, and to obey His leadership and His word.

Conclusion

These key factors, coupled with the fervent and ongoing prayer of the worker continues to produce fruit in the expanding of this Church Planting Movement. But we are all still learning about Church Planting Movements and how God is using us in cultivating, sowing, watering and harvesting to reach large numbers of people. I pray that we will all continue to learn how we can be better workers in His harvest for His glory.

Chapter 6

Organic Churches and Church Planting Movements

Neil Cole

Our Story

In 1999 my family moved to Long Beach California to start new churches among urban postmoderns and to simultaneously start Church Multiplication Associates (CMA). We came with some strategy, which had proven very effective in previous ministry, but a far greater asset was our desire to learn and hearts willing to listen to what the Spirit had to say to the churches. The churches that God started did not look like our plans, but as we followed the leading of the Lord of the harvest, we discovered ways to start churches that were healthy and reproductive. These new churches were small and met mostly in homes. I never went out to start "house churches" and am always a little surprised when I am considered an authority on such. As a result we began 10 new churches in our first year.

These churches were different from others we had been a part of. They were the result of planting the seed of the gospel in good soil and watching the church emerge more naturally... *organically*. These organic churches sprung up wherever the seed was planted—in coffee houses, campuses, businesses and homes. We believe that church should happen wherever life happens. You shouldn't have to leave life to go to church. Because we were approaching church as a living entity, organic in essence, we followed certain natural phases of development. The result was reproduction at all levels of church life—

133

disciples, leaders, churches and ultimately movements. In all of life, reproduction begins at the cellular level and eventually morphs into more complex living entities. Life reproduces and usually develops from micro to macro. The Greenhouse movement has developed in just such a manner. As we learned, we shared our learning with others and soon organic churches were starting all over the States and the world.

Our first plan was an original, one-of-a-kind idea to start a coffeehouse. We had the whole scenario worked out—who would bake muffins and pastries, who would brew coffee, and who would play guitar and sing cool Jesus songs in the corner. We even had a space rented to turn into the business. Then the Lord stepped in and whispered in my ear: "Why start a coffeehouse to attract lost people?" "Why not just go to the coffeehouses where they are already?" That was a turning point for us. *Our original strategy required us to convert people from the coffeehouses they already loved, to our coffeehouse so that we could then convert some to Jesus*. The Lord of the harvest, once again, had a better idea for His harvest. This simple transitional lesson meant the difference between becoming just another attraction-oriented "y'all come to us" form of church and actually becoming a missional and incarnational church that goes to the lost. The implications have reverberated now to 16 states and 12 nations in just five years.

Most Christians today are trying to figure out how to bring lost people to Jesus. **The key to starting churches that reproduce spontaneously is to bring Jesus to lost people**. *We're not interested in starting a regional church but rather to church a whole region*.

The momentum was beyond our expectations. In our second year, CMA started 18 churches. The next year 52 new starts were added. In 2002, we averaged two churches a week being started and had 106 starts. Last year (2003) we saw around 200 starts in a single year. Today there are probably more than 400 churches in 16 states and 12 nations around the world. These churches were small (averaging 16 people) and simple. The term "simple church" began to gain popularity. We discovered the profound truth that if you lower the bar of how church is done and raise the bar of what it means to be a disciple, church will empower the common Christian to do the uncommon works of God. The result is churches that become healthy, fertile and reproductive.

The organic or simple church, more than any other, is best prepared to saturate a region because it is informal, relational, and mobile, not financially encumbered with overhead costs and is easily planted in a variety of settings. It also reproduces faster and spreads farther because it can be a decentralized approach to a region, nation or people group and is not dependent upon heavily trained clergy.

CMA's mandate is clear and simple: ***reproduce healthy disciples, leaders, churches and movements to fill the earth with God's kingdom***. We have developed some very simple ways to release the power of multiplication at each of these levels of kingdom life and growth. Each system is simple and reproductive. As the layers develop, movement as a whole appears more complex, but in reality it is made up of much that is simple. Saturating the globe with healthy and vital disciples is our mandate. It appears that God is fulfilling our deepest desires.

One evening at one of my own churches (called Awakening Chapels), Milton (who paints houses for a living) asked me about the church we had on Gaviota Street in Long Beach. Gaviota is only a few blocks from where I lived at the time. I told him that we don't have any churches on Gaviota. He smiled and said, "Yes you do." He told me that he had been painting a house and noticed that cars started coming to the house across the street and people would pull out guitars, bongos and Bibles and go into the house. He went over to introduce himself and mention that he had a church meeting in his home as well. When they saw him they recognized him and said that they were also a part of our network of churches. A church had started only a few blocks from my home and I didn't even know about it. When I heard this story I felt like we had finally reached a goal of spontaneous reproduction. We were beginning to see things out of control. We still have much to learn but God seems to be showing us the way to release spontaneous multiplication.

A couple of us from this Awakening Chapel started a new church in an apartment complex in the barrio of East LA. On a Saturday we went to the apartments to have a barbeque and baptize new believers. When we arrived I was surprised to see one of our other church planters there. He was also surprised to see me. It happened to be that he lived on that same block and led a church that he had already started there in Spanish. Now there are two churches on that block, one in Spanish and one in English. Could it be that we are now bumping into each other?

I went recently on a trip to Asia with Phil Helfer, one of our key leaders and co-founders of CMA. On our return flight we met a flight attendant who was expecting her first child. As we talked we found out that she was a Christian who until just recently lived in Long beach. What we didn't find out until a few weeks later is that she was a part of one of our churches. It blows my mind that we are bumping into people in our movement all over the place in such a short time.

Our Assumptions about Church

Church is a living organism, not a static institution

Just as God breathed life into all living creatures in the beginning of time (Gen. 2:7), He also breathed life into His church in the beginning of a new age (John 21:21-23; Acts 2). Church is alive, she is organic.

God's very first command given to man had nothing to do with a tree or tending to a garden. It was more basic and has been repeated and never repealed. It is one command we have actually fulfilled, even in our fallen state: Be fruitful and multiply and fill the earth (Gen 1:28; 9:1,7). He has given that same command to the church (Acts 1:8).

Most of the metaphors and explanations of the kingdom of God and the church in the New Testament use natural concepts for identification and descriptions. The body, the bride, the branches, the field of wheat, the mustard seed, the family, the flock, leaven, salt, and light. When the NT uses the building as a metaphor of the church, it is quick to add that it is made up of living stones.

Mark chapter four describes the beginning, growth, and end of God's kingdom in natural parables. The beginning of the kingdom life starts organically (Mark 4:1-20). The kingdom grows in a natural manner (Mark 4:26-29). And finally, the results of God's kingdom influence is an organic picture, albeit as supernatural as it is natural (Mark 4:30-32).

We would do much better as leaders in the church to learn at the feet of the farmer rather than to study the CEO of a corporate business. It is time that we see the church starts in the fields, not in the barns (Prov. 24:27). We spend so much time building nice barns with padded pews, air-conditioned halls, and state-of-the-art sound systems, yet we have neglected the fields. We are as foolish as the farmer who builds a barn and then stands in the doorway calling all the crops to come in and make themselves at home.

Church is so much more than a building, a service or a place

How did we ever get to the place where church was nothing more than a one and a half hour service on a single day of the week at a specific location? I assure you, in Jesus' eyes church is much more than that! He doesn't limit His church to a building, a location of a time frame.

At least four times in the Bible the Scriptures come out and say plainly that God does not dwell in buildings made by human hands. The first dwelling place God designed for Himself was a tent because He wanted to be on the move with His people. David strove to build a more permanent home for God but was resisted. Finally, David's son built the first Temple. At its' inauguration, Solomon stood in the shadow of this great building and said, "But will God indeed dwell on the earth? Behold, heaven and the highest heaven cannot contain

Thee, how much less this house which I have built (1 Kings 8:27)!'"

Isaiah 66:1 says clearly: "Thus says the Lord, 'Heaven is My throne, and the earth is My footstool. Where then is a house you can build for Me? And where is a place that I may rest?'"

Fast forward to Acts chapter 7 and we arrive on one of the most pivotal scenes in the history of the kingdom of God. Stephen is found preaching the gospel to a group of Jewish leaders under the shadow of another wondrous Temple, this one built recently by King Herod to please the Jews. He recounts most of the Old Testament Scriptures to a very attentive audience, when finally he says, "the Most High does not dwell in houses made by human hands." Then he quoted the very words mentioned above from Isaiah. He went on to say, "You men who are stiff-necked and uncircumcised in heart and ears are always resisting the Holy Spirit you are doing just as your fathers did." Upon hearing this, they were so agitated that they took up stones in the presence and blessing of Saul, and executed Stephen there on the spot. This began a movement orchestrated by God to decentralize His church via persecution.

Fast forward ten more chapters and we find Paul preaching before the stoic philosophers of Athens at Mars Hill. This is a pagan audience, unfamiliar with much of the Old Testament. Nevertheless, in the shadow of a great temple which still stands today—the Parthenon—he says, "The God who made the world and all things in it, since He is Lord of heaven and earth, does not dwell in temples made with human hands; nor is He served by human hands, as though He needed anything, since He Himself gives to all people life and breath and all things (Acts 17:24, 25)."

Jesus did not seem to have plans for buildings. One day, Jesus was walking in the shadow of Herod's beautiful temple and the disciples were straining their necks enamored by the magnificence of this building, thinking to themselves "Surely God dwells here!" Jesus responded with a remarkable prophecy, "I tell you that before this generation passes away, not one of these stones will be left upon another." He wasn't impressed. Sure enough, in 70 AD the Romans so destroyed the temple that no two stones were left on top of one another. It wasn't until the third century that the church first owned a building and it was a small room looking much more like today's lounge or living room than a temple or cathedral.

One dry hot day, Jesus had an interesting conversation with a Samaritan woman. When she discovered that He was indeed a prophet, she brought up one question that had occupied her thoughts all her life (John 4:20-24). "Our fathers worshipped in this mountain and you people (the Jews) say that in Jerusalem is the place where men ought to worship." Jesus responded, "Woman, believe Me, an hour is coming when neither in this mountain, nor in Jerusalem, shall you worship the Father. You worship that which you do not know; we worship that which we know, for salvation is from the Jews. But an hour is coming, and now is, when the true worshippers shall worship the Father in spirit and truth; for such people the Father seeks to be His worshippers."

We are always asking the wrong question — *Where*? All along, the right question is — *Who*? Where you worship is nothing compared to who it is you worship! Jesus instructs the woman (and us as well) that the reality is not that we need to go and seek God in some special place, but that He has been seeking us right where we are—even at an old well outside of a Samaritan village. We work to create what we call "seeker services" but all along the Bible tells us "there is none who seeks God no not one". A true Seeker service is one that focuses on the Father who is *seeking* His worshippers in Spirit and in truth!

The Kingdom of God was Always Meant to be Decentralized

Just as God has always intended for mankind to be spread out and fill the earth with His glory (Gen. 1:28; 9:1, 7). This is true of His church as well (Matt. 28:19-20; Acts 1:8). The people in the early days tried to settle in one place and started a building project in direct disobedience to God's design and God had to force decentralization with the confusion of languages (Gen. 11:7-8).

The first apostles struggled in the same way. When Jesus revealed His true incarnate self to His inner-circle of leadership (Matt 17:1-6) Peter's response was classic: "This is a good place to be, let me start a building project right now!" The Father rebuked Peter by telling Him to listen to Jesus' command. This rebuke is still relevant to this day!

It seems that mankind always wants to settle—in a single location and also for lesser things. Jesus commanded the first disciples in Acts 1:8 to spread out from Jerusalem until the ends of the earth are filled with the power of God. Instead they all stayed in Jerusalem. Just as God forced decentralization in Genesis 11 with languages, he forced decentralization in Acts, this time with persecution (Acts 8:1). One of the ironies of the Bible is that under persecution everyone from the Jerusalem church went out except the "sent ones" who were given the command in the first place. "Apostle" literally means "sent one" and they were the only ones who didn't go when persecution struck the church.

The Lord of the harvest had to raise a different set of apostles to finally get the job done (Acts 13:1-3). Nevertheless, by Acts 15 we still see the original "sent ones" in Jerusalem where they gave their blessing to the new apostles.

By Acts 21 Paul returns to the Jerusalem church and finally the "sent ones" are gone. But look at this model church. Paul was taken aside and told in private that he shouldn't be there because the church was overrun with legalists who would attack Paul if they saw him (Acts 21:20-26). Sure enough, he is attacked, arrested and this church tried to kill the author of half of the New Testament! When we disobey God's will (whether in outright defiance or the more subtle neglect) the consequences are an unhealthy church that has messed-up priorities.

By 70 AD this church was dead and gone forever. The only lasting effects this church left behind were "accidental" moves of the Spirit in alternative ministry ventures, with second tier leaders and lay people that eventually spread to become healthier expressions of the kingdom that would actually obey Jesus' original command to fill the earth.

Can you imagine what it was like to be one of the twelve disciples following Christ around for three years? Every morning you would awaken wondering what marvelous miracles you would see that day. You would have witnessed Him walking on water without a surfboard, healing a man born blind and feeding roughly 20,000 people with only the contents of school boy's lunch box. Imagine the feeling you would have if you had seen Him walking across the Sea, faster than the boat filled with twelve men (many professional fishermen) straining at the oars could go! You would have seen Him calm a storm with a single command or lay hands on an unclean leper only to see him cleansed instantly! You would have even seen Him raise someone from the dead! Imagine then that one day He says to you, "I am going away, and it is good for you that I leave." What would you think? How would you respond? Would you, like Peter, try to correct Him? How can it possibly be better if Jesus leaves? He tells us, "But I tell you the truth, it is to your advantage that I go away; for if I do not go away, the Helper shall not come to you; but if I go, I will send Him to you. And He, when He comes, will convict *the world* concerning sin...and righteousness...and judgment."

We must ask three important questions when considering this statement by Jesus to understand the significance of what His plan is:

1. Before Jesus was born, where did people have to go to gain direct access to the holy God of Israel? The answer was the temple, the Holy of Holies, and there only one man could enter one time every year.

2. When Jesus was walking on the planet, where did people have to go to be in the presence of God? Wherever Jesus was, whether that was on the shores of Galilee, on a boat in the sea or taking a midnight stroll across it.

3. Finally, after His death, burial, resurrection, ascension to heaven and Pentecost, where do people need to go to be in the presence of Almighty God? Wherever His people are, there the presence of the Holy God is. That is the rich prize that came at an incredible cost on the cross. Jesus died so that we can be spread out all over the globe. We can find God's presence with us in Southern California, but at the same time He is present with His children gathered in Costa Rica or Cairo, Belize or Beijing! Now the kingdom of God can enter into every neighborhood and every nation simultaneously. In Jesus' mind, this truth is so valuable it was worth dying for. We should hold on to it with much value and care.

We are God's Temple and We Each Carry His Service of Worship with Us

The New Covenant established by Jesus' own blood spilled as a sacrifice, was to release a decentralized nation of priests who would multiply and fill the earth with His presence. Ezekiel 37: 26-28 says:

> *"And I will make a covenant of peace with them; it will be an everlasting covenant with them. And I will place them and multiply them, and will set My sanctuary in their midst forever. My dwelling place also will be with them; and I will be their God and they will be my people. And the nations will know that I am the Lord who sanctifies Israel, when My sanctuary is in their midst forever."*

Jesus died a horrific death in order to retire the old system and establish a new one. He tore the veil between God and man from top to bottom removing the separation of God from His people. He has established a new nation of priests (1 Peter 2:8-9) to cover the globe with His power, His presence, and His glory.

Why then do we work so hard to reestablish the old ways with centralized buildings, priests and constant offerings to appease the system?

God indwells His people, all of them from the smallest to the biggest (1 Cor. 3:16; 6:19). Our hope of glory is not in the buildings in which we are, but in the Master who is building His life in us. Christ in us is the hope of glory (Col. 1:27). The world is not so impressed with our sacred houses of worship. In fact, other religions have built more beautiful ones. Let them see something they cannot reproduce, a new life in Christ.

The only time "worship" and "service" are put together, has nothing to do with a meeting on Sunday mornings, sound systems, pews, sermons or worship bands. It is a 24 hour a day, seven days a week expression of Christ's life in us. In Romans 12 Paul writes that we are to present our own bodies to be His temple. He writes, "I urge you, brethren, by the mercies of God to present your bodies a living and holy sacrifice, acceptable to God, which is your spiritual service of worship. And do not be conformed to this world, but be transformed by the renewing of your mind, so that you may prove what the will of God is, that which is good and acceptable and perfect."

Do not be "men who are stiff-necked and uncircumcised in heart and ears and are are always resisting the Holy Spirit" lest we be guilty of doing just as our fathers did. Jesus paid a huge price to set His people free, to take His presence everywhere. Don't let the seductive magnet of glamorous buildings and religious hierarchical systems bound us to a place and form of church that cannot spread His glory across the planet. Recognize, once again, the beauty of the New Covenant—a decentralized nation of priest bringing the presence of Christ all over the world!

What Is Church?

When it comes to church, most people ask the wrong questions. What church do you go to? How big is your church? Where is your church? What kind of music do you have at your church? How does your church grow?

I remember standing in front of a district conference for my denomination, as the one they had entrusted to start churches, with a different question. I honestly asked them (four years into our charge to plant churches): *What is church?* It doesn't induce confidence when the one who is supposed to start churches doesn't even know what one is. But when I asked the question it caused others to reflect and realize they may not really know what church is. Oh sure, we all know what our experience is. We all know what our traditions are. We speak as though we obviously know the answer to this question. But in reality, most of us never took a moment to ask the question. Rather than starting with the question of what church is, we start by asking how we can make it bigger, better or start more of them. As a result, we are trying to grow something without understanding what it is.

The temptation is to define church according to our own experience, so that we are assured we are always right, but that is a cheap solution that will perpetuate all our current problems. To define church and not take an honest and courageous look at the Scripture is a mistake. If you will ask this dangerous question, however, it may lead you down a path that you don't expect.

While I was an impressionable seminary student I was given a definition of church that was really more of a description. Church was explained as: (1) A group of believers who gather together regularly; (2) That consider themselves a church; (3) That have qualified elders present; (4) That regularly practice the ordinances of baptism and communion; (5) And have an agreed upon set of doctrinal beliefs (or an evangelistic persuasion).

While I admit that these are good qualities, they are missing something very important. I often ask groups what is missing from this description? After a few minutes of responses I usually tell them what I think is missing if they haven't already found it.

Jesus is missing!

One of my most respected mentors, a theologian and career missionary, once told me that Jesus is assumed in the definition because it is *believers* who are gathered. My response was, "Why would you assume Jesus' presence but make sure that a qualified elder is present?"

This indicates a problem in our churches, a very serious one. The church is more about what we bring to the table than what God does. I am convinced that if God were to pull the Holy Spirit out of our churches, many would carry on without even a pause. I heard of a Korean pastor who came on a tour and at the end of his visit he summarized his observation by commenting: "It's amazing what you people can do without the Holy Spirit."

As the world looks at our churches in the West, they see only what people have done and they are not impressed. We scheme, "What can we do to make our church more appealing to the people in our community?" This is, once again, the wrong question. When the world begins to see Jesus in our midst many more people will be attracted to our churches. A better question is: "Where is Jesus at work in our midst?"

If Jesus is missing in our understanding of church, He will likely be missing in our expression of church as well.

In Acts chapter 1 we find all five of the qualities mentioned above. But church doesn't really begin until chapter 2. In fact, Jesus instructs the people to stay shut in the upper room and not to do anything because they are not competent. What is the difference between the group in chapter 1 and chapter 2 of Acts? God joined the group, and what a difference that makes! With Jesus missing from the very core of our understanding of church we are no different than any other religious group, Kiwanis Club or the Moose Lodge.

We have a saying in our movement: *The church must be conceived in heaven before it is born on earth. It must first be a glimmer in our Father's eyes.*

As we approach a better understanding of what church is, I believe we must begin in heaven, not earth. The heavenly ingredient is so much more significant than the earthly ones. In fact, it is the heavenly ingredient that makes the earthly ingredients of any significance at all. Therefore, to minimize or even eliminate the heavenly from our definition is like a computer without a power source or a body without a circulatory system.

In our movement we have come to understand church as:

The presence of Jesus among His people called out as a spiritual family to pursue His mission on this planet.

Granted, this is very broad, but I like a broad definition of church. The Scriptures don't give a precise definition, so I'm not going to do that which God has not. For my understanding of church, I want something that captures what the Scriptures says about the Kingdom of God. In one of only two places where Jesus mentions church in the gospels, He says: "For wherever two or three are gathered together in my name, there I am in their midst." His presence must be an important element of church.

A threat in Revelation 2 and 3 for disobedient and unhealthy churches is that the lamp stand (representing the churches) would be removed from Jesus' presence. The presence of Jesus is crucial to what church is.

In many of the churches in the West ministry is done _for_ Jesus, but not _by_ Jesus and there is a big difference. If we evaluated churches, not by attendance or buildings, but by how recognizable Jesus is in our midst, our influence would be far more reaching and our strategies would be far more dynamic. Unfortunately, it is possible to do more and more of the things that make up the five qualities above but not demonstrate anything of the person or work of God in a neighborhood. But if we start our entire understanding of church with Christ's presence among us, then we will want to see something much more.

Imagine for a moment, three of the most powerful and dynamic people you can think of in 200 years of history. Now select one of them and ask yourself, "What difference would it make if this person was on your church leadership team?"

I read an article once that explained how Michael Jordan came to the Chicago bulls because of a simple flip of the coin a year earlier. Would the Chicago Bulls of the 90's, who went on to win six NBA championships have been different if Michael Jordan had not been on the team? Of course they would. Adding a single, powerful ingredient can make all the difference. Now I ask: how would your church be different if Jesus Himself was placed on your leadership team? Would that raise your expectations? I hope so.

Unfortunately, we look around the boardroom table at the faces present on our team and start there without realizing that God Almighty is also at the table. And we set standards, goals and expectations that we think these visible people around the table can accomplish without taking into account the fact that the most powerful person in the universe is also on board.

Phil Jackson, as coach of the Bulls in the 90's began building his team around his best player. Everyone else was evaluated by how they supported Jordan. Our churches should allow Jesus to be the best player on our team and set expectations accordingly.

Someone may say, "Well of course we recognize Jesus is on board, it is assumed. We even pray about our decisions."

But the real test is if you conduct ministry business expecting Jesus to carry the load—carry the team. Or do you practice church as though Jesus doesn't need to do anything and everything is done *for* Him instead of *by* Him. This would be like the Bulls, having Jordan on the team, and never passing him the ball!

We need to take on the challenges of God's kingdom with the confidence that Jesus Himself is on the team. What would you do differently if you had complete confidence that God was with you in your decisions? Is Jesus merely the owner, the coach, or is He also the most valuable player as well? It is time to pass the ball to Jesus and see what He can do.

If The Church Is Indeed Organic, She Has A DNA
What Is The DNA Of Christ's Body?

In the organic world, whether crickets or churches, the DNA becomes the internal code that maintains the integrity of each multiplied cell. In every organism the DNA is that which encodes each cell with its proper process and place in the body. In the expansion of the kingdom of God, it is the DNA that will maintain the strength, vitality and reproductivity of every cell in Christ's body. The DNA is exactly the same in every single cell of a body. In the same way, it is important that the whole DNA of the kingdom be found in every cell of Christ's body…the church. The DNA is the pattern of kingdom life from the smallest unit (the disciple in relationship to Jesus and others) to the largest unit. The pattern is the same and its expression remains constant.

The church is the body of Christ. It has one head and is one body and therefore has one DNA that must be the same for all of its members.

After some research and thinking, I have come to understand the DNA of the church to be simplified to three things. These three things are needed in every part of the church, from its smallest unit to its largest. These are the three things that make up the DNA of the kingdom of God:

Divine Truth: Truth comes from God. It is the revelation of God to man. It is best seen in the person of Jesus and the Scriptures. In both cases, there is a mysterious connection of both God and man. Jesus is both God and human and the author of Scripture is both. Nevertheless, they are without blemish.

Nuturing Relationships: Man was never created to be alone. We are social creatures and have a natural and intrinsic need for relationships. Our relational orientation is a reflection of the image of God in us. God is Himself relational and exists in a community—Father, Son and Holy Spirit. God is love because God is relational.

Apostolic Mission: Apostolic means sent as a representative with a message. We are here for a purpose. We have been given a prime directive to fulfill—to make disciples of all the nations. This part of us also comes from who our God is. Jesus is an Apostle. He is the chief cornerstone of the apostolic foundation. Before He left this planet, He spoke to His disciples and said, "As the Father has sent me, so send I you."

DNA is only potent as it is together. Once the component parts of the DNA are unraveled they bear little to no significance. It is the same in the church. Most chruches will gladly exclaim that they have all three portions of the DNA, but what they have done is unraveled it into separate compartments and lost its power. "We have excellent preaching on Sudays which is where we have the divine truth," one will say. "And we have small groups during the week which are our nurturing relationships and a strong missions committee which is our Apostolic mission." The key is not in having a separate ministry committee or program to handle each area. DNA must be whole, intact and in every cell. In other words, every meeting, every ministry, every disciple must have all three components at the same time. To breakdown the DNA into separate components and place them into different places in the body is to unravel the DNA and life and all that comes with it is lost.

If this is truly the DNA of the body of Christ then you would think that Jesus would emphasize them. He did just that. He said that the greatest commandment of all is to "love the Lord your God with all your heart, mind, soul and strength." This is the Divine Truth instilled in us.

Jesus said that the second greatest commandment is to "love your neighbor as yourself." This, of course fulfills the Nurturing Relationship component of the DNA.

Finally, Jesus' last words on earth before He ascended to heaven was the Great Commission where He said, "Go therefore and make disciples of all the nations..." This is an Apostolic Mission, the third component of the DNA.

Why is this so important to structure a spontaneous church multiplication movement? There is a risk in spontaneous reproduction without controls. For instance, a photo copy of a previous copy will lose some definition in the image. Another generation of photocopying will become even more corrupted. Every succeeding generation of photocopying will pass on the flaws of all the previous generations. Eventually, the copy will be indistinguishable and the image is lost. Many will object that loose expansion without controls will lack substance and quality, and every succeeding generation will get worse.

The solution to multiple photocopies is to copy from the master rather than other copies.

In the natural world, scientists have discovered something they call "Imprinting". This is described as a chemical process in the brains of birds, especially noticable in ducks and geese, where the first moving object they focus their eyes on upon hatching, they imprint upon this as their mother. God designed this as a way of forming a strong bond between mother geese and her babies so that they can follow her, be protected and nourished by her and also trained in how to be a goose.

One of the problems with this is when the goslings imprint on something other than a goose. The movie *Fly Away Home* is based on this phenomenon, where a young girl finds a nest of hatchlings and they imprint on her. At first this is lovely. She finds loyal companions and they find their needs met by this loving care giver. Wherever she walks she is followed by a gaggle of young geese expecting her to feed them, protect them and teach them how to be a goose. That last part is the challenge. As much as she loves them, how can she teach them to fly south in the winter? In the movie, her dad finds a way for her to do that but it is unnatural.

One big problem in the church today is that believers are imprinting upon other believers rather than upon Jesus. I am convinced that what we do with a new convert in the first 24-48 hours is of utmost importance. This is a very vulnerable stage of life where it is important for the life of the new child of God to imprint upon their Maker and Savior.

Usually, when people are first born again, we tell them things like, "You're just a baby. You're vulnerable, weak and there is so much you don't know yet. There is a mean and wicked enemy who wants to destroy you. You need some good teaching and help, so don't worry about anything but learning right now. Go to church, make friends with Christians, after you've grown we will talk about getting baptized and serving, but for now, just soak up as much as you can."

We imprint upon these fresh souls that they are helpless, needy and unable to fend for themselves without our help. We also teach them that their nourishment, protection and training must come from other Christians. The result is that we now have churches full of baby birds with their mouths wide open every Sunday waiting to be fed. They remain helpless consumers, stuck in their nests, who have no idea what it means to take off and fly. They have imprinted upon other men rather than God and most will spend the rest of their lives soaking up more knowledge and doing little with it.

In the book *Dedication and Leadership*, Douglass Hide describes how he used to train good committed communists. When new converts to communism were found they wouldn't try to protect them, but rather, would send them out on a street corner to pass out tracts and paraphenalia to support communism, despte the fact that they knew next to nothing. As people would question them and even attack their new belief, instead of weakening their resolve it forced them to learn faster and better what they needed to know. It also caused them to be even more committed to the cause.

I think we are guilty of protecting new believers from having to have a dependency on God. If we were to follow Christ's example and employ new believers immediately in ministry we would see how quickly they would be forced to pray, trust in God, listen to the Holy Spirit, find answers and solidify their commitment. New disciples will imprint on God rather than upon other men in such a case. They will have an unbreakable bond to the head of the body—Jesus Christ.

Perhaps this is why baptism is done so quickly in the New Testament, it is a chance for a brand new believer to make a stand publicly for their new Lord. I fear, once again, we have wandered too far from the plain truth of the Scriptures with dire results.

Every disciple we reproduce, every church that is birthed, and every movement that is ignited must be directly connected to the Master Himself in a context of growing relationships and mission. The DNA in like manner, gets passed on to each and every generation thus maintaining the connection needed to the master. This DNA is the quality "control" for the body, whether we speak of our own bodies or Christ's body. The DNA can maintain the integrity of the growth without needing human management or controls. In fact, it probably will maintain better integrity because it is connecting to the Lord for its strength rather than any human agency.

I feel comfortable releasing control of disciples, leaders, churches and movements as long as I know that each unit is connected to the Master. This is as it should be.

Chapter 7

From Cell-Based Churches
To Church Planting Movements

Harold Bullock

In January of 1978 my wife and I along with 13 other friends started an innovative Southern Baptist church in Fort Worth, Texas. We wanted to develop a new approach to church life that might make it easier to win unchurched adults to Christ and also see significant character change in believers. We thought a different approach to worship, utilizing a conversational style message and contemporary Christian music, might make it easier to invite non-churched friends to church. We were convinced that the right kinds of small groups would be far more effective in seeing the character of people grow than would the usual Sunday School class. Were we to develop such a church, we wanted to train people to start such churches in other cities of the U.S.A. and the world. We anticipated that, as we focused on the unchurched, other Christians may discover us and want to join. But we intentionally did *not* try to drain off members from other churches, especially Southern Baptist ones.

Today about a thousand people are regularly involved with us in Hope Community Church, which I still pastor. Sunday morning services at Hope usually have about 750 people in attendance. Special outreach Sundays will gather about 1100. Between 40 and 45 percent of the congregation is from the unchurched ranks. The other part of our church has come from a wide variety of church backgrounds. Our in-town transfer rate from other Baptist churches is about 6-8 percent.

Former members of Hope Church have started more than 80 churches in the U.S.A. and other countries. In July 2003 Hope celebrated its twenty-fifth anniversary with a reunion. About 250 people returned from ministries across the U. S.A and from other countries to celebrate the goodness of God over the twenty-five-year stretch.

In the following pages I would like to address the powerful effect of involving God's people in ministry to one another through the use of small groups in contrast to the traditional Sunday School approach. Autonomous house churches also involve people in direct ministry to one another. However, our experience with such direct ministry in decentralized groups, suggests that some unique challenges may face those who desire to develop House Church Movements in the United States and other free countries.

The Benefits of Cell Groups

In starting Hope, we intentionally wanted to work with both small groups and a larger worship service, anticipating that the small groups would not be able to meet all the members' needs for relationships. We felt we would gain some advantages by doing some larger group activities built around the "life-situation" of the people: singles' activities, college student activities, marriage and parenting seminars and conferences, etc. However, to best help with discipleship and character growth, we felt the small groups of 6-12 people needed to be the heart of our church life.

Ability to Involve People

Indeed, our utilization of small groups over the years has been a significant part of our ability to see new converts grow into mature believers and become aggressive lay ministers. The small group's advantage lies in its ability to involve people in one another's lives. A typical Sunday School class tends to take place in a more formal setting (classroom) and a shorter time frame (30-45 minutes), encouraging cordial but more distant relationships.[124] Small groups meet in homes (informal, let-your-hair-down settings) and usually last for an hour to an hour-and-a-half with refreshments following. The informal atmosphere and longer time frame encourages people to open up to one another in a deeper way over time. Groups may also carry on social life or ministry projects outside the regular meeting time.

In a typical class, *information* passes from mind to mind through a lecture or discussion. *Character*, however, is acquired differently from information. People acquire character in much the same way people get measles: they get into close, continuing contact with those who have it.

Transmission of Character

Small groups facilitate the transmission of character. By putting more mature believers and newer believers together in a group with an accepting atmosphere, the newer ones get a clearer picture of what the Christian life looks like, as they see the example of the more mature believers. The rest of the group provides practical and emotional support for newer believers as they grow. The group leader functions as a mentor to coach newer believers in applying the Scriptures to difficult situations in life.

Older believers who are part of the group have an opportunity to pass on what they have learned of walking with Christ, which deepens their own faith. They also have an immediate realm of ministry, meeting needs among members of the group. And they have an opportunity for outreach as they get involved in each other's circles of non-churched friends.

Over the years, our small groups have been effective in shaping lives toward Christ-likeness. For example, a married couple in their mid-twenties came to Christ and got involved in a small group led by the couple who had shared Christ with them. Toward the end of his third month as a Christian, the man approached the group leader and asked for prayer for the following Saturday. He explained that, before he had come to Christ, he had been in financial straits and had stolen a friend's motorcycle and sold it to pay his bills. He and his wife had been saving money and now had enough to repay the man. On Saturday he intended to take the money to his friend, confess the theft, pay his for the stolen cycle, and ask the friend's forgiveness. He was doing it because he had seen the group leader ask forgiveness in relationships in the group when he had offended people. He assumed that Christians just did this kind of thing. Unless he were in a close enough relationship to the leader to see the leader make mistakes and clear them up, he would likely have gone on for years with the theft on his conscience.

Groups allow the leader and older believers to mentor people who are struggling in their marriages or jobs. Many marriages have been vastly improved or healed as the couple gradually opened up and revealed to their leaders the distress in their marriage. Over time leaders have been able to coach them, problem by problem, to a healthier marriage.

Pastoral Care

Groups also provide a context for newer people to learn how to minister to others. As they participate in meetings they learn how to pray, how to open up to others, and how to work together harmoniously on group projects. As the leader involves them in helping out with ministry to others, they are coached in doing ministry.

Groups provide a fantastic amount of individual "pastoral care" for large numbers of people in the church. Much of it occurs *without* the *involvement or* even the *knowledge* of the church staff.

About eleven o'clock one night I received a call to come quickly to the hospital. A young mom in childbirth had begun hemorrhaging after delivery. She faced an imminent hysterectomy. Since I lived close to the hospital, I moved quickly and got to the waiting room ten minutes later. I was informed by the husband's group leader that the crisis was past. He and the wife's group leader had drawn all present to prayer just after they called me. "By chance" the attending doctor "happened to try a procedure that stopped the bleeding," and the hysterectomy was not needed.[125]

I found out that both group leaders had been at the hospital for about three hours. The husband's group leader had met the men of the husband's family and shared the Gospel with some of them. The wife's group leader had been working with the women. The leaders told me to go home; I was not needed any more. I led everyone in a prayer of thanksgiving and left.

Groups minister in other ways also. In the early days of our church, my wife and I restored an old home in the older part of Fort Worth. The project took several years and dozens of friends. One day I was in my yard when a group leader rolled up in his pickup truck and asked if I had anything for the garage sale. I ask which sale. He told me that a young couple in his group had just found out that they had miscalculated their taxes. At the same time, their medical insurance refused to pay part of the bill for their recent difficult child-birth. Suddenly, the couple was about $5000 in debt with the IRS and the hospital was demanding their money. The dollar amount would be perhaps $10,000 today. The couple was feeling hopeless.

The leader told me that people in a couple of groups had put together about $1000 to help them out. Our congregation was small and most of our people were younger and thus lower income. The $1000 was a significant amount of money. Then someone had the idea for a garage sale for the couple. Several groups had pitched in together to make the sale go. So the leader had come by to see if I had anything to contribute.

He and I loaded some of my unused building supplies on his truck, and the leader took off to collect more items. Money from the sale netted another $1500. The couple arranged to pay off the remaining $2500 over time. Over time they grew into strong leaders in our church life.

I could go on and on with stories like these, stories of God's people taking the initiative to deal with situations of ministry through their groups. By utilizing groups and training leaders who develop others, we have been able to involve a large percentage of our people in real ministry. And, we have been able to see large numbers of members' lives mature to a depth beyond what church often produces.

The Challenges of Cell Group Ministry

While small groups can be quite an effective way to build people and churches, they create their own challenges for the ministry leaders.

Group Training

Training group leaders is more complex than training Sunday School teachers, for the group leaders have to handle *more complex situations.* Sunday School classes usually occur on the church campus with higher status leaders, such as the church staff members or the pastor, close by if things were to get out of hand. However, small groups usually meet off-campus, so the leaders are "on-their-own" and must lead the meeting and deal with people without immediate higher-level back-up.

Group leaders must also learn to deal with people on a much *deeper level* than merely information transmission. Participation in a group where people get to know each other more deeply is a much more intense experience than a Sunday School class provides. Group leaders must learn to lead things in such a manner that dependent relationships do not develop. They have to deal with difficult people in the group who may be hogging discussion time or generating conflict in the group. And, they need to learn how to help people work through difficult problems and to refer people for greater help when their problems are sufficiently complex.

Character of the Leaders

Since the groups meet off-campus and leaders are significantly involved in the lives of the members, it is crucial that the character of the leaders be sufficiently developed before they are put into spiritual leadership over others. One wants to deploy leaders as soon as possible to multiply groups, not to delay forever until the leader reaches perfection before he is entrusted with leadership. But some matters represent crucial bottom lines. Paul addresses this issue in his profile of an overseer's qualifications in 1 Tim. 3:1-7 and Tit. 1:5-9. The vast majority of the qualifications are primarily character traits, not merely knowledge or skills. They do not resemble the characteristics of young graduates from theological school in the West, but they do resemble the characteristics of many mature men converted in "third-world" settings.

Paul understood that leaders must be sufficiently trustworthy before being entrusted with the spiritual leadership over others (2 Tim. 2:1-2). He also understood their role in providing a model for their flock. The leader's way of life carries tremendous instruction for their followers (Tit. 2:7-8, 1 Thess. 2:5, 10-12, 14; see also Heb. 13:7). Also, in the Christian arena, one's authority flows out of his initiative in setting a godly example in both speech and conduct (1 Tim 4:12). Thus, the immature leader, promoted into leadership too early, falls into traps that destroy his leadership (1 Tim 3:6-7).

This is quite true today. A leader transmits his values and character to his followers. Since small groups enhance this transfer, would-be group leaders must develop a godly way of life. Those who train group leaders must deal with values and practical Christian living in a way that is not necessary for the usual Sunday School teacher. And, just as the group leader's life impacts his followers, the trainer's life must set the right example for the rising leader. This necessitates a personal relationship between the trainer and the emerging group leader.

Maintenance

Not only is leader training more complex, group life also *requires more "maintenance"* than does a Sunday School. The shallower relationships in a typical Sunday School and its shorter time frame means that the teacher can focus primarily on the content of the lesson. However, the fact that people are actually getting to know one another in the cell groups raises the possibility of *a greater number of relational "messes."* Longer-term Christians who lack sensitivity to new believers can easily "burn" newcomers in the group and cause them to leave. Then again, since people are actually getting to know each other, they may get into a conflict that can flare into misunderstandings among several people. Or, as people get to know one another, sometimes skeletons are brought out of the closets—and leaders need help knowing how to handle difficult or complex situations. For example, if a husband or wife reveals that they have had a *physical* fight, the group leader feels that he needs to do more than simply say, "We'll pray for you."

The rise of such relational problems allows the opportunity for group members to work through issues that would never be effectively dealt with by a sermon alone or that would probably not come up in a typical Sunday School class.

However, such problems do not resolve themselves. High-level leadership must be assigned the task of coaching the group leaders and helping them sort out and deal with the situations that arise. Over time, the group leaders themselves can coach other rising leaders. But the whole system requires more maintenance than a Sunday School. It also yields richer life change in the participants.

More maintenance is also required because *groups can become pathological.* Groups can be more vulnerable to heresy than a typical Sunday School class, since they operate off-campus away from immediate supervision by higher leadership. Or, they may become a power-base for cunning, rebellious leaders.

Rebellious Leaders

We try to prevent the rise of rebellious or heretical leaders by *adequately teaching* the church members. A part of our new member instruction deals with "Seven Crucial Heart Attitudes."[126] These seven commands from the New Testament form a framework for our relationships in the church. The membership covenant reads:

- "I realize that often, as a part of Hope, I will have to: (1) Put the goals and interests of others above my own (Phil. 2:3-4 John 13:34-35); (2) Live an honest, open life (Eph. 4:25; Col. 3:9); (3) Give and receive Scriptural correction (Heb. 3:13 KJV, NKJ, RSV, NLT); (4) Clear up relationships (Matt. 5:23-24); (5) Participate in the ministry (1 Pet. 4:10-11); (6) Support the work financially (2 Cor. 9:6-8); (7) Follow spiritual leadership within Scriptural limits (Heb. 13:17).

- I am willing to work together with the church toward these."

Leaders are required to actually set the example in living out these attitudes. We also practice them as we work together on ministry projects.

Occasionally arrogant or rebellious people have come into the church and attempted to gain leadership or create a faction. Because of a widespread awareness of these New Testament teachings on genuine Christian fellowship, the arrogant or rebellious people "stick out like a sore thumb." So far, people simply have not followed them. After a while, the rebels get frustrated and leave.

Another preventive in the rise of illegitimate leaders is our *leader selection process*. We select leaders who have *already* demonstrated the Heart Attitudes as well as leadership potential. Group leaders, who know their group members, suggest new leaders. But, before a leader is appointed, we get feedback from peers who know the person to see if the candidate has evidenced the heart attitudes. We also ask their peers if they would actually want to follow the potential leader.

A final "safety feature" is that group leaders are *appointed* by the church staff, not elected by the congregation. Since they are appointed, they can be "dis-appointed" if need be. *However, over the years we have never had to dismiss a leader for heresy or rebellion.*

Burnout

Besides deploying qualified leaders, another challenge is keeping leaders from burning out. We have used small groups for twenty-five years. In the long run, *many leaders get tired and need a break*. Staying in contact with leaders lets us know who may need a rest before they begin to develop serious fatigue. A leader in training can step into the leader's role while the leader gets a vacation.

Long-term Membership

Another challenge is long-term group membership. Not only leaders, but also *group members grow tired*, especially in periods of intense work on their job or in times of family stress. Some members get bored with their group. The life situation of others changes: they may get married or have children. For many different reasons, people sometimes desire to find new relationships and join a different group.

Having the weekly worship service and other training and social events allows people to get to know a wide range of people and be aware of other groups they may want to explore. Without these other larger meetings in which people can network and possibly explore other groups, it would be a challenge to retain people in the same group they felt was not meeting real needs in their lives.

Group life is a powerful way to see lives change and to draw large numbers of people into ministry. However, it is not "as easy as falling off a log." It requires intentional development of people into leaders over time and training, and coaching them into effectiveness.

Implications for House Church Movements in the U.S.

Our experience with a wide range of people in small groups over the years leads me to some thoughts for those seeking to develop House Church Movements (HCMs) in the U.S.A., and in other free societies.

Leadership

Since House Churches are decentralized and involve people in one another's lives, they can be a powerful tool in the development of people. However, they will also be subject to many of the same problems as our cell groups: the rise of illegitimate leadership, interest of the members in broader activities than merely the one unit, long term weariness or boredom, changes in the life-situation of members that create a disconnect with the unit and relational messes that must be resolved—some of which will be quite complicated. However, the HCM, as usually explicated in the West, does *not* have a larger organizational or institutional framework to help deal with these problems.

Decentralization

Most plans for a House Church Movement that I have encountered intend a string of autonomous house churches led by a pastor, with no *formal* organization or hierarchy above the house church level. The experience of the members is restricted, primarily, if not exclusively, in the house church meetings and ministry with their friends in the house church to outsiders.

Many schemes for house church life usually include an infrequent worship service (once a month or less frequently), made up of several house churches meeting together. As a unit grows too large for a house, a leader would be chosen from the group to begin a new unit with some of the people from the existing house church. The hope is that house churches will multiply rapidly out of conversion growth and dramatically impact their locale, as they have done in some settings overseas.

Mentoring of a house church leader is usually intended to be done by his previous pastor, the leader of the mother unit from which his house church emerged. As the individual house churches multiply, they each become autonomous, voluntarily cooperating with one another but focusing primarily on their own ministry through their own house church.

House Churches in the Presence of Very Oppressive Governments

To date most rapidly expanding House Church Movements have developed in countries antagonistic to the spread of Christianity. In some more moderate but still quite antagonistic countries, house church movements have developed in the villages of rural districts where a strong sense of community binds people together, individuals are well-known by their peers, and a natural leadership structure exists in the village elders or chief. In such cases tested, proven leadership is already available in the person of the newly-believing chief or elders.

In countries that are highly antagonistic to Christianity, inadvertently, these oppressive governments have prevented several problems from developing in the HCMs that would otherwise hinder their progress and rapid spread. Those prevented problems, however, are likely to go unrestrained in a free society. Those wanting to foster HCMs in the U.S.A need to be aware of these.

Results in a More Mature Convert Who Can More Quickly Fill Leadership Roles

HCM's often use very new believers to establish a new house church. The presence of an oppressive government raises the bottom line for calling oneself a Christian. The real possibility of persecution creates a pool of more serious new converts from which to draw leaders for a rapidly expanding movement.

However, in the U.S.A., a "convert" is often a long way from being a dedicated follower of Christ. It often takes some time before new converts have dealt with enough issues in their personal lives that they are prepared for spiritual leadership.

In oppressive societies, a person seriously counts the cost before deciding to become a Christian. He makes a "Lordship" decision. He is likely to have thought through the consequences of being found out by the government before he commits to Christ. And, when he decides to become a Christian, he is probably committing to suffer for Christ if necessary. He is miles ahead of the usual new convert in the U.S.

If an HCM is expanding rapidly and newer converts are needed to head up new house churches, converts under an oppressive regime are already at a point of spiritual development perhaps three or four years ahead of new Christians in the U.S. An eight-month-old "Christian" in the U.S. is far more likely to fall into the demonic trap of pride and arrogance that Paul described in 1 Tim 3:6-7. The oppressive government helps assure more committed believers who will be able to rise more quickly to lead in a rapidly expanding HCM.

Unless extraordinary measures are taken, the U.S. is not likely to produce such quality converts as quickly, causing the HCM to slow down or too quickly put under-developed people into leadership.

Culls the Arrogant or Predatory
from Leadership

Paul warns the Ephesian elders that "savage wolves will come in among you and will not spare the flock. Even from your own number men will arise and distort the truth in order to draw away disciples after them" (Acts 20:29-30 NIV).

In a free society predatory people are drawn to church leadership and to professional ministry as a means to exploit people. The recent pedophile situation among Catholic priests is an example of this, though the Protestant Church also abounds in examples of sexual and financial predators achieving leadership and preying on the people who trusted them.

Arrogant people also strive to rise to leadership in churches, often doing battle with the pastor or church staff for control of the church. Once in power they rule like "little tin gods" (1 Pet 5:3-5 Philips). Diotrephes was an example in the early church (3 John 9, 10).

Under an oppressive government, the arrogant and predatory (who do *not* want to sacrifice for the Gospel) are likely to avoid becoming a Christian leader like one would avoid the plague. The arrogant wants a realm in which to shine and to be admired without having to actually serve or sacrifice for his leadership. The predator wants gratification of his own desires, not sacrifice *for* others. To serve as a house church leader where the government is oppressive is not really of benefit to the predator or the proud. Leading a house church represents only the possibility of sacrifice and imprisonment. Rapidly expanding HCMs in oppressive societies not only have more devoted converts to draw on for potential leadership; they have a built-in governmental screen to discourage the arrogant and the predatory from desiring leadership.

In a free society, church ministries are targets for the arrogant and the predatory. Small groups systems are especially vulnerable to such illegitimate leaders. But, in churches built on cells there is a hierarchical shepherding system that can discourage their approval as leaders.

A rapidly expanding network of autonomous house churches in a free society, however, would also be vulnerable to the arrogant and the predatory, but would not have an adequate hierarchy to discourage their rise. As the HCM pushes for the rapid multiplication of new units, it could promote the talented, but also arrogant or predatory, to leadership of an autonomous unit. Once in power, these illegitimate leaders can damage others before they are detected or dislodged, and thereby slow or destroy the church.

Those who intend to foster the HCM must come up with a way to detect and deal with these destructive people lest they "participate in another man's sins" (1 Tim 5:22, 24-25).

Keeps Expectations of the
Church "Program" Minimal

The presence of an oppressive government means the house church will focus on a limited number of activities, with multiplication at the core of the focus. When Christians must meet in secret gatherings, people do not expect much more of "church life" than genuine fellowship, prayer and encouragement. These things can be accomplished in a house setting. No one is dreaming of starting a public worship service or perhaps a choir that could be used to draw people to public concerts for Christ.

In a free society, however, people tend to expect more out of church life. As they marry and raise children they tend to look to church for more than just close fellowship. Though I think Maslow's Hierarchy of Needs has several flaws, it does communicate a general human tendency: when needs are satisfied at one level, other things rise to motivate people. As people's fellowship needs are met, other needs will arise that they may seek to fulfill through the church.

A church using cell group methods can construct other activities or organizations to help deal with those needs. In contrast, an assemblage of autonomous house churches meeting infrequently for a larger worship service does not have a mechanism for doing this. Indeed, were it to try, it would likely lose its focus on multiplication.

As the HCM movement ages, it will likely have trouble remaining an HCM and be pressured to transition into another form of church in order to deal with increasing felt needs of members. Leaders of the HCM need to be prepared to deal with this.

Reduces Relational Stress Within the Group

The presence of an oppressive government minimizes the number of distracting internal relational issues and allows the house church to stay on focus in spreading the Gospel and multiplying.

People who face a common enemy band together far more tightly than people without one. We saw this effect in the days after the 9-11 disaster at the World Trade Center in New York. Quite diverse groups were suddenly unified under the enemy attack. As the months dragged on after the attack, however, the flush of unity began to wane. Separate agendas of the different political and ethnic groups became to creep back to the forefront and generate conflict once again. A common enemy increases social cohesion and demotes individual agendas that could lead to division.

As imperfect people get to know one another closely, they can greatly strengthen one another. They can also create lots of messes. Lacking the higher quality converts of oppressive societies, the house church in the U.S. will have to deal with a lot of relational problems. Without the presence of a common, oppressive (obvious) enemy, members of the church will be more susceptible to conflicting personal agendas that diminish effectiveness in evangelism and multiplication. House church leaders will need both training and continued coaching as they deal with a wide variety of relational issues. In addition, an intervention system may be needed if the problems within an autonomous unit become destructive.

Limited Cross-Cultural Application:
A Case In Point

The power of God to work through his people is just as alive today as it was in the first century. It seems God especially works through the close fellowship of his people both to grow them and to reach new people around them. In Hope we have experienced this through our small groups. Indeed, God has wrought it in HCM's in oppressive societies.

However, it may be that free societies, particularly Western ones, will turn out to be less fertile soil for HCMs. That turned out to be true for another methodology with dramatic record of growth in a different culture.

In the late 1970's and early '80's, Dr. Cho, the founder of Full Gospel Central Church in Seoul, Korea, toured the U.S. and fired the imaginations of pastors as he told the story of the rise of his church beyond 50,000 members. (The church today has more than 600,000.) Key to Cho's strategy was a system of cell groups.

It was clear to leaders of the time that the American church was "losing the war" in evangelizing and congregationalizing Americans. It appeared to many leaders that cell groups could be the answer to the American church's need, the tool that would

176

result in a fantastic acceleration of evangelism and lead to the discipling of America.

Hundreds, perhaps thousands, of U.S. pastors zealously attempted to re-create Cho's success by imitating the cell group process that Cho had used.   Large numbers of the attempts failed entirely.   Some pastors were able to create churches of several hundreds in groups.   Years later, the most successful pastor had only made it to about 5,000 members—far shy of the hundreds of thousands at Cho's church.

An American friend studying theology in Korea sent me a copy of 16 factors in Korean church growth that did *not* translate well into the American culture.[127]   One of the most obvious was the Korean respect for authority.   Dr. Cho could be quite directive as he made the hard decisions that would lead to the creation of the huge church.   The culture supported his authority and encouraged his followers to support him.   Korean respect for authority also helped strengthen a long chain of authority stretching from Cho down to each individual cell leader.   It was highly unlikely that insubordinate leaders would rise to challenge Cho and rip the church apart.

However, a pastor who wants to be so highly directive in an American church usually has a fight on his hands.   He has to constantly earn his authority, and is easily challenged by arrogant people.   American culture does not support highly directive leadership.   Indeed, the culture undermines it.   Even if a large audience gathers to hear the pastor's sermons, few of them consider themselves "under his authority."   Nearly every person in an American church feels free to question the pastor's decisions and resist his authority.   Few western churches have reached five thousand, much less hundreds of thousands.

The work of God through Cho in Korea was real and valid. God, however, did not do the same thing in the U.S.A. Cho's fabulous cell system produced only limited results in the U.S., not the dramatic results it had in Korea. In a similar manner, House Church Movements have prospered dramatically in some non-American societies—usually antagonistic, oppressive societies. Will HCM's prosper as dramatically in a non-oppressive, free society rooted in western individualism? It remains to be seen. Only time and effort will tell.

Endnotes

[124] We acknowledge that there are some Sunday School classes that have many of the functions of a cell group.

[125] We truly feel that this was an answer to prayer

[126] The "Heart Attitudes" are our "bottom line" on church membership. A CD with information on the balance we are seeking in these areas is available at haroldbullock.com.

[127] Unfortunately, I do not currently have a copy of the list. However, it included other societal factors. One was the presence of a large number of university educated wives with few jobs available for them in the Korean economic structure. Many of these devoted their time to leading Cho's cell groups. In America, however, educated women had easy entry into the job market. Another factor was that Korean Christians had for decades educated their children, and in the Korean society, the educated were held in higher regard. Thus Christianity was perceived as having status. In the USA, however, Christianity is increasingly perceived as a questionable matter.

CHAPTER 8

GlocalNet and NorthWood Church:
A Church Planting Movement

Ebbie Smith

Christians have used missionary strategies since the New Testament period.[128] The Christian movement has seen some of the long-used strategies return to favor in recent years. One such strategy, clearly visible in New Testament teachings, is receiving a contemporary revival in the methodology that has come to be called, "Church Planting Movements."

This chapter seeks to establish that forms of church planting movements are not only possible but actually operating in North America today. In fact, authorities can point to several movements in North America that exhibit many of the characteristics of church planting movements. One such group that clearly shows the characteristics of a church planting movement in North America is the GlocalNet group that has grown out of NorthWood Church in Keller, Texas and the leadership of Dr. Bob Roberts

Church Planting Movements

David Garrison of the International Mission Board of the Southern Baptist Convention has given recent expression to this newly revived strategy in his initial book, *Church Planting Movements* and the expanded version *Church Planting Movements: God's Way of Redeeming the World.*[129]. This work may well be the most significant missiological writing since Donald A. McGavran's, *The Bridges of God* in 1955.

179

Garrison not only describes church planting movements but also outlines some of the ways God is blessing these movements around the world.

According to Garrison, a church planting movement is *a rapid and exponential increase of indigenous churches planting churches within a given people group or population segment.*[130] The essence of the strategy is to introduce Christianity by starting churches that will in their own strength (empowered of course by the Holy Spirit) start other churches. God has granted unusual harvest to many of these movements around the world.

The strategy of church planting movements has rightly received acclaim as a significant strand in the methodologies for Great Commission Missions in the 21st century. Some have, however, raised the question as to the possibility of applying the methodology in areas where churches already exist. The questions especially addressed the problems that might arise in starting churches with this strategy in areas where subsidy had been used extensively. An even larger question considered the possibility of church planting movements in North America.

The possibility of church planting movements in North America must be approached from several standpoints. First, no strategy can or should be simply moved from one environment to another. Church strategists should not expect or attempt to use the method in exactly the same way it is used in other countries. Context is different.

Second, no *strategy should be considered the one and only way to engage in the multi-faceted mission that God has given the Church.* God has many plans for reaching many people and peoples. He will reach his will for people and peoples by means of various approaches. In most circumstances, methods compliment rather than replace.

Third, using any strategy calls for adapting the basic means of reaching people and starting congregations to local situations. The aim is never to reproduce the methodological pattern but seeking the results. A church planting movement in North America might not reproduce every aspect of the church planting movement methodology from other countries but would seek the constant of reaching of people and the starting of congregations that would then start still other churches.

its founding pastor, Dr. Bob Roberts, have supported and spawned the starting of at least 150 congregations both in North America and beyond. God has accomplished a church planting movement in North America though His use of NorthWood Church and its family of congregations.

The NorthWood/GlocalNetwork Story

That God has used NorthWood Church in a significant way cannot be questioned. Are NorthWood and the GlocalNetwork that has grown out of this congregation's ministry a church planting movement in North America? I believe that the results of its ministry indicate that this church and its church-starting emphasis clearly indicate that it is indeed a church planting movement. NorthWood Church, Pastor Roberts, and the dedicated servants of God who work with him have lived out the conviction that *every church should be a church-starting center.*

Not only does NorthWood itself show the characteristic of starting other churches but the churches it starts in turn plant new congregations. When the convictions and practices of NorthWood Church is combined with the development of the network they call GlocalNet (hence GlocalNet), the presence of a church planting movement is evident. God has uniquely used this pattern to inspire many in regard to the imperative spirit of church multiplication.

God planted the seed for NorthWood Church in the heart of Pastor Bob Roberts and nurtured the seed through the ministry of Bob Roberts Jr.'s father, Bob Roberts Senior. The elder Roberts pastored for over 25 years and has done extensive missionary work in other countries, especially Belize, South America. The younger Roberts speaks of the influence of his father saying, "My Dad introduced me to the world—something I wish to do for my children."[131]

The seed thus planted and nurtured sprouted and began to grow into a strong church start in 1985 when Bob Roberts and a core group of some 43 adult Christians started NorthWood church in Keller, Texas, an area just to the north of Ft. Worth. The new sprout, fertilized by the influence of many examples such as Rick Warren, Tom Wolf, and Robert Logan began to flourish with the conviction that *every church should be a church-starting center*

NorthWood began to produce fruit naturally. By 2006, in some 18 years, NorthWood had reached a membership of over 2500. Additionally, the ministry of NorthWood has been directly involved in spawning over 100 other churches in North America and in other countries. The first church-type new start came into being less than seven years after the beginning of

NorthWood. Using resources for outreach rather than for facilities, NorthWood did not provide permanent facilities until 1996, eleven years after its birth.

A strong plant not only produces fruit for eating each year but also seed that can lead to other plants and other fruit in many different places. Much of the NorthWood story must be seen though the other churches and their spread. In 2006 the NorthWood story (along with the stories of the congregations that have grown out of NorthWood) included over 300 congregations of various kinds and in various places. Roberts sometimes calls these other congregations that have grown out of NorthWood "bloodlines."

A major part of the vision of Roberts lies in the finding of gifted persons and turning them loose to start reproducing congregations. *Roberts teaches that God's people should become more concerned about the advance of the Kingdom than just the growth of their church.* He seeks to implant the idea of transformation. Roberts laments that we have many converts but few transformations. The concept of reproduction looms large in the heart of Pastor Roberts. Roberts says "I had rather be a little horse than a large mule."[132] The idea is that horses can reproduce while mules cannot.

The saga of NorthWood Church and the rise of GlocalNet began with the departure from the traditional approaches to a pattern that certainly has eventuated in a church planting movement. The beginnings of this movement rested in the answer to a question the Holy Spirit obviously placed in the mind of Bob Roberts, "When will Jesus be enough?"[133]

In answering this seminal question, Roberts found the direction away from the "old school" approach to one that now reaches virtually around the world. Roberts came to realize that God is the center of the church and that Christians and church leaders serve in His power. The pattern came to incorporate the concept of transformation. The GlocalNet works through "T Cells" (transformational cells) and "T Communities" (transformational communities). The "T Church" and "T Groups" look to transform, in the power of God, human individuals, communities, and the world by guiding to what is called "T Life" or transformed and transforming life.

The worldwide vision of GlocalNet can be clearly seen in a series of three-fold goals. On the local level, GlocalNet supports seek connection with the unchurched, conviction, and community. This trio of goals leads to a result of "T Life" or transformed life. The pattern is not about conversion without change but transformation to Christlikeness.

The local congregation serves the community by receiving new believers, equipping them for service in and through their relationships, deploying them through their stewardships, watching over and supporting them as they serve, and treating those injured in the process. The GlocalNet pattern does not, however, stop with the local church and its needs. The pattern involves community development, church multiplication, and nation building. The GlocalNet vision is worldwide. The NorthWood vision is pictured in the following visual.

The symbol pictures a basic aspect of the GlocalNet approach. The point is that the church is based on the concept of transformed life. The center of the symbol shows the goal of transformed life for the persons who come into the influence of the churches. The point is transformation rather than conversion without any real change.

From the fellowship involved in T-life in the church, the GlocalNet pattern moves to outside the congregation to seek T-world. The pattern is nation-building by contributing to the inner structures of nations, community, development by contributing to the needs of the peoples in the communities, and then church multiplication. In the concepts of T-life and T-world one finds an important facet of the ministries of these congregations.

The NorthWood Church story is most vividly seen in the churches that have grown out of its ministry and influence. The Bear Valley Church formerly under the leadership of Pastor Sam Carmack, for example, became the first of the church groups growing out of the ministry of NorthWood. Beginning in 1992, Bear Valley Church reached a membership of some 800 by 2006. The church met in a movie theater, schools, and other temporary facilities until the congregation purchased land and constructed a permanent facility in 1999. Most exciting, Bear Valley Church has helped start at least

185

eight other churches and these congregations actively start new churches.

Brian Lightsey first came under the influence of Bob Roberts around 1992 when Roberts spoke in an evangelism class at Southwestern Baptist Theological Seminary. Lightsey became the first intern to join with Roberts for inspiration and training. Brian told Roberts he would work with him in any capacity—including cleaning toilets and was, he says, somewhat surprised when this was exactly some of his first duties at NorthWood. While he was under the mentorship of -to-door surveys Bob Roberts, the Holy Spirit gave Brian Lightsey convictions and commitment to become a church starter.

The Lakeline Church in Austin, Texas was conceived in 1996 without a core group, such as had been available to the Bear Valley Church. The Lakeline Church began by seeking in doorinterested persons. The first public worship services were held in 1997. The church met in, and still meets, in rented facilities. These facilities have been a movie theater and storefronts. They rented a storefront but look forward to seeking permanent facilities in the future.

Lakeline Church has not only experienced growth in Austin but has had a part in starting other churches. Among their church starts are an African-American congregation in Austin, an urban downtown church in Austin, Texas, a church in Mission, Texas, and a church in Greensboro, North Carolina. The church has also done extensive missionary work in other countries.

The Fellowship of the Parks, another church that has grown out of NorthWood, began its story in the spring of 1993. Pastor Doug Walker responding to the God-given challenge of the need for a church in North Tarrant County began meeting with a small group in a home. The beginning church received financial support and spiritual encouragement from three other churches—NorthWood, Bear Valley, and First Baptist Church in Euless. Public worship services began in September 1993 using rented facilities in a local hotel. The beginning church group faced a number of trials relating to the facilities.

The church moved into other rented quarters in a school, then to space in another church, in a leased facility, back to the school, and finally God provided the land and a facility. The opening in the new facility was on January 6, 2002. Today, over 800 persons join in the worship services.

A most significant aspect of the church planting movement nature of NorthWood's ministry is seen in the creation of the fellowship that has been given the name of GlocalNetwork or Glocalnet. The purpose and intention of this network is to bring together, empower, and guide leaders and congregations to incorporate the vision of guiding congregations to become church-starting centers that aim to achieve, through God's power, the transformation of persons, churches, communities, and nations.

The vision of GlocalNet lies in starting and developing churches that become biblical fellowships and move toward relational, spiritual, and missional communities. The network, under the direct leadership of Roberts and Glenn Smith, seeks to train church leaders who will start and develop reproducing congregations. Glenn Smith declares:

> Our training is not about any model! Our training is designed to challenge you to think carefully about what you are starting! To be truly successful you need to create a model that uniquely fits you and your context, and you need a clear picture of the kind of disciple you intend to produce![134]

In describing the kind of congregations that the GlocalNetwork envisions, Smith shows that the churches are to be incarnational—that is, groups who bring the kingdom and its King into every corner of human life simply by fully living in the Kingdom with Jesus. This quality in a congregation will lead the church to become *missional. A missional church is a reproducing body of authentic disciples, being equipped as missionaries, sent out by God, to live and proclaim His kingdom in their world[135]*.

The missional church does not exist for itself but for the world. This kind of church expresses its nature as a missional body. The purpose of GlocaNet is that of glorifying God by mobilizing people and resources to transform lives, communities, and nations. The pattern centers on four guiding principles—personal and relational transformation, serving passionately, having sustainable impact resulting in effective ministry, and maintaining integrity without boundaries.

The GlocalNet pattern accepts a vision. The one-year vision statement is,

By January 1, 2005, the Global Impact Team will be a high performance, dynamic leadership team utilizing sound management and effective marketing to mobilize 200 glocal volunteers. We will create a local program that mirrors the same passions found in our international outreach. Our alumni's passion will ignite the NorthWood community to the next level of commitment and obedience to further God's Kingdom.[136]

Glenn Smith suggests that the missional churches envisioned in the Glocal pattern involve seven distinctives. The first is multiplication. This group thinks in terms of churches that reproduce and avoids any group that is sterile. The GlocalNet plan also calls for behavior-based discipleship. The churches do not teach simply facts and ideas but rather guide people to live out the biblical teachings.

The third distinctive in the GlocalNet vision is diversity. The group sees the world made up of a diversity of peoples who will only be served adequately by a diversity of churches. No one model is presented as "the" way. A fourth distinctive lies in the concept of a local importance. The church should be involved in the community and in service to the community. If the church were removed from the community, the community would recognize a loss. Glocal churches seek community transformation through biblical influence.

An equally important distinctive (the fifth) is global involvement. This global involvement involves a "front door approach." Christian influence in exerted through direct involvement with nations and the leaders of nations and services to the people. Members of Glocal churches realize that they go to other cultures to serve.

A sixth distinctive of Glocal churches includes the idea of total church mobilization. All members are drawn into the ministries of the church. Every spiritual gift is utilized. All talents and abilities are brought to bear on what the church is trying to do. GlocalNet churches and leaders are convinced that the Great Commission is given to all Christians rather than to a select few designed to serve as "missionaries."

Finally, Glocal churches show the distinctive of strategic relationships. These churches will partner with other acceptable groups who are serving the kingdom. Partnership and networking continue to occupy a central position with GlocalNet churches.

Space denies the temptation to chronicle many other congregations that have grown out of NorthWood's ministry and training. Bob Roberts is reluctant to claim as a church start some congregations realizing that new starts sometimes do not actually become new churches. He is unwilling to give unfounded statistics. But one can verify at least 150 congregations that have grown directly and indirectly out of the efforts of NorthWood church and Bob Roberts and the people who have been trained, mentored, and inspired through the efforts of this church. A legitimate question is, "How has it happened?"

Elements in the NorthWood Pattern

Every church that comes out of the NorthWood pattern does not exhibit the exact, same features. Roberts sees the necessity of a diversity of churches to reach the diverse peoples of the world. Still, the reproducing ministry of GlocalNet Churches grows out of and is based on several characteristics or elements that allow for and stimulate ongoing church expansion. In general these characteristics will be found in GlocalNet churches.[137]

The Element of Vision

Bob Roberts follows the vision of a church that is grounded on a passion to reach the world for Jesus. He shares with the congregation the vision that includes a kingdom understanding. The church should always be more than just one congregation. The vision of NorthWood is of a church that is both local and global that serves its own community while at the same time envisioning the entire world.

Bob Roberts is convinced that the church's vision should include the concept that the church is on a journey. A reproducing church, he says, must follow a journey that always has a goal but never has an end. The goal is that of providing needed congregations that will in turn reproduce themselves. This journey should continue until the returning Lord declares the mission to be complete.

Resting the church on a definite vision is a characteristic seen in the churches that spring from NorthWood. For example, Lakeline Church in Austin, Texas has the vision statement of *Know, Grow, Go*. Pastor Lightsey explains that this vision is not simply about the church increasing. Lakeline Church exists to develop unchurched people into followers of Jesus Christ who KNOW Him, GROW to be like Him, and GO tell others about Him. The vision is that the unchruched will come to Know Christ in salvation experience, Grow in Christ likeness, and then Go to the others who need Jesus.

The Fellowship of the Parks began with the vision of sharing Christ with the unchurched in North Tarrant County. The congregation responded to the vision of fulfilling the will of God to reach the people in Tarrant County but also to reach out beyond to the people of the world. The Fellowship vision is that of being faithful to God and helping people relate to God and to others.

Such vision is essential for a missional church and is seen in these congregations.

The Element of a Winsome Spirit

Relating to leaders in the GlocalNet churches one is impressed with the spirit that is evident. These leaders have joy, sincerity, commitment as evident characteristics. One is impressed with the absence of pride, self-seeking, or arrogance. These leaders fully believe in and committed to the plan of GlocalNet ministry but do not hold any position that it is the only way to do Kingdom work. This spirit that pervades the movement is perhaps the most noticeable and important features of GlocalNet.

The Element of Expanding Ministry

NorthWood Church has never been about one single congregation. Pastor Roberts from the beginning envisioned a local church with a worldwide ministry. By moving all ministries and training to an "on the field" design, the

NorthWood pattern has indeed proved expandable to the world. "NorthWood Church shows how a local church that is committed to reproduction can thrive in its own locality while still contributing to church starting efforts in other areas—in the United States and in other countries"[138]

NorthWood Church has on-going ministries in other nations. A great deal of this ministry is done by providing opportunities for lay members to use their abilities and resources to live and practice their faith in other cultures. These ministries proving most effective for outreach are using methods different from traditional missionary strategies. The local situations make public discussion of these ministries ill advised. Pastor Roberts declares, however, that he approves of no ministry methods that violate any national laws or ethical principles.

The Churches that have flowed out of the NorthWood family all have expanding ministries to other regions of the United States and to other nations, focusing on unreached people groups. Bear Valley Church ministers in the Philippines and India—sometimes using medical services. Persons from Bear Valley Church have started congregations among the Rizalian people in the Philippines and among business caste persons in Delhi, India. They have also been active in New York City and Atlanta, Georgia.

Lakeline Church in addition to its work in the United States continues ministry in India, among the *Yadav* people. The church has been active in Haiti, where they have helped provide a school for a congregation. Pastor Lightsey points out that in Haiti the public school situation is such that a church with a school has a great advantage in evangelism.

Lakeline Church also will soon be working in Guatemala. This expanding ministry is typical of the NorthWood network pattern.

In this element of an expanding ministry, the NorthWood pattern most clearly shows the characteristic of a church planting movement. Each "bloodline" in the Church builds into their outreach congregations this same DNA of expansion. Presently, the GlocalNet vision is expanding to New York City where Paul Gomez is training local ministers in the vision and practice of GlocalNet patterns.

The Fellowship of the Parks that started in the spring of 1993, now has planted seven other congregations. The congregation has sent out ministers and church starters. A ministry among the *Garifuna* people of Honduras also is among the ministries of this congregation.

Expansion is attained by intentionally implanting the church multiplication DNA into the churches from the beginning. Roberts encourages the new congregations to early in their experience begin to think in terms of starting new churches. This planning to the church starting DNA is, according to Sam Carmack, essential to the movement.

The Element of Constant Encouragement

Leaders and members of GlocalNet churches point to the constant encouragement from the movement as a major reason for the effective ministries that are seen. Brian Lightsey speaks of the frequent phone calls and the constant encouragement from Bob Roberts. Lightsey remembers contact with Roberts almost weekly. Even during the early days of the church's life, Pastor Roberts repeatedly inquired if Lakeline Church had an Unreached People Group with which to work and encouraged him to find them.

Carmack recalls that in his initial talk with Bob Roberts on structuring their relationship, Roberts suggested, "Let's be friends." Carmack says that the regular meals and other contacts were indispensable to one engaged in the lonely task of launching a new congregation. Perhaps most important, Carmack indicates that this encouragement continues and focuses on personal matters but also church multiplication and unreached people groups.

The Element of Cultural Accommodation

Cultural accommodation is essential to the movement according to Pastor Carmack. The churches respond to the huge cultural shift involved in globalization and postmodernism. The worship services and other activities are designed to attract and appeal to the vast unchurched neighborhoods that are the target of their ministries.

Lakeline Church promotes a relaxed and casual atmosphere where people are welcomed just as they are – no matter their background. They strive to be a church for the 21st Century by utilizing innovative approaches to present the timeless message of Jesus Christ in a contemporary and relevant way through our live band, videos, dramas, multi-medias, and other art forms. Lakeline Church is especially open to "unchurched" or "dechurched" people who have for whatever reason never gone to church or who have dropped out along the way. Their goal is to create an atmosphere where people, who might have been "turned off" by church in the past, can come and feel comfortable, relaxed, and welcome.

These congregations never lose any biblical truth in their efforts to accommodate to the cultures they serve. They faithfully maintain the Word of truth while they adjust so as to make the unchanging Message plain and attractive to the changing masses. Cultural accommodation without compromising biblical truth is a strong point of the churches as it must be for any church that desires to reach the lost and unchurched.

The Element of Small Group Activity

Small group activity forms another essential element in the methodology of GlocalNet churches. Bear Valley has over 100 small groups meeting. In these small groups the congregation finds its most effective means of discipleship and education. These functions best happen, according to Pastor Carmack, in groups smaller than 12.

Small groups meet regularly with the common purpose of developing friendships, learning biblical principles, serving together, caring for one another, and having fun in a relaxed and informal setting. They are designed to be a simple expression of the biblical church. They are all about relationships and doing life together. Small groups are the primary places of really connecting with others as well as giving and receiving care in Lakeline

Church. They are the best means for authentic community and genuine life-change.

The congregations associated with the GlocalNet approach should not be viewed as what has come to be known as "Cell-Group Churches." They rather should be viewed as churches that use cell groups. Cell group activities are integral parts of these churches but not a central as would be the case in actual cell-group churches. In most GlocalNet churches one will find small group activities holding an important place.

The Element of Conversion Growth

Churches related to the Glocalnet group center on reaching the unchurched. Conversion growth occupies the center stage of the ministries. Roberts reports that of the new members who come into NorthWood congregation, one-fourth are Christians from other congregations, one-half are new Christians, and one-fourth are Christians who have left the organized churches and been reclaimed. In other words, NorthWood is clearly an missional church that seeks and wins the unchurched. Over half of Lakeline Church's members joined through baptism.

Sam Carmack indicates that 80 percent of the members of Bear Valley Church come from the unchurched rather than from other churches. Over 50 percent of the adult members have been baptized at Bear Valley Church. This congregation baptizes 8.5 adults for every child they baptize. They grow from conversion growth.

Carmack *uses the phrase, "We try to congregate people before converting them."* By this he means,

"Discipleship before conversion" *and* "they need to belong before they believe." He explains that the method is a way to relate to the "Post Modern" mindset that usually discerns truth as relational or experiential. This fact significantly informs preaching style and also suggests a better way for church to relate to the unchurched. Pastor Carmack explains that his congregation has designed their church so that a non-Christian can belong as a "seeker." Formal membership occurs when committed believers are willing to accept the church covenant. Carmack says, "We constantly verbalize the fact that we value the involvement of the seeker in every area of the church."

The pastor continues by pointing out that the church allow a seeker to hold just about any position in the church, as long it doesn't involve teaching. We include seekers in our worship team and drama team as part of the teaching ministry of the church. Seekers are encouraged to hold service positions but this service first requires an interview and verification that there is nothing in their lives that would embarrass the church. Carmack says, "Our growth by conversation is a little higher than most other churches. I believe the principle of 'congregating before converting' is a main reason. There are, however, many other reasons as well."

Membership in the Lakeline Church in Austin, Texas, is composed mostly of younger, professional adults who have come into the fellowship through conversion growth—from unsaved and unchurched people. The Fellowship of the Parks has drawn the bulk of its members from the ranks of the unchurched. Conversion growth stands as a central fact for the movement of the GlocalNet churches.

The emphasis on conversion growth and reaching the unchruched is so great in the GlocalNet congregations that they rightfully could be termed, Missional Churches." These churches do not use that terminology about themselves. They do, however, incorporate the basic features of purposely designing their approaches so as to enable them to reach the lost and unchurched.

The Element of Training

Internships at NorthWood project into training church starters. The training involves personal involvement in the ministries at NorthWood but also direct involvement with Christian leaders from other areas. Each year, the GlocalNet conference brings members of the GlocalNet team and other leaders for a two-day conference. Interns gain inspiration and knowledge at these meetings.

These congregations follow the pattern of Eph. 4:11-12. The leaders train, inspire, and lead people to the empowering presence of Jesus Christ. People who are thus led by the infilling Holy Spirit go out to minister in many ways. No lack of training is seen in the GlocalNet pattern. More important, the training closely resembles what has come to be known as "Obedience-based training."

This strong component of training leads to the possibility of the incorporation of lay involvement in the ministries of the congregations. Pastor Carmack declares lay involvement as central to the ministry efforts of the Bear Valley congregation. Over one-half of the staff members of the church were first lay leaders. Most of the ministries were started and are led by lay workers who are trained, discipled, and empowered by the church staff.

The Element of Christian Discipleship

Training in Christian growth and living holds a major place in the ministries of NorthWood Church and its associated congregations. Pastor Roberts and his staff in Keller, Texas promote the NorthWood University that meets on Wednesday evenings. Among the subjects of these seminars are: *Journey of Desire*, a book study by John Eldridge; *First Place*, A Christ-centered health program for all ages; Journey of Encouragement, A support system concerning topics women deal with daily; *Making Your Remarriage Last*, recognizes & addresses the unique challenges remarried couples face n building a godly marriage; *Honor Based Parenting*, say good-bye to whining, complaining, bad attitudes in children and kids; *Prayer Team*, fellowship with God; *CROWN Ministry*, God's view of finances and debt; *Perspective on World Missions*, explores foundational concepts behind our *glocal* identity; *and multiple support groups.*

The other churches that have grown out of the NorthWood network also promote study groups for members—many of which meet on Wednesday evening. Bear Valley Church provides its members with the Bear Valley Institute. This institute offers seminars on *Frequently Asked Questions; Introduction to the Bible; World Religions; and Spiritual Warfare.* Monthly one-evening seminars guide church members in developing skills, behaviors, and knowledge that help them become more effective witnesses. The actual sessions are most often led by trusted and trained lay leaders.

Lakeline Church holds the Lakeline Institute that offers seminars in eight basic focus areas.

Lakeline Church utilizes eight focus areas for developing KNOW-GROW-GO Followers of Jesus Christ:

Worship: KNOW-GROW-GO Followers of Jesus Christ worship on a regular basis.

Membership: Followers of Jesus Christ join a church body and become active participants who strive to live godly lives that honor God.

Relationship: KNOW-GROW-GO Followers of Jesus Christ cultivate healthy and authentic relationships within families and between friends as they participate in small groups and other church ministries.

Discipleship: KNOW-GROW-GO Followers of Jesus Christ mature in their faith through spiritual disciplines.

Stewardship: KNOW-GROW-GO Followers of Jesus Christ submit their time, talents, and treasures (tithes and offerings) to God.

Workmanship: KNOW-GROW-GO Followers of Jesus Christ are ministers who discover, develop, and deploy their gifts on ministry teams to creatively serve others.

Ambassadorship: KNOW-GROW-GO Followers of Jesus Christ communicate their faith to unbelievers in a style that fits them.

Leadership: KNOW-GROW-GO Followers of Jesus Christ follow the leaders of their church and invest in others to lead them to become KNOW-GROW-GO Followers of Jesus Christ.

Small groups contribute to group discipleship. These gatherings have the goal of individual discipleship and the equipping of the members of the church for Christian growth and ministry.

Training of church members obviously holds a central place in the lives and ministries of GlocalNet churches. The provision of this on-going training enables these congregations to continuing growing better as they grow bigger.

The NorthWood GlocalNet Future

The NorthWood GlocalNet ministry has not reached its zenith. The quality of the ministry, the dedication of the workers, the soundness of the plan, the spiritual fervor of its approach all point to continuing growth and service. Doug Walker speaks for all GlocalNet congregations saying God has provided the facilities, the power, the field, and the vision. The future of our church (and he could have said of GlocalNet churches) is bright and exciting.

Every Christian group is constantly faced with the efforts of Satan to harm, delay, obscure, weaken, destroy, or pull down. GlocalNet will not be immune to these evil attacks. Any relationship with these congregations and their leaders gives assurance that they are aware of the dangers but committed to the One who can give them strength to overcome the evil efforts. GlocalNet will, I believe, continue to serve with effectiveness in North America and beyond. May God be praised.

GlocalNet and Church Planting Movements in North America

The most important single feature about NorthWood Church is that it exists! This church, beginning only 21 years ago already has been used of God to significantly impact its community and its world. This church continues to guide unchurched people into relationships with Jesus Christ, motivate believers to become disciples and disciples to be turned into apostles. The influence of this congregation reaches around the world through the dedicated ministries of Pastor Roberts and those who have gone out from NorthWood. But what exactly does NorthWood Church teach about church planting movements in North America?

NorthWood Church shows that a movement that incorporates most of the essential elements of church planting movements can thrive in North America and is indeed thriving in North America. It demonstrates the possibilities of such a movement in North America.

What exactly does NorthWood Church teach about church planting movements in North America? These imperative lessons for the world Christian movement can be summarized in the following statements. We can safely say that NorthWood Church's experience teaches us that:

- *Church planting movements can thrive in North America and are indeed thriving in North*

America even though such movements may differ in some respects from church planting movements elsewhere in the world. Church planting movements in North America incorporate most of the essential elements of these movements even as they differ in some factors. These differences do not disguise the fact that GlocalNet and other examples of church planting movements in North America exist and are, therefore, possible.

- *Church planting movements in North America, as in every other region of the world, depend on a compelling vision that understands divine planning and expectation.* The three prong approach of church multiplication, community development, and nation building is one expression of this vision. Every church planting movement will need some expression of this vision. The GlocalNet vision is not the only example.

- *Church planting movements in North America must incorporate congregational reproduction into the DNA of every group of believers.* Churches must start with the conviction that every congregations that lives in conformity with the basic nature of a biblical church will by its make up seek to reproduce.

- *Church planting movements in North America, as in every other region of the world, must carefully guide believers to obedience to Christ and service to humanity.* Church planting movements center on church multiplication but do not neglect community development and nation building. A genuine concern for the needs of humankind is a vital and imperative factor in church planting movements.

- *Church planting movements in North America depend on dedicated leaders who are fully committed to the concept of continuing congregational reproduction.* Any concern with personal kingdom building renders Kingdom building impossible. The commitment demanded to perpetuate a church planting movement calls for total commitment to and involvement in continuing church multiplication

- *Church planting movements in North America insist on carefully on discipling and training believers in Christian living and service.* Reliance on the leaders at the top can never produce and sustain a church planting movement. Discipleship and training of believers in something like T-Life and T-ministry is a necessity

- *Church planting movements in North America will center on conversion growth and reaching the unchruched.* Churches that fit into church planting movements are in every sense of the word, *Missional Churches.* Assurance for the Kingdom task rests with churches that demonstrate the "Missional Character" in this day.

- *Church planting movements in North America will only be possible to group willing to accommodate to the cultural segments they seek to reach.* It is most doubtful that we will see a church planting movement in North America, or elsewhere, that seeks to perpetuate nothing more than traditional church structures. Church planting movements demand a cultural accommodation to the people served. The NorthWood experience has been primarily among the young, professional, affluent, upper educated groups. We need to see other church planting movements among the poor, the working class, and perhaps the very affluent with congregations patterned to fit the exact needs of each population.

- *Church planting movements in North America can produce congregations that remain in fellowship with other church bodies (such as associations and conventions) while serving in their own new patterns of life and ministry.* These churches do not isolate themselves from other ministries. They tend to network in every way possible.

- *Church planting movements in North America provide the most viable means for reaching the goal of the Great Commission in this nation.* Church planting movements have many characteristics in common with the movement of the Early church as seen in the Book of Acts. This kind of expansion is needed to evangelize and congregationalize the people of the world— including the people of North America.

Conclusion

Church planting movements can indeed happen in areas already served by existing churches and church bodies. Congregations growing out of church planting movements are springing up. The answer to the question as to the possibility of such movement in North America has actually been answered. The ministries of churches such as NorthWood and its network of congregations and ministries is adequate assurance that church planting movements can indeed happen here are in fact happening here!

Notes

[128] Roland Allen, *Missionary Methods: St. Paul's or Ours?*, American ed. (Grand Rapids, MI: William B. Eerdmans Publishing Company, 1962).
[129] David Garrison, Church Planting Movements, Richmond: International Mission Board, 1999 and *Church Planting Movements: How God is Redeeming a Lost World,* Richmond: WIG Take Resources, 2004.
[130] David Garrison, Church Planting Movements, Richmond: International Mission Board, 1999, 7
[131] Interview with Bob Roberts, May, 2004.
[132] Ibid.
[133] Ibid.
[134] Glenn Smith, "A New Kind of Church: Glocal," unpublished paper, 2003, 1.
[135] Ibid., 2
[136] Interview with Bob Roberts, May, 2004.
[137] Ibid..
[138] Daniel R. Sanchez, Ebbie Smith, Curt Watke, *Starting Reproducing Congregations*, Atlanta: ChurchStarting Network, 2001, 424.
www.churchstarting,net

Chapter 9

Church Planting Movements Among Oral Learners

Jim Slack

The place of orality in a people group is claiming an increasingly central place in the thinking of those associated with these movements. Beyond the sovereign acts of God that providentially initiate a Church Planting Movement, numerous lesser, or secondary, influences also contribute to a CPM's emergence, health and progress. *This chapter considers the significance of orality and literacy on potential, emerging, or occurring Church Planting Movements.*

Observation reveals that God has worked for decades, if not centuries, among a particular ethnic group, moving His witnesses among them so that the lost within the group could have the opportunity of experiencing a Church Planting Movement. Conversely, these same observations have revealed that often a Church Planting Movement lurked beneath the surface of the lost people group's experience but did not occur. Sometimes it was, as in Jesus' ministry, that the people simply ignored or refused the witnesses to accept the Gospel. In others a CPM waited below the surface and did not break out because God's children were not obedient in witness, or they practiced very poor and contradictory mission methods.

Definitions of Orality and Oral Communicators

This discussion correctly begins by explaining the concept of orality and oral communicators. Orality, following the strict definition, deals with societies which do not use any form of phonetic writing. In general, orality refers not only to the level of literacy among the people but the extent to which oral communication, teaching, learning, and daily activities interact in the culture. Workers with Church Planting Movements see the necessity of understanding the dynamics of these movements among people who are habitually oral preference communicators and learners.

In more detail, orality, according to Webster's dictionary, consists of the quality or state of being oral. *Primary Orality*, according to Dr. Walter Ong in *Orality and Literacy,* is the state of persons totally unfamiliar with writing, who live in settings where most of the people around them are illiterate. Traditionally, orality has been defined as a person who is in a state of being illiterate. In this traditional orality, persons are described as illiterate if they are unschooled, non-readers and non-writers, meaning oral persons.

Functional illiterate must be added to the category of illiteracy to include the basic scope of orality and oral communicators. Functional illiteracy describes generally those who function at eighth grade competencies or less, who have been introduced to reading and writing, but who have not normally developed abilities to handle through reading and writing skills, conceptions, abstractions, logical conclusions, and other literate skills, at the level of a functional literate.

The importance of recognizing orality in a culture is clearly expressed by Tex Sample, a sociologist, demographer, and theological professor. Sample thinks that the issue and extent of persons with oral orientation makes this matter of orality a significant factor in church life in North America. He writes:

> It is my contention that about half of the people in the United States are people who work primarily out of a traditional orality, by which I mean a people who can read and write--though some cannot--but whose appropriation and engagement with life is oral. More than this, I am convinced that most churches have a clear majority of their membership who work from a traditional orality....When one moves out of the United States into most of the rest of the world, the mass of oral-cultures, both primary and traditional, looms even larger. Two-thirds of the people in the world are oral.[139]

An oral communicator is one who prefers to hear, learn and communicate through predominantly aural/oral means rather than through reading and writing. Oral communicators learn and communicate best and more comfortably, through oral narratives or stories. They do not easily understand and adequately handle presentations in the form of outlines, lists, ideas, guidelines, steps, principles or abstractions. They house important information and treasured personal facts in stories and narratives. Thus, when issues or topics arise, they remember and tell the story that reminds them of these issues and topics, and participate in the discussion.

The state of being an oral communicator covers the academic levels of illiteracy (inability to read and write) and functional illiteracy (reading and writing competency between grades 1-8). Semi-literate (competencies equal to grades 9-11) is the educational transition level for oral communicators moving into the state of being a literate communicator. For example, an oral communicator cannot read with understanding the Bible or other similar textual documents. Jonathan Kozol in *Illiterate America* said: "Most educators and workers among illiterates and others on the way to becoming literate do not like the term 'functional illiterate.' However, this term has been the best that orality, literacy, and educational specialists have been able to come up with, so it is still in use since it was first coined over 100 years ago." The same is true of the pejorative word "illiterate," which implies that a person is ill if they cannot read.

At this time, at least 45-55% of all USA residents function as oral communicators, and not at a literate level. This is also true of most of 30 other Western nations such as Canada, Great Britain, Germany, and France. The global oral communicator percentage is at least 66%, and likely higher when country-by-country educational demographics and local literacy studies are considered. Around 65-75% of the unreached peoples in the world are oral communicators. This fact brings us back to the issue of orality and Church Planting Movements.

Wycliffe Bible Translators, also known as the Summer Institute of Linguistics, have accepted the task of working with at least 5,000 languages and dialects, preferably those with a population of 100,000 or more, who have no written language. They are working at some level with close to 2,500 of the 5,000 and estimate that it will likely be close to 150 years before they have those individual heart languages reduced to writing, with literacy primers, a few literates, a literacy training process, and at least a New Testament translated into each of those languages. New Tribes is also involved in reducing languages to writing and bringing literacy and Scriptures to oral societies.

When all people group languages and dialects are considered, even those that have as few as 5,000 people in them, there are close to 8,000 languages and dialects with no written form of their language or dialect. Also, at this point in time, a whole Bible exists in only 417 languages or dialects and about 2,000 languages and dialects have a New Testament, a Bible book, or some Scriptural verses in their language or dialect.

The Development of the Method Of Ascertaining the Orality of a People

Jim Slack has led the IMB study group in a methodology to ascertain the place of orality in Church Planting Movements, as the on-site CPM Assessment is conducted. He explains the process, saying that a number of trained workers go on-site and study Church Planting Movements up close. These on-site looks at a particular CPM are usually accomplished through hundreds of interviews which allow the group to see what God has been doing and as said above, opened the way for the experience of a Church Planting Movement.

Orality, Oral Communicators and Church Planting Movements

The importance of orality and oral communication factors became obvious as the broader CPM studies continued. Oral learners respond slowly to a Western approach to teaching and proclamation. The problems created with people who function on the basis of oral communication and life is seen as imperative factors in the Western world as well as the non-Western.

The Extent of the Problem of
Orality in Church Planting Movements

Within six of the seven completed CPM assessments orality was, and still is an issue of significant magnitude. The movements were within an Indian Hindu people, a Cuban group, a Buddhist contingent, an African traditional religion people, an Islamic-oriented North African people group, another Indian, Hindu-Tribal group; and another Islamic people group population. Five of the movements assessed were found to be actual Church Planting Movements. Only two of the seven--the Buddhist group and the traditional religion African people group—failed to meet the assumptions, definition, and description of a Church Planting Movement.

Of the people in the seven groups assessed, six were experiencing significant problems concerning orality and oral communicators. The level of concern, by the time of the assessment in each of the six that possessed significant orality and oral communicator issues, had reached the level of being at risk of plateauing, or facing the development of unhealthy characteristics within the movement. The only assessment that did not possess serious or significant orality and oral communicator issues was the Cuban Church Planting Movement. Functional literacy was generally at such a high level in Cuba in most places that no serious percentage of the population was at risk due to unaddressed or unsolved orality or oral communicator issues. This is not to say, however, that no oral communicators exist in Cuba.

Space does not allow for a more detailed examination of the findings concerning orality and oral communicators within each of the seven CPM assessments. Therefore, issues that are common within most of the seven will be highlighted and described. At least eight orality and oral communicator issues were found to be common in at least six of the seven Church Planting Movement assessments.

The Most Common Issue.

A basic issue concerning orality and oral communicators existed in six of the seven assessments and currently exists in over 90% of the unreached people groups where a CPM could likely emerge. This issue exists in the USA and other Western nations whether or not a CPM emerges. The fact is that a commonly high percentage or oral communicators live within each ethnolinguistic people group. Those working with such people need to ascertain the possibilities of approaching the people by following these suggestions: (1) Determine the scope of orality and the percentage of oral preference people within the people group's population; (2) Understand the learning style which determines understanding, remembrance, and reproduction of what the lost and saved hear; (3) consider the witness approaches and techniques employed by the evangelizers; (4) Investigate the presence and possession of Scripture--an oral or written Bible; (5) seek to ascertain the leadership potential, abilities, and supply among the people; (6) Find the level of the ability and speed to spread the Good News--the Gospel--to the growing edges and beyond; (7) Examine how to free a CPM from having to depend only upon literates.

A number of assessments reveal that a CPM was often hindered in emerging. God initiates CPMs but He extends to evangelizers major roles in the emergence of the movements. The evangelizers contribute much by working in harmony with God's plans and activities among a people. Studying the peoples' history and worldview helps evangelizers see more clearly how God is at work, or desires to work among a people and the potential for the emergence of a CPM. Sadly few evangelizers are willing to invest the time in historical and worldview studies to find out where God is at work in order to join Him in that work.

In any setting, a CPM or not, identifying and understanding the orality and literacy status within each people group, or population segment, is critical. Knowing the peoples' orality and literacy status is pivotal to evangelization. This understanding is not just the concern for missiologists; it is an imperative concern for pastors, lay leaders, Strategy Coordinators, church planters, strategy planners, prayer partners, people group team members, or others evangelizing a people.

Orality and Literacy Issues and Questions Affecting Church Planting Movements

When considering and evaluating the issue of orality within a particular CPM, workers should ask numerous important questions. The leading questions include:

Question 1: What is the Status of Scripture Within The People Group?

The witness or evangelizer should ask this first question that in each setting where evangelism and church planting are to occur. Scripture, God's Word, in the language of the people is the foundation for witness. Workers must know if the people within a people group personally have access to the Christian Scriptures. They also need to know to what degree they possess their own religion's scriptures and the Christian Scriptures.

If a people group is Islamic, it should be known to what degree the average Islamic person knows the *Quran*. Can they read it? Or, are they unable to read it, but have memorized it? Few things affect the future of witness, discipleship, church planting and a church planting movement as much as the possession of, or lack of possession of, the Bible in their heart language. Without God's Word, how can a people experience conversions, churches, and a church planting movement? Many witnesses, evangelizers and strategy planners fail at this point by not asking this question up front.

This first question relates to the possession of the Bible in the people's heart language. If the reader is not familiar with this issue and the process related to answering it, help should be sought immediately before engaging in evangelization of the people group, or before evangelization continues. This issue is that crucial. Never approach a people to evangelize before finding out the status of the Christian Scriptures among them.

Evangelization is possible if the evangelizer and the hearers within a people group have the Scriptures, the Bible. If the Word of God is not a possession of those within the people group, evangelism and church planting will be very difficult and seriously handicapped. Also, syncretism, and likely heresy, will lurk in the wings.

Again, the Scripture needs to be in the heart language of the people. A person and thus a people acquired their worldview through their heart language. Evangelizers can interface successfully with the people's worldview and lead them by Scriptural presentations to Christian truth only if they can share the Bible in the same language of the people's worldview--their heart language.

These questions should be asked on the basis of the expectation and desire that the presence of Scripture and evangelization be conducted in the heart language of each engaged people group. Beyond the previously mentioned worldview issue, maximum understanding occurs when evangelism, church planting, discipleship and leader training occurs in a people's heart language.

Ministry results decline as one moves away from a people's heart language to a different tongue, especially one with a low cognate ratio to their heart language. The workers should relate to this matter in a positive fashion. They should committ to evangelizing in a person's heart language. This approach is modeled for us in the Scripture in such passages as Acts 2.

Hopefully, the reader can understand this hierarchy of Scripture questions and understand their importance. In six of the seven supposed CPMs that have been assessed by the IMB, the emergence of a CPM hinged on the positive presence of the Scriptures.

At the same time, the assessments have shown that a church planting movement can and has emerged with the presence of the Christian Scriptures being only in the hands or heads of the initial evangelizers. In those cases where the people were oral, not literate, the continuance of the CPM found itself immediately in jeopardy of continuing due to the lack of access and possession of the Scriptures.

Table 1
Availablity of Scriptures

This understanding should be a wake-up notice to evangelizers who are praying for and are working toward a CPM. Assessing the status of Scripture in the initial stage of evangelization and the availability of Scripture among the common people should be an up-front question during people group planning sessions.

Question 2: What is the orality and literacy Status of the people within the people group?

A second question relates to what percent of the people group population is able to read and write at a functional, conceptual level. Knowledge of the various orality and literacy levels commonly used by educators in dealing with orality and literacy is necessary. This question will be only summarily and briefly laid out. If one is not familiar with this educational hierarchy, that reader should seek help from various sources mentioned in this presentation.

219

In progressing from primary orality to high literacy the following are the formal categories used by educators in the field. Upon understanding them, evangelizers and strategy planners should not assume the people are literate, for in most cases they are not. The facts concerning the people's orality or literacy should be determined and never assumed. Most of the world's people are oral, or oral preference people. Among unreached peoples, 75% or higher of them are oral and therefore they are not literate enough to handle the Scriptures in their written language, even if a written version of their language exists.

Learning Grid Categories & Grade Levels

Level 5: High Literacy (College Level Performance)

Level 4: Literacy (12th Grade Performance)

Level 3: Semi-Literacy (9th-11th Grade Performance)

Level 2: Functional Illiteracy (1st-8th Grade Performance)

Level 1: Illiteracy (Never Introduced To Writing)

Learning Grid Categories & Grade Levels

A brief description of the levels should assist one in understanding this educational hierarchy of categories or levels of progression. These are the levels or phases of progression that a person hopefully moves successfully through when entering school and moving through the successive grades to the status of functional literacy at or near Grade 12. In some settings where entering school is not possible, individuals have enrolled in a literacy program, and by discipline and intensive work, move through the various levels to the point of functional literacy as represented in the Grid at Level 4. The successive levels along with a brief explanation of each are:

Level 1: Illiteracy means that those in this category are non-readers; they are known as primary oral communicators. Their function in society and their interface with others in society depends totally upon an oral, not literate, interface. Consequently, for illiterates to possess the Scriptures, they must possess them orally. This may be accomplished either through memorizing the Scriptural texts, or through narrative, story formatted presentations such as Chronological Bible Storying. Persons who are not literate must have an oral Bible in order to possess and use the Scriptures personally or in ministry.

Level 2: Functional Illiteracy exists when people have attained an educational status between the first and eighth grades. France defined this term in the late 1890s. Most western nations did not become that familiar with the term and its implications until the 1970s or after. Since the 1970s, voluminous research has resulted in defining and enumerating the status of functional illiteracy in at least thirty nations, mainly in the USA and Europe.

The reason for these studies is the ignorance of the population and the serious nature of this category. Those who have been educated to any point on the learning grid from the first grade through eighth grade appear to be literate but they are not functionally literate. Functional literacy comes normally at the end of twelve grades of school, which is the true, or functional literacy category.

Since those who have gone through some or all of the grades from one to eight appear to be literate because they can sound and even read at whatever grade level they are, a number of evangelizers who are not familiar with orality and literacy issues are confused. France and others found out that if a person drops out of school before moving beyond the eighth grade, that person has not progressed enough in educational attainment to correctly recognize and handle concepts, ideas, steps in a process, guidelines, or expositional presentations.

These skills are finally developed in a student during the semi-literate and literate stages of education. Therefore, it has been found that a student who drops out of school prior to the eighth or ninth grade competency level will, within two years, revert back to an oral learner's level and style. Educationally, those persons function as an illiterate through oral means and not literate means.

These individuals should be treated as oral communicators for they learn and communicate through oral means--narrative, story presentations. Functional illiterates have not progressed in educational competencies to achieve typical literate, expositional, inductive, conceptual, reasoning means of learning and communicating. This is a critical issue for evangelizers who assume that people who can sound words and sentences are literate and thus interface with them as literates.

It is true that conceptualization in students begin to occur and emerge between grades four and eight. But, it is somewhere between grades seven through nine that conceptualization begins to be a normal, successful activity among students. One does need to realize that being an oral communicator has nothing to do with intelligence or ability.

They can learn most any concept if it comes to them through narrative means.

Level 3: Semi-Literacy means that the person is now moving educationally in his or her competency and performance skills beyond oral learning status to the beginning or threshold stage of literacy. Semi-literate, like illiteracy, is not the most desirable, or best descriptive term. But, it is a term that the U.N. has used for more than fifty years. A semi-literate is not yet fully literate in all of his or her competency or performance capabilities, but is positively moving that way. This is the first level where a person is able to successfully handle basic concepts, analysis, inductive studies, expositional presentations and other literate level activities. They can understand them at this level better than they can engage in initiating them. At this level a person should be able to read the Bible himself or herself with a significant level of understanding. That comes more completely at the literate level but is initially gained at this level, but not at the levels below semi-literacy. Conceptualization becomes a functional reality within persons as their education takes them into this level and the following level, level 4.

Level 4: Literacy means, readers will remember, that the person is functionally at grade 12 level where literacy in narrative, mathematical, and comprehension should have been functionally achieved. Anyone connected with education knows that simply being exposed to and passing through the grades from one to twelve does not guarantee that a person will truly be a functional literate at grade 12. This depends upon aptitude, attitude, application, and their teacher's skill, the learning environment, learning tools, physical condition and family support, among other variables. Twelve grades supposedly do a literate make in most school settings.

These oral and literate levels are mathematically computed and often are presented visually. The reader should keep in mind that the following graphic displays the best case scenario for these entities. It does not mean that students who have moved into the listed levels can actually perform at that level. Even so, this graphic should assist the reader in further understanding one way whereby the levels of students can be computed. The data in the following table comes from United Nations educational data provided each year to the U. N. through UNESCO. As you study the table, remember that in most of these countries the Primary and Secondary levels are below ninth grade level. So, one should look under the Tertiary (high school level which is usually 10th grade and above) for the first mathematical literacy level of the students.

Region	Gross Enrollment Primary	Gross Enrollment Secondary	Gross Enrollment Tertiary	Gross Enrollment All Levels
E Asia & Oc	118.00	66.30	10.80	67.90
S. Asia	95.40	45.30	7.20	52.00
Less Dev Cty	71.50	19.30	3.20	46.40
Dev Country	102.70	100.10	51.60	86.30
Europe	104.70	99.20	42.80	83.30
Arab States	84.70	56.90	14.90	57.90
Arab Sts (F)	76.90	52.30	12.40	52.60
Africa	80.70	34.0	6.90	47.40
America	110.40	74.80	37.10	79.00
Asia	106.00	56.90	11.10	60.80
Croatia	87.0	82.0	28.0	No Data
Albania	No Data	No Data	12.0	No Data
Turkey	107.0	58.0	21.0	No Data

Table 3.
Educational Levels

For instance, based upon actual government school enrollment reports in East Asia and Oceania, somewhere close to 10.80% of the people are literate. In the Arab States in general, close to 14.9% of the people are literate, but only 12.4% of the women are literate. In America, based upon the actual educational records submitted by the educational system to UNESCO, a maximum of 37.1% are likely to be literate at a tertiary level.

As stated previously, at least 75% of the unreached people groups in the world are predominantly illiterate or functionally illiterate. The men within unreached people groups tend to be more literate than the women. This is especially true in Islamic settings.

Therefore, even if the people have written Scriptures, the majority may not be able to read the Scriptures or to read them with understanding. Moreover, they likely will be unable to handle literate styles of preaching and Bible study. Orals need to hear the Scripture through narrative or story means to understand and facilitate their memory and accurate reproduction of the Scripture. This question needs to be asked and the implications of the answer be understood to more fully comprehend the dynamics that are occurring in most CPMs.

Question 3: Are the Approaches Compatible with The Learning and Participation of the Less Literate Peoples

Asked another way, are the evangelism, discipleship and pastoral approaches that are being used compatible with oral and literate learning and participation styles of the common people, and not just the literates? This question follows the first two in logical succession. If the people have no written

Scriptures in their heart language and a majority of the population is oral, this question becomes a highly important one for evangelization planners.

Implied in this question is the understanding that if the population does not posses the Scripture and if they are oral, then the evangelizers need oral forms of evangelism, discipleship, church planting and leadership training. If this does not exist, then a church planting movement may never emerge. If the evangelizers who are planting the churches are literate and use their literate means to plant churches, the predominantly oral people who make up the churches will not possess the Scriptures in a form they can use.

This principle means reproduction of the local churches will not occur or it will likely move only among the literates. If this eventuality happens, one rejoices for the literates, but grieves over the majority population of orals for whom the CPM was denied. They are sealed off from the CPM because of their orality and because of the singularly literate methods and approaches used by the evangelizers.

Question 4: Are the Approaches Reproducible By the Oral People?

Do the currently used evangelization approaches have every chance of being reproduced by the common people and does the CPM have the opportunity of moving comfortably and compatibly among the oral people? As the CPM moves, as it should, beyond missionary, Strategy Coordinator, or any other foreign evangelizers, can the grass-roots people comfortably replicate in indigenous fashion the evangelization approach used by outside evangelizers ministering to them?

The answer is, only if oral evangelism, discipleship, church planting, and leadership training methods and approaches exist. Failure to provide for the oral peoples simply frustrates the emergence of a Church Planting Movement in most cases. Literates and orals deserve to be part of a CPM, and especially the orals if the majority of the people are oral learners and communicators.

Findings From CPM Assessments
Related To Orality Issues.

When all people group languages and dialects are considered (10,600 of them), even those that have as few as 5,000 people in them, at least 6,000 languages and dialects with no written form of their language or dialect continue to exist in the world. Also, at this point in time, a whole Bible exists in only 420 languages or dialects. About 2,000 languages and dialects have a New Testament, a Bible book, or some Scriptural verses in their language or dialect. SIL/Wycliffe and New Tribes have at least 5,000 language groups on their priority list to be reduced to writing and Scriptures provided for them in each of those heart languages. Many of these peoples make up the Last Frontier. These are at the top of the list for missionary agencies, or any New Testament evangelizer to engage for evangelization as soon as possible.

Finding and Examples of Orality
in Actual Church Planting Movements

Without giving the names of the people groups and the exact location of the CPMs, we will mention five examples. Within these five case studies, the oral and literate issues will be highlighted with enough history of the movement for the reader to hopefully see the implications of the issues. Assessments of movements have revealed a number of findings related to orality, and especially related to the four previously stated questions. The number of orality issues, questions, and thus findings in the reports, are too many to cover completely in this presentation. Therefore, only selected items will be included.

An Islamic Example

The issue is that initial evangelism occurred through leading active Islamic individuals who knew well the *Quran* (many who had memorized it) being taken through the *Quran* looking at *ISA* (Jesus) passages. In progressing through the Isa passages, the Christian believers naturally bridged to the *Engil*--the Christian Gospels--which are somewhat sanctioned by Islam, due to a reference of them in the Quran. At least 80% of the people in this country are poor and illiterate, with only a few functional illiterates among the 80%.

First, this was an oral and literate based approach within a very familiar setting--Islam and the Quran. Second, the method did cater to literates who would tend to come to the foreground (or "…come forth") in the process. Third, the evangelism method continues to be very effective, but now that they have thousands of converts who need discipleship and leadership training, they have no Scriptures to use due to the high percentage of orality among the general population. Technically, they do not possess the Christian Scriptures due to their orality. They now need an oral Bible. This CPM is so large, and the Church Planting Movement has spread so far through this very effective strategy that a solution to the lack of Scripture is paramount

A Buddhist-Hindu Example

Another CPM began to emerge within a somewhat mixed Buddhist-Hindu religious setting. The results of a previous war had left the average grade level of the entire population at a 3rd to 6th grade level—clearly a functionally illiterate level population. The movement, in order to continue, now needs evangelism, discipleship, and training approaches in an oral format such as Chronological Bible Storying.

The basic issue is that the initial evangelizers used mostly literate approaches and methods when they were teaching, modeling evangelism, and church planting. They led the new national coverts, most of whom were literates, to evangelize. To the credit of the same initial evangelizers, a narrative approach, Chronological Bible Storying, was modeled some before the literate leaders by very competent narrative, storying trainers, mainly James O. Terry.

The narrative model was, however, a secondary model to the literate models that the initial evangelizers, people group pastors from the states, and itinerant trainers from the region, used when they came from time to time to provide assistance in training. As a result, the literate model was not reproducible for there were not enough literates in the places where churches needed to be planted.

To maintain a literate approach meant denying evangelization participation to 80-90% of the population, thus putting a ceiling on new church starts. The current expatriate leaders know they need to train their local church leaders in Chronological Bible Storying, which is now very difficult. The literate pastors and evangelists have become comfortable with the literate models they were taught.

An Animistic and Hindu Tribal Setting

A third CPM setting emerged in a very rural, agricultural, tribal setting, where the religion of the people is a mixture of animism and Hinduism. This very significant movement has emerged over the past 4-6 years. The people groups are some of the poorest in the country and are highly illiterate, with few functional illiterates, fewer semi-literates, and even fewer literates except for the wealthy land owners and business men.

The orality issues are quite unique within this particular CPM. The expatriate Strategy Coordinator (SC) came to answer a request for evangelization direction and agricultural expertise from a small, long-established base of Baptist churches. The existing Baptist churches had become, due to partnering with other Episcopal polity churches during a period of government pressure, very traditional. The expatriate Strategy Coordinator came and instituted agricultural projects coupled with Chronological Bible Storying as the evangelism and church planting means.

The SC used the illiterate and functionally illiterate common people to establish hundreds of agricultural projects coupled with storying the Scriptures. The agricultural projects were highly successful economically and socially, and the storying led to many converts and hundreds of new church starts--the emergence of a genuine CPM. However, during the CPM assessment, it was discovered that most of the older, established Baptist church pastors who had previously affiliated with the other denomination held a poorer understanding of the new birth and some deviant doctrinal positions when assessed from a Baptist perspective. Syncretism existed among many of the older, traditional Baptist pastors who were trained in the schools of the other denomination.

The lay pastors of the new churches, who had come to Christ and to leadership through the agricultural projects and the Chronological Bible Storying sessions held clearer new birth understanding and few, if any, syncretistic beliefs. Consequently, the SC had to begin pulling together stories to add to the story set that would obliquely correct the former, more educated pastors`, syncretized doctrinal positions.

Among the Maasai in Africa

A potential, but not yet actual, CPM among the Maasai in Africa rested, at the time of the CPM assessment, in the hands of expatriate missionaries, literate Swahili, or literate Maasai (Maa speaker) pastors. Over 100,000 believers existed among them, a testimony of significant response and aggressive missionary and Strategy Coordinator-team faithfulness.

Some of the finest missionaries have served as evangelists and trainers among the Maasai, and the Maasai have been very responsive for more than a decade and a half. The missionaries, Swahili evangelists, and few literate Maasai evangelists, continued to baptize all of the new believers in the churches. The missionaries, US volunteers, and Swahili and Maasai evangelists responded to local church suggestions that new church plants were needed in specific villages near and far from them. Some, but not a majority of the new church plants were initiated and conducted by local church pastors and members. Even when local pastors and their members did start new churches, baptism and other local church matters were not passed on to the local leaders.

The SC and other team members used oral models among the Maasai regularly. They were introduced to oral communication approaches such as Chronological Bible Storying. At the same time, the churches and their leaders saw the more educated literates retain leadership roles as literate models were respected more than the oral ones. Oral models, as well as local church responsibility was not, at the time of the CPM assessment, placed in the hands of the local churches and their leaders. Maasai believers and leaders had amply demonstrated their ability to handle the responsibility but it remained in literate hands.

Among Hindu People in India

A huge movement in India among a large, historic, mostly Hindu people group in India began in the early 1990s and expanded to well beyond 5,000 churches in less than 10 years. Those behind the movement were mostly converted Hindu believers led by partner Strategy Coordinators, one an Indian Baptist and another a Baptist from America.

Like in one of the other CPMs, there were Baptist churches and leaders in existence when the two SCs began working toward a CPM among this people group. Unlike the other CPM where there were existing Baptist churches, these Baptists and their churches were very conservative and followed Baptist teachings in their church structure and doctrine. Here, like others, over 80% of the people within this people group were oral, not literate.

To their credit, the very literate Strategy Coordinators introduced both literate and oral methods (Chronological Bible Storying) to the early leaders before the movement showed any signs of emerging. At the same time, the partner SCs used literate means themselves during their training and evangelization modeling sessions. Obviously, many of their early converts and consequently leaders were literates. However, as the movement emerged and literally exploded from 28 existing Baptist churches into thousands of new church starts over a ten-year period, most of the members and many of the pastors were oral communicators--illiterates and functional illiterates.

During the CPM assessment, a number of the pastors said during interviews, that the training sessions were still led using literate formats rather than oral ones. Many of the pastors said they understood what the literate leaders were saying and were profited personally from the literate formatted (non-narrative) sessions. At the same time, these same leaders said they could not remember the literate, expositional presentations, and thus could not take them home and share with their members and other new church leaders. These leaders remembered and knew enough about orality and Chronological Bible Storying to say they really needed to be taught by the oral methods and not the literate ones.

The movement had moved well past 4,369 churches and 14,144 outreach groups before the SCs secured and provided oral Scripture modules such as cassettes and videos in their heart language. As a result, the movement has moved well beyond utilitarian servicing of it with the proper oral methods. In a persecuted and poverty-stricken setting, how does one get to 4,369 churches and model and train them in a new methodology that replaces an older, familiar, yet much less effective model?

Conclusion

Those reading this presentation should now understand, at an introductory level, the value of considering oral preference people when praying and planning and participating in a church planting movement, should God grant one. CPM strategists should have at least a basic appreciation for and understanding of the characteristics of, and the learning and communication status, and styles of oral communicators. In light of high orality preference levels in developed and undeveloped ethnolinguistic societies, witnesses should sense the need to think of orals as evangelism, discipleship and leader training styles and content are chosen. It would be tragic indeed, should God grant multiple and continuing Church Planting Movements among numerous ethnolinguistic people groups, to find us who cooperate with Him in initiating them neglecting half to three-fourth of their populations who are oral. This awareness of the issues and presence of oral preference people should move us to develop oral evangelization skills as a second option to our literate, expositional evangelization skill.

Notes

[139] Miles Smith-Morris, ed., *The Economist Book of Vital World Statistics* (New York: The Economist Books Ltd., 1990), 210.

Chapter 10

Ethno/Linguistic Factors
in Church Planting Movements

Daniel Sanchez

What are the intercultural dimensions of church planting movements? What is the glue that binds people together and facilitates the transmission of the gospel along their natural communication networks? In this chapter we discuss factors that need to be taken into account in starting church planting movements among ethnic groups in North America. *Due to the fact that church planting movements have spread along existing communication networks, it is crucial to know what these networks are and how they work.* To facilitate this discussion, we focus on a sociological definition of ethnicity, an analysis of factors that contribute to assimilation, an analysis of assimilation stages, and the implications of assimilation for church starting strategies.

A Sociological Definition of Ethnicity

The term "ethnic" is a derivation of the Greek word *ethnos,* which means race, tribe, or nation.[140] Milton Gordon defines ethnicity simply as "a group with a shared feeling of peoplehood." [141] *The International Encyclopedia of Sociology* adds to the definition such factors as a common cultural tradition, common language, common religion, and distinctive customs.[142] An even more comprehensive definition is given by R.A. Schermerhorn, who defines an ethnic group as:

A collectivity of people having a real or putative common ancestry, memories of a shared historical past, and a cultural focus on one or more symbolic elements defined as the epitome of peoplehood. Examples of such symbolic elements are: kinship patterns, physical contiguity (as in localism or sectionalism), religious affiliation, languages or dialect forms, tribal affiliation, nationality, phenotypical features, or any combination of these. A necessary accompaniment is some consciousness of kind among members of the group.[143]

For many years, the International Mission Board (hence IMB) has recognized the value of "identifying ethnolinguistic peoples, people group segments, and homogeneous units (substrata of society) whose bonding is stronger within that designated grouping than within other variables that describe or fragment them."[144] Their priority has focused on targeting existing unreached ethnolinguistic people groups prior to targeting sub-groups (such as a sub-dialect), strata of society or homogeneous units.

The North American Mission of the Southern Baptist Convention (the successor of the Home Mission Board), has been the most effective evangelical mission agency in North America in reaching ethnolinguistic groups with the gospel and starting churches among them. One of the reasons for this is that its mission strategists (e.g., Oscar Romo, Gerald Palmer, Wendell Belew, etc.) have carefully studied the sociocultural characteristics of each of these groups and have taken them into account in designing their strategies.[145] In the 1960s and 1970s, while many Protestant denominations were employing unilateral integration strategies (closing ethnic churches and mandating that their members join Anglo congregations) Southern Baptists were starting hundreds of churches among ethnic groups. This coincided with the arrival of many refugees (e.g., Cubans, Vietnamese, etc.) and a trend among ethnic groups toward cultural revitalization. Many of these groups were seeking to return to their ethnic roots.

Southern Baptist strategy took this trend into account and the methodology was instrumental in the establishment of large numbers of ethnic churches. Aware of the fact that some ethnic groups had been in North America for generations, Southern Baptists were flexible enough to encourage the development of bi-lingual congregations for the younger generations. In order to be instrumental in initiating church planting movements among the numerous ethnic groups in North America, church planters need to be knowledgeable not only of the general characteristics of each of these groups but also of the pilgrimage they have experienced in becoming a part of the North American scene.

An Analysis of Ethnicity

In seeking to understand these ethnic groups, it is helpful to do an analysis of the mode of entry, mood of the host country, socioeconomic level at the point of entry, ethnicity and class, hence, eth/class category, cultural congruity, patterns of residence, proximity to native land, length of residence, and rate of immigration.

Mode of Entry

A factor that needs to be considered in an effort to understand ethnic groups and their relation to predominant societies is their mode of entry. How did this group arrive at its current status as an ethnic group in this particular society? There are several ways by which groups arrive at their ethnic status.

Annexation

Annexation basically means that the territory in which this group lived was incorporated by another group. This generally happens as a result of war, the purchase of land, or the signing of treaties. In the United States, for example, those affected by annexation include Native Americans, Hispanic Americans of the Southwestern U.S., and the residents of the territory of Louisiana, Alaska, Puerto Rico, and Hawaii. These are groups that became U.S. citizens when the territory in which they lived officially became a part of the United States.

Forced Migration

Some groups have been forcefully moved from their country to another country. Some examples of these are Koreans who were transported to China, Germans to Russia, and Africans to the United States.

Voluntary Migration

The list of those who came to this country voluntarily includes political refugees, documented immigration, and undocumented Immigration.[146] Political refugees obviously do not leave their country voluntarily, however their decision to go to a particular country is voluntary. Documented and undocumented immigrants make a voluntary decision to leave their place of origin and come to this country. Some could be considered economic and or disaster related refugees.

Each of these modes of entry carries with it a cluster of historical, social, political, and economic factors which affect

238

the ethnic group's self-perception as well as the predominant society's attitude toward it. This means that the pilgrimage of each of these groups is very different. This has significant implications for church planting. The experiences that people in a group have had during their pilgrimage have implications for the manner in which the gospel is presented to them. Their experiences with the predominant society will also influence their willingness or reluctance to participate in the same congregation with them.

Mood of the Host Country

The mood of the host country at the time of arrival also affects the experience of the immigrant group. In times of economic prosperity and expansion, the country is generally very happy to receive people from abroad. During World War II, laborers were needed so badly that they were actually recruited in other countries. Conversely, during times of economic depression, the country is not receptive to people coming from abroad. This is also true in areas where there is already a heavy saturation of immigrant groups. The mood of the country at the time of the entry will invariably affect the experience of a particular immigrant group.

Socio-Economic Level

The socio-economic level at the point of entry of an ethnic group also has significant implications regarding its self-perception and the way the predominant society perceives the group. For example, the first wave of Cubans who fled communism was mainly made up of professional and business people. Once they brushed up on their English and validated their credentials, many of them were well underway toward a

239

fairly prosperous life as doctors, lawyers, educators, politicians, etc.

The second wave that left Cuba decades later through the "Mariel boat lift" was principally made up of people on a lower socio-economic level with limited job-related skills. Their experience has been very different from that of the first wave of refugees even though they belong to the same socio-cultural group. A comparison of some highly educated Asian immigrants (such as the Chinese and Koreans professionals and business people) with some of the Southeast Asians who arrived as refugees and who were agricultural workers also points out this distinction.

Socioeconomic level at the point of entry, therefore, signals a different pilgrimage for each of the immigrants in terms of the status they occupy in the predominant society, the jobs available to them, the distance they have to go to arrive a middle class lifestyle (it may take generations), the image they have of themselves, the ability they have to communicate with people in the predominant society, and the image the predominant society has of them.

Ethnic/Class Dimensions

"Ethnic/Class (Eth/Class or Ethnic groups , may belong to the lower, middle, or upper socioeconomic level of society. Assimilation is often influenced by ethnic group identity as well as the socioeconomic level to which it belongs. Ethnic groups who have a similar socio-economic level with the majority in the predominant society (and with other ethnic groups who are on the same level) have a narrower gap to fill than those who do not. For example, since many people in the United Sates consider themselves "middle class," ethnic groups who are also middle class have more in common with them than ethnic groups who find themselves in the lower socioeconomic level.

A middle class status contributes to the ethnic group's progress in the assimilation process. Conversely, ethnic groups who are at the lower socioeconomic level when they enter the United States generally have a wider cultural and socioeconomic gap to fill in their efforts to relate to the predominant society. Ethnic persons may have more in common with others who are on the same socioeconomic class (predominant society or other ethnic groups) than with persons of their own ethnic group but who are in a different socioeconomic class. Information as sought in Figure 1 can be utilized to indicate which ethnic groups are present in a given community and the commonalities they have with one another as well as with the predominant society in terms of their social class and status.

Figure 1

Ethnic/Class Dimensions

Class	Predominant Society	Ethnic Group A	Ethnic Group B	Ethnic Group C
Upper Class Upper_____ Middle_____ Lower_____				
Middle Class Upper_____ Middle_____ Lower_____				
Lower Class Upper_____ Middle_____ Lower_____				

241

Cultural Congruity

The congruity between the culture of the immigrant group and that of the receptor country is also a significant factor. Generally the greater the similarity between the two cultures, the easier the adjustment on the part of both. For instance, the earlier immigrations of Northern Europeans brought people to this country who were a part of a common cultural basin. Their culture was influenced largely by the Greco-Roman empire. Their religion was basically Christian. Their worldview was somewhat similar. Even their languages belonged to a common family of languages. This facilitated their adaptation. Conversely, the arrival of people who have vastly different cultural backgrounds, increases the challenge of adaptation. The greater the differences in language, worldview, customs, and religion, the broader the gap will be between ethnic groups and predominant societies. Cultural congruity and incongruity, therefore, will need to be considered in designing church planting strategies. One cannot generalize on the basis of the experience of one group.

Patterns of Residence

Patterns of residence also accelerate or retard the assimilation process. Ethnic persons who arrive in their host country and decide to live within the enclave of their cultural group will generally experience a slow rate of assimilation. This is due to the fact that these immigrants will find themselves in an environment in which they can communicate with most of the people around them in their mother tongue, socialize mainly with people from their own group, and even seek assistance from professionals (e.g., doctors, lawyers) with whom they have a common ethnic identity. On the other hand, ethnic persons who establish their places of residence in communities where the majority of the people are from the predominant society will experience a significantly faster rate of assimilation. Patterns of residence, therefore, often influence the rate of assimilation that ethnic groups experience.

Proximity to Native Land

Proximity to native land is also a factor that influences the assimilation process. There are people who travel so far to their host country that they seldom, if ever, go back to visit their homeland. Some of these appear to make a conscious decision to adjust to their host country because they will probably never see their homeland again. On the other hand, there are other ethnic groups who live just across a border from their native land. This makes it possible for them to stay in constant contact with their relatives and to visit them frequently. Generally one can say that the closer the homeland, the slower the assimilation process.

Length of residence

Length of residence in host country also influences the assimilation process. Generally speaking, it can be said that the longer an ethic group has resided in a host country the greater the degree of assimilation it will experience. This factor can be off-set, however, by some of the other factors discussed above. Unless the ethnic group is totally isolated, which is highly unlikely, the second and succeeding generations of the ethnic group will experience an increasing degree of assimilation into the predominant society.

Rate of Immigration

Another factor which influences the assimilation of an ethnic group is the rate of immigration that continues to occur after the ethnic group has arrived in the host country. There are some ethnic groups (e.g., Germans, Irish) who migrated to the United States in one or two major waves. Once these occurred, the rate of assimilation dropped significantly or virtually ceased. On the other hand, there are groups (e.g., Hispanic Americans) whose immigration rates have continued at a steady pace for decades. This has resulted not only in the steady increase of its population figures, but also in the constant reinforcement of linguistic expression (their mother tongue) and cultural values. This constant reinforcement of the group's cultural identity often retards the assimilation process.[147]

Factors the Contribute to Assimilation

In seeking to reach newly arrived immigrants, the task of identifying them, ascertaining the language they speak and designing strategies to establish contact with them and to communicate the gospel with them is indeed a challenging one. The task, however, becomes more challenging once the group has been in an area for a number of years and the second and third generations begin to experience assimilation into the predominant society. An understanding of the assimilation process becomes essential if one to be successful in reaching the various generational segments. It is, therefore, important to seek to understand the factors that contribute to assimilation.

Sociologist Andrew Greeley states that *schooling, mass media, and peer pressure are the principal factors that contribute to the assimilation of Immigrant groups.*[148] While most adult immigrants do not go to school or spend much time being exposed to the media of the predominant society, they have to make an effort to learn enough of the language of the predominant society to be able to function on the job. They also have to cope with the peer pressure that children experience in school and in their neighborhoods to conform to the predominant society. It is important, therefore, to understand the process of assimilation on the part of adults and on the part of their children as well as the implications of this for church planting efforts.

Adult Assimilation

Unless the immigrant group lives and works in total isolation from the host group, a certain degree of assimilation is needed. Immigrant persons often find it necessary to learn the language of the host group in order to find employment and function adequately in the new environment. Language learning may relate primarily to that which is needed to carry out the requirements of a job and to function in the basic activities of life related to travel (e.g., getting a driver's license), to financial dealings (purchasing goods) and to avail themselves of needed services (e.g., medical, legal). For adult immigrants, a basic understanding of the language and customs of the host society, therefore, is essential for life in the new cultural setting. It must be kept in mind, however, that there is a difference between the "trade language" and the "heart language" of ethnic groups. Even though adults may learn enough of the language of the predominant society (for them the trade language), they can best be reached with the gospel message in their heart language.

245

Child Assimilation

For the children of immigrant parents, the process of assimilation is even stronger and more extensive than for adults. As stated above, there are three factors that contribute to assimilation among the children of immigrants: 1) Schooling; 2) Media; and 3) Peer Group.

Schooling

As soon as the immigrants arrive, the law requires them to enroll their children in school. Immediately upon enrollment, children are faced with the task of learning the language of the predominant society. Even schools that have bilingual programs require students to learn the predominant language as soon as possible. That, along with the fact that children have a great capacity to learn languages, contributes to the fact that within a short period of time they can become proficient in their new language. As soon as the children of immigrant parents begin to attend public school (or private schools run by the predominant society), they begin to learn the language and the culture of the predominant society. Schooling, therefore, is an acculturation instrument. In addition to language learning, students learn the values of the predominant society. Very soon the children may even become interpreters for their parents, not only of the language, but often of the acceptable customs of the predominant society.

Media

An additional factor that contributes to the rapid assimilation of the children of immigrants is the media. This means that children have an opportunity to learn the language of the predominant society in the television programs and movies they watch, the music and other programs they hear on the radio, and the books and magazines they read. This, in addition to the reading assignments that children do in school, contributes toward a preference for predominant language in the things that they hear and read. Mass media contributes to the assimilation process not only in terms of *language* utilization but also with regard to the *cultural values* of the predominant society. These values (e.g., morals, dating, parental authority) are at times in conflict with those of the Ethnic Group.

Peers

The children of immigrant families, like all other children, are greatly influenced by their peers (friends, classmates, and those of their own age in society in general). This peer-group influence relates to they way they dress, comb their hair, relate to others, and talk. Because the children of immigrant parents are surrounded by other children who speak the language of the predominant society and have some of the characteristics of the predominant society, they soon become very much like the predominant society.

Assimilation Stages

The work of several sociologists (e.g., Andrew Greeley,[149] R.A. Schermerhorn,[150] and Susan Keefe[151]) calls attention to the fact that ethnic groups are not homogeneous. Different segments are generally found at different stages of assimilation into the predominant society. These provide a graphic way of analyzing the various segments of an ethnic group.[152]

Greeley's "mosaic with permeable boundaries" model posits the following stages of assimilation: (1) nuclear ethnic, (2) fellow traveler ethnic, (3) marginal ethnic and (4) alienated ethnic.[153] By *nuclear ethnic*, Greeley means persons for whom ethnic identity and background is of controlling importance in many areas of their lives. By *fellow-traveler ethnic* Greeley means persons for whom ethnicity is a relatively important part of self conscious identification but not absolutely important. By *marginal ethnic* Greeley means persons who occasionally think of themselves as ethnics. For these persons ethnicity is normally not an important part of their identity. *Alienated ethnics* are those who self-consciously exclude themselves from their ethnic heritage.

A typology which considers assimilation in church planting efforts is needed. In the following chart we have substituted *Total Ethnic* for *Nuclear Ethnic*. While it is acknowledged that no group can be totally isolated, the term *Total Ethnic* indicates the highest degree of ethnic enclosure possible. *Median Ethnic* connotes a moderate degree of ethnic enclosure and conversely a moderate degree of integration into the predominant culture. *Marginal Ethnic* connotes greater participation in the predominant culture than in the ethnic (ethnic) culture. *Alienated Ethnic* connotes total participation in the predominant culture, hence, alienation from the ethnic culture. *Revitalized Ethnic* connotes a reversion into the native culture.

Employing the stages posited by Greeley (as modified) produces the following chart that indicates the level of assimilation and the generation most likely to be in that category. Some groups assimilate more rapidly than others, therefore, the designation for generation will vary for each group. The stages of assimilation also provide clues as to the types of assimilation which the various segments of an ethnic group are experiencing. It is important, therefore, to analyze the various types of assimilation which ethnic groups experience (see Figure 2 .

FIGURE 2
STAGES OF ASSIMILATION

Level	Generation
Total Ethnic	First
Median Ethnic	Second
Marginal Ethnic	Third
Assimilated Ethnic	Fourth

Assimilation and Church Models

As is true of traditional congregations, the assimilation level of ethnic groups needs to be taken into account in simple church strategies.

Total Ethnic

If the target group is made up of total ethnics who speak only their mother tongue and have all of their social contacts within their ethnic community, what is needed is a multiplicity of ethnic churches that utilize the mother tongue of the group and utilize the normal associational patterns of the group. If exponential growth is to take place, the local leaders of the simple churches need to be Total Ethnics. In the development of urban or regional strategies, Median or Marginal Ethnics may be able to serve as bridges of communication between the Total Ethnic community and other ethnics as well as members of the predominant society.

Median Ethnic

If the target group is made up of median ethics who having a working knowledge of the Predominant Group's language and have some social contacts with others outside their own cultural group, bilingual churches may be needed. The fact that the Median Ethnic group is still more proficient in its own language may suggest that the stronger emphasis may need to be ion its own mother tongue in the Bible studies and other activities of the simple church. Due to the assimilation process, however, it is very likely that the younger generation may need their ministry (e.g., Bible studies, Fellowship activities) in the language of the Predominant society. By virtue of the fact that they are bi-lingual, Median Ethnics are perhaps in the best position to serve as leaders that facilitate communication within their own group, with other ethnic groups, and with the predominant society.

Marginal Ethnic

In light of the fact that Marginal Ethnics are more fluent in the Predominant Group's language and most of their social contacts are outside of their own group of origin, bilingual churches with a greater emphasis on the Predominant Group's language may be needed. The leaders of these churches will need to come from this sub-cultural group if exponential growth is to be experienced.

Assimilated Ethnic

Due to the fact that Assimilated Ethnics do not want to be identified with their group of origin, they are the best prospects for churches that utilize the language of the predominant society. If the inclusion of these is to be successful, it must be ascertained that they are experiencing structural as well as cultural assimilation. If they already participate with many people from the predominant society in primary group type activities (e.g., birthdays, anniversaries, and special day celebrations), they will be included quite naturally in small church gatherings.

The following chart combines the level of assimilation with the type of church that needs to be considered. As is true of any taxonomy, there will be instances in which exceptions will be in order. The point that needs to be made, however, is that *different types of churches are needed for the various levels of assimilation in which ethnic groups find themselves. Another way of stating this is that one size does not fit all.* It also needs to be pointed out that while it is appropriate to designate the English language as the language of the predominant society in North America, adjustments need to be made for other parts of the world.

251

Figure 3
Assimilation and Church Model

	Assimilation Level	Outside Social Contacts	Language
Total Ethnic	0 – 10%+	Mother Tongue	Ethnic Church
Median Ethnic	25%+	Bi-lingual: MOTHER TONGUE (dominant) English (secondary)	Bi-lingual Church MOTHER TONGUE (dominant) English (secondary)
Marginal Ethnic	50%+	Bi-lingual Mother Tongue (secondary) ENGLISH (dominant)	English Language/ Ethnic Culture Church or Multi- cultural Church
Assimilated Ethnic Church	85 - 100%	English (dominant)	Existing Anglo Churches

Cultural and Structural Assimilation Model

After an extensive study of assimilation in the United States, Milton Gordon has posited the theory of cultural and structural assimilation.[154]

By "cultural assimilation" Gordon means "*a change of cultural patterns to those of the host society*."[155] This means that the immigrant group acquires *some* of the cultural traits of the predominant group. These may include the use of the trade language, adoption of predominant modes of dress, and some of the customs that are considered appropriate in the work place.

By "structural assimilation," Gordon means "*large scale entrance into the cliques, clubs, and institutions of the host society on the primary group level.*"[156] This signals the social integration of the ethnic group into the predominant society. In order to have a better understanding of this factor in the assimilation process, it is helpful to discuss the significance of primary and secondary relationships in more detail.

Primary versus Secondary Relationships

A Modern Dictionary of Sociology defines primary relations as "*social relations that are lasting, are based on frequent and direct contact, and are characterized by deep personal and emotional involvement*". Primary relationships generally take place between family members and close friends. These are the people who are invited to important celebrations (e.g., birthdays, religious holidays, family reunions).

Secondary relations are defined by Theodorson as "*impersonal, without emotional involvement and specialized, that is, generally limited to performance of specific activity or activities.*"[157] Secondary relationships generally take place in the work place where people perform tasks together but do not socialize with one another after work hours.

By experiencing only *cultural assimilation* the immigrant group absorbs numerous cultural traits from the host group without losing its own cultural identity or entering the area of primary (personal, informal, intimate, usually face-to-face, involving the entire personality)[158] relationships of host group. This means that, while there may be some cultural or behavioral similarities, the immigrant group maintains only secondary social relationships. Gordon explains:

> The evidence we have examined indicates that, apart from the sub-society of the intellectuals, intimate

253

primary group relations between members of different racial and religious groups in the United States remain at a minimum level. This structural separation provides for the retention of a core of differentiated religious beliefs, values, and historical symbols to the loyal members of the faith. To this extent one is entitled to say that structural pluralism in America is accompanied by a moderate degree of cultural pluralism as well.[159]

Distinguishing between the different types of assimilation has significant implications for church planting. *If there is extensive contact between ethnic groups and the predominant society at the primary group level, there is a greater possibility that the people in that community will be receptive to the idea of becoming a part of a multi-cultural church[160]*. If, on the other hand, people from the ethnic groups and those from the predominant society relate to one another principally at the secondary group level, the task of reaching the un-churched and bringing them into a common congregation will be very difficult if not impossible in certain contexts.

Assimilation Variables

The distinctions which Gordon makes between structural and cultural pluralism are based on his paradigm of assimilation variables. [161] In it he posits seven variables of assimilation:

1) Cultural Assimilation is one in which the minority group adopts some of the cultural patterns of the predominant society. This includes utilization of the trade language, adopting some of the dress styles of the predominant society, and accepting the customs that are considered appropriate in the work place.

2) ***Structural Assimilation*** is one in which there is large-scale entrance into the cliques, clubs, and institutions of the predominant society on the primary group level. This means that people from the various ethnic groups and the predominant society get together socially to celebrate such special events as birthdays, holidays, and community wide events.

3) ***Marital Assimilation*** is one in which there is large-scale intermarriage between people from the ethnic groups and the predominant society.

4) ***Identificational Assimilation*** is one in which there is the development of a sense of group identity based exclusively on the predominant society. Identification, therefore, is defined in terms of the broader community (e,g., country, state, city) over against rather than one's ethnic group.

5) ***Attitude Receptional Assimilation*** is one in which the minority group does not encounter prejudiced *attitudes* on the part of the predominant society.

6) ***Behavioral Receptional Assimilation*** is one in which the minority group does not encounter discriminatory *behavior* on the part of the predominant society.

7) ***Civic Assimilation*** is one in which there is political participation of the minority group with the predominant society.

By distinguishing between the variables of assimilation, Gordon is able to ascertain with some precision the kind of accommodation that is taking place between the minority group and the predominant society. This includes a clearer understanding of the social spheres in which assimilation is occurring (i.e., primary or secondary groups). This typology also helps in determining the degree of assimilation, which a group has experienced. Structural assimilation, for instance, indicates a deeper degree of assimilation than cultural assimilation. To some extent the stages of the assimilation process are outlined in this paradigm. Generally cultural assimilation precedes the other types and may take place even when the other types do not occur.[162] Cultural assimilation, in some cases, may continue indefinitely. Once structural assimilation has occurred, however, the other types of assimilation generally will follow.[163]

Analysis of Goal Orientation

As additional factors are considered a clearer picture of the interaction between ethnic and predominant groups can be obtained. One of these factors relates to the goal orientations of the predominant and of the ethnic groups.[164] These goals are either centripetal or centrifugal.

Centripetal tendencies foster assimilation. They are "cultural trends such as acceptance of common values, and life styles, as well as structural features like increased participation in a common set of groups, associations, and institutions."[165] Centrifugal tendencies "foster separation from the predominant group or from societal bonds in one respect or another."[166]

Four ways in which these tendencies are expressed are: (1) when the predominant as well as the ethnic groups, have centripetal goals (this leads to assimilation); (2) when predominant and ethnic groups have centrifugal goals (this leads toward cultural pluralism and autonomy); (3) when the predominant group has centrifugal goals but the ethnic group has centripetal goals (this results in forced segregation with resistance); and (4) when the predominant group has centripetal goals but the ethnic group has centrifugal goals (this leads to forced assimilation with resistance).[167]

Situations 1 and 2, therefore, tend toward integration while 3 and 4 tend toward conflict.[168] When the factor of goal orientation is combined with the stages of assimilation the dynamic relationships between the ethnic and the predominant cultures can be seen with greater clarity.

FIGURE 3

GOAL ORIENTATION AND STAGES OF ASSIMILATION

ETHNIC GROUP	ADAPTATION	PREDOMINANT

Total Ethnic

Centrifugal--------------------Pluralism----------------Centrifugal

Centripetal----------------Forced Segregation-----------Centrifugal

Median Ethnic

Centripetal--------------Partial Assimilation------------Centripetal

Centrifugal--------------Forced Assimilation-----------Centripetal

Marginal Ethnic

Centripetal-------------Extensive Assimilation---------Centripetal

257

Assimilated Ethnic

Centripetal------------Total Assimilation--------------Centripetal

In this scheme, the factor of goal orientation is viewed from the perspective of the ethnic group as well as the predominant culture. When combined with the various stages of assimilation, it provides a heuristic device to examine the extent to which goal orientation encourages or discourages assimilation.

Conclusion

As we seek to discover and understand the people groups in a given area, we need to take several facts into consideration. First, ethnic groups are made up of individuals with a shared feeling of peoplehood. Second, the mode of entry of an ethnic group carries with it a cluster of historical, social, political, and economic factors which affect the ethnic group's self-perception as well as the predominant society's attitude toward it. Third, in seeking to understand these ethnic groups, it is helpful to do an analysis of the mode of entry, mood of the host country, socioeconomic level at the point of entry, eth/class category, cultural congruity, patterns of residence, proximity to native land, length of residence, and rate of immigration. Fourth, it is important to seek to understand the factors that contribute to assimilation. Fifth, the various levels and types of assimilation need to be taken into account in selecting church starting models. We need to design our strategy in accordance with the patterns of association of the target group. A church planting movement should be built around the natural lines of relational patterns and fellowship between the members of an ethnic group and those of the predominant society.

Endnotes

1. *The World Book Dictionary*, 1978, s.v. "ethnic."

2. Milton Gordon, *Assimilation in American Life* (New York, NY: Oxford University Press, 1964), p. 24.

[142]. *The International Encyclopedia of Sociology*, 1984, s.v. "ethnicity," p. 135.

143. R. A. Schermerhorn, *Comparative Ethnic Relations*, (New York: Random House, 1970), 12.

[144] Jim Slack, "Levels of Segmentation," Power Point, 2003.

[145] Oscar I. Romo, *American Mosaic: Church Planting in Ethnic America*, Nashville: Broadman Press, 1993; Wendell Belew, *Missions in the Mosaic*, Atlanta: Home Mission Board, 1974. Gerald Palmer, Winds of Change, Atlanta: Home Mission Board, 1970.

[146] For a discussion of these types of migration see R. A Schermerhorn, *Comparative Ethnic Relations* New York: Random House, 1970).
[147] For an updated study on this subject, see Robert Suro, Jeffery S. Passel "The Rise of the Second Generation," Pew Hispanic Center, October, 2003.
[148] Greeley, "Is Ethnicity Un-American?," 106-12.
[149]. Greeley, "Is Ethnicity Un-American?," 106-12.

[150]. Schermerhorn, *Comparative Ethnic Relations*, 131.

[151]. Susan E. Keefe and Amado M. Padilla, *Chicano Ethnicity* (Albuquerque, NM: University of New Mexico Press, 1987), 14-18.

[152]. It is acknowledged that typologies are never totally adequate to describe a social phenomenon. Groups do not generally fall neatly under the various categories devised by the sociological researcher. Being cognizant of this,

however, a sociological researcher, can find typologies useful for heuristic purposes.

[153]. Greeley, "Is Ethnicity Un-American?" 107-9.

[154]. Gordon, op. cit., 3-18.

[155]. Gordon, op. cit., 71.

[156]. Gordon, op. cit., 71.

[157]. *A Modern Dictionary of Sociology*, 1969. s.v."primary relations." *A Modern Dictionary of Sociology*, 1969. s.v. "secondary relations."

[158]. This is Gordon's definition for "primary group." The secondary group would be the obverse of this. Gordon, op. cit., 31.

[159]. Gordon, op. cit., 239.

[160] For the purpose of this discussion we are going to define a multi-cultural church as one that is composed of individuals who come from a variety of cultural groups. Conversely, a multi-congregational church is one that is composed of several congregations representing a different cultural group.

[161]. Gordon, op. cit., 71.

[162]. For a more detailed discussion of this see Gordon, op. cit., 77.

[163]. Gordon, op. cit., 81.

[164]. Schermerhorn utilizes the idea of paired concepts found in Bendix Reinhard and Bennett Berger, "Images of Society and Problems of Concept Formation in Sociology," in Llewellyn Gross ed. *Symposium on Sociological Theory* (New York, NY: Harper & Row, 1959).

[165]. Schermerhorn, *Comparative Ethnic Relations*, 81.

[166]. Schermerhorn, *Comparative Ethnic Relations*, 81.

[167]. For further details see Schermerhorn's "Congruent and Incongruent Orientations toward Centripetal and Centrifugal Trends of Ethnics as Viewed by Themselves and Superordinates." Schermerhorn, *Comparative Ethnic Relations*, 83.

[168]. The integration trends hypothesized in cases A and B and the conflict trends in cases C and D Schermerhorn explains are "based on what knowledge we have of these situations from the research literature, and as gross distinctions have a face validity that can serve as a springboard for future testing." Ibid., 85.

Chapter 11

Assessment of Church Planting Movements

James B. Slack

The Existence of Church Planting Movements

Church Planting Movements are a reality in our generation. Calling a movement by a certain designation is not just a neat, innovative, organizational way to describe previous church growth activities, events and results such as revivals, awakenings, or even record harvest times. *In other words, a Church Planting Movement is not a new name for old movements.* Christians have, still are, and we pray will continue to identify and observe Church Planting Movements wherever they emerge.

To say it in still another way, a "church planting movement" is not just a name attached to other historic types of church growth. It is a legitimate and needed name that serves to *describe a very distinct and important way in which Christianity has spread and grown.* And, a Church Planting Movement is not a recent phenomenon. When trying to review church history to identify Church Planting Movements in the past, we do not have historical knowledge passed on to us that was gathered and presented from today's church planting movement perspective.

We have clearly observed within the New Testament what seems to have been embryonic Church Planting Movements. It is likely that what we read about in the book of Acts, in terms of the growth of the churches among the Gentiles, is a description of a church planting movement. Church Planting Movement historians and assessors recognize the descriptions of the first Christian churches in Jerusalem and Antioch were not descriptions of a church planting movement. Jerusalem and Antioch would more closely fit the modern description of a mega-church rather than a church planting movement. By contrast, the way Luke described how the early churches among the Gentiles grew as a result of Barnabas' and Saul's (Paul's) missionary journeys, look very much like a church planting movement.

Some ask today, then why do we need the term Church Planting Movement, and why do we use it? Christianity has faced this same kind of issue before. There is never the mention of "missionary" as a type of minister in the New Testament. However, Christians recognized that Barnabas, Paul and others were missionary in character and activity, so Christians created the term "missionary" as both a description of how they functioned, and later as a title for what they were. "Revival" and "Great Awakening" are not New Testament terms. However, they are terms that have been created in modern times by Christians to describe events that Christian's have observed in the Bible or more commonly in history. "Harvest Movement" and "Church Growth Movement" are not found as descriptive or title terms in the Bible, but they are valuable to us today when talking about and describing the kind of movement and activities we see occurring where God is working among people in this world.

A Church Planting
Movement Defined

A Church Planting Movement is as Dr. David Garrison, and consequently the International Mission Board, SBC has described it—*"a rapid and multiplicative increase of indigenous churches planting churches within a given people group or population segment."* Stated in another way, a church planting movement is a situation wherein local churches have matured to the point of taking the initiative to plant multiple other local churches, who in turn plant other local churches within the same people group or segment of peoples.

A Church Planting Movement is characterized by multi-generational local church planting. And, it is understood as part of the meaning of the term that this *is occurring with little to no outside instigation or assistance, or without needing outside assistance to occur or continue.* In a church planting movement, one observes indigenous church planting, and understands from observations of other Church Planting Movements that *outside assistance would only serve to slow down, redirect, or place a ceiling on the continuation and spread of the movement.* The church planting is occurring on its own, and lives within its own environment of peoples—making it indigenous. This repeated and carefully stated definition seems redundant. If it is, then redundancy is necessary when it comes to describing and assessing whether or not a movement in the field is a church planting movement or not.

Due to the confusion of Church Planting Movements with other historical movements, it is necessary to provide a more exact and refined definition. We are aware, of course, that what we say about Church Planting Movements in this early stage of observation and definition will surely be corrected and refined as more of them are observed and more carefully assessed.

Many individuals use the term, church planting movements, loosely, confusing the method with other church growth terms and descriptions. This confusion is more obvious when Christians identify growth among a certain people group and tell others that the growth represents a church planting movement. After extensive, on-site, in-depth and random interviews, two of the illustrations in the International Mission Board's (*IMB) booklet on Church Planting Movements were found not to be a Church Planting Movement.* They were close, and could possibly develop to be a Church Planting Movement, but they were not one at the time of their assessment. Neither of the two fit the most basic part of the definition, that of "local churches planting other local churches."

So, when talking, teaching and writing about a Church Planting Movement, there is the need for a clear distinction between a Church Planting Movement and other movements such as: a Great Awakening; a Harvest Movement; A Quickening; A Revival; a People Movement, or a Church Growth Movement. The planting of multiple local churches by different entities among a people group such as hired evangelists, missionaries assigned to the people group, or by itinerant evangelists who go out on their own, do not qualify as Church Planting Movement characteristics. They may be the precursor to a movement. *But, a Church Planting Movement is in existence only if a majority of the existing local churches own the lostness of their friends and neighbors (near or far) and who themselves go out as lay and pastoral leaders of those local churches to start multiple other local New Testament churches.*

For instance, if multiple evangelical agencies place church planters among a people group, or even one agency places multiple church planters among a people group, and they start dozens or even hundreds of churches over a short period of time, that is not a Church Planting Movement, or even a type of Church Planting Movement. Such growth is good and can be seen as a Church Growth Movement, but that is clearly by definition not a Church Planting Movement. A Church Planting Movement might, arise out of such an experience, but would only be a Church Planting Movement *when Christian fervor or life within many or most of those local churches reaches the point where they almost simultaneously, and very naturally from their own spiritual initiative send their local church members out to plant other New Testament churches like theirs.*

When observers come to assess the status of the movement they will see that local churches are planting multiple other local churches that are themselves going out to plant other New Testament churches like themselves. That clearly fits the part of the Church Planting Movement definition saying: *a rapid and multiplicative increase of indigenous churches planting churches...* **After local churches starting other local churches reaches second and third generation status, that warrants being called a Church Planting Movement.** Convention evangelists, itinerant evangelists and expatriate missionaries may be planting some churches, but it is a Church Planting Movement only when the majority of the local churches within that people group are being planted by other local churches that expand to second and third generations of local churches planting local churches. Until then, call it what you will, but it is not a Church Planting Movement.

When local churches, old or new, reach out and regularly evangelize people and bring them in to a decision for Christ, baptizing them into their existing churches in ever increasing numbers, however many, you likely have a Harvest Movement, but a Church Planting Movement does not yet exist. If a Gospel witness sweeps through a village, a territory, or a country through lay witnesses or preachers or evangelists and thousands come to Christ, thus changing the entire spiritual fabric of the region, you likely have a Quickening or a classic People Movement, but you do not have a Church Planting Movement. If one describes a Church Planting Movement in any other terms, or with greater latitude, then the term is synonymous with other historically defined movements, and the term Church Planting Movement is neither warranted nor valid.

As a result of the singling out and setting forth of the initial definition of a Church Planting Movement, and after some on-site and extensive field assessments have been conducted of some supposed Church Planting Movements, this polishing or careful defining of a Church Planting Movement has become necessary. To this point in time, the IMB has fielded missiologically-seasoned teams to assess the status of church growth within at least seven people groups where it was thought that a Church Planting Movement was occurring. Those teams strictly followed the IMB's Church Planting Movement booklet, the criteria developed only from that booklet in order to develop interview instruments tailored to determine if the criteria was present in Church Planting Movement terms within those people groups. An on-going Church Planting Movement was observed in five of the seven people groups. And, one must be quick to say that the other two were phenomenal and significant growth movements, just not a Church Planting Movement. And, not being a Church Planting Movement does not mean that they are a second-class movement.

A Call for Patience and Decorum

And, as this sorting-out process is conducted and continues, we must be very patient with those who say they are working with a Church Planting Movement. Many are working without having the benefit of the more exact definition and interpretation, or all the materials and reports coming from the field studies. They have not unknowingly misrepresented the growth experiences they have been connected with and should not be labeled as having done so.

Our having before us both the history of the terms and the intricate on-site field research allows us to define a Church Planting Movement more accurately. Do notice that to this point in time, nothing has been changed in the IMB's Church Planting Movement document concerning the definition or description of a Church Planting Movement.

Church Planting Assessments

The International Mission Board has commissioned the Global Research Department of the IMB with the task of identifying supposed Church Planting Movements and assessing them. That task has been placed in the job description of Dr. James Slack, Global Evangelism and Church Growth Consultant within Global Research.

To this point in time seven (7) supposed Church Planting Movements have been assessed. At least five others (5) others have requested that an assessment team come and assess the status of the growth there. By the end of this year, two to three more of these on-site assessments will have been completed and an extensive report of the findings produced. Most of these reports are highly confidential due to the people group situation concerning persecution within them.

The Assessment Process

The current edition of the IMB's Church Planting Movement booklet written by Dr. David Garrison and intricately critiqued by the administrative staff of the IMB prior to publication, is serving as the basis for all of the current assessments. Upon being assigned the task of leading in the assessments of the supposed CPMs, Dr. Jim Slack developed a first draft edition of Church Planting Movement Criteria as seen in the IMB's Church Planting Movement booklet. Since that booklet contained the IMB's only stated definition and interpretation of a Church Planting Movement, that document was used as the only basis for developing the assessment criteria. Slack called upon the assistance of Curtis Sergeant and a number of other missionaries, including numerous SBC seminary missions' professors to assist in either developing or critiquing the stated criteria. Each one who assisted was asked to read carefully the CPM booklet and develop only criteria that could be found within the booklet. Each of these individuals was asked to identify criteria in the document, positive or negative, which was restated and organized into a set of positive criteria for assessing a supposed CPM.

Once the Church Planting Movement Criteria document was revised to the point of being an acceptable mirror of the Church Planting Movement booklet, a questionnaire was developed for use in the field when interviewing pastors, members and church leaders within the supposed Church Planting Movement.

A questionnaire was developed that represented in question form, but not in the same sequence, all of the criteria within the criteria document. This instrument was not designed for use as a sociological instrument but as an anthropological type instrument. The questionnaire was not designed to be given to any respondent to be filled-out and turned-in to the researchers. The instrument was designed to be used by an experienced missionary or field sensitive team member, who would administer it by means of a personal interview. A verbatim log would be kept by each team member, recording all that was said during each of the interviews. Sometimes it was possible to capture the interviews by means of tape recordings, which would be transcribed. In most of the assessments, the interviews were captured by writing down what each respondent said during the interview. In numerous settings, it was not appropriate for a tape recorder to be used. In none of the CPM assessments has it been appropriate to use a computer in order to more directly enter the information gained during the interviews.

After all the interviews are conducted, a report based upon the data secured from each interview is shared with the Strategy Coordinator and each team member. Data from the interviews are put into a database. The team then consults among themselves concerning their interpretation of the interviews, the data in the database and other records secured during the assessment, and a report containing the findings of the Church Planting Movement Assessment team is produced. The report is then shared with the Administrative staff of the IMB, which includes the Regional leadership of the region where the CPM assessment was conducted. At appropriate times, and in appropriate ways, the information gained during the CPM assessment is formatted and shared with Seminary professors of missions who assist in educating potential and actual IMB missionaries.

Conclusion

The assessment method outlined above has been and is being employed to investigate movements in order to classify them as church planting movements or to understand them as some other manifestation of church growth. These assessing efforts are important in order to help workers know the exact nature of the works with which they have contact. This understanding helps in attempting to aid the beginning of other movements that could become church planting movements. The processes of assessment of church planting movements continue to develop and further refinements are certain to follow.

Chapter 12

Worldview Identification and Church Planting Movements

Jim Slack

Why should we take the time to identify a people's worldview?[169] Can't we just preach the Gospel to a people group and let the Holy Spirit do His work of wooing and winning? Or, can't we just gather the basic demographics and some sociological information about the people and get on with the urgent task of evangelization? Is this talk of the need to identify a target people's worldview anything more than an academic endeavor? Is worldview identification more than a fad within our leadership? Are any others in the evangelical community involved in worldview identification?

An initial answer is that worldviews, with a long and very reputable history in anthropological circles, has come of age in secular, business and especially religious circles. Even so, questions concerning "why engage in worldview identification" are legitimate, necessary, and appropriate for those who are anxious to "get on with the evangelization task." Consequently, this presentation is an attempt to address those questions about the importance of worldview studies. *The central question being addressed is why should a Strategy Coordinator-led team identify its target people's worldview as a basis for evangelism, curriculum development, discipleship, theological mentoring, church planting, and/or any other ministries aimed at initiating a church planting movement?*[170]

Perspective Concerning Worldview

To address any topic, the avenue of approach or perspective is very important. This topic of the need for worldview identification could be and already has been addressed from an anthropologist's perspective, from an academic seminary professor's perspective, from an evangelical organization's perspective, from a historical perspective, from a curriculum developer's perspective, and from a business perspective. I will address the issue from the perspective of Southern Baptist's missiological focus on ethnolinguistic peoples and homogenous strata of society. Each of the aforementioned perspectives will also be cited.

In the 1970s I was serving as a missionary in the Philippines and had regular contact with Summer Institute of Linguistics (Wycliffe Translators). SIL is the world's most accomplished agency for reducing oral and thus unwritten languages to writing and producing literacy and educational tools in those languages. SIL is a legend in the eyes of many governments and for sure in the eyes of religious agencies who are working among those peoples whose language has been reduced to written form. SIL missionaries are professional linguists and cultural specialists with generations of practical experience in the most primitive settings.

After getting to know SIL missionaries and their excellent work, I realized that they had legal and diplomatic relationships with each respective government that gave them permission to enter and work with primary oral communication peoples who had no written language. In many settings, this was the only way they could gain entry to these peoples. While satisfying government needs for educational progress among their peoples who gained a written version of their language and the opportunity to become literate in their heart language. The religious community gained Biblical texts in each of the languages that SIL produced in writing.

This meant that, even though SIL personnel were all missionaries, they were not free to engage in church planting. In most cases, due to their visa status and the contract they had with each of the governments, they were free to witness as individual Christians but they were not free to engage in church planting. Realizing this, I also noticed that in most cases, SIL in Asia tended to invite Christian and Missionary Alliance (C&MA) missionaries to come behind them to pick up on any evangelism they were able to initiate and to follow SIL with church planting activities. In most cases SIL was able to leave behind believers who were ready to be gathered into churches. This continually put C&MA missionaries at the forefront of people-group work, and gave them a literate base with freshly produced Biblical materials as they entered.

In the 1970s, during a meeting with SIL leadership from its headquarters, I asked why they tended to invite Christian and Missionary Alliance (C&MA) missionaries and not Southern Baptist Convention (SBC), International Mission Board (IMB) missionaries to to conduct follow-up after their translation work. The leader asked if I really wanted to know, which perked my interest even more. He went on to say: *"We do not invite you because you Southern Baptists have no stomach for identifying a people's worldview and using it as a basis for learning how to present Christ's Gospel to the people."* He followed that statement with another by saying: *"You Southern Baptists tend to get off the plane preaching without learning the local people's worldview and the questions they ask. And, you preach the same sermons and teach the same Bible studies that you preached and taught in southern USA."*

I was stunned, to say the least, but very much aware of the truth of his statements. In further conversation he said he and others observed that Southern Baptists would "take off the denominational shelf," materials and programs designed to speak to people in southern United States without asking if they were in any way compatible with the worldview issues the foreign people faced. In many cases, he cited, Southern Baptists often translated those US materials directly into the local language without worldview adaptations, and many times without professional linguistic assistance in choosing appropriate words for the translation.

As a result, much misunderstanding or lack of understanding arose from this use of materials created from the perspective of one worldview yet presented in the context of a people with a very different worldview. The SIL evaluator was not an anti-SBC person. He went on to say: "Most of our SIL missionaries are Baptist, and if you folks could come to the point of identifying the target people's worldview (ethnography) and use it as a basis for your ministries, we would be thrilled to allow you to follow up our translation work." His final statement was: "Until you gain an appreciation for the target people's worldview and the issues local cultures struggle with, SIL can't afford to invest all of the time, money, and expertise into these peoples and their society and then pass it on to folks that work without a local worldview orientation."

I, who had anthropological and sociological training, was very much aware of the truth of his evaluation. That event became a defining moment in my life and ministry. The bottom line was that in our haste to get on with the evangelization task Southern Baptists generally did not identify local worldview issues and address them appropriately by means of the Scripture. To be honest, Southern Baptists have known this to be very true. And, that is becoming ever more obvious in a pluralistic USA where various worldviews abound.

But, "because SIL said we should," is not the answer to this chapter's question as to "why identify a target people's worldview?" The SIL discussion provides a focus for this enquiry. Rather than wait to the end of the chapter to speak of the current SIL-SBC relationship, due to changes within SBC circles, SIL is actively partnering with SBC missionaries today.

Meaning and Use of the Concept of Worldview

"Worldview," as a word, a descriptive noun, and as a secular and religious term, is of recent ascendancy. The original term is "ethnography." If one is interested in a more in-depth look at SIL and ethnographies see James P. Spradley's work.[171] Technically, an ethnography is a graph of an *ethne*. Spradley defines ethnography as "the work of describing a culture. The essential core of this activity aims to understand another way of life from the native point of view." Spradley goes on to say: *"Rather than studying people, ethnography means learning from people"*[172]

One should notice that the author has talked about worldview identification and not worldview study. The two are admittedly close, but the emphasis on learning a worldview is intended. An ethnography is an enquiry into the culture, life, and lifestyles of a specific ethnolinguistic people group. There are many sister terms such as "ethnographer,"one who identifies the "ethnography." Masters and doctorate dissertations in the field of anthropology are focused on identifying the ethnography of a specific ethnolinguistic people group. In academic history, there have been only a few exceptions to this practice. The IMB is party to one of those rare exceptions within the anthropological community, but that is not pertinent to this presentation. The IMB's Jenkins Library has on file that very interesting worldview exception.

"Ethnography" as a term, did not become that popular outside the academic world. As a result, a more popular term--world view--developed as a substitute. From the 1950s until the 1990s the term "world view" was increasingly used as a common substitute both within and beyond anthropological circles. Until the mid-1990s this term was two words--world view. In England and Europe the word was hyphenated, world-view and probably will continue that way until it has been in Webster's and other dictionaries for some time. That is very much in keeping with their worldview. By the mid-1990s, however, the term began to be used in secular life and in anthropological circles instead of ethnography and now appears as one word, worldview.

Worldview is a very common word today, used in many environments such as business, religion, anthropology, sociology, and religion. Again, an ethnography, or worldview, is the way a specific people act, think, believe, function, and relate. Simply, it is a people's view of the world. A people's worldview is how people try to function as a result of how they think the world functions and the way they think it should function. To identify a people's worldview is to intimately understand them. Well, so much for semantics.

Worldview is a term and function that has come of age. The value and use of a worldview can now be observed in many forums. Worldview identification has become a common commodity in business, secular, and religious life. Perhaps the most interesting citation as to the extensiveness of the use of worldview technology is that anthropology graduates who can identify and explain worldviews (ethnographers who identify ethnographies) are now in great demand in the secular world, especially in corporate America.[173]

This situation was highlighted recently in a newspaper article entitled "Hot Asset In Corporate Life: Anthropology Degrees." The article said: "...as companies go global and crave leaders for a diverse workforce, a new hot degree is emerging for aspiring executives: anthropology. The study of man is no longer a degree for museum directors. Citicorp created a vice-presidency for anthropologist Steve Barnett. Not satisfied with consumer surveys, Hallmark is sending anthropologists into the homes of immigrants, attending holidays and birthday parties to design cards they'll want. Anthropology and the identification of worldviews have moved into the business world big time. That article and other related articles cited numerous CEO's in the business world who came to that position due to their success within the organization through identifying and adequately addressing worldviews of their personnel and clients.

Of greater interest in the religious world are the numerous evangelical teachers, leaders and writers such as David Hesselgrave, Donald McGavran, Ralph Winter, Peter

Wagner, Paul Hiebert, Rick Warren, Ebbie Smith, Steven C. Hawthorne, Charles Kraft, Eugene Nida, John Apeh and others who, out of experience, have given worldviews a prominent place in their work, writings, and teaching. Worldview studies are promoted by these and a host of other evangelical teachers as a needed, up-front, activity for all who engage in cross-cultural evangelism. In fact, David J. Hesselgrave, at the occasion of his retirement, also in his address to the Evangelical Missiological Society, and in consequent letters to his colleagues, said he wanted to devote major time to writing and urging the missionary and cross-cultural evangelism communities to engage in worldview studies as a basis for their work.

Worldview development has not occurred in a corner and it is not an unproven and untested fad. It is important to note that worldview awareness has developed on the frontiers of lostness and in the hard-nosed arena of the workplace where appropriately addressing the issues with maximum understanding is paramount.

Worldview Proponents Speak.

Across the spectrum of Missiological thinking, authorities have been increasingly speaking on the issue of worldview identification as a component in missionary strategy. In January of 1978, in the context of the Lausanne Movement and the Committee on World Evangelization, the "*Willowbank Report*" was presented as a consensus of the evangelical community's task on world evangelization. At the heart of that report, the group stated directly, "*No Christian witness can hope to communicate the gospel if he or she ignores the cultural factor.*" The group continued,

280

Sensitive cross-cultural witnesses will not
arrive at their sphere of service with a pre-
packaged gospel. They must have a clear
grasp of the 'given' truth of the gospel...It is
only by active, loving engagement with the
local people, thinking in their thought
patterns, *understanding their world-view*,
listening to their questions, and feeling their
burdens, that the whole believing
community (of which the missionary is a
part) will be able to respond to their need.[174]

In the same vein, C. Peter Wagner says the paradigm
shift that includes identifying and understanding the peoples'
worldview holds a most significant place in bringing
missionaries more in touch with the worldview of the men and
women to whom they are attempting to communicate the
Gospel. [175]

David Hesselgrave says worldview is simply the way in
which a person 'sees' the world." He quotes Norman Geisler
who says: "people do not see things as they are, but as they
appear to be through glasses tinted by their world view.[176]

Charles Kraft devotes major sections of his new
anthropology textbook to worldview. Kraft says a society may
chart its course according to a single map of reality—which we
call a worldview. Worldview, says Kraft, constitutes the core of
a culture. It functions on the one hand, as the grid in terms of
which reality is perceived, and, on the other, as that which
provides the guidelines for a people's behavioral response to
that perception of reality. A worldview consists of assumptions
(including images). Since many, perhaps most, of a peoples'

underlying assumptions are stored in their brains as pictures or images, it is important to note that these images are kinds of assumptions. [177] Obviously, worldview constitutes a vital understanding for those sharing the Gospel.

N. T. Wright is a contemporary contributor to the subject of worldview biblical sources and among those who respond to the biblical sources. In one of his latest works, *The New Testament and the People of God,* which is used in many major seminaries, centers on worldview as a major issue as Christianity confronts lostness in the world today.[178] The first 143 pages of this 535 page work uses worldview as the focus for discussing his perspective on the New Testament, Christianity and witness today.[179]

Paul Hiebert, a professor at Trinity Evangelical Seminary, has written much about the importance for cross-cultural ministers to identifying worldviews of the target people. He calls worldview an encompassing blueprint and contends that the biblical worldview helps
us see the big picture of reality present in Scripture and in nature. Hiebert sees worldview as serving like glasses in shaping how people see the world around them. Because people in other cultures have different worldviews, he teaches, they see reality differently at even the most fundamental levels.

Hiebert contends that worldviews are largely implicit. This fact makes it difficult for us to see our own worldview. Our worldview assures us that what we see is the way things really are. Any who disagree with us, says Hieber, are not only wrong, but out of touch with reality. If our worldview is shaken, we are deeply disturbed because the world no longer makes sense to us.

Worldviews, teaches Hiebert, serve several important functions. On the cognitive level worldview give people the rational justification for their beliefs and integrates them into a more or less unified view of reality. Worldview, on the level of values, validates our deepest cultural norms. In short, our worldview is our basic map of reality.

Worldviews, according to Hiebert, change over time. At times a peoples' worldview no long makes sense of their world. If another and more adequate explanation of the world is presented to them, they may reject the old and adopt the new...Such worldview shifts, says Hiebert, are at the heart of what we call conversion.[180]

Rick Warren, a well-known Baptist pastor in California, is a good illustration of a practitioner who identifies and addresses a target people's worldview. Even though he tends not to use the term "worldview, he speaks to the issue of worldview throughout his workshops and in his book. Warren's Saddleback Sam and Saddleback Sally are classic worldview illustrations. I wish that every witness, pastor, curriculum writer and missionary would identify their "Sams" and "Sallys." In one particular section entitled "How Do You Define Your Target" he says that if a church leader is serious about having his church make an impact the pastor must become an expert on the community. Warren declares that no missionary to a foreign land would try to evangelize and minister to people without first understanding their culture. It is equally important for workers in North America to understand the culture in which they minister. One of the major barriers to church growth, says Warren, is 'people blindness'--being unaware of social and cultural differences between people. Warren is convinced that there is no substitute for getting a feel for the community through one-on-one interaction. [181]

These few illustrations in the use of the term worldview, the meaning of worldview, and the concept of worldviews from the business, academic, and religious community, underline the fact that "identifying worldviews" has become a common commodity in our world. A large amount of professional research has been conducted on worldviews and the results have served to highlight the necessity of conducting worldview research. Courses on worldview studies are in every major academic institution, including every one of our Southern Baptist Seminaries.

Each of the SBC seminaries is using the IMB's worldview identification instrument as the basis for their worldview research. Ebbie Smith, Daniel Sanchez and others at Southwestern Baptist Theological Seminary have been developing a worldview orientation and identification course module for correspondence and on-site use. Numerous articles in the latest edition of *Perspectives,* highlight the need to identify a target people's worldview as a basis for working with them or evangelizing them. In fact, almost every article in *Perspectives* on strategy and cross-cultural work mentions worldview consciousness as important to achieving evangelization goals. The phrase "cultural studies" is often defined by the quoted writers as "worldview studies." Numerous scholars see a people's worldview as the "core of their culture."

Being educated in today's schools, and reading recent publications has in itself provided many with the reasons why cross-cultural workers need to be worldview conscious and

284

worldview learners. This approach also indicates the need to use worldview information in addressing the target people at the point of their everyday assumptions, beliefs, values, and questions. Worldview understanding is a necessity rather than a luxury in contemporary missional strategy.

Reasons for Identifying
a People's Worldview

Thus, the basic question is before us. Why do we need to be worldview conscious and why do we need to engage in worldview identification of our target people?

Worldview Identification
Is Essential in Witnessing

First, let me start with a bottom line reason for those who apply the Gospel based upon worldview understanding. Wright speaks to this issue in the introduction of his book. Kraft devotes an entire chapter to this issue in his new book. As quoted earlier, Wright says all people in every society possess stories at the very basic level of their understanding of reality which contain what they believe about reality, life, and the way the world should function for all things to be as they should be, that is, normal. He goes on to say that Christians, of all people, are at the basic level of witness, pitting their story--Christ's story--and His claims against the lost person's stories--their perceptions of reality and normality.

Witness is the act of presenting all of the truth that can be presented in any format, but mainly that of the Biblical story, with the belief and prayer that the Holy Spirit will work to assist the lost person or persons in accepting Christ's story as the ultimate reality and thus the norm for life. Wright says the only way one ever knows that the lost person accepted Christ, is not in terms of stated beliefs, going to church, or joining any group. Even though these are good, and hopefully subsequent Biblical choices that a new believer makes, they should follow a rearrangement of a new believer's core beliefs as a result of their new birth in Christ. If not, syncretism is sure to result. He says one has a fairly clear understanding that the other person has accepted the Christian worldview when that person now witnesses as a result of totally rearranging his or her own story and resultant arguments in favor of Christ's story and His arguments and lifestyle. *Thus, when their worldview has given way, under the Spirit's impetus, to a deliberate and positive choice of Christ's worldview that is evidenced in their life and witness, one can be quite sure that new birth has come to those individuals.* The obvious change in the worldview is one of the indicators. This is brought about, in part, through the active identification and resultant addressing of a target people's worldview. It is sometimes sad that the business world picked up on this faster than the Christian world. Surely, understanding the lost person's perception of reality, so a relevant witness can be presented, is more important than "making a buck" in the market place.

The basic aim for identifying a person's worldview is to know how to tell or share Christ's story with the lost person, in light of their worldview so the Gospel will make sense to them. Basic witness demands that we understand the worldview of the target people. Therefore, a witness learns the target people's worldview so they will be better prepared to present Christ's claims, to know what specific issues should be covered in discipleship and how to train pastors to serve within the setting of that worldview.

Worldview Identification
Helps to Recognize Barriers

The second reason flows out of the first one. It is necessary to know a target people's worldview, in order to identify the issues within the worldview where the lost people's worldview produces conflicting barriers to the Christian worldview. Kraft in his latest book says:

> Worldview assumptions underlie all sociocultural behavior. These are the basic principles, the foundation for the rules and regulations from which social control techniques flow. *Since people tend to be quite protective of their worldview assumptions, these provide the primary barriers to change.* These worldview barriers are in the patterning, the script that people follow. At a personal level, however, lies another formidable set of barriers, the social barriers. These flow from the fact that we ordinarily behave habitually and unthinkingly, according to the patterns we have been taught."[182]

Kraft emphasizes that each barrier must be identified, addressed very tactfully and positively or change is unlikely. Kraft, like N.T. Wright argues that, *"significant culture change is always a matter of changes in the worldview."* That is the task of the witness, once the worldview barriers are identified.

A number of other reasons as to "why one should identify a people's worldview" are associated with this second reason. Evangelizers, and especially those who desire to initiate a church planting movement, need to know those serious "touch points" within the worldview of the target people's culture or worldview that are in direct conflict with the Christian worldview. Once those are identified, the Christian evangelizer is able to put the Christian Gospel together in ways that will adequately address the conflicting worldview issues within the lost people.

These "barriers to the Gospel" can only be identified through the identification of the target people's worldview. The opposite of this is what SIL highlighted when I asked why Southern Baptists were not used to follow up SIL's work. SIL leaders said Southern Baptists preached a *generic Gospel.*

I have come to increasingly understand that the Gospel. Southern Baptists often preach and teach is based upon God's word, but the content of the sermons and Bible studies are fashioned to answer questions that existed within American worldviews and not those of the target people. Those sermons and Bible studies often adequately answer many of the worldview barriers within Americans. They need to address each worldview of the people being evangelized.

Many evangelizers assumed two things. One, because they were not aware of worldviews, they assumed that the sermons and Bible studies were straight out of the Bible with no cultural overhang. Few were aware they had taken Bible truth and rightfully fashioned it to speak to American people in the pews and in the street. Second, they assumed that those same culture oriented sermons and Bible studies would universally in answering anybody's questions in any culture. As a result, many who were called and shifted to work in cross-cultural settings were not able to apply the Gospel to the target people until they did identify the target people's worldview.

What is interesting is that even in the United States pastors and church members have argued that a lot of the literature produced in Nashville by the Baptist Sunday School Board (BSSB) was generic and did not speak to the specific issues of people in very different settings in the United States, and especially those who came to the U.S. from other cultures. That problem was a worldview problem, but was not understood as such. Therefore, they made the same mistakes when they moved to address others in different cultural settings. As literature became more and more generic or general in its presentation, it became less and less specific for any people group. If the teacher could not apply the literature's content to the worldview of the local people, it was often seen as very true and good but it was seen by those with other worldview questions as being irrelevant to them and their situation.

Therefore, in order to apply the Gospel to each people group's specific worldview, and in order to answer all of the questions and conflicting issues of the people, worldview research must be conducted. Anything less leaves major questions unanswered by those who prepare curriculum or presentations in evangelism, discipleship, leadership training and church planting. Culture specific ministry comes from knowledge of each culture's worldview.

Worldview Identification
Avoids Syncretism

A third reason flows out of the first two reasons--the entry of syncretism into the churches via new members. If the barriers, i.e., the conflicting issues between the people's worldview, and the New Testament worldview, are not identified, those worldview positions remain within the lifestyles of the converts and come into the church in the form of syncretism. If differences are not addressed in evangelism, discipleship, and leadership training, confusion will result. Numerous studies in secular and religious circles have revealed that generic Gospel presentations leave the target people who receive them, unable to identify the specific barriers in their own worldview. Being unable to know that if I trust this Jesus, I must change my worldview in these specific ways, leaves much of the old worldview in tack as they come into the church. As a result, syncretism exists within many Christian churches. Lately, syncretism has been found to be alive and well within many Baptist churches.

Of course, the classic anthropological and religious example is Roman Catholicism in Latin America. In fact, Rome says the Latin American Catholic Church is by no stretch of the facts, Roman Catholic. They say it does not resemble Roman Catholicism because it is a wedding of ancient Latin American animism and Catholicism. Some argue that Roman Catholicism, during the early centuries was the result of the same kind of syncretistic evolution where early Christianity was wedded with local practices.

The idea then emerges that every SC-led team must identify the worldview of their target people to discover the barriers so that they can be addressed and syncretism minimized. If not, a church planting movement may be slow in coming, or may come laden with syncretism.

Worldview Identification
Averts Ethnocentirsm

A fourth reason is that Gospel presenters, if they do not know the worldview of the target people, will present the Gospel based upon their own worldview. Ignorance is thought by some to be the most deadly situation. In most cases not many of the cross-cultural target people's worldview is close to that of a southern American's worldview. As a result, the Gospel presenter often shares, as the Gospel is shared, in the wrappings of his or her own worldview.

This is especially true concerning church polity and daily Christian lifestyles. The development of an institutionalized church is usually the result of a lack of worldview orientation. For many American Christians, worship services should be at 11:00 A.M. every Sunday morning. Therefore, Gospel presenters need to know the worldview of the target people in order to compare it with his or her own worldview so as to avoid sharing his own "church trappings" as the Gospel is shared. Snyder's book on wineskins is a valuable source for further study on this issue.

Worldview Identification
Prevents Cultural Distortion

A fifth reason is that after two to three generations of Christianity among a people, the church entity that emerges develops its own worldview. It becomes problematic in that the new and developing worldview becomes institutionalized, developing its own church member's lifestyles and structures. Some of those are not characteristically New Testament. The leaders and members of those churches often identify their worldview with the lost population's worldview and "pass it on" as such.

When the newly arrived Gospel presenter, preacher, volunteer, missionary, or other type of Christian worker asks these leaders and church members what the people are like, the church leaders and members give them their own worldview, which is in almost every case very different from the actual worldview of the lost people. Worldview identification is necessary to distinguish these two local worldviews from each other and to interrupt this cycle of exchanging one inappropriate worldview for the previous one. In these settings the New Testament worldview has little chance to emerge unless worldview identification is conducted.

Worldview Identification Allows Focusing

A sixth and very subtle reason for identifying a worldview is found in the Biblical ethnolinguistic focus that many evangelicals have rediscovered. Why should evangelizers narrow the focus on an ethnolinguistic people group rather than targeting an entire country or large grouping of ethnolinguistic peoples? Ralph Winter highlights this in one of his articles in *Perspectives*. This choice, according to Winter, is underlined and clarified by worldview identification.

One narrows his/her focus to concentrate on one ethnolinguistic people group because of its distinctives--its worldview distinctives. One narrows to take on one ethnolinguistic group or a stratum of society because that group or stratum is different from other peoples and strata. And, it is most difficult to try to answer a number of different worldview positions at the same time. Just how different two ethnolinguistic or social strata are, is determined by means of the identification of their worldview. To narrow the target on an ethnolinguistic people group but not identify their worldview is stopping short of actually going to one's target.

Worldview Identification
Facilitates Contextualization

The seventh reason is a very practical one. For those cross-cultural workers who have for a long time worked without considering the worldview of their target people, it is imperative they give deliberate and guided attention to worldviews. It will be most difficult for them to move away from long-standing generic preaching and teaching to target a people in light of their worldview. Such a paradigm shift seldom occurs normally and naturally at any point without their engaging in definite worldview identification.

Shifting from a long-term traditional approach within a very institutional church setting can only be changed through guided worldview identification. Even then, it will not be easy for them to make the change. The temptation will continually be that of using generic, off-the-shelf materials, and reproducing the institutional church structure and lifestyle in each of the new settings. In these settings identifying a target people's worldview cannot be optional if success is expected. If this is not done, cooperating with the Holy Spirit in initiating a church planting movement will be most difficult.

Conclusion

In summary, there are at least four worldviews that are simultaneously operational in most cross-cultural settings. The first is the worldview of the target people--the unevangelized. They have their set of assumptions, values, beliefs, questions and lifestyle habits that define what is normal for them. The second is the worldview of the Gospel presenter--the cross-cultural evangelizer. He or she has come to the scene with a worldview that has been shaped by the culture and the churches from which he or she came. It is very normal for them to desire and work toward developing churches just like the ones they knew in their home culture. The third is the worldview of the New Testament, that is hopefully the worldview being presented to the target people for acceptance.

Studies have shown, however, that those who are not worldview sensitive and who have not deliberately compared their own worldview with the New Testament are, in a sense, programmed to reproduce their own worldview in whatever setting they work. If these individuals come from American and traditional mission settings, and they do not have worldview skills, the end result is obvious. The fourth is the worldview of the local denomination or churches and their leaders and members. They exist, and church as they have developed it, is the norm for them and they want foreign cross-cultural workers who have joined them to plant and develop churches as they now exist. And, worldview studies themselves have shown, that as a cross-cultural workers live and work within a developed church setting, those cross-cultural workers tend to accept and defend the local denomination's worldview as right and best even when it differs greatly from the New Testament worldview.

In *Perspectives*, Kietzman and Smalley speak to this issue of multiple worldviews in operation at the same time. They say:

> The missionary's role in culture change, then, is that of catalyst and of a source of new ideas and new information. It is the voice of experience, but an experience based upon his own culture for the most part and therefore to be used only with care and understanding. *Part of the value of anthropological study, of course, is that it gives at least a vicarious experience in more than one cultural setting.* By study in this field, missionaries can gain awareness of the much wider choice of alternatives than their own culture allows."[183]

Thus, the cross-cultural Gospel presenter should be aware of the distinctive features of the four worldviews. This is necessary as the Gospel is being formatted for presentation to the target people during evangelism, discipleship, curriculum development and theological training. Basic to all of this is the identification of the target people's worldview which must be the focus of these ministries. Worldview identification is necessary for this to occur.

How Much Time Should Be Given To A Worldview? Worldview identification, as defined in this document is a learning experience. Learning experiences are dynamic, occurring over a period of time. Obviously, one can be a victim of not knowing important things about a target people's worldview. The cost of such unawareness can easily result in poor or improper presentation of the Gospel. In fact, all of the worldview promoters quoted in this document, argue that it is almost certain that those who fail to engage in at least basic worldview identification will suffer the consequences outlined in the reasons section.

An SC-led team should use the Country and People Profile instruments and the Worldview Instruments in order to begin learning about the target people's worldview. Obviously, once a basic understanding begins to be seen, plans should be constructed and implemented. A complete worldview will often not be in hand as the multi-year plan is begun. As new awareness comes to the evangelizers that would impact the plans, the changes should be made and implementation should be continued in light of the changes.

Formal anthropological worldview identification, which is part of academic master's and doctorate studies take two years to identify and write-up in order to fulfill academic requirements. No one would suggest that a Strategy Coordinator-led team should take two years of full time work to identify a people's worldview. There are generally five guidelines with accompanying options.

The first is that all SC-led teams should be obligated to seriously identify the worldview of the target people and use it in developing endvisioning (Is this word right or should it be two words?) and the master plan. Second, each SC-led team should check the academic, business and religious community for existing worldviews of the target people. Hundreds of worldviews exist that have been completed. Do not reinvent the wheel if one exists for the people. Some of these are old, but simply need to be updated. Third, not being professionals, the SC-led teams should use the instruments that SIL and other anthropological professionals have assisted the IMB in developing.

These instruments have been used effectively for a number of years in identifying target people's worldviews. Working alone on a worldview project is seldom productive. Fourth, a segment of the SC-led team's time, or one or two designated individuals, should be given the task of working at least half-time on identifying the target people's worldview. *That can be comfortably completed at an entry-level within six to nine months.*

A fifth option or guideline is to secure professional help from local or foreign individuals who are trained in identifying a people's worldview. Such help can be secured through a partnership with a school or with a professional who is a church member who is willing to give time to this endeavor. Another avenue is an International Service Corps, Journeyman or Associate assignment for a professional who can join the team for a time to assist in guiding local people in identifying the target people's worldview.

SC-led teams should be encouraged that most new individuals who, in the future, come on their teams will be more and more familiar and comfortable with identifying a people's worldview. More and more missionaries have undergraduate degrees or minors in anthropology. Few individuals go to school today in the West, and for sure in America who are not exposed to worldview issues. This is even more the case with those trained and experienced in the business world. It should not take the average group more than six to nine months to gain a very accurate worldview of the target people. However, ignoring worldview identification flies in the face of current Christian and evangelical experience and teaching. Worldview identification is a task whose time has come.

Even so, the bottom line is learning the target people's worldview in order to present the Gospel, to disciple, to train leaders and to plant the church in the most culturally appropriate way while not compromising an accurate presentation of Christ and the New Testament church as the focus of their attention. A process and an instrument for constructing worldviews are provided in appendix7

Chapter 13

Suggested Shifts in Preparation for Church Planting Movements In North America

J.D. Payne

This chapter addresses some of the necessary missiological shifts required for the North American Church to be in the position to experience spontaneous church expansion.[184] The discussion also includes some of the hindrances to this spontaneous expansion. The spontaneous expansion of the Church is not something that can be manufactured by mankind. Not even the best missiological formulae or shifts alone will produce the church growth that many desire. A spiritual dynamic constitutes an indispensable component for church multiplication. The movement of the Spirit both on the churches and on the masses is required.

Some Presuppositions

Several imperative presuppositions form a foundation for this chapter. First, change is needed for the North American Church to experience spontaneous expansion. This chapter is not to be taken as a prescription for how to create church multiplication. Nevertheless, it is written to advocate that paradigmatic shifts are necessary if the Church is going to be in the position to experience a church multiplication movement or church multiplication movements. These shifts, as related to church planting, are found in the areas of theology, strategy, and methodology.

The second presupposition is that by its very nature, the Church is designed to grow and reproduce. Robert E. Logan noted that the Church will grow and reproduce, "unless we do something that hinders that from happening."[185] Though at times the rate of the growth of the Church will vary, nevertheless, it is God's will for growth to occur.

The third presupposition is related to the receptivity of North America to the gospel. Donald A. McGavran observed:

> Peoples and societies also vary in responsiveness. Whole segments of mankind resist the Gospel for periods—often very long periods—and then ripen to the Good News. In resistant populations, single congregations only, and those small, can be created and kept alive, whereas in responsive ones many congregations which freely reproduce others can be established.[186]

It is assumed that North America is receptive to the gospel. Indications are, however, that North America is not receptive to many of the traditional cultural expressions of the gospel and the Church. The postmodern cultural shift has created an openness to the spiritual and is supernatural in ways that did not exist 20-30 years ago.[187] One problem, however, is that the Church has become isolated from the culture-at-large. Wilbert R. Shenk was correct when he observed that the Western Church:

> "takes its culture for granted. The fact that the church has for so long been defined by the social classes in which it was embedded indicates that, far from having a critical knowledge of its culture, the church speaks largely with the accent and idiom of the class(es) with which it is identified."[188]

This cultural ignorance has resulted in many individuals rejecting the gospel because of the manner in which the gospel has become packaged. Instead of rejecting the truth, many have rejected the evangelistic methodologies and consequently have never even listened to or heard the truth.[189]

In light of this receptivity that the cultural shift has produced, a related assumption must be made. As noted in the opening paragraph, unless God in his sovereignty moves upon the Church and the masses, the spontaneous expansion is impossible. The Church should be praying for continued and heightened receptivity, and in McGavran's words, be on the lookout for the changes and adjust accordingly:

> Unless churchmen are on the lookout for changes in receptivity of homogeneous units within the general population, and are prepared to seek and bring persons and groups *belonging to these units* into the fold, they will not even discern what needs to be done in mission. They will continue generalized "church and mission work" which, shrouded in fog as to the chief end of mission, cannot fit mission to increasing receptivity. An essential task is to discern receptivity and—when this is seen—to adjust methods, institutions, and personnel until the receptive are becoming Christians and reaching out to win their fellows to eternal life.[190]

A fourth presupposition is that the contemporary denomination should not be discarded. The Lord has used North American denominations in a powerful way to establish hundreds of thousands of churches on this continent. He will continue to use those Churches who remain faithful to His Word. Denominations will continue in their existence, and will reach many more for Christ. They are organized institutions that can guide and educate future church leaders concerning

301

pitfalls to avoid and the correct paths to pursue. Though their resources are to be used with discernment and caution, denominations have much to offer North American church planting.

In relation to this presupposition, however, a disclaimer must be offered. Most denominations will not make the necessary paradigm shifts required for church multiplication in the twenty-first century. The three major shifts suggested in this chapter are in all likelihood too radical for many contemporary denominations. Too many unsettling changes in the current infrastructures will eventually occur if the necessary changes are made. Rather than make the necessary adaptations, out of fear and concern for control, many will continue to remain on their present course of action. Jonathan Stuart Campbell's observations describe the current situation and problem:

> The major reason church reproduction has not been envisioned for Western contexts, is simply because the church is still captive to the Christendom paradigm. It still considers Western society as basically "churched." There is virtually no attempt to apply principles of group conversions, people movements and spontaneous church planting in Western cultures. The current emphasis continues to be on building bigger and bigger institutions instead. Since organic reproduction is not valued, there is no expectation for it. "Spontaneous" church reproduction in Western contexts is almost exclusively limited to church splits.[191]

Though many denominations will continue to experience church planting by addition, church multiplication will remain only a dream. For those desiring church multiplication but also desire to continue in their established paradigms, great allowances must be made for *avant-garde* church planters.

A fifth presupposition is that all church planting to some degree is cross-cultural. North American Church leaders, therefore, have much to learn from missionaries and missiologists from outside of North America. While discussing the importance of culture and church planting, Robert Logan was correct when he stated that:

> it is important to realize that it is essential to be culturally relevant even if you are not going cross-culturally. Because the fact is that even when we are crossing over from light into darkness *that is a cross cultural experience* [emphasis mine].[192]

Though not only in a spiritual sense, North American church planting is a cross-cultural experience even if the church planter is of the same culture as the target group. Membership in the North American Church generally entails a form of separation and isolation from the rest of the unchurched world. Though the Church is *in* the world, it is to keep *from* the world as much as possible to not be *of* the world. The Church, unlike its biblical predecessor, has created a subculture in which most believers are expected to function in the areas of work, education, entertainment, ministry, and socialization as much as possible. In most cases, the Church is out of touch with the culture of the unchurched.

For the professional church planter who has been educated in Christian Academia, the North American missiological experience is even more of a cross-cultural endeavor. Cultural readjustment is necessary after being isolated for several years in classroom education. Even readjustment is required for a church planter to return to one's own people to minister

303

effectively. Roland Allen, who has been credited as coining the phrase "spontaneous expansion," was concerned with the Christian education of his day since it established an unhealthy chasm between the national believers and the unchurched population.

Many writers recently have observed that Western Missiology now demands cross-cultural thinking and practice. Writing from a European perspective, Stuart Murray observed:

> As we conclude our discussion of the task of the church, the fundamental point is that, whatever diverse shapes the church assumes, church planters and church leaders in a post-Christian context are required to operate according to principles which have been common among cross-cultural missionaries for many years. The paradigm shift that underlies this requirement is the recognition that all church leadership in Europe should be missionary and cross-cultural, and that the shape of the church should reflect this. Church planting requires the same missionary encounter with surrounding culture and the same concern about developing appropriate forms and structures as is evident in areas of the world that have been regarded as the 'mission field'. Complex issues of indigenization, inculturation and contextualization need to be addressed. The local community is now the 'mission field' and missiological perspectives and skills are required.[193]

Eddie Gibbs made a similar observation on doing mission in Western civilizations in general, and North America in particular:

> The majority of church leaders throughout the Western world find themselves ministering in a rapidly changing cultural context that is both post-Christian and pluralistic. Consequently their outreach ministries are as crosscultural as those of their

more traditional missionary counterparts seeking to make Christ known in other parts of the world. Consequently they are in as much need of missionary training to venture across the street as to venture overseas.[194]

Elsewhere, Gibbs noted, "Our post-Christian, neopagan, pluralistic North American context presents crosscultural missionary challenges every bit as daunting as those we would face on any other continent."[195]

Also, displaying similar lines of thinking, Wilbert Shenk stated:

Preparing for mission in the region of "Jerusalem, Judea and Samaria" that comprises our Western culture will require that we approach this frontier in missional rather than pastoral terms. In this respect, the cross-cultural mission reserves for us a basic model of how the church is to relate to the world in all times and places. We assume that the cross-cultural missioner must treat the host culture with sensitivity and respect, starting with learning the language and the various symbol systems that comprise a culture. As modern societies have become increasingly pluralized, this "cross-cultural" perspective becomes ever more imperative for all Christian witness. Ministry always emanates from a particular vantage point, with the disciple serving as ambassador of the kingdom of God to a culture. The motif of the resident alien, found in both Old and New Testaments, is another way of expressing the fact that the church is to be "in but not of the world."

We must come to grips with a culture that is in crisis and transition. At the same time we should become more self-aware of the assumptions that have controlled mission studies and missionary action up to the present. The cross-cultural experience of mission over the past two centuries represents an invaluable resource for the training of missiologists and missionaries to Western culture. Indeed, mission should be conceived of as an inherently cross-cultural action, a movement mandated by the Triune God into territory that does not acknowledge the reign of God. Geography and nationality are entirely secondary concerns.[196]

Though the Church has been established in North America for a few centuries, this region has recently become a pioneer territory for the Church. Though the continent is not like other areas of the world that have few or no churches, cultural shifts and maintenance-oriented congregations have contributed to this predominately unchurched region of the world. The presence of over 300,000 churches does not negate the need for the spontaneous expansion of the Church.

As will be discussed later, a sixth presupposition is that much contemporary church planting is founded on a shallow ecclesiology. Tradition, cultural relevance, and pragmatism, rather than biblical moorings primarily shapes this ecclesiology itself. It is a shallow ecclesiology that produces unhealthy churches and contributes to hindered spontaneous expansion.

A seventh presupposition is that church multiplication is the best approach to North American missions. Church planting by addition is good, but not the best. An exponential increase in the number of disciples, and thus congregations, is needed for North America. In light of this presupposition, Church leaders must begin to strategize in terms of reproduction. Methodologies developed and applied must therefore reflect the value of reproduction.

A final presupposition is that the spontaneous expansion of the North American Church will take place through congregations that are yet to be planted. Most established congregations and many recently planted congregations are entrenched in theological and cultural paradigms that are counter-multiplication. A disclaimer needs to be made: it is possible that a catastrophic event could occur which would force the already established churches to make the needed paradigmatic shifts. May the Lord forbid that something of this nature should happen; in all likelihood, church planters will lead the way to spontaneous expansion. While addressing the post-modern cultural shift that has occurred, and continues to occur, Gibbs stated:

> Generally, those most aware of the cultural shift from modernity to post-modernity are people who are not locked into the power structures. Those who shoulder the responsibility for the functioning and survival of hierarchies and local churches tend to be too preoccupied in bailing out the boat to be setting a new course. Change agents are most likely to be pioneering church planters who have no congregational history to deal with and who are immersed in the cultures of the people they endeavor to reach.[197]

Three Paradigm Shifts

If the North American Church is going to experience spontaneous expansion, what are the needed changes that must occur? This section addresses three necessary paradigm shifts in the areas of theology, strategy, and methodology. The theological shift is specifically related to the areas of ecclesiology and pneumatology. All church planters have some type of ecclesiology whether good or bad. Church planters must return to the Scriptures for the necessary ecclesiological irreducible minimum that needs to be translated to new believers. In light of this ecclesiological shift, North American church planters need to practice a missionary faith as advocated by Roland Allen. Again, a return to the Scriptures will assist in developing a proper pneumatology to foster the missionary faith.

The strategic shift required will focus on developing a philosophy of reproduction. Instead of church planters focusing on planting a single congregation, the focus must be on church multiplication, or as Logan noted: planting churches which plant churches which plant churches. From the beginning, all that the church planter does is to be related to church multiplication through disciple-making and the corollary, leadership multiplication.

The methodological shift is closely related to the other two shifts. All church planting methodologies should be evaluated in light of three areas. First, the methodology must be effective in translating to the people group the gospel and the ecclesiological irreducible minimum. Second, the methodology should be effective in multiplying disciples and leaders. Third, and closely related to the second area, there should be a high reproducibility potential related to all that the church planters practice before the target people. The target people should be able to reproduce the pattern of church planting established by the church planters.

Theological Shifts

By far, the greatest need in contemporary North American church planting is a theological shift from a pragmatic ecclesiology or a paternalistic ecclesiology to a biblical ecclesiology that focuses on multiplication. Twenty years ago, Charles Brock noted the need for a healthy theology:

A proper theological basis and practical principles of church growth are of major importance to the church planter. An education in various strategies and methodologies is of little value unless there is a corresponding and preceding theology. The greatest need today lies in this area of renewed theological thinking. A proper theology will produce a proper methodology. For the church planter the proper methodology will be natural and inevitable to the degree that it issues strictly from biblical theology.[198]

At the Baptist World Alliance International Conference on Establishing Churches held in 1992, Denton Lotz observed:

One of the crises of the church today is ecclesiology. What is the church? Is the church a building? Is it where two or three are gathered together? Is it where there is a bishop and a diocese, or a pope and a Vatican with apostolic succession? Is it one man or woman in communion with God? Is it where signs of the kingdom, such as justice and peace and shalom, are initiated? Is it where a community of peasants form a cooperative? Is it when a group of youth walk for hunger? Where senior adults demonstrate for more pension? On and on the questions go, perhaps strange to some, but serious questions to others.[199]

Though much research is being conducted in the area of ecclesiology and North American missions, church planters have yet to heed Brock's words and answer Lotz's questions concerning the essence and nature of the church.[200] Murray was correct when he noted: "An inadequate theological basis will not necessarily hinder short-term growth, or result in widespread heresy among newly planted churches. But it will limit the long-term impact of church planting, and may result in dangerous distortions of the way in which the mission of the church is understood."[201]

As mentioned above, there are at least two ecclesiological dangers facing North American church planters. The first danger is a pragmatic ecclesiology. This ecclesiology sacrifices the big picture of seeing local church multiplication for the immediate satisfaction of seeing one church planted or only a few planted by addition.

In an unhealthy manner, a pragmatic ecclesiology focuses on the results. Those who adopt this understanding of the church begin with a church planting model usually because it produces quantitative results. Contentment is related to the large size of the churches planted. Since a particular model of church worked in one region of the country or world, therefore, the model should be applied to other church planting endeavors. The model becomes a panacea. The rationale is usually as follows: Because the model of church reached many for Christ among the middle-class, suburban population of one particular community, therefore it will work in other middle-class, suburban populations throughout the nation.[202] The model is selected in light of the culture, and then the understanding of the church develops (see Figure 1).

The rationale also assumes that since the model of church reached many people in a particular culture, then an ecclesiology must be designed to support the model. The next step in this phenomenological approach is to turn to the Scriptures to find support for why the particular church functions as it does. Though not referring to a pragmatic ecclesiology, Murray sounded an alarm of caution related to theologizing as he observed: "Designating an approach as 'a theology of' an issue may represent careful reflection on experience and an attempt to engage theologically with contemporary issues, but sometimes it is little more than an attempt to provide theological justification (or a few proof texts) for practices or structures that are already established on other foundations."[203]

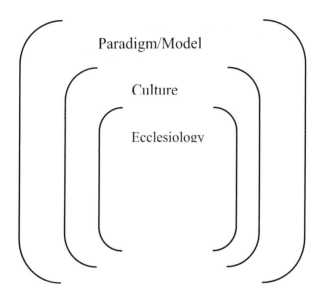

Figure 1. Pragmatic Ecclesiological Paradigm

The end result is that the congregation has "biblical" evidence for seeker-sensitive, contemporary worship services, cell groups, nurseries, recovery classes, and marketing.[204] Campbell observed the danger of pragmatism when he noted:

Pragmatism is preoccupied with effectiveness, success and measurable results. Practical and cultural perspectives are emphasized over biblical revelation. Meaning is determined through practical or experiential bearing in contrast to theological bearings.[205]

Paul G. Hiebert observed, "We are often more interested in techniques than in consequences, in success than in outcome, in doing than in being."[206] Os Guinness stated, "Christians who know only trends, and not where they came from, will always remain uncritical. Heads may nod sagely, hands may scribble furiously, but minds will be only in neutral."[207] It is this uncritical mentality that is a hindrance to spontaneous expansion. The model becomes the focus, and the ecclesiology must be developed to support the model. Not only does the pragmatic ecclesiology paradigm look toward the culture to develop the nature and essence of the church, but also it teaches the membership of the congregation to do likewise.

A pragmatic ecclesiology is very similar to cultural syncretism as described by Bruce J. Nicholls:

> It may result from an enthusiastic attempt to translate the Christian faith by uncritically using the symbols and religious practices of the receptor culture resulting in a fusion of Christian and pagan beliefs and practices. . . . A contemporary example of cultural syncretism is the unconscious identification of biblical Christianity with "the American way of life." This form of syncretism is often found in both Western and Third World, middle-class, suburban, conservative, evangelical congregations who seem unaware that their lifestyle has more affinity to the consumer principles of capitalistic society than to the realities of the New Testament, and whose enthusiasm for evangelism and overseas missions is used to justify noninvolvement in the problems of race, poverty and oppression in the church's neighborhood.[208]

As will be noted later, this quotation does not negate proper contextualization. The problem is that if any model used, as selected in light of the target culture, is antithetical to a proper biblical ecclesiology, even if numerous conversions are produced and churches are planted, that model must be discarded. Whenever the culture determines the church, not only is the ecclesiology based on a tenuous foundation, but it also hinders spontaneous multiplication.

Many church planters would agree that they should not cater to a culturally determined theology proper that advocates a less than sovereign God; even if it is the only way to be seeker-sensitive. If church planters are unwilling to compromise on issues such as theology proper, christology, and soteriology, then why compromise ecclesiology for the sake of planting a church? As will be noted later, unless the people can reproduce the model, then in the church's mind, church multiplication is not a possibility.

The second theological danger facing North American church planters is a paternalistic ecclesiology. This ecclesiology advocates that the church background and church culture of the church planters must be projected onto the new believers. Because the church planter prefers having a large group worship experience with praise music, Sunday school classes, newcomers' classes, and a sermon offered by a single individual, then the new church must also have these elements for it to be a healthy congregation. This understanding of the church begins with the culture of the church planter. A model of church is then selected for the target group. This model usually will be one which the church planter is most familiar. Finally, the Scriptures are consulted to find support for why the model of church exists and functions (see Figure 2).[209]

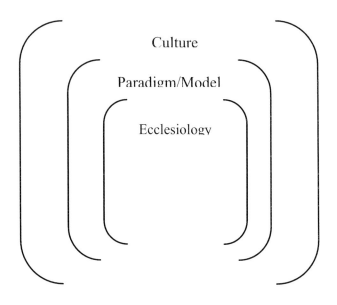

Figure 2. Paternalistic Ecclesiological Paradigm

A corollary of this paradigm is that the church planter tends to see the new believers as being incapable of existing as a church under the sole guidance of the Holy Spirit. Because the neophytes are not more mature in the faith, the church planter cannot remove himself or herself from the congregation. A practice such as the apostle Paul utilized is seen as impossible in North America.

Not only is the new congregation viewed as spiritually immature, but also untrained, uneducated, and incapable of maintaining the institution that the church planter helped establish. A professional is required for the institution to exist and function as a church. The planting of an institution, rather than a church, is actually a sign of a much deeper-rooted problem plaguing many in the North American Church, institutionalism. Shenk observed this problem and noted:

> The integrity of the church in the West is under siege because of the extent to which institutionalism has overtaken the church. There are observable signs of this condition. One is the sheer proliferation of programs and activities. Driven by the advice of consultants who tell churches that they must cater to the needs of their publics, churches are operating a veritable supermarket of specialized services to meet the whims and demands of a consumer society. Not to do so is to lose out in the competition for a growing membership.[210]

Campbell made several observations regarding how the Church has been impacted by institutionalism:

> Beginning in Christendom, living images of the church (e.g., the Body of Christ and family of God) were displaced by non-living models as it came under increasing political-institutional controls. The shift was gradual and subtle because it followed the culture shift. Now the church defines itself predominately in institutional terms. Institutionalism assumes that the church is an inanimate, linear, cause-and-effect system that is constituted by its organizational structure. From a sociological perspective, an institution is a stable, constructed system of social roles and resources designed to perpetually accomplish some end beyond the lives of its members. Inescapably, it has a life of its own, which is often not easy to   change. . . .
>
> This organizational paradigm was further influenced by the development of bureaucratic organizations and industrialization of the modern era. Institutionalism is built on the basis of a humanly determined set of regulations, programs, policies, traditions and goals. Churches accommodated to this trend by

developing their own privatized, institutional center (or compound) within the culture. . . .

For the most part, religious structures birthed in modernity have been organized to conserve and control for the sake of the institution rather than empower and release for mission [emphasis mine].[211]

The concern with this ecclesiological paradigm is not the eventual institutionalization of the newly planted church. History has revealed that over time many religious groups become more and more organized and structured. [212] Institutionalization usually occurs. If the new church desires to develop technical and elaborate structures and organization, then that is her prerogative. The concern is that the paternalistic ecclesiology begins with institutionalization already in place. Even before the congregation comes into existence, the church planter already has the infrastructure and organization in mind.[213] From the beginning, the new church is taught how to function as an institution that exists to perpetuate the institution. Within the genetic code of the congregation, the church planter establishes the paradigm of how the congregation will exist and function as a church for the following generations, regardless of whether or not the new believers are capable of overseeing and maintaining the organization. Shenk stated that structures themselves are not an evil, but rather cannot define the local church. He writes:

Structures per se are timebound. Invariably structures undergo change in response to the environment, which itself is continually changing. Those that do not prove flexible and adaptable are soon regarded as obsolete and must be discarded. But the process is never easy. Enormous resources can be used up in defending and preserving archaic structures. The church, like all human enterprises, readily looks to its structures to ensure the continuity of the faith. But the New Testament emphasizes the fundamental identity and purpose of the church as the people of God. This peoplehood is what the Holy Spirit uses to give life and move the church forward. The church cannot exist without institutional arrangements, but it is the Spirit alone who gives the people of God life and renews them in their identity and purpose.[214]

To import the model of church onto the people is to place the proverbial cart before the horse. This paternalistic ecclesiology can be seen in North American church planting today when church planters enter into the field to plant a purpose-driven church, a cell church, a seeker-sensitive church, a Gen X church, a post-modern church, or a traditional church.[215] To determine the model beforehand, even in light of demographic and psychographic research, is presumptuous and detrimental to the multiplication of indigenous churches. Church planters should keep the models in mind and even create new models, but models should be held onto ever so lightly and only used in light of a proper biblical ecclesiology and proper contextualization.

Guder stated, "We must establish clearly the church's nature and ministry before we proceed to design organizational forms to concretize both in a specific cultural context. Unless we do so, we may fall subject to the illusion that managing the organization is equivalent to being the church."[216] According to Nicholls, this ecclesiological paradigm is also a form of cultural syncretism. He noted that "it is the spirit of the Pharisees and Judaizers who sought to force their cultural forms of religious conviction on their converts. Its modern form is often seen in mission or denominationally founded churches, as enforced ecclesiastical structures, or in social standards of right conduct and worldliness totally alien to the local culture."[217]

Even if the church does become capable of functioning on its own, it is not necessarily an indigenous church. While discussing the cultural implications of an indigenous church, William A. Smalley noted the misconceptions with the three-self formula. According to Smalley, the concept of self-government was subject to misinterpretation. He wrote:

> It may be very easy to have a self-governing church which is not indigenous. Many presently self-governing churches are not. All that is necessary to do is to indoctrinate a few leaders in Western patterns of church government, and let them take over. The result will be a church governed in a slavishly foreign manner (although probably modified at points in the direction of local government patterns), but by no stretch of imagination can it be called an indigenous government. This is going on in scores of mission fields today under the misguided assumption that an "indigenous" church is being founded.[218]

William Smalley also noted a misunderstanding of the concept of self-propagation. He observed:

> Of the three "selfs," it seems to me that of self-propagating is the most nearly diagnostic of an indigenous church, but here again the correlation is by no means complete. In a few areas of the world it may be precisely the foreignness of the church which is the source of attraction to unbelievers. There are parts of the world where aspirations of people lead them toward wanting to identify themselves with the strong and powerful West, and where the church provides such an avenue of identification. Self-propagation in such a case may be nothing more than a road to a non-indigenous relationship.[219]

In relation to North American church planting, it could be noted that the "foreignness of the church which is the source of attraction to unbelievers," contemporary music, casual dress, use of technology, marketing, may mislead many Church leaders into believing the church is indigenous. In reality, however, the people are attending and joining because of the novelty.

International missionaries and missiologists for years have been refuting the notion of importing Western cultural constraints onto new congregations. Over a century ago, John L. Nevius questioned the practice of projecting missionary structures onto a new congregation and encouraged examining the Scriptures for the organizational principles. Nevius declared:

> Is it not this, that practical experience seems to point to the conclusion that present forms of church organization in the West are not to be, at least without some modification, our guides in the founding of infant churches in a heathen land? If it be asked, What then is to be our guide? I answer, The teachings of the New Testament. If it be further asked, Are we to infer, then, that all the forms of church organization in the West are at variance with Scripture teaching? I answer, By no means. . . . The all-important question is, What do the Scriptures teach respecting church organization? Do they lay down a system with fixed and unvarying rules and usages, to be observed at all times and under all circumstances? or a system based on general principles, purposely flexible and readily adapting itself, under the guidance of God's Spirit and providence and common sense, to all the conditions in which the Church can be placed? I believe the latter is the true supposition.[220]

Allen also admonished missionaries to avoid projecting their own structures and organizations onto the new congregations. He said:

The missionary can observe the rule that no organization should be introduced which the people cannot understand and maintain. He need not begin by establishing buildings; he need not begin by importing foreign books and foreign ornaments of worship. The people can begin as they can with what they have. As they feel the need of organization and external conveniences they will begin to seek about for some way of providing them.[221]

Though believing that there is a place for various institutions in peasant churches, while discussing church planting in peasant societies, Paul G. Hiebert and Eloise Hiebert Meneses admonished against cultural projection. They observed:

On the social level, western [sic] leaders have a culturally shaped drive to create formal, highly organized institutions. We create roles such as teacher, doctor, nurse, and preacher, organize committees, set goals, pay leaders, and formulate rules. This tendency to high organization can have a negative effect on church planting. First, we are in danger of creating specialized institutions the people cannot maintain. . . . Second, the hidden message behind bureaucratic organizations is that life is divided into segments and specialists are needed in each. Medical care is entrusted to doctors, education to teachers, and church ministries to trained pastors. There is little room in this model for an empowered laity.[222]

While discussing church planting in band societies, elsewhere, Hiebert and Meneses noted that church planters must separate the gospel from their own culture. They noted that one important principle in ministering to bands is to distinguish between the gospel and our own culture. They note:

We naturally assume that Christianity is what we believe and practice; consequently, we expect converts in other cultures to do the same. We translate our songs into their language, expect them to listen to sermons based on logic, and teach them how to elect a pastor democratically. We are surprised and confused when they say that to become Christian, they must leave their own culture. . . . The church needs to adapt its modes of organization to the social practices of people as far as biblical teaching allows. In many ways the loose, egalitarian nature of band organization is more compatible with Christian teaching than the western Christian bureaucratic, pragmatic, and management-by-objective type of leadership that we have borrowed from the world.[223]

Murray attributed this projection of church organization onto a new congregation, to a variety of elements. He noted, however, that the end result tends to be a cloned congregation, rather than a newly planted community of believers.

I suspect that the creativity needed to engage in such ecclesiological renewal is already present among contemporary church planters, but that this is frequently stifled by inadequate training in the process of theological reflection and contextualization, and such pressures as time-related goals and denominational expectations. The result is all too often that churches are *cloned* rather than being planted. Cloning, the exact duplication of an organism is a technique once associated primarily with science fiction, and the scary notion of producing human beings through replication rather than reproduction. . . . In the context of church planting, then, cloning describes the process of replicating the structures, style, ethos, activities and focus of one congregation in another. The location of the church may change, but its shape remains the same.[224]

The alternative to the two harmful ecclesiological paradigms facing North American church planters and hindering spontaneous expansion is an ecclesiology which begins with the Scriptures, and in light of the target's culture, allows for the development of a reproducible church planting methodology. This alternative is a biblical ecclesiological paradigm (see Figure 3).

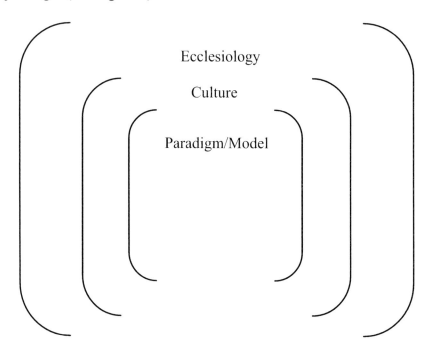

Figure 3. Biblical Ecclesiological Paradigm

As previously noted, Brock emphasized the need for the church planter to begin with a healthy theology. By beginning the church planting process at the proper starting point, a biblical ecclesiology, the potential for church multiplication increases. He also observed:

The resounding conclusion is that a fresh New Testament theology must pervade the life of an indigenous church planter. What one believes about the Bible, salvation, ministry, and the church, as well as other great biblical teachings, is very important. The strategy employed in planting and nurturing a church will depend greatly upon what a person believes. The planter's belief about planting a reproducing church will be reflected in his strategy.[225]

The church planter must develop a clear understanding of the nature and purpose of the Church, before attempting to plant a church. Until the questions, about the nature of the Church and the mission of the Church are answered satisfactory in light of New Testament teachings, then the possibility of adopting a pragmatic or a paternalistic ecclesiology exists.[226]

In relation to the above biblical exercise, the church planter must also come to understand the irreducible ecclesiological minimum that must be present for a church to be a church. By understanding the nature and purpose of the church, from a biblical perspective, the church planter will come to understand the least amount of components necessary for the church to exist.[227] It is this irreducible ecclesiological minimum that must be translated in church planting to the target group. Anything less than this minimum produces something other than a New Testament congregation. Anything more than this minimum, though not necessarily heretical, begins to run the risk of hindering the ability of the new believers to multiply themselves.

Since it is impossible to become completely objective while conducting research, the danger of developing a biblical ecclesiology intertwined with cultural values is always present. Despite this challenge, through proper hermeneutics, it is possible to make distinctions between the New Testament ecclesiological prescriptions and the Western Church's description. The result is that which can be contextualized into any given society. John E. Apheh noted, "It is imperative that a cross-cultural church planter be able to understand what it means to separate his culture from his message and communicate instead a contextualized message to his hearers."[228] Tom Steffen made a similar observation when he encouraged church planters to learn to think long term as well as short term. Steffen declares:

> We must take time to reflect and rectify what we're doing, or plan to spend significant time later doing the same. We must learn to define the gospel, guard it, and strip it of cultural clothes. We need to ask ourselves what components of the message are nonnegotiable, and how we can eliminate cultural biases from the message.[229]

Nicholls offered a pattern towards healthy contextualization. He noted:

> There is always a dynamic tension between the supra-cultural universals of the church common to churches worldwide, and the cultural variables peculiar to each national church. In relation to the supra-cultural nature of the church as the body of Christ there must be a "formal correspondence" among all churches to the divinely appointed concept of the church as given in the Scriptures. In relation to the particular cultures in which the church is contextualized we expect the gospel to make a dynamic impact on their design for living equivalent to the impact that the biblical people of God made on their own societies. Unless the creative tension is maintained between the "formal correspondence" of the universals and the "dynamic equivalence" of cultural variables, there will be no true contextualization of the church.[230]

It is difficult to separate a biblical understanding of the nature and purpose of the Church from a biblical understanding of the Holy Spirit. Along with a biblical ecclesiology, the church planter must have a biblical pneumatology. For it is by a proper understanding of the Church and the Holy Spirit that the church planter can manifest a missionary faith required for the spontaneous expansion of the Church.[231]

Allen understood that most missionaries of his day feared the notion of spontaneous expansion. North American church planters face a similar fear. In an article entitled, "Spontaneous Expansion: The Terror of Missionaries," he wrote of the solution to overcoming the ungodly fear. Allen taught:

> For myself, then, I faced this terrible monster and I found here my answer to it: it is a compound of fear of the weakness of men which ignores the strength of Christ, and trust in the power of our own authority which ignores the grace of Christ; and I decided once for all that it was a monster which the Christian man ought to face and to defy in the name of Christ. Then I began to perceive its weakness. I saw that we did not escape from the evils with which it threatened us, moral and spiritual failure in our converts, by our exercise of authority. I saw that spontaneous expansion is not for a Church guarded and protected by a long training under foreign direction only, but for the most infant Church as a very condition of its well-being in Christ; I saw that spontaneous expansion was necessary for our faith and for the glory of Christ, that the power might be of God, not of us. I wish that all missionaries would face this question and decide once for all, whether they believe that the spontaneous expansion of the Church is a thing to be looked forward to only in ages to come, whilst now they must rely upon their training and discipline and government to prepare the Church for the future liberty; or whether they believe that we

must go forth in the faith of Christ and expect spontaneous expansion now, to-day; and abandoning our control, give full authority to the native Churches, and be content to assist them and to encourage them.[232]

Until church planters develop a healthy biblical ecclesiology and pneumatology and learn to translate the ecclesiological irreducible minimum to the target group, spontaneous church multiplication will always remain a future possibility.

Shenk's words are appropriate to close this section.

We can only pray that the church everywhere increasingly will develop an identity that consists of two things. First, the church exists for mission to the world, and its identity is authentic only when it is worked out in genuine missionary encounter. Second, the church always stands under the judgment and mandate of the gospel. It is the church's privilege to be the bearer of the life and love of Jesus in the world, to be the instrument of good news. But it is always incumbent on the church to allow the fullness of that life to be expressed rather than seeking to reduce it to fit a formula convenient to the times and context.[233]

Strategy Shifts

The second paradigm shift necessary to prepare the Church for spontaneous expansion is a shift from a strategy of church planting by addition to a strategy of church multiplication through reproduction. As Samuel D. Faircloth observed: "Church planting in any situation must make a high priority of the goal of *reproduction*—the multiplication of local churches throughout the land. Church planters must not be satisfied with the mere birth of an infant congregation."[234]

Strategies need to focus on the church planter modeling reproduction at all levels in the church planting process. Following a discussion of the philosophy of modeling reproduction, this section will note three areas of the strategic shift that are needed: multiplication through disciple-making; multiplication through leadership development; and phase-out activities.

Reproduction Modeled at All Levels

The unifying theme that is found throughout the three areas of the needed strategic shift is that each area is founded upon the philosophy that the church planter must model reproduction before the target people. Brock noted:

A church's view of reproduction will be learned early. Every action of the church planter becomes part of a lesson learned by the church, even during its birth. The planter's relationship to the church can be likened to a parent-child relationship. The child is learning from every action of the parent even though the parent isn't consciously teaching and the child isn't consciously learning. (Sometimes through his actions the parent teaches the child things he never intended to.) If the church planter is fully aware of the need for "thinking reproducible" in everything done, he will more likely plant a church capable of reproduction.[235]

What then are the areas in which the church planter should be "thinking reproducible?" Brock discusses at least three critical areas.

First, the planter must "'think reproducible'—*in the use of material things.*"[236] All the material items that the church planter uses to plant a church convey to the people that those items are necessary for a church to be planted. If the church planter uses a guitar, then the use of a guitar will be seen as a necessary component in church planting. If the church planter uses a high-quality promotional mailing, then a promotional mailing will be seen as a necessary component in church planting:

The planter should not use anything which the people cannot provide for themselves. . . . Long before the new church thinks of reproducing itself in another place, it must decide how to continue and how to attract and feed the people without the things used by the church planter. The church members will be tempted to give up because they can't do it like the planter did. The material "crutches" used by the missionary appeared to be a blessing, but stymied, stunted, irreproducible growth becomes a tragedy. . . . The planter should take himself, his gospel seed, and little else.[237]

Related to the use of material things is the notion of importing ecclesiological structures onto the new church. As previously noted, this importation also hinders reproduction. The reproducibility theory states that as the number and/or complexity of imported ecclesiological structures increase, the overall reproduction potential for the people to reproduce that model of church decreases (see Figure 4).

The second area in which the church planter must "'think reproducible'" is "*in every detail of strategy used.*"[238] The strategy must be contextualized to the target group, and capable of being used by the group to start other churches. David J. Hesselgrave noted that church planters should take advantage of the study of culture and missions history, but "If our dependence is on the overall strategy and the method of its

328

implementation rather than on the wisdom and power of the Holy Spirit, we cannot claim to be true to New Testament precedent nor will our witness be as effective as was that of those first-century believers."[239]

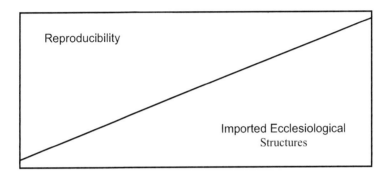

Figure 4. Model Reproducibility Potential

By using a non-reproducible strategy, the church planter "has made it very difficult for that church to plant another church."[240] The technicality of the strategy will affect the ability of the congregation to reproduce the strategy (see Figure 5). The reproducibility theory states that as technicality increases, the reproducibility potential decreases.

The third area in which the church planter should "think reproducible" is "*in the kind of leadership used*."[241] Though the concept of leadership will be addressed later in this article, here it is necessary to note that the model of leadership used by the planter will affect the actions of the leaders raised up from the new church. According to Brock the group should shortly be able to reproduce everything the planter does in teaching, praying, and singing.[242]

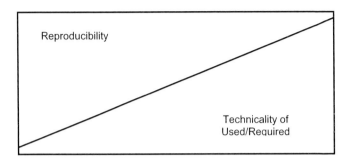

Figure 5. Strategy Reproducibility Potential

In regard to leadership, as the technicality of the strategy used goes up, reproducibility of the movement goes down. This truth points out the danger of using technology and training above that of most of the people in the group served. Reproducibility is enhanced by methods most of the people are capable of using.

If the church planter manifests a leadership style which can only be developed through years of theological education and ministerial experience, then few within the new church will desire or even be capable of taking over the leadership responsibility of the church. While advocating an indirect form of leadership, Brock offered the following statements to show how leadership style can limit church reproduction:

> Direct leadership is often leader-centered. Indirect leadership centers attention on the group. The spotlight is on the leader in direct leadership, while it is on the group in indirect leadership. Many churches have been planted by church planters using direct leadership methods. This often includes traditional evangelistic crusades. This kind of leadership may have its

place in church planting, but because such a critical spotlight beams upon one person, the leader, the number of people capable of such successful leadership is very limited. . . . It is quickly apparent that many ordinary people would be disqualified. Most will not have the talent to plant churches if strong direct leadership is required.[243]

Again, the reproducibility theory states that as the technicality of leadership style increases, the leadership reproduction potential decreases (see Figure 6).

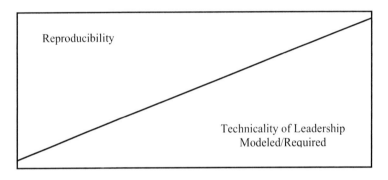

Reproducibility

Technicality of Leadership
Modeled/Required

Figure 6. Leadership Reproducibility Potential

Three Areas of Strategy Shift

At least three areas constitute the needed strategy shift. First, strategies need to focus on church multiplication through disciple-making at the individual level.[244] As Charles L. Chaney experienced while working with the Illinois Baptist State Association, "We were convicted that churches always begin small. If you multiply churches in your fellowship, you must expect to have small churches around."[245] Though it has been argued that there are several advantages to planting large churches from the beginning, it is highly unlikely that those churches will ever experience church multiplication.[246]

Second, and closely related to the first area of the strategy shift, is the need to focus on church multiplication through leadership development. As Logan has noted, there is a great need to raise up leaders from the harvest and then send them back into the harvest.[247] As long as the professional clergy is needed for church planting to occur, spontaneous expansion will always remain a future possibility.

The third area of the strategy shift is related to the concept of phase-out activities. Church planters need to consider planting several churches and raising up indigenous leadership to oversee those churches. Phase-out passes the baton of leadership from that of the church planters to the new believers.[248]

Church multiplication through making disciples.

Instead of thinking first about reproducing the macro structures which include, but are not limited to, the ever popular seeker-sensitive services, church planters should begin by thinking about the "multiplication of the smallest units of Christianity" and "then congregationalizing what God is doing. Building it from the bottom up, not from the top down."[249] Just as Allen advocated that the missionary should place priority on evangelism, contemporary church planters should do likewise. Brock noted that even before the establishment of indigenous churches *"The first objective is to lead individuals to saving, transforming faith in Jesus Christ as the only hope of an abundant life."* Reginaldo Kruklis resounds a similar ideology:

We do not preach church planting. We preach Jesus and Him crucified. We don't go around the world inviting people to church, as good as that may be. We are calling people to know Jesus, Savior and Lord. We call them to be part of His family. We preach the kingdom of God. He provides the answers to our problems and challenges regarding church planting and corrects our preconceived ideas. The emphasis must be on the fact that Jesus is God, and He is risen from the dead. We must make a fresh declaration of dependability on the power of Jesus. That is the beginning and the end of our mission.[250]

As with the New Testament example, the church planter should make disciples and then congregationalize those disciples, regardless of their numerical size, property owned, or lack of organization and education. When the church planter begins with evangelism at the individual level, an ideology is created within the newly converted that advocates personal evangelism as a healthy and reproducible strategy for planting churches. When the church planter begins with event evangelism, in all likelihood, he or she is modeling a non-reproducible disciple-making strategy.

Logan, while discussing the harvest model of church planting (also understood as planting at the grass-roots level or in a pioneer territory), urged church planters that as they design a culturally appropriate planting process, to refrain from a top-down approach:

> Most commonly, I think when missionaries think about planting a church they often are thinking congregational in their structure. And so we are talking and thinking finished product in the sense of very well educated pastors, with church buildings, all sorts of kinds of programs, and a fairly sophisticated level of leadership in the midst of all of that. And

if that's the starting point, [it] can lead you to some inappropriate designs when you are thinking about church planting.

Rather than start at the top, I would suggest you start at the grassroots. And that you think through, "What really are the essential activities." And even translate it one step further, "What are the ordinary people going to be doing?" "What's the ordinary believer going to be doing in this new church?" You know, what are the essential activities that they are going to do individually. What are they going to be doing in their family? What are they going to be doing together in their small groups? How are they going to be ministering to each other? How are these groups going to be functioning in the communities in which they are found?

And so, instead of thinking about a top-down model, think about a bottom-up model. Because in church planting, especially with the harvest model, you're building it unit-by-unit, piece-by-piece from the ground up. And so you're letting the church emerge, but you have to clarify what are the essential activities.[251]

Church multiplication through leadership development

Leadership development must not only be reproducible by the new church, but leadership development must also be a process of multiplication. The goal is to see leaders multiply leaders. Without leaders, spontaneous expansion is impossible.

In the field of leadership development in new churches, Logan's research and philosophy surpasses all others. His passion is to see leaders raised up from the harvest to be sent back into the harvest for disciple making. It is this ongoing process of leadership multiplication which is crucial to church multiplication.

Logan noted the need for leadership multiplication when he stated:

> When you see thousands and tens of thousands of new people coming to know Christ, it quickly outstrips your capacity to be able to service those people and to serve those people with existing leaders. There must be a way to raise up leaders from the harvest. And so church multiplication movements utilize leadership development strategies that are integrally woven into the evangelism process.[252]

When the spontaneous expansion of the church is occurring, potential leaders
are being trained for multiplication as they are coming to Christ. A strategic shift in how leadership is understood and developed for North American church planting must occur. Logan's comments note the problem with the traditional understanding of teaching leadership development in the classroom.

> What is learned first, is learned best. And the second principle is what is learned first shapes all future learning. And I would also say, the way in which you've learned you'll have a tendency to reproduce that in the next place that you go. Thus, that's why the classroom model in particular, is one of the worst models for pre-service training of leadership. Here me say "pre-service training" because I'm all for higher education. But training people in a classroom to do evangelism and disciple-making is like trying to teach people how to swim in a classroom. You know the way to learn how to swim is to get into the water, try some stuff, then get some instruction, then go try some stuff, get some more instruction.[253]

If a church leader must be required to have a formal theological education, then church multiplication will be limited by educational requirements. If a church leader must leave his job and become a full-time paid pastor, then the number of congregations that can financially support a full-time pastor will limit church multiplication.

Leadership cannot be limited to a professional clergy. In fact, professional church leaders should be seen as the exception, rather than the norm. If the spontaneous expansion of the North American church is dependent upon the number of professional clergymen who can pastor new churches, then the expansion will be greatly limited to the number of available clergymen. What about formal theological education? For Logan, formal training is more of an in-service experience, rather than a pre-service experience. He noted:

> Formal training is a good option for many people. But we find that it's more effective to use it as an in-service training after they're already out being a pastor, church planter, or a missionary and it simply enhances their development through theological reflection. I know from the teaching that I do in the seminary, that those that are involved actively in ministry ask far more perceptive and relevant questions than those that have not had ministry experience. And so I encourage people wherever possible to get formal training, but do it after God has already validated and proven your ministry. And after you've already been a proven leader, and after you already have the basic orientations down through the non-formal or informal ways of training, and then take one class a quarter and keep going after that new degree.[254]

As seen in the reproducibility theory in Figure 6, as the technicality of leadership required increases, the reproduction potential of leaders decreases.

A much better approach to leadership development is on-the-job training, beginning with the church planter's initial contact with the individual or group. Even prior to the group's conversion, by modeling a reproducible leadership style, the church planter begins the training. While looking to Jesus as a model, Logan stated that church planters should allow the people to start where they are and help them continue to be involved in the process. Then raise them up as leaders as they do the evangelizing and discipling and grow into the role. But do not strive toward more than what they themselves can do.[255]

By beginning with where the people are in their spiritual journey, the church planter's leadership style is to be influencing them to influence others. Logan states that as long as the leader is influencing persons to move more toward Christ and toward the will of Christ in their lives, the exact point of the leader on the maturity scale does not matter. Less mature people can perform acts of leadership and lead. Witnessing in its very simplest form is a leadership function. Because the Christian already knows more and is [in] the Kingdom of light he/she can lead at least in that area.[256]

This process of beginning leadership training with people where they are in their spiritual journey is very beneficial for spontaneous expansion. As Logan noted, leadership develops through on-the-job training and faithfulness to Christ. This process allows for the development of valuable leaders, as the church is being planted and experiencing growth.[257]

Phase-out activities

Tom Steffen has significantly developed the concept of phase-out activities. While serving as a missionary in the Philippines, Steffen was discouraged when he noticed that after almost 25 years his mission agency had not "successfully phased out of their ministries so that nationals could control their own churches." [258] After conducting research and analyzing the data, Steffen noticed a number of factors that contributed to this problem. Upon further investigation, he came to realize that the church planters' strategies lacked an integrated approach which brought closure to the missionaries' involvement.[259] Steffen wrote:

> Individual team members, possibly because of the lack of an overall field strategy, tended to focus more on "phase-in" activities (e.g., evangelism and discipleship) than on "phase-out" activities (e.g., activities that would empower nationals to develop leadership among themselves with an eye toward ministry that reproduces). Team members, following the lead of field leaders, followed suit. They implemented the piecemeal activities individually instead of taking the stated objective of planting churches that reproduce and then integrate all the various activities, directing them toward that one goal. Team members tended to view ministry with "phase-in eyes" rather than "phase-out eyes."[260]

Though phase-out activities also entail raising up leaders from the harvest. These Local leaders take leadership responsibility for the development to another level by when the church starters completely turning over the congregation to the believers. The church planter begins the process with the end in mind. Steffen defines phase-out "as programmed absences by the church planters that encourage nationals to take up their rightful responsibilities as leaders and multipliers of the church planting movement."[261] Within this process the church planters are to "*work themselves out of a job, but not out of relationships.*" [262] Just as following his departure, Paul maintained contact with the churches he started, contemporary

338

church planters should do likewise. For church planters, phase-out activities must be determined prior to arriving on the field.[263]

The reason the phase-out activities are to begin before the church planters enter into the ministry context is because

> Responsible phase-out begins with a *strategy of closure* for the overall people group, and for each subculture within that community. Well-honed phase-out strategies call for planting clusters of churches that have a contagious enthusiasm for reproducing themselves. Moreover, it encourages the national believers immediate freedom to execute this. . . . Responsible phase-out strategies create believers whose allegiance remains on the Holy Spirit, not team members.[264]

Obviously, the importance of phase-out activities preclude the assumption that an incarnational approach to church planting is necessary in postmodern societies. Because most postmoderns long for community, some fear that phase-out activities will sacrifice the community that the church has with the church planters.[265] The actual truth is that phase-out activities do not sacrifice the relationships between the church planters and the new church, but rather strengthen the relationships.

First, phase-out activities keep the church planters from viewing the new church as spiritually inferior and incapable of standing on their own as a congregation. Church planters believe in the power of the Holy Spirit to oversee the believers, and look forward to the day when the group will take over the leadership. Though the new believers will always be the spiritual children of the church planters, they will not always be viewed as infants in need of adult supervision. Church planters hasten the day when the new church will work alongside them in multiplying other churches. Abandonment is never an option with the use of phase-out activities. As Steffen wrote:

> Church planters should inform the nationals about their departure plans in a judicious manner. Like Jesus, they must inform them at appropriate times, revealing only what is necessary for the moment. Church planters must also convince them that the departure will be to their advantage. To overextend the stay would be to steal the nationals' rightful power to grow and reproduce on their own.[266]

Continuing, Steffen noted:

> In the majority of cross-cultural church plants, an abrupt pull-out will not be the most appropriate response to reactions regarding the departure announcement. Following Jesus' post-resurrection example, church planters should return periodically to visit the nationals. They should bring encouragement, answer questions, review basic biblical truths, and have some meals together. This will rekindle the nationals' enthusiasm as they assist a second generation of disciples to mature in Christ and ministry, and reach out to the world. Programmed absences will help the disciples overcome the feeling of abandonment.[267]

The church and the church planters will always be a family.

Second, phase-out activities strengthen the community and fellowship of the new church. Since leaders are being raised up and the church planters are gradually doing less and less direct ministry, the church must rely on one another. A dependent mentality focused on the church planters, is swiftly converted into a dependent mentality focused on the Holy Spirit and one another. The community must grow together as they reach others for Christ.

Methodological Shifts

The field of church planting is action-oriented. As a methodology for evangelization, the world of church planting naturally contains numerous "how-to" books.[268] Methods in and of themselves are not an evil, but a necessity. The practioners are the experts and need to be heard by the Church. Though there is a place for the academic study of church planting and missions, the classroom cannot be an end in itself. A problem exists unless actual churches are being multiplied. Academic study is not enough. Church planting is a pragmatic field; the Church must know what is and is not working to multiply churches. Thom S. Rainer observed:

> We must not view pragmatism as an inherently evil approach. Christians make decisions daily based on "what best works" without violating scriptural truths. The danger, rather, is replacing theology with pragmatism.[269]

As long as the Scriptures take precedence over the methodology and the target's culture, church planters are beginning in the correct place.

The purpose of this section is to address some of the needed methodological shifts to prepare the North American Church for spontaneous expansion. The first shift discussed is the erroneous assumption that because one methodology worked well to produce a certain model of church in one region, it will work well in other similar regions.[270] North American culture is far from being homogenous. Though cultures may appear similar because of like socio-economic attributes, ethnicity, and language; word-views and lifestyle create much diversity.[271] Edward R. Dayton and David A. Fraser observed:

> We must approach our evangelism with the realistic awareness that we know very little about how to sow the seed, or water and harvest the crop. We will have to do far more than simply sensitize ourselves to the cultural dimensions so that we can know how best to plug in our standardized solutions. Completely novel approaches which have never been taught in seminary or college and which are not written up in any missiological journal may have to be devised. We need to be ready and flexible to do just that.[272]

Just because a methodology worked well to plant a church, does not mean that
methodology will work well to plant a church which continually multiplies itself. As Brock noted:

> The indigenous church is a goal and not a method. The goal remains fixed and attainable by various methods. It should be strongly emphasized that certain indigenous methods lead more easily to the goal.[273]

Though a plethora of methodologies exists, prayerful discernment, flexibility, and experimentation are required to determine what will work best to result in church multiplication. A shift is required from the ideology that assumes just because there is action, therefore, the best thing is being accomplished. Too much of the North American Church has substituted actions for faithfulness. Just because churches are being planted does not necessary mean the Church is best accomplishing the Great Commission. The Church needs to practice a critical discernment.

In light of the necessary discernment, the second methodological shift needed is a shift toward much more research in the area of North American church planting. Literature and seminars abound with various isolated church planting success stories and anecdotal evidence.[274] Though these illustrative elements are good for praise, morale, and encouragement, research needs to be conducted to determine what God is blessing with rapid growth, moderate growth, slow growth, and no growth.

History has shown that many will uncritically adopt the methodologies of the few isolated success stories that occur in the realm of church planting. Whenever this adoption occurs, the exceptional methodologies become a panacea, and those who do not follow the exceptions become the exceptions in and of themselves. What is exceptional methodology becomes the norm until many realize that the exception is just that, an exception.

In conjunction with the need for research is the need for Church leaders to encourage innovation in church planting. Church planters should be free to try new and different approaches to making disciples. There is much in church planting circles that discourage innovation. As Murray noted, "Time pressures, denominational expectations, the concern for numerical success, and the temptation to clone rather than plant all militate against such innovation. A further problem is the tendency to marginalize or patronize creative alternatives, to regard these new forms of church life as interesting but peripheral experiments, and to continue to endorse as "normal" forms of church life with which we are more familiar."[275]

The words of Dayton and Fraser need to be heeded:

In the history of debates about methods one thing is certain: those who innovate a new and successful methodology invariably carry the day and the next generation of evangelists. It is difficult, in a pragmatic world, to argue against results, especially when one cannot show equal or better results from alternative methods. Logically, it is also difficult to try to argue that there is little or no connection between mean and ends, even if they are evangelistic means and ends. We may not know a great deal about how methods are causally connected to the conversion of unbelievers and the growth rates of churches, but we cannot conclude that methods are irrelevant to the communication of Christ or the conversion of the lost. We reap what we sow here as in the other departments of human endeavor. We *know* methods are relevant because of the experience and study of the church world-wide.

Yet we cannot be so naïve or messianic about our methods as Finney and some of his descendents appear to be. There is far more to evangelization than simply the right use of the right means. We are not dealing with the operation of physical and organic laws, but with people who are far less uniform and predictable than plants. We have already alluded to the fact that human factors are involved (personality, competencies, gifts, rapport, etc.) in evangelism in a way that can have major impact on the effectiveness of a given methodology. However, we approach the question of methods, we must be humbly aware that they are only *one* of the components of a strategy. True, they are an important and critical part, but they are not sufficient in themselves to guarantee effectiveness or success. The right methods do not insure a large response to the gospel.[276]

The third methodological shift that is needed in the area of church planting is that methodologies need to be evaluated based on at least three areas: (1) the translation of the gospel and the ecclesiological irreducible minimum, (2) the multiplication of disciples and leadership, and (3) the reproducibility potential. As noted above, uncritical methodological evaluation is detrimental to church planting in general and spontaneous expansion in particular.

First, methodologies must be evaluated on how well they translate the gospel and the ecclesiological irreducible minimum. Do the methodologies add cultural requirements to the biblical teachings concerning the nature of the gospel or the churches? These additions can demand belief and practice that are not scriptural but rather cultural. An example of this error would be the early missionaries in Hawaii demanding New England type clothing for people living in the tropics. Church planters must practice excellent hermeneutics in determining the difference between Scriptural prescriptions and cultural additions.

Second, methodologies must be evaluated on how well they multiply disciples and leaders. Are disciples being made and leaders raised up from the harvest? Do the church planters expect the new believers to be involved in personal evangelism immediately following their conversions? Is this expectation being communicated to the people in both verbal and nonverbal manners? Are the new believers required to assist in the ministry from the very beginning? Are the church planters giving the new believers more and more responsibilities? Are the church planters practicing phase-out activities?

Third, methodologies must be evaluated based on the reproducibility potential. This potential for church reproduction diminishes with an increase in the technicality of the approach the church planters use. An increase in the cultural expectations added to the gospel and the ecclesiological irreducible minimum likewise adds to the difficulty of reproducibility. Are the church planters using a methodology that can be reproduced by the ordinary individuals of the target group? Are the church planters modeling a simple and reproducible leadership style? Does the methodology require resources that the target group cannot provide for themselves or would have a difficult time providing for themselves?

Conclusion

From a humanistic level,[277] changes must occur within North American church planting circles before spontaneous expansion of the Church becomes a possibility. The most important and immediate shift required is theological in nature. Church planters must develop a healthy biblical ecclesiology rather than a list of proof-texts concerning the Church, a pragmatic ecclesiology, or a paternalistic ecclesiology. Within this biblical ecclesiology, the nature and purpose of the Church must be addressed. A corollary to this ecclesiological development is the need to develop a biblical pneumatology addressing the nature and purpose of the Holy Spirit. It is only by returning to the Scriptures that church planters will develop the missionary faith as advocated by Allen.

Strategy shifts are also needed for the possibility of spontaneous expansion to occur. Logan's philosophy of reproduction needs to permeate church planting circles. North American Church leaders would be wise to learn more from Logan's harvest paradigm. For the church planters, reproduction must be modeled at all levels. The reproduction of disciples and leaders is of the utmost importance. In conjunction with this philosophy, church planters need to incorporate phase-out activities into their strategies. The new churches must stand on their own to reproduce on their own.

The necessary methodological shifts reflect the values derived from a biblical ecclesiology and pneumatology and a reproducible philosophy and practice. Present and future methodologies must be subjected to critical analysis in light of the necessary theological and philosophical parameters. More research is needed in the area of church planting. Instead of relying on exceptions and anecdotal evidence, the Church needs to better understand what is effectively working and not working the area of spontaneous expansion.

Endnotes

[169] Dr. James B. Slack, Global Evangelism and Church Growth of International Mission Board, Second Edition
March 1999. Used by permission of the author.

[170] The International Mission Board of the Southern Baptist Convention utilizes the term "Strategy Coordinator" for a person who designs and coordinates church planting efforts in a designated region. The North American Mission Board uses the term "Strategic Catalyzer" for a person who performs a similar function in North America. See, Joe Hernandez' chapter in this book entitled: "Rapid Church Multiplication."

[171] Spradley, James P., *The Ethnographic Interview* (New York: Holt, Rinehart and Winston, 1979).

[172] Ibid., 3.

[173] USA Today, February 18, 1999, 1B.

[174] Winter, Ralph & Hawthorne, Steven (Editors), *Perspectives* article "The Willowbank Report: The Lausanne Committee for World Evangelization" (Pasadena: William Carey Press)pp. 483-506.

[175] Winter, Ralph & Hawthorne, Steven, Editors, *Perspectives On The World Christian Movement* (Pasadena: William Carey Press, 1999), 538 and 539 of the article "On The Cutting Edge" by C. Peter Wagner..

[176] Hesselgrave, David J., *Planting Churches Cross-Culturally* (Grand Rapids: Baker, 1980), 177.

[177] Kraft, Charles H., *Anthropology For Christian Witness* (New York: Orbis Books, 1996), 51-53.

[178] Wright, N.T., *The New Testament And The People Of God* (Minneapolis: Fortress Press, 1992)

[179]Apeh, John, *Social Structure & Church Planting* (Shippensburg, PA: Companion Press), 9 and 10.

[180]Hiebert, Paul G. and Meneses, Eloise Hiebert, *Incarnational Ministry: Planting Churches in Band, Tribal, Peasant, and Urban Societies* (Grand Rapids: Baker, 1995), 13 and 41-42.

[181]Warren, Rick, *The Purpose Driven Church: Growth Without Compromising Your Message & Mission* (Grand Rapids: Zondervan, 1995), 162, 164-166.

[182]Kraft, 381.

[183]Keitzman, Dale W. & Smalley, William A, "The Missionary's Role in Cultural Change" An article in *Perspectives* (Pasadena: William Carey Press), 480-482.

[184]Unless otherwise noted, I will always refer to the local church with a lowercase "c" and the universal, national, or denominational church with an uppercase "C".

[185]Robert E. Logan and Steven L. Ogne, "Expand Vision for Church Multiplication," in *Churches Planting Churches* (n.p.: ChurchSmart Resources, 1995), cassette.

[186]Donald A. McGavran, *Understanding Church Growth* (Grand Rapids, MI: William B. Eerdmans Publishing Company, 1970), 216.

[187]Numerous Christian publications have revealed the heightened receptivity that affects postmodern cultures to spiritual needs and issues. For example, see Stanley J. Grenz, *A Primer on Postmodernism* (Grand Rapids, MI; Cambridge, U.K.: William B. Eerdmans Publishing Company, 1996); Tom Beaudoin, *Virtual Faith: The Irreverent Spiritual Quest of Generation X* (San Francisco, CA: Jossey-Bass Publishers, 1998);Thom S. Rainer, *The Bridger Generation* (Nashville, TN: Broadman and Holman Publishers, 1997); Todd Hahn and David Verhaagen, *Reckless Hope: Understanding and Reaching Baby Busters* (Grand Rapids, MI: Baker Books, 1996);Todd Hahn and David Verhaagen, *GenXers After God: Helping a Generation Pursue Jesus* (Grand Rapids, MI: Baker Books, 1998); Dawson McAllister with Pat Springle, *Saving the Millennial Generation* (Nashville, TN: Thomas Nelson Publishers, 1999); Jimmy Long, *Generation Hope: A Strategy for Reaching the Postmodern Generation* (Downers Grove, IL: InterVarsity Press, 1997); Kevin Graham Ford, *Jesus for a New Generation: Putting the Gospel in the Language of Xers* (Downers Grove, IL: InterVarsity Press, 1995); Leonard Sweet, *Soul Tsunami: Sink or Swim in New Millennium Culture* (Grand Rapids, MI: Zondervan Publishing House, 1999).

[188]Wilbert R. Shenk, *Write the Vision: The Church Renewed* (Valley Forge, PA: Trinity Press International, 1995), 63-64.

[189]For example, much contemporary evangelism is event evangelism based on the unregenerate coming to a seeker service and usually listening to a monological sermon. Many people do not desire to participate in this type of experience. On another note, it is interesting to observe that much of what is currently being hailed as contemporary innovations in church planting and church growth circles closely parallel many of the contemporary innovations of the crusade evangelists of yesteryear (i.e., Charles Finney). Though the methodologies have worked since the nineteenth century, past success does not guarantee their continued effectiveness.

[190]McGavran, *Understanding Church Growth*, 232.

[191]Jonathan Stuart Campbell, "The Translatability of Christian Community: An Ecclesiology for Postmodern Cultures and Beyond" (Ph.D. diss., Fuller Theological Seminary, 1999), 297-98.

[192]Robert Logan, (classroom lecture, MC 525—*Starting and Multiplying Churches*, 27 January 1998), audiocassette.

[193]Stuart Murray, *Church Planting: Laying Foundations* (Carlisle, United Kingdom: Paternoster Press, 1998), 128.

[194]Eddie Gibbs, *Church Next: Quantum Changes in How We Do Ministry* (Downers Grove, IL: InterVarsity Press, 2000), 27.

[195]Ibid., 36.

[196]Shenk, *Write the Vision*, 90-91.

[197]Gibbs, *Church Next*, 33.

[198]Charles Brock, *The Principles and Practice of Indigenous Church Planting* (Nashville, TN: Broadman Press, 1981), 9.

[199]Denton Lotz, "The Holy Spirit and Establishing Churches," in *Five Till Midnight: Church Planting for A.D. 2000 and Beyond*, ed. Tony Cupit (Atlanta, GA: Home Mission Board, 1994), 2.

[200]Research which already has been produced include the following: Charles Van Engen, *God's Missionary People: Rethinking the Purpose of the Local Church* (Grand Rapids, MI: Baker Book House, 1991); Darrell L. Guder, ed., *Missional Church: A Vision for the Sending of the Church in North America* (Grand Rapids, MI; Cambridge, United Kingdom: William B. Eerdmans Publishing Company, 1998); George R. Hunsberger and Craig Van Gelder, eds., *The Church between Gospel and Culture: The Emerging Mission in North America* (Grand Rapids, MI; Cambridge, United Kingdom: William B. Eerdmans Publishing Company, 1996); Craig Van Gelder, ed., *Confident Witness—Changing World: Rediscovering the Gospel in North*

America (Grand Rapids, MI; Cambridge, United Kingdom: William B.
Eerdmans Publishing Company, 1999); Darrell L. Guder, *The Continuing
Conversion of the Church* (Grand Rapids, MI: William B. Eerdmans
Publishing Company, 2000); Craig Van Gelder, *The Essence of the Church:
A Community Created by the Spirit* (Grand Rapids, MI: Baker Books, 2000);
and Jonathan Stuart Campbell, "The Translatability of Christian Community:
An Ecclesiology for Postmodern Cultures and Beyond" (Ph.D. diss., Fuller
Theological Seminary, 1999).

[201]Murray, *Church Planting*, 30.

[202]Aside from other problems, the fallacy committed in the above logic is
that it reveals an assumption that middle-class suburban areas in North
America are fairly homogeneous in nature.

[203]Murray, *Church Planting*, 28.

[204]A note of clarification is necessary. Churches should base all of their
practices on biblical principles as much as possible. In light of culture, there
are some areas in which Scripture is silent and therefore, the regenerate Body
has the liberty to practice as the Spirit guides. The problem arises when
church planters who project contemporary Christian practices onto first
century believers teach congregations poor hermeneutics. It is much better
for a church to practice something just because it is the way they desire to
function and to offer no biblical support for lack of Scriptural evidence,
rather than proof-texting unbiblical practices.

[205]Campbell, "The Translatability of Christian Community," 38.

[206]Paul G. Hiebert, "Planting Churches in North America Today," *Direction*
20, no.2 (Fall 1991): 8.

[207]Os Guinness, *Dining with the Devil: The Megachurch Movement Flirts
with Modernity* (Grand Rapids, MI: Baker Book House, 1993), 79.

[208]Bruce J. Nicholls, *Contextualization: A Theology of Gospel and Culture*
(Downers Grove, IL: InterVarsity Press; Exeter, England: The Paternoster
Press, 1979), 30-31.

[209]For the purpose of discussion, I have listed scriptural consultation as the
last step in this process. In all likelihood, prior to their arrival on the field,
church planters already have Scripture passages in mind that support their
cultural views of the church. The point being made here is that the church
planters' cultural understanding of the church takes precedence over the
scriptural prescription.

[210]Shenk, *Write the Vision*, 73.

[211]Campbell, "The Translatability of Christian Community," 25-26, 29.

[212] Even some groups which began with a counter-denominationalism philosophy in mind have become highly structured and even have become denominations (i.e., Association of Vineyard Churches).

[213] A manifestation of this ideology can be seen in the premature development of a church's web page and name. I am amazed at the number of church planters who develop web sites, names, logos, and promotional pieces even before the churches come into existence. These subtle creations support the argument that a church can be in existence as an institution, but not as a regenerate body of baptized believers.

[214] Shenk, *Write the Vision*, 84-85.

[215] This statement is not to suggest that there is no place for models. Church planters should be familiar with what approaches are working and not working in North America. The problem is when the planter without regard to the Scriptures and the cultural context of the target people determines the model implemented. For a process of selecting an effective church planting model, see Tom A. Steffen, "Selecting a Church Planting Model that Works," *Missiology* 22 (1994): 361-76.

[216] Guder, *Missional Church*, 72.

[217] Nicholls, *Contextualization*, 31.

[218] William A. Smalley, "Cultural Implications of an Indigenous Church," in *Readings in Dynamic Indigeneity*, ed. Charles H. Kraft and Tom N. Wisley (Pasadena, CA: William Carey Library, 1979), 32.

[219] Ibid., 35.

[220] John L. Nevius *Planting and Development of Missionary Churches* (n.p.: The Presbyterian and Reformed Publishing Company, n.d.), 56.

[221] Roland Allen, *Missionary Methods: St. Paul's or Ours?*, American ed. (Grand Rapids, MI: William B. Eerdmans Publishing Company, 1962), 161.

[222] Paul G. Hiebert and Eloise Hiebert Meneses, *Incarnational Ministry: Planting Churches in Band, Tribal, Peasant, and Urban Societies* (Grand Rapids, MI: Baker Books, 1995), 244-45.

[223] Ibid., 77-78.

[224] Murray, *Church Planting*, 124-25.

[225] Brock, *The Principles and Practice of Indigenous Church Planting*, 15.

[226] It is well beyond the scope of this chapter to attempt to answer these questions or attempt to develop some theological framework for church planting. Stuart Murray's *Church Planting: Laying Foundations,* 24-86 and Jonathan Stuart Campbell's Ph.D. dissertation, "The Translatability of Christian Community: An Ecclesiology for Postmodern Cultures and

Beyond," are two excellent works which attempt to address the nature and purpose of the Church in relation to church planting.

[227]In some contemporary church planting circles numerical size is a determining factor as to whether or not a church is considered a legitimate and healthy congregation. Unless some arbitrary critical mass is achieved, then the "group" is viewed as a substandard congregation at best. In other circles, a church is only considered legitimate whenever it "goes public" and has a public worship service. It is commonplace to hear of the birth of the church referred to as the "launching" of the new congregation at this first service.

[228]John E. Apeh, "Socio-anthropological Implications in Cross-cultural Church Planting," *Asian Journal of Theology* 11 (1997): 285.

[229]Tom Steffen, "Flawed Evangelism and Church Planting," *Evangelical Missions Quarterly* 34 (October 1998): 434.

[230]Nicholls, *Contextualization,* 64.

[231]This concept of "missionary faith" is from the thinking of Roland Allen. According to Allen, many missionaries lacked faith in the power of the Holy Spirit to protect, empower, and guide new churches to fulfill their God-given responsibilities. Because of this lack of faith, Allen noted that many missionaries were holding back the growth of the natural expansion of the church by practicing a style of leadership that was heavy-handed and dominating. For more information regarding this notion of faith see my work "An Evaluation of the Systems Approach to North American Church Multiplication Movements of Robert E. Logan in Light of the Missiology of Roland Allen," Ph.D. diss., The Southern Baptist Theological Seminary, 2001, 61-64.

[232]Roland Allen, "Spontaneous Expansion: The Terror of Missionaries," *World Dominion* 4 (September 1926): 222-23.

[233]Wilbert R. Shenk, *Changing Frontiers of Mission* (Maryknoll, NY: Orbis Books, 1999), 189.

[234]Samuel D. Faircloth, *Church Planting for Reproduction* (Grand Rapids, MI: Baker Book House, 1991), 34.

[235]Brock, *The Principles and Practice of Indigenous Church Planting*, 55.

[236]Ibid., 56.

[237]Ibid., 56, 57.

[238]Ibid., 58.

[239]David J. Hesselgrave, *Planting Churches Cross-Culturally: A Guide for Home and Foreign Missions* (Grand Rapids, MI: Baker Book House, 1980), 54, 55.

[240]Brock, *The Principles and Practice of Indigenous Church Planting*, 58.

[241]Ibid., 61.

[242]Ibid.

[243]Ibid., 73.

[244]In reality, since making disciples is both an event and a process, all the strategic shifts could fall under the heading of making disciples. For ease in understanding the shifts, I have separated them into the three components as noted above.

[245]Charles L. Chaney, *Church Planting at the End of the Twentieth Century*, revised and expanded (Wheaton, IL: Tyndale House Publishers, 1991), 73.

[246]David Putman, "Getting Off to a Big Start," in Charles L. Chaney, *Church Planting at the End of the Twentieth Century*, revised and expanded (Wheaton, IL: Tyndale House Publishers, 1991), 179-210.

[247]See Robert E. Logan and Neil Cole, *Raising Leaders for the Harvest* (n.p.: ChurchSmart Resources, 1992-1995).

[248]Phase-out as discussed in this article does not negate the legitimacy of someone planting a church and then pastoring that congregation. Since the topic of discussion is church multiplication through reproduction, phase-out must be addressed. If the international context is reflective of the North American context, then the likelihood of church multiplication occurring whenever the missionary pastors the church is rare. As noted earlier in this article, the professional clergyman who has been a believer for years, has to cross social and cultural barriers to plant a church in a non-Christian context. The notion that the church planter and the unchurched people are "the same type of people" because of socio-economic and language similarities, in reality, is a myth. The worldviews and lifestyles are radically different, hopefully.

[249]Robert Logan, (classroom lecture, MC 525—*Starting and Multiplying Churches*, 6 February 1998), audiocassette. It should be noted that Logan was referring to the harvest model (church planting at a grass-roots level, or pioneer territory) when making this quote.

[250]Reginaldo Kruklis, "Christ, the Source and Goal of Church Planting," in *Five Till Midnight: Church Planting for A.D. 2000 and Beyond*, ed. Tony Cupit (Atlanta, GA: Home Mission Board, 1994), 9.

[251]Robert Logan, (classroom lecture, MC 525—*Starting and Multiplying Churches*, 5 February 1998), audiocassette.

[252]Robert E. Logan and Neil Cole, "Envisioning the Harvest," *Raising Leaders for the Harvest* (n.p.: ChurchSmart Resources, 1992-95), tape 1, cassette.

[253]Robert Logan, (classroom lecture, MC 525—*Starting and Multiplying Churches*, 3 February 1998), audiocassette.

[254]Robert E. Logan and Neil Cole, "Harvesting: Church Multiplication Movements," *Raising Leaders for the Harvest* (n.p.: ChurchSmart Resources, 1992-95), tape 6, cassette.

[255]Logan, (classroom lecture, MC 525—*Starting and Multiplying Churches*, 3 February 1998), audiocassette.

[256]Logan, (classroom lecture, MC 525—*Starting and Multiplying Churches*, 6 February 1998), audiocassette.

[257]Logan, (classroom lecture, MC 525—*Starting and Multiplying Churches*, 5 February 1998), audiocassette.

[258]Tom A. Steffen, *Passing the Baton: Church Planting that Empowers* (La Habra, CA: Center for Organizational and Ministry Development, 1993), 2.

[259]Ibid., 2, 3.

[260]Ibid., 3.

[261]Ibid., 9.

[262]Ibid., 19.

[263]Tom A. Steffen, "Phasing Out Your Work: Make It a Plan, Not a Crisis," *Evangelical Missions Quarterly* 27 (July 1991): 284.

[264]Steffen, *Passing the Baton*, 20.

[265]As Stanley Grenz noted: "With its focus on community, the postmodern world encourages us to recognize the importance of the community of faith in our evangelistic efforts. Members of the next generation are often unimpressed by our verbal presentations of the gospel. What they want to see is a people who live out the gospel in wholesome, authentic, and healing relationships. Focusing on the example of Jesus and the apostles, a Christian gospel for the postmodern age will invite others to become participants in the community of those whose highest loyalty is to the God revealed in Christ. Participants in the inviting community will seek to draw others to Christ by embodying that gospel in the fellowship they share" (Stanely Grenz, *Primer on Postmodernism* [Grand Rapids, MI; Cambridge, U.K.: William B. Eerdmans Publishing Company, 1996], 169). Though I believe Grenz's quote tends to diminish the importance of a verbal presentation of the gospel which is necessary in any cultural context, nevertheless, his words need to be heeded by all contemporary North American church planters.

[266]Steffen, *Passing the Baton,* 218.

[267]Ibid. Steffen also commented that "Jesus' post-resurrection revisits to the disciples did not continue indefinitely. *While Jesus left the disciples*

geographically, he did not leave them relationally (John 16:16). Today's church planters can keep their relationships intact through periodic letters, phone calls, video tapes, e-mail, prayer, and an occasional visit" (218). It is my assumption that North American church planters can contextualize phase-out activities so that they will not have to move from the geographic area. By starting numerous churches in a given location, church planters can remain in one location all their lives.

[268]For example: Jack Redford, *Planting New Churches: Nine Well-tested Steps for Starting New Churches* (Nashville, TN: Broadman Press, 1978); David T. Bunch, Harvey J. Kneisel, and Barbara L. Oden, *Multihousing Congregations: How to Start and Grow Christian Congregations in Multihousing Communities* (Atlanta, GA: Smith Publishing, 1991); Floyd Tidsworth, Jr., *Life Cycle of a New Congregation* (Nashville, TN: Broadman Press, 1992); Melvin L. Hodges, *A Guide to Church Planting: Practical "How to" Information on Establishing Mission Churches* (Chicago, IL: Moody Press, 1973); Robert E. Logan, *The Church Planter's Toolkit: A Self-study Resource Kit for Church Planters and Those Who Supervise Them*, rev. ed. (n.p.: ChurchSmart Resources, 1991); Dick Scoggins, *Planting House Churches in Networks: A Manual from the Perspective of a Church Planting Team*, rev. ed. (Pawtucket, RI: The Fellowship of Church Planters, 1995); George Patterson and Dick Scoggins, *Church Multiplication Guide: Helping Churches Reproduce Locally and Abroad* (Pasadena, CA: William Carey Library, 1993); Rick Warren, *The Purpose Driven Church: Growth Without Compromising Your Message and Mission* (Grand Rapids, MI: Zondervan Publishing House, 1995); Paul G. Hiebert and Eloise Hiebert Meneses, *Incarnational Ministry: Planting Churches in Band, Tribal, Peasant, and Urban Societies* (Grand Rapids, MI: Baker Books, 1995); Thomas Wade Akins, *Pioneer Evangelism: Growing Churches and Planting New Ones that are Self-supporting Using New Testament Methods* (Rio de Janeiro, Brazil: n.p., n.d.); Ray Register, *Back to Jerusalem: Church Planting Movements in the Holy Land* (Enumclaw, WA: WinePress Publishing, 2000); Charles Brock, *Indigenous Church Planting: A Practical Journey* (Neosho, MO: Church Growth International, 1994); Greg Livingstone, *Planting Churches in Muslim Cities: A Team Approach* (Grand Rapids, MI: Baker Book House, 1993); Samuel D. Faircloth, *Church Planting for Reproduction* (Grand Rapids, MI: Baker Book House, 1991); Tom A. Steffen, *Passing the Baton: Church Planting that Empowers* (La Habra, CA: Center for Organizational and Ministry Development, 1997); David J. Hesselgrave, *Planting Churches Cross-culturally: A Guide for*

Home and Foreign Missions (Grand Rapids, MI: Baker Book House, 1980); Aubrey Malphurs, *Planting Growing Churches for the 21st Century: A Comprehensive Guide for New Churches and Those Desiring Renewal*, 2nd ed. (Grand Rapids, MI: Baker Books, 1998).

[269]Thom S. Rainer, *The Book of Church Growth: History, Theology, and Principles* (Nashville, TN: Broadman and Holman Publishers, 1993), 319.

[270]A distinction needs to be made between a model and a methodology. A model of church is a form or pattern which gives the congregation its structural appearance, and generally affects the way the church views itself and conducts its ministry (i.e., cell church, house church). Models are needed, but must be derived from the target people. A methodology, on the other hand, is a way to achieve a desired result. It could also be a way to produce a particular model of church. What is being advocated in this section is that church planters should develop and select methodologies that will result in spontaneous multiplication, rather than the planting of a single church model. Just as it is harmful and unhealthy to import a model onto a target people, likewise, it is problematic to use a methodology which is counterproductive to spontaneous expansion.

[271]Research is needed in understanding and applying people group principles to North America.

[272]Edward R. Dayton and David A. Fraser, *Planning Strategies for World Evangelization* (Grand Rapids, MI: William B. Eerdmans Publishing Company, 1980), 294.

[273]Brock, *The Principles and Practice of Indigenous Church Planting*, 12.

[274]The classic example of claims made without clearly delineated research findings is the internationally famous statement by C. Peter Wagner, "The single most effective evangelistic methodology under heaven is planting new churches" (C. Peter Wagner, *Church Planting for a Greater Harvest* [Ventura, CA: Regal Books, 1990], 11). To my knowledge many church planters and denominational leaders constantly cite Wagner and build philosophies and missiologies off of this statement, though Wagner never offered any well documented research to support his claim.

[275]Murray, *Church Planting*, 164.

[276]Dayton and Fraser, *Planning Strategies for World Evangelization*, 265-66.

[277]Regarding the movement of the Sovereign Lord across the globe to produce church multiplication movements, see the booklet David Garrison, *Church Planting Movements* (Richmond, VA: International Mission Board, 1999).

Chapter 14

Church Planting Movements
In Urban Areas

Kenny Moore

Our Urban Challenge

I have chosen to address an urban Church Planting Movement (CPM) strategy with the metaphor of war. We are without a doubt engaged in a spiritual battle, a deadly battle, a battle where ultimate victory is assured of course, but certainly none-the-less a battle of cosmic proportions. As is much of the world, Colorado has become a mission field and battlefield that is increasingly urban. This urban environment in Colorado is characterized by a great diversity of people groups and needs (Over 90 percent unchurched and never churched). It is my personal belief that this "urban challenge" is perhaps the most important and exciting "battle theatre" of the twenty-first century.

Our goal, therefore, must be gospel saturation through a saturation church planting movement (CPM). In order to create an environment where every urban dweller can hear the good news of Christ and have an opportunity to respond, we are validating all kinds of churches---campus based churches, cell churches, and simple churches (relation-based churches in homes, apartment communities, schools, parks, market place, etc.). We will now investigate some of the battles, battle strategies, and barriers of waging urban warfare.

The Battle Field

George Hunter, in his book *The Celtic Way of Evangelism*, describes the church in the western world as a population that is increasingly "secular"—people often with no Christian memory who often do not know what we Christians are talking about. These populations are increasingly "urban"--out of touch with God's "natural revelation." These populations have graduated from Enlightenment ideology and are more peer-driven, feeling-driven and "right-brained" than their forebears. ("forebears" does not mean someone who came before.) The good news is, however, that these populations are increasingly receptive to "spiritual" things, but often are looking "in all the wrong places" to make sense of their lives and find their soul's true home.

Hunter's observation that populations are increasingly "urban" is exactly ours (does the author mean "exactly like our observation"?) in Colorado and affirmed by colleagues around the country. There is an increasing migration, a reverse migration if you will, back into the urban core/central city. Young professionals, empty nesters, singles, starter families and ethnics are gravitating back into urban America for the vitality and vibrancy of city living, growing dissatisfaction with the suburban dream (commuting, suburban ghetto mentalities, etc.), desire for diversity, community driven architecture and neighborhood design, and the possibility for concentrated options of employment.

The demographic of urban America in general and for Colorado in particular is one of great diversity. There are literally hundreds of ethnic/racial groups represented and many affinity/culture groups. The opportunities to engage cultures that are totally outside and often antagonistic to the story of Jesus are gargantuan in the urban context.

A Battle to Win

In 1941, the United States became embroiled in World War II. This war would (changed tense, should be "was" instead of "would be") be fought on many fronts by the combined efforts of men and women in the Army, Navy, Air Force, Coast Guard, and Marines. The battles in fronts in the South Pacific and North Africa, and in Europe required massive amounts of personnel and materials. The battle to liberate Europe from the evil Nazi regime of Adolph Hitler affected millions of people—many who were designated for extermination because of their ethnicity such as Gypsies and Jews. When the battle for Europe was finally won, not only were countries liberated, but also many people groups ("nations") who were immigrants in those countries. Who were these liberators? Were they the generals and staff commanders? Yes, most would admit that the Allies possessed some of the greatest military leaders ever. The consensus, however, explained that the battle for Europe was won not just by having great leaders, but also by an army of "citizen soldiers" quickly mobilized by their countries to be equipped, trained and deployed into battle.

These "citizen soldiers," willing men and women from every walk of life who performed a variety of tasks, modeled a liberating force the likes of which had never been assembled before in modern warfare and most likely will never be seen again. They willingly fought to protect their country and their families, but many also fought because they knew from personal experience what freedom and liberty were like and wanted it for others.

In much the same way, evangelicals in general and Southern Baptists in particular are involved in a spiritual battle to set the captives free and release those outside the story of Jesus from the bondage of sin and death. There is not a greater need to fight a battle for freedom than in urban America. World War II's strategic goal was the liberation of Europe, and our strategic goal should be the total saturation of every urban context in Colorado and America with the gospel of Jesus Christ. The essence of this strategic plan is total gospel saturation—nothing less than a saturation church planting movement.

Every strategic battle is won by the utilization of many tactical skirmishes as well as major engagements with the enemy. If the spiritual battle is to be won in urban America, it will benefit from major invasions of the enemy's territory with traditional campus based churches, cell churches and hybrid models where the cells function as mini-churches. However, ultimate victory may be achieved by mobilizing an army of men and women teams (this does not read right. Does the author mean "men's and women's teams" or co-ed teams?) planting networks of simple churches to penetrate the thousands of pockets of lostness and people groups ("nations") that make up the urban battlefield. We must engage the enemy with a variety of personnel and material, from seminary-trained leaders of large campus-based churches to emphasizing the enlistment, training/equipping, and deployment of a huge "citizen" army of volunteer men and women ministers planting thousands of small, simple relation-based churches in urban neighborhoods, apartment complexes, mobile home parks, high-rise condos, affluent loft communities, business towers, retirement communities or wherever the followers of Christ gather to engage the enemy, i.e. the lost culture where God has placed them.

When the battle is won, the victory will not be measured by the size of the combatants or their weapons, but by the aggregate. In the battle for urban American, there must be a parallel strategy for defeating darkness---prayer and the saturation planting of all kinds and sizes of "churches." For like the invasion of Europe with huge battleships and tiny landing craft to heavy bombers and light wooden gliders, it is the aggregate that becomes monumental in its impact against the enemy.

A Battle to Lose

As we think of mobilizing an army of men and women to wage urban warfare, there are old weapons and strategies that must be scrapped and shredded. One of the most crucial of all strategy questions for waging a war against lostness is how to fund the war effort and where to direct financial resources.

Unfortunately there is a mentality that has made church planting dependent upon financial resources that come from outside the particular pocket of lostness where the freedom battle is being fought—for example from: sponsoring churches, associations, denominations, etc. The problem with dependence upon outside resources rather than those found in the local context is that they subvert and dilute the capacity needed to receive an outpouring of God's Spirit. I believe that a church planting strategy dependent upon external aid is destined to *mediocrity* and *possible* failure and an intentional saturation church planting movement dependent upon external aid is *absolutely* doomed to failure.

We have for too long "battled" hard to win access to denominational coffers in order to wage the spiritual battle against the powers of darkness instead of depending upon and looking for personnel and material that the "Harvest Master" wants to provide free---*if we ask*. Most non-strategic funding decisions, particularly from a missiological perspective, occur in two areas---as regards church planter compensation and in relation to land and buildings.

The first funding battle that needs to be lost is the strategy to fund church planter salaries. Here are just a few of the problems that occur with funding that comes from outside the local harvest, particularly in regards to planter salary support:

1) There is not enough money from the national mission agencies/state conventions/associations, Church planting positions, etc. to pay a living wage to a church planter, particularly in an urban context, and still have funds for training, projects, and expenses for indigenous catalytic "harvesters." There is not enough money in the world for "soldiers pay" necessary to fight the cosmic battle we are engaged in instead of utilizing volunteer "citizen soldiers" to fight the war.

2) There is not enough money to give salary assistance to all of the potentially gifted church planters with whom God wants to start churches---so the "have nots" feel slighted or even worse, they become angry and feel disenfranchised.

3) There is an inherent unfairness in asking some planters to be bi-vocational/self-supporting, if needed in the

church planting process, and not others, particularly if circumstances, personnel, etc. are equal.

4) There is always the potential, particularly in some ethnic and lower socio-economic groups, for the new developing congregation to look to denominational sources for the support of their leader instead of embracing the leader as their responsibility from the outset.

5) There is always the danger, particularly with some ethnic and lower socio-economic groups, to create a salary scenario that is non-reproducible by the contextual environment where the new plant is being planted. Once the phase-down or whatever the plan of salary assistance has run its' course, several things happen:

6) There is a danger when the money is no longer available

   a. The leader leaves when the money stops
   b. The leader stays, but there is bitterness when the subsidy stops
   c. The recipients are reduced to beggardom after the convention/association/ sponsor church money runs its course----"Can you just help us a little more to do this or that? Can you just help us with this particular emergency?" ETC!
   d. The planter and the new congregation's self-esteem is lowered, which results not only in bitterness towards the "benevolent provider," but bitterness also toward themselves for becoming involved with people they feel have wronged them.

7) There is a climate created where stewardship is not encouraged because there is no immediate pressure on the new congregational expression to feel responsible for their leader's personal support needs.
8) There is not the exercise of entrepreneurial gifts and dependence upon the Spirit, on the part of the planter and/or the new congregation, when <u>direct</u> salary assistance is available.
9) There is a major preoccupation, which can be a huge distraction, on the part of the planter in any salary phase-down scenario, as they see their subsidized livelihood declining.
10) There is direct evidence that salary subsidies minimize the need to disciple people in the blessings of stewardship and dependence upon the local harvest field for ultimate resources.

The second funding battle that needs to be lost, but one that continues to be fought, *emphasizes the need for land and buildings.* In almost all urban contexts there are often huge expenditures of energy, preoccupation, and mental anguish to battle local and national agencies for help to purchase land and build buildings. However, because of the high cost of land in urban environments and the increasingly high cost of construction, it is arguably impossible to have independently owned facilities to address the thousands of pockets of lostness and people groups that are in need of gospel penetration.

Thus it is my considered opinion that we will never experience a CPM in urban America, or for that matter, in suburban or exurban America, as long as we have a strategy to penetrate lostness that depends upon or is driven by finances. If for this reason alone, the growing interest for a "simple church" strategy to provide the capacity for receiving God's Kingdom will have to be validated because the need for outside financial resources will sabotage the war effort.

To wage a battle against lostness, and experience a victory via a saturation church planting movement that is organic and gives glory to God, we must *lose the battle* to fill our respective war-chests with funding that does not originate from and that is not sustained by the local harvest—macro and micro.

Barriers to Waging War
in an Urban Context

In order to successfully wage a war on lostness in an urban context, we must first examine what has gone wrong in past battles and how these mistakes can be mitigated. The following strategic failures must be dealt with in order to breach the barriers that sabotage the utilization of our most effective weapons and demoralize our fighting forces.

There has been a failure to make prayer the overarching emphasis for whatever we do. To engage an enemy that is so firmly entrenched in so many pockets of lostness, our prayer effort is one that is specific and continual for "harvesters" as in Luke 10:2b, and it will have to be as persistent and unrelenting as the widow woman in Luke 18.

Southern Baptists as a denomination have generally failed to define "church" in terms of the lowest common denominator as Jesus describes in Matthew 18:20---church that is not determined by form (buildings, land, time, clergy, etc.), but by function (fellowship, worship, discipleship, evangelism, prayer, ministry and reproduction).

One of the biggest failures has been to not validate the aggregate. To engage in a spiritual battle in an urban environment against a formidable enemy, we must embrace the reality that our strategy must include all kinds and sizes of church and celebrate that it is the aggregate of all expressions of church that will be monumental in their impact on defeating darkness and liberating those in bondage. If we fail to experience validation for a simple church strategy from the top down, total gospel saturation is doubtful. Until our mission agencies have the will to validate and emphasize a simple reproducing organic strategy to penetrate lostness and reduce unbelief more rapidly than we have been doing, a saturation church planting movement will most likely not catch on with our denominations as a whole.

A failure to reduce clergy culture and congregational culture hinders the needed mobilization of volunteer ministers. The debilitating factor here is that there is a mentality among some clergy that they are special and the contributing factor is often congregations who make them feel special, i.e. where the cleric becomes the only minister and the congregation does not embrace their ministry role to be on mission.

There has also been a failure to deemphasize funding strategies in favor of a more organic strategy for mentoring and training. The tendency to rely on funding and overlook more spiritual elements in urban church ministries has seriously hindered the efforts to start and equip urban churches.

Lastly, we have failed to adequately value small expressions of "church." We are still a denomination where size counts. We usually justify this by saying that size simply means more saved people. But while large churches may indicate more believers, they can never accomplish alone the spread of the gospel into all areas of lostness. Once we see that what is simple and small is the easiest to reproduce and has the best potential for multiplication, we will value these small expressions of church as an effective means to address a culture as varied as is found in the urban context.

The Battle Plan

When a war is waged, the effort is almost always waged on multiple fronts and with multiple strategies based on the geography, the strength of the enemy, and the resources available--to name just a few. Nowhere is this approach more applicable than in urban warfare where the task is penetrating urban lostness. There will be major campaigns and many tactical skirmishes. Strategies will vary and the tactics to accomplish them will be varied depending upon the urban environment. So must it be with us as we wage a spiritual war for a territory and stronghold that presently is under the control of the enemy---urban America.

The battle plan for Colorado urban centers is driven by the non-negotiable goal of completing the Great Commission. The four major strategies that we have chosen in Colorado for this end vision are: *prayer, research, contextual strategy, and Spiritual power.*

Prayer

In order to achieve our goal of completing the Great Commission, we feel that the means must be total gospel saturation that utilizes a total involvement in church planting philosophy. The strategic need that flows out of this vision is for an army of "harvesters"---indigenous, apostolically gifted and Spirit prepared workers who will not just be church planters, but who will be very catalytic in their function and organic in their methodology.

We have chosen that most organic of all approaches for personnel (workers/harvesters) acquisition---*prayer*. We believe that Christ's words in Luke 10:2b are to be our most strategic activity. When Christ sent out the seventy-two in teams, he gave one overarching set of marching orders as they invaded enemy territory---to ask the Harvest Master for the personnel (harvesters) to bring in a harvest that waits for His called-out harvesters.

By intentionally encouraging an organic/grass-roots effort to pray Luke 10:2b, we are seeing the Colorado army of God form without being program driven. God is not just rising up and calling anybody, but indigenous "harvesters" who are gifted, wired and inspired to engage the enemy where they live. It has been our Christian "M.O." (This needs to be spelled out with the first usage.) to pray for a season, but then default to activity---activity of trying to force the enlistment of our invasion/fighting forces rather than waiting for the Harvest Master to thrust out His chosen workers to engage the enemy and liberate the captives. We believe that if Jesus told those He was deploying in Luke 10 (it is an imperative in the original language) to pray/ask the Harvest Master to connect them with the people resources needed for the harvest, then it must be in God's heart to answer this type of prayer. So a prayer movement, particularly a very organic prayer movement for Luke 10:2b workers, must be the precursor and foundation for all of our strategic activities to address lostness. *Here the battle will be won or lost!*

Research

Any invasion, particularly campaigns against urban strongholds, of necessity demands as complete an understanding as possible of the wiles of the enemy, the context in which the battle will be fought, and the profile of the people who are being held captive. Reconnaissance/research must be carried out in order to begin to grasp the context, culture, world-view, etc. of the indigenous people we are trying to rescue. They in turn will become the resistance fighters who will engage the enemy in their personal *oikos*/urban context, which they know so much better than the invading forces. This necessary information and insight comes largely through Spirit-led research.

As we think of research, people profiles, master plans for evangelism, and church planting, we face a major battle with ourselves---a battle to keep the research process simple and not default to complicate. We are committed to develop a simple research process and master plan strategy that is reproducible, sustainable, and not esoteric in its training process. This process and strategy must be utilized by God-provided (Luke 10:2b) indigenous harvesters with passion and culture orientation not available in enlisted volunteers. We need a simple template that asks the basic questions that will result in the

369

exegesis/information needed for the harvesters that God provides to begin a process leading to an urban saturation CPM.

Contextual Strategy

As mentioned earlier, Colorado has chosen to have a saturation CPM mentality that mandates not being dependent upon or driven by outside financial resources or a preoccupation with the need for buildings and land. Our strategic vision is to promote a strategy that creates an environment that would allow God to trust us with a revival, because we had (changing tenses in the same sentence. "had" should be "have") the capacity to receive a movement from Him. We believe that we have reduced our credibility with the Father and hampered the possibility for a saturation CPM because we have historically elected to create a gospel delivery and receiving strategy that is dependent upon professional clergy and facilities.

We are, therefore, drawing battle plans for a "guerilla" campaign to penetrate our urban centers by mobilizing and enlisting an army of volunteer ministers to plant hundreds and hundreds of "simple churches" that can meet anywhere and at anytime and whose leadership are indigenous to the urban context where they live, work, go to school, and play. Even in a day of nuclear weapons with a mind-blowing array of "smart" weapons and international diplomacy, we are seeing that to take an urban context from the enemy requires intensive house-to-house combat and winning the hearts of the indigenous inhabitants. In a nutshell, this is our strategy.

At the end of this chapter, you will see a visual of one of our major blueprints for penetrating lostness. We will continually develop other blueprints/strategies/tactics as the urban war is waged. I will try and explain the following visual. (Does the author go immediately into this visual?)

First, we need to deal with some statistical and philosophical realities. Reliable research declares that evangelical America is addressing only 10% of the population. This same research indicates that only 4% of evangelical churches in America are intentionally missional and that given the rapid growth in Colorado specifically, particularly in our urban centers, we continue to fall behind in addressing the lostness that surrounds us---much less experience a measurable gain on this lostness.

In the modern church era, we predominately ask one question, "What would it take to get people to *come* to our church event?" This "come" question, because of its' focus on the event, has hindered the existing traditional and contemporary churches from asking the possibly more important question, "What would it take for us to go and take the gospel beyond our conventional Sunday morning church setting and into the urban community?" Because of these two different mind-sets, we have evaluated these approaches by strengths and challenges.

The strengths of the "come" form of churches lie in their potentials. These more traditional churches can be sending platforms for propelling God-called leaders into the local harvest. They can be equipping centers for these called-out leaders and an environment where the emphasis can rest on training to train trainers. The "come" churches can be a major source of validation for their lay men and women whom they are sending out to address lostness. They can be prayer

371

advocates and intercessors for the sent ones and petition God to connect these missionaries with indigenous harvesters. They can be staging areas to mobilize church planting teams. They can be the logistical center for whatever resources are needed in the on-going battle for urban gospel saturation.

However, *the challenges of the "come" form of churches are that they: are complicated because of such things as staff, programs, budgets, facilities, etc; are often dependent upon a high level of performance (preaching, worship, programs, etc.) to get people to come.* They have high stress levels for professional clergy and for lay leadership and require increasing levels of funding. Usually these churches are mostly homogenous and exhibit and foster a church culture that is more "come" than "go;" and usually grow only by addition. The "come" churches require high levels of energy from all levels of participants, are facility intensive, and have difficulty validating and releasing the laity to be on mission.

The strengths of the "go" churches are that they are simple in structure and this inherent simplicity is easier to reproduce. They are very participatory and do not need to rely on extraordinary performance by leadership. Consequently, they are less stressful than the event-centered church, require little or no funding beyond themselves, lend themselves to the diversity of their local context, and are characterized by conformity to native (indigenous) culture. The "go" churches have the built-in potential for growth by multiplication, are relaxed and do not experience worker burn-out, can meet anywhere and at anytime, and they can naturally validate and release emerging leaders/planters.

The "go" churches, like the "come" congregations, also face challenges and limitations. The challenges the "go" churches face include the fact that they are not perceived as legitimate by established church culture and even by some who are outside of church culture. Often, outsiders, including the existing church cultures, perceive the "go" churches as being short lived in their ministry, utilizing leadership that is spiritually immature, and being difficult to measure as to their scope and impact on lostness in the short run. At times, the "go" churches even elicit a fear for doctrine from some church leaders;

Colorado's strategy is to pray/ask God for catalytic church planters who will breach cultural, socio-economic, and geographic barriers and move into the unchurched and never churched mission field that makes up urban Colorado. As God provides the emerging harvesters, trained catalytic personnel will identify them, enlist them, train them, mentor them, and then deploy them into receptive pockets of lostness where God is already working preveniently. (Webster doesn't even give a definition for this word. Only that it is an adjective.) Some of these venues where God is already working will be in the workplace, in the growing area of high density housing-- (45/50% of metro Denver), and in low density housing.

Obviously strategy will be guided by the enemy's response, the resistance to our efforts by urban native culture, and the new opportunities for victory. We do not intend to try and figure out a "fits-all/all-at-once" strategy for the spiritual battle in our urban centers. Rather, we will develop strategy in-route as we connect with the harvesters God is providing and as we learn more about the battlefield and gain a better understanding of the many strongholds presently in the hands of the enemy.

Spiritual Power

Urban environments in Colorado are characterized by a multiplicity of idols and distractions that hinder the spread of the redemptive plan of Jesus. These idols and distractions debilitate, distract, and strike fear in the hearts of our "citizen solders" and the new combatants who are being saved and who are joining the war against darkness.

In the summer of 2000, I heard Bob Logan tell about case study of a recorded CPM in a large valley in Latin America. Thousands of people came to Christ in a relatively short period of time and not only were personal lives spiritually transformed, but entire communities were changed. The missionaries did a post-CPM study to see if they could determine the factors that provided the impetus for this movement of God. The researchers discovered that there were two overarching components that fueled this particular CPM--- *immediate baptism of new converts and teaching them immediately about their new identity, i.e. their union with Christ in His death, burial and resurrection.*

There is a growing belief on the part of some of us that to see a saturation CPM that is manned and led by indigenous emerging harvesters and new converts there must first be recognition of who they are in Christ. Then, there must be a belief, just as there was among the New Testament churches who read the letters of Paul that these converts are new creations, that they are seated in the heavenlies in union with Christ, that they have been crucified with Christ, and the life

374

they now live is Christ's life working in them and that they must choose to live out of these realities moment by moment.

We realize that the spiritual principles of "Christ in us" are apprehended by the work of the Holy Spirit in the life of the believer. However, we are incorporating as part of our church planter/catalytic leader/harvester training a biblical reminder of the spiritual power available to the believer. Only when God's army that is battling the enemy in urban warfare understands that they are not only saved by grace but that they can only live a victorious and powerful Christian life by grace, then and only then can they be the effective freedom fighters necessary to liberate the urban context with the gospel of Christ.

When an indigenous force with an understanding of their union with Christ engages the enemy on their home turf, the enemy is then put on the defensive. As we design and implement varied strategies for training existing urban church planters and emerging planters, the training will also include learning the biblical truth of their identity in their oneness with Christ and how to begin to experience that reality. As with prayer, here the battle will be won or lost!

An Intentionally Late Battle Strategy

I would like to describe a battle strategy that must permeate all of our war efforts if we are to experience victory on the urban battlefield. We in Colorado are working to provide an environment to receive what God wants to send (Acts 2:47) by utilizing a biblical strategy that could result in a CPM---a multiplying process of saturation church planting. As an industrial and technological western society, we function as an economy where inventories and production are based on "on-time delivery" and on research that is obsessed with being cutting edge and innovative---to be first. We are a culture in which not being ahead of the curve is to be considered backward.

In the same way, ("In the same way" as what? Is this referring back to the previous paragraph?) the Southern Baptist Convention, the North American Mission Board, state conventions, and local churches seek to be cutting edge and innovative. We work to be ahead of the times in strategy, promotions, programs, research, in enlistment of missionaries, and procurement of financial resources. Because of our desire to be edgy and ahead in the areas listed above, we have a default mode that moves us perpetually from the simple to the complicated. As a result, our goal to see a CPM of relation-based "simple churches" is crippled because in the minds of some, "simple" and "small" are denominationally incorrect while "complicated" and "large" are, often with the best of intentions, embraced as our desired models. (This sentence is confusing.)

Similarly, our church planting strategies focus on doing activities that we initiate rather than tolerating a level of un-comfortableness that comes from being "intentionally late" as we wait on God's provision for harvesters and to respond to the receptive pockets of lostness where He is working preveniently. (Again I think a better word can be found instead of "preveniently".) Only with this strategy will God have any opportunity to get the glory and only then will we be victorious in battling the enemy.

As mentioned earlier, our Great Commission goal is for "every person in Colorado and every visitor to our state to be able to hear the gospel, have an opportunity to respond, be discipled, and worship the most high God." However, our penchant to default towards the complicated results in battle strategies that are neither reproducible nor sustainable nor indigenous and definitely do not possess the spontaneity requisite for a CPM in our urban neighborhoods.

Should we choose to make prayer our primary focus and couple it with a strategy of being intentionally late, we will be exactly on time as we connect with the different ethnic and cultural groups God has prioritized us to address. As a result of this sort of prayer movement, we will not have to prioritize people groups or pockets of lostness, but rather focus our battle efforts on the people groups that God has chosen for priority and engage the enemy with harvesters that God has impassioned and prepared for their particular harvest field.

Battles Being Won In Metropolitan Denver

The setting

Metropolitan Denver is diverse geographically (urban, suburban, exurban [plains, mountains]). It is also ethnically diverse (over 100 language groups) and culturally diverse (literally hundreds of sub-culture groups [Goths, Bohemian mix, cowboys, bikers, etc.]). Politically the community is conservative. While the area is mostly unchurched/never churched, a high level of spiritual seeking pervades. Unfortunately, however, this seeking is not a seeking for Christ.

The Objective

The objective of church planting leaders in Denver is to see the Kingdom of God brought near to every "ethne" in the Denver metro area by means of a Church Planting Movement. This objective is not beyond the possibilities of a Spirit-led people who are empowered by the living God.

The Strategy

The strategy is to reduce unbelief rapidly by facilitating a multiplying process of saturation church planting (CPM), having prayer as foundational, and utilizing multiple models (campus based churches. The plan utilizes cell churches and relation-based churches in homes, multi-housing, work place, school, parks, etc.), (The sentence shouldn't be ended and another one started within parentheses.) while emphasizing and implementing indigenous, reproducible, and sustainable principles.

Who is being reached?

- Traditional church planting (seeker, event, performance, facility, programs, etc.) is reaching a portion of suburbia and ethnic populations, but not really effective in the inner and central city areas nor in reaching multifamily housing and exurban subdivisions
- Simple/organic models are showing more potential to be effective (particularly because of value for multiplication) in densely populated areas of inner and central city, isolated exurban and gated communities, with the lower socio-economic groups, the very affluent, and the myriad of sub-culture and ethnic people groups

What's Not Working?

- Seeker strategies (event, performance, etc) are not working as well as they used to do
- Funding dreams instead of seeing fruit first (CP assessments not proving adequate)
- Strategy driven by time and outside financial resources (Mission agencies – national, state, local etc)
- Strategy dependent upon imported leaders (seminary, out-of-state, etc.) versus indigenous leaders emerging from the harvest

What is working—key factors to how the gospel is spreading?

- Praying for harvesters (Luke 10:2b) with apostolic skills and a plan/vision from God to become traditional church planters and simple church network leaders---**praying is the most important activity we are doing**
- Encouraging hybrid church plants, that plan to be traditional event and program centered, to utilize a cell approach, but where the cells function as house churches (valuing multiplication) which are intentionally missional----not a means to an end
- The development of simple/organic church (house, multi-housing, etc.) **networks** that value and implement the functions of: fellowship; worship; discipleship; prayer; ministry and reproduction---**any CPM we experience will flow from this strategy**
- The Rocky Mountain Campus of Golden Gate Baptist Theological Seminary emphasizing (in addition to traditional campus based models) a simple/organic way of being church (house, apartments, etc.) This effort under

direction of Allan Karr, Nehemiah professor, is yielding a new crop of students with a CPM mentality

- Simple Church Basic Training (weekend retreats for potential simple church planting leaders) that is part of Allan Karr's efforts
- Indigenous harvester strategy (praying Luke 10:2b) versus planting simple churches with the "saints"---**any CPM we experience will flow from this strategy**
- Greenhouse retreat (weekend for simple/organic church leaders and network leaders) led by Neil Cole—CMA----recent Denver event had ninety participants
- Eighteen-month follow-up process to the Greenhouse to develop network leaders; simple/organic church planters; who will develop other leaders who develop other leaders---This (If "This" is going to be capitalized, then the dashes should be removed and a period inserted.) would be similar to the North American Mission Board's Church Planting Networks. (This period should be removed or add them to the end of all bullets.)
- ACTS Training Center—to equip lay ethnic men and women to be church planters in their *oikos* with an emphasis on addressing pockets of lostness with small reproducing simple churches (Luke 10:2b; MAWL; etc.)---we are wondering if a CPM in Colorado may be led by/started in the ethnic community (What does MAWL mean? Should it be spelled out?)
- Multiplying Church Networks---gatherings of regional pastors and church planters to pray Luke 10:2 b; to instruct these pastors on how to map their church fields; how to discover and identify pockets of lostness and how to prioritize addressing them through traditional church-type plants and a simple/organic church planting strategy

- Developing a very simple Master Plan process that the emerging harvesters (Luke 10:2b) can do themselves. Instruct in a simple beginning plan (one page) that deploys them rapidly into their target people group.

Church planting in Denver---Facts and Figures

- There are 2.5 million people in metro Denver (700 thousand Hispanics; many Asian groups, etc.). Of these 90/95% are in the category of "unchurched or never churched."
- We are working with over twenty language/ethnic groups. There are over one hundred in our area
- There are 98 churches and missions in Denver Metropolitan Baptist Association
- In the last eight years, 70 churches and missions were started in Denver
- In the last eight years, 10% of the churches planted have ceased to exist
- In the last eight years, 10% of plants have reproduced
- The goal for traditional church plants in 2003 was 15(I can't figure out why I can't remove this empty line. But if this empty line is needed then the following bullet should not be a bullet.)
- *God's activity* over the last *eight* months with simple church networks

*By April of 2003 there were 7 networks started with approximately 27 simple churches in networks. The goal for 2003 was that these seven networks and others planned would result in 50 simple churches and in 2004 to have 90 simple churches in multiple reproducing networks

* By April of 2003, 10 simple churches had been started with ethnic laity from ACTS Training Center. The goal for 2004 is that these 10 simple churches will result in 4 networks with 18 simple churches

* The goal for 2003 was that at least 5 reproducing networks would start out of a Greenhouse training event leading to the starting of 25 simple churches.. From this start our goal for 2004 is for this group to have 13 networks with 65 simple churches

Our summary of goals for 2004 is:
Simple churches   90
Ethnic simple churches   18
Greenhouse simple churches   <u>65</u>
Total simple church goal 2004   173

With a conservative estimate of 10 participants in each church this will give us a total of 1730 participants in these simple churches. We are praying that the year 2005 will be the tipping point in which we will began to see a greater multiplication of simple churches.

We believe that to receive the CPM that God wants to send, we must first be ready to receive a harvest that is already ripe. Then we must have a battle strategy to discover, connect with and deploy indigenous harvesters, who are provided by the Harvest Master, and who will then continue the cycle of discovering, connecting with and deploying more harvesters until the harvest is finished.

At the risk of being redundant, it must be repeated that the church culture of today is not ready to receive a movement of God because of its dependence on buildings and professional leadership. So perhaps our biggest challenge, before God is willing to pour out His Spirit on the urban battlefield, is to redefine what can be "church." One definition that we are using, among others, is "*A gathering of obedient followers of Jesus worshipping together, nurturing one another, ministering to unbelievers, growing in Christ's likeness---who perceive themselves to be a church.*" This definition has freed us from the prevailing model of church where the event, building and clergy orientation shackles the possibility of rapid multiplication. This new definition allows for a more organic model (Acts 2:42-46) that can receive whatever spontaneous outpouring of God's Spirit (Acts 2:47) He chooses to send.

As we seek to reach our urban areas for Christ, prayer plays the overarching role. Our entire urban battle hinges upon a prayer movement being the precursor to a CPM. Without an intentional focus and value on prayer, we will be left to our own biases, templates and stereotypes of who can be a harvester. We will then fail miserably to connect with the host of harvesters God has already prepared to engage in urban warfare and an *urban CPM.*

Chapter 15

Associational Strategy for Church Planting Movements

Tom Billings

When Tony Perkins of ABC's Good Morning America gave the weather report, he gave the national weather picture. He showed major weather patterns—storm developing in the Caribbean, cold front coming down from Canada, or heat wave across the south. He showed how these movements would affect the national weather scene. Then he segued to the local station saying "That's what's happening across the nation. Now, here's what's happening in your neighborhood."

At that moment, a local reporter tells what's happening in the viewing area. Viewers quickly learn that national trends may or may not affect local weather. There may be a storm brewing in the Caribbean, but the weather in Phoenix won't be affected by it. Viewers in Miami, however, may need to brace for a hurricane.

This chapter focuses on major trends affecting cities and considers the potential impact of these trends on the work of associations and/or judicatories. (Webster doesn't give a definition for this word. The closest association is judicature or the act of judging. Will the readers know this word or the meaning?) It is not the intent of this writer to describe or prescribe something for all associations or judicatories for they are not all alike. Open country associations and mega-city associations do not function the same way. The reader is encouraged to consider what is happening on a larger scale and see what potential impact and application it may have on a local level. To illustrate this we will look closely at one association and see how these trends are affecting it. Finally, we will consider how associations can help facilitate church planting movements in North America.[278]

God's Heart for Cities

God has a heart for the city. The Bible begins in a garden (Genesis) but ends in a city (Revelation). The epicenter of the Christian movement was the city of Jerusalem. From there Christianity spread to major metropolitan regions of the Mediterranean: first to the cities along the coast of Syria (Caesarea, Tyre, Sidon), then into Asia Minor (Colossae, Laodecia, Pergamum, Ephesus, Troas), to Greece (Philippi, Thessalonica, Corinth) and ultimately to Rome, the heart and soul of the Roman Empire.[279]

God has a heart for all people. Peter discovered "God does not show favoritism but accepts men [and women] from every nation who fear him and do what is right" (Acts 10:34-35, N.I.V.). From its inception, the Christian movement embraced people of every nation, tongue and tribe. At Pentecost "God-fearing Jews from every nation under heaven" were present and "each one heard them speaking [the gospel] in his own language" (Acts 2:5-6). Pentecost was a prelude to what would happen next as the gospel moved beyond Jerusalem, the heart of Judaism, to the God-fearers, to the Greeks, and ultimately to people from many nations around the earth.

God, who is the same yesterday, today and forever, still has a heart for the city and for all the peoples of the earth. The early church wanted to go where the people were so they went to the big cities. Rome, the mega-city of Paul's day, is small

compared to the major metropolitan regions of today. [280]
Whereas the early church had to travel across land and sea to
encounter all the nations of the earth, now one only needs to
walk the streets of a major metropolitan area in North America
to encounter the nations because the nations have moved into
our neighborhoods. This is one of many trends that will
significantly affect the work of the association.

National Trends

A trend is a general tendency or direction in which
something is moving. There may be a general trend toward
smaller cars, more women in the workplace, or higher interest
rates. Some trends are not much more than fads that come and
go quickly with little or no affect on our lives, like the hula-
hoop or reality television. Other trends, like demographic shifts
or a depressed economy, develop over time and may
significantly impact society for an extended time period.

There are several trends which will impact the work of
the association in the future. In this chapter they are divided
into two broad categories. *Major trends* are undeniable and
widespread throughout North America. *Minor trends,* while
still significant, may affect fewer people or may be just
emerging and not fully developed.

Major Tends

The world is becoming more urban every day. Consider
these key findings cited in the *World Urbanization Prospects:
the 2001 Revision,* prepared by the United Nations Population
Division:

1. The world's urban population reached 2.9 billion in 2000 and is expected to rise to 5 billion by 2030. Whereas 30 per cent of the world population lived in urban areas in 1950, the proportion of urban dwellers rose to 47 per cent by 2000 and is projected to attain 60 per cent by 2030 (table 1). At current rates of change, the number of urban dwellers will equal the number of rural dwellers in the world in 2007.

2. Virtually all the population growth expected at the world level during 2000-2030 will be concentrated in urban areas (figure 1). During that period the urban population is expected to increase by 2.1 billion persons, nearly as much as will be added to the world population, 2.2 billion (table 1). [281] (Where are figure 1 and table 1? Nothing is identified as such. Also later we have some graphs but nothings is identified with a label.)

Mission strategies during the twenty-first century must recognize the majority of the world's population lives in the cities.

Urban areas are places, but urbanism is a mindset, a way of looking at life, that extends beyond the city into all areas of the country. Consequently, strategies developed in the major metropolitan areas could have significant impact on smaller cities and even open country areas where the urban mindset predominates.

Cities are becoming more ethnically and culturally diverse. From 1995 to 2000, 7,495,846 people migrated to the United States from abroad. The majority of these (two-thirds) migrated to the south and west and settled in cities like Miami, Houston, Dallas and Los Angeles.[282] New York City has been the most ethnically diverse city in the world since 1640.[283] In Houston, the second most culturally diverse city in the United States, researchers have identified approximately 230 ethnolinguistic people groups. Similar research is now being conducted by the North American Mission Board of the Southern Baptist Convention and other groups. This will help provide a better picture of the ethnic diversity in cities all across North America.

America has been a nation of immigrants since its inception. What is so significant about immigration? In the past, America was a melting pot. Today it is more of a cultural mosaic. As people migrate to the United States they tend to cluster with people like themselves. Driving across any major metropolitan area one will find large communities of Chinese, Mexicans, Vietnamese, Asian Indians, Koreans, Somalians, and other ethnic groups. By clustering together immigrants are more likely to maintain their national and cultural distinctives, e.g., language, religion, customs, and traditions. No major American city is without an Islamic center.[284] In Harris County (Houston, TX) Muslim mosques and Buddhist temples are being built as fast or faster than Baptist churches.

Associational mission strategy must take into account the diversity and complexity of working with various people groups. Strategies which work in one culture may not work effectively in another. Established churches must embrace a missional mindset which recognizes that people may be culturally distant while also being geographically proximate, that missions is not just something that happens around the world but it must also happen across the street.

The impact of the gospel is diminishing in our cities. The growth of the Church has not kept pace with the growth of the population in major metropolitan areas. This has been evident for some time in Europe and Great Britain. Now it is also true in North America. Though the theologically conservative, evangelical side of the Church is growing, Tom Sine asserts "we are witnessing the incredible shrinking [of the] Western church."[285]

While much of the American population claims to be Christian, the Christian church's impact on the culture also appears to be declining. Sine argues "the reason we have so little influence on the larger, modern secular culture is that we have allowed that culture, instead of our faith, to define what is important and of value."[286]

What does all this mean for associations and associational missions? Cities in North America, including those in the Bible belt, have become major mission fields.

Minor Trends

In addition to these major trends there are other trends which will need to be factored into an associational mission strategy. Some of these trends have been around for a while; others are just now emerging. Rather than elaborate upon these trends, we will simply list them:

- The importance of denominational identity is diminishing. This is especially true among younger Anglo pastors and churches. The concept of "the kingdom of God" has become more important than denominational identity.

- The church may experience a reformation of structure in the twenty-first century. First, the house church may emerge as a viable alternative to the institutional church. [287] Second, city reaching and the concept of the church in the city may emerge as more significant than church growth. [288] This second trend is particularly consistent with the emphasis on the kingdom of God. (These bullets are outside the bounds of the page.)

What are we to conclude from this? The world is becoming more urban every day. Urban environments are complex, complicated and constantly changing. Mission strategies that worked successfully a decade ago may not work today. Though the institutional church is well-established in North America, it is losing ground in the city. To successfully reach the diverse population of North America, the institutional church must become missional in purpose and programming.

Those are some national trends. Now let's consider how these trends affect one association—the Union Baptist Association (UBA) in Houston, Texas.

One Association's Story

In October 1840 a call went out to churches in the Republic of Texas. Eleven messengers from three churches met in Travis, about twelve miles south of Brenham, for the purpose of forming a Baptist association. One man, Rev. T. W. Cox, was the pastor of all three churches whose combined membership totaled forty-five folks. The messengers voted unanimously to form a missionary association. This was the first Baptist association formed in Texas. In the beginning it was known as "the Association." Eventually the name "Union" was attached because they spoke so much about union and unity.

From such humble beginnings, Union Baptist Association (UBA) began. UBA has grown to become the largest association in the Southern Baptist Convention serving more than five hundred congregations. In the beginning, the three congregations were virtually alike. Today UBA is one of the most culturally and ethnically diverse associations in Baptist life.

Demographics

Houston is the fourth largest city in the United States and one of its most ethnically and culturally diverse. When the city began in 1840, approximately 2,000 people resided in Harris County. The population grew steadily until 1960 when it reached 1.2 million people. At that juncture, the city began to grow rapidly. "Between 1970 and 1982, almost one million people moved into the metropolitan area. They were coming at the rate of some 1,300 per week. Every day on average, 250 motor vehicles were being added to the streets and freeways of Harris County."[289] Today the population of Harris County is nearing four million people making it the third most populated county in the United States.

As the population of Harris County grew, it diversified. [290] Houston has not always been so ethnically diverse according to at Rice University professor in Houston Stephen Klineberg, who writes:

Throughout virtually all of its history, Houston was essentially a biracial Southern city dominated and controlled by white men. In just 20 years [since approximately 1980], it has been transformed into one of the most ethnically and culturally diverse cities in America. More than a decade ago, a cover story in *Time Magazine* (Henry, 1990) used this city to illustrate the new America. "At the Sesame Hut restaurant in Houston," the author wrote, "a Korean immigrant owner trains Hispanic immigrant workers to prepare Chinese-style food for a largely black clientele."[291]

The following chart indicates what has happened in Houston since 1960.

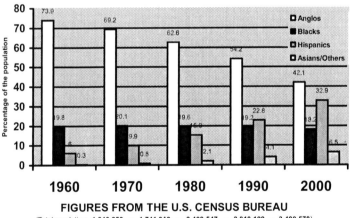

FIGURES FROM THE U.S. CENSUS BUREAU
(Total population: 1,243,258 – 1,741,912 – 2,409,547 – 2,818,199 – 3,400,578)

Note that in 1960, Anglos claimed the majority of the population (73.9%) in the county. In spite of a numerical increase of more than half a million people from 1960 to 2000, the percentage of Anglos dropped from 73.9% to 42.1%. During the same period Hispanics increased from 6.0% to

32.9% (from a total population of approximately 75,000 to 1,119,000). If these trends continue, the Hispanic population will soon be the majority ethnic group in Harris County.

The Asian population also enjoyed significant growth. Though Asians comprised only 0.3% of the population in 1960, they were 6.5% of the population by 2000. This makes them the fastest growing ethnic population in Harris County.

Broad ethnic categories, like Asian and Hispanic, are convenient groupings but they do not adequately describe the complexity of the city. All Asians are not the same. Asians come from many countries. They speak many languages. They have diverse cultures, practices and worldviews. Nor are all Hispanics the same. Though the majority shares a common language, they may come from countries with different cultures and customs. This diversity surfaced in a meeting the writer had with Hispanic church leaders when one person complained (in Spanish), "Why is it that every time we have a dinner on the grounds in my church, we have to have Mexican food? That's not what we ate in my country!"

As helpful as ethnic or ethnolinguistic distinctions are, even they cannot adequately express the diversity and complexity of the city. For this we need to identify the various groups of people that share common bonds other than language or ethnicity. Generational distinctions help, so we speak of boomers and busters. Social distinctions help, so we speak of lower, middle and upper class. Religious heritage helps, so we speak of Christian, Hindu, Buddhist, and Muslim. Philosophical distinctions, like the modern and postmodern worldview, help further identify the people in the city. Marketers have other ways of identifying and grouping people according to location, lifestyle and habits. (That's why I get sales promotions on Fords, not Cadillacs!) Products like Prism[292], Mosaic[293] and SCAN-US help identify these groups of people. These distinctions are helpful in describing who lives in the city and for developing strategies designed to reach all the people groups and population segments in the city.

The Association

The growth and development of Union Baptist Association (UBA) is closely connected to the growth and development of the city. As the city grew, the number of churches in the association grew.[294] As the city diversified, the congregational makeup of the association diversified. [295] *Unfortunately, the growth of the churches in both numbers and diversity did not keep pace with the growth and diversification of the city.* This realization in the 1990s created a crisis which led to a change in the way the association functioned.

Prior to 1990 UBA, like most other associations, was a conduit of denominational programs to the local church. In the early 1990s the focus of the association shifted its emphasis to developing customized programs intended to develop healthy, growing congregations. UBA focused on leadership development, strategic planning, conflict management, partnership missions, and other strategies designed to strengthen the local church.

This change in approach served UBA congregations well and resulted in significant growth for the association as the following charts reflect.

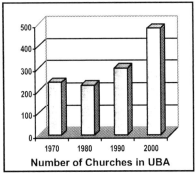

Number of Churches in UBA

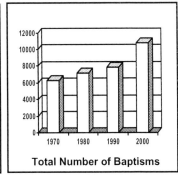

Total Number of Baptisms

As impressive as these gains were, however, the growth of UBA churches still did not keep pace with the growth of the city! From 1960 to 2000, the population of Harris County grew from 1,243,258 to 3,400,578 (a growth factor of 2.75). Yet the number of churches grew from 238 to 480. (I would include the growth factor for the churches as a comparison.)

The number of baptisms reported grew from 6,264 to 10,783. In order to keep pace with the growth of the population in Harris County, there needed to be 651 churches baptizing 17,132 people! UBA's overall strategy has improved the situation but it is not enough. The future holds great challenges

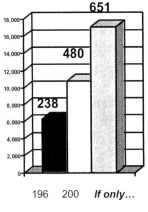

Number of Churches

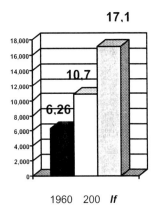

Number of Baptisms Reported

396

and the Association trusts the unlimited God who through His Holy Spirit can enable the harvest to be reaped. Note the charts above.

If modern American cities have become world cities, perhaps the answer to reaching our cities lies in doing what missionaries are doing to reach others around the world. The association of the future will need to be more missional and less programmatic.

The Missional Association

Albert Einstein is credited with saying the definition of insanity is to do the same things over and over while expecting a different result. If churches and associations in North America continue in their present strategies, Southern Baptists in North America will continue to lose ground. An ever-decreasing percentage of the population will be believers. The church will become even more marginalized in society. This outcome is unacceptable to church leaders.

If associational leaders are going to rise to the challenge of a changing metropolitan environment and reverse the current trends, they will need to consider new strategic approaches. The association will need to recapture its missional nature. Established churches will need to develop aggressive church planting strategies. Strategies must be developed for engaging ethnolinguistic people groups and identifiable population segments. Boundaries between foreign, home, and associational missions must be eradicated. More flexible definitions of "church" must be considered. New structures and forms of church must be positively embraced. Associational leaders must develop strategies which benefit from church planting movements happening throughout the world and facilitate church planting movements at home and abroad. In short, we must do whatever it takes to penetrate lostness, exponentially multiply the number of disciples for Christ, and turn new believers into missionaries and church planters.

The International Mission Board of the Southern Baptist Convention has adopted a people group strategy for world missions. Rather than focusing attention on a specific geographical region, missionaries concentrate on reaching people groups no matter where they live in the world. The results in new believers and new churches have been unparalleled in recent church history. [296] If America is becoming more and more like the world mission field, perhaps associational leaders should consider what's happening on the mission field and learn from it.

What would a people group strategy look like? How would it be implemented in an association? As of this writing attempts are being made to contextualize a people group strategy for North America, but it is so early in the process the approach has not been successfully implemented. Consequently, the most that can be written at this point is what is being considered and tried.

If a people group strategy is to be implemented, several key considerations will need to be kept in mind.

1. *The focus must be on penetrating lostness and making disciples.* The focus should be on mission first, strategy second. Jesus said, "As you go, make disciples of all nations πάντε τὰ ἔθνη refers more to people groups than geographic regions (Matt.

28:19). This is the mission of the church. The end result should be that every tongue, tribe, people and nation will be reached with the gospel of Jesus Christ (Rev. 5:9). Church planting and church planting movements are critical components of a strategy for accomplishing the church's mission.

2. *A people group/church planting movement approach is more than a new program to implement. It is a paradigm shift.* A paradigm is a way of understanding life.[297] We base our actions on our paradigms (assumptions). When people thought the world was flat, it made a difference in what they thought and what they did. Learning the world was round, not flat, was a major paradigm shift. It required thinking and acting differently. Implementing a people group strategy will require new ways of thinking as well as new ways of acting. This will be true at every level of church life: the local church, the association, state conventions, and national mission agencies.

3. *The institutional church can be a bridge or a barrier to successfully implementing a people group and church planting strategy.* The idea of "church planting" connotes competition and diminished resources for the institutional congregation. Many congregational leaders will be apprehensive or even fearful of such a strategy. Still the institutional church can be a tremendous resource of trained leaders; mature, passionate believers; prayer support; resource development and financial strength. By keeping the focus on penetrating lostness and

making disciples, the fear of competition from starting other churches should be lessened.

What might be involved in a people group strategy at the associational level? How could associational or judicatory (?) leaders implement a church planting/people group approach? Since there are no examples of successfully implementing such an approach in North America, the most we can consider is what might work. The reader will need to discern prayerfully God's leadership for his specific situation before developing a plan or strategy.

1. **Know your city.**

Research is important. Know who lives in the city. Cities change, sometimes dramatically in a short period of time. Data can be gleaned from reports like those provided by the U. S. Census and SCAN-US. School districts maintain records of their students and make reports available on what languages are spoken by students and the countries of origin included in the school population. Local colleges and universities often have departments which keep local demographic, sociographic or ethnographic data. Still, much will need to be determined by local field research, e.g., windshield surveys and interviews with key ethnic leaders.

Study the impact of your congregations on the city. Compare church growth to the growth of the city. As a whole, are churches keeping up with the growth of the city, or losing ground? Are there churches among all the ethnic and language groups in your city, or are there pockets of lostness across the city?

2. Cast a clear, compelling God-sized vision.

God desires that none should perish but all should have a redemptive relationship with Jesus. This means *all* the people in your city. This means *all* the people groups in our world. Growing churches is not enough! Help pastors and congregational leaders see the need for reaching all the people groups in the city, then extending beyond to reach them in other cities in the United States and around the world. A vision and a strategy which does not have a global focus is a strategy for disobedience.

3. Create a sense of urgency among church leaders.

It will be impossible to implement significant change unless Christians feel a compelling sense of urgency. Urgency is created by comparing God's vision with current reality. While God's desire to see all people live in redemptive relationship with him is clear, congregational leaders may not have a clear view of current reality. They may lack an understanding of what's happening throughout their greater metropolitan area.

In Houston, the UBA staff suspected many pastors who lived in the suburbs were not aware of the extent of the major demographic shifts throughout the city. So we took pastors and congregational leaders on day-long tours of the city. Pastors who had lived in the city for years came away saying, "I never realized how much our city had changed." Up-to-date statistics, stories and experiences like city tours help create a sense of urgency.

4. Develop a strategy that connects local congregations with

a people group(s) in the city, across the nation and around the world.

The International Mission Board (SBC) has developed the role of strategy coordinator. The primary function of the strategy coordinator is to facilitate the development of church planting movements among their specific people group wherever they live in the world.

In order to accomplish this, the strategy coordinator must "marry" the assigned people group. To "marry" implies a high level of commitment and an intimate level of knowledge. The strategy coordinator must be committed to accomplishing the Great Commission mandate among his people group no matter what it takes. The strategy coordinator must spend time getting to know his people group intimately—language, worldview, lifestyles, social roles, values, customs, mores, taboos, religious beliefs—and then develop a strategy for reaching them.

A local congregation could function in the role of a strategy coordinator for a particular unreached people group in their city. The church's aim should be to see the Great Commission accomplished within their people group. The strategy should include praying for the people group. The church (or a group within the church) would learn everything they could about the people group.

Church members could build relationships with people in the people group. Compassion-based ministries, if appropriate, could be focused on the specific people group. The church could make sure the Scripture is available in the heart language of their people group. Hopefully, through these initiatives people within the people group will be led to faith in Christ. Small groups of new believers could be formed where they would be discipled and taught to share their faith with friends and loved ones. As these new believers do business with folks from their people group in other cities, or as they travel back and forth to their homeland, they could share their faith, disciple new believers, and other small groups could be formed in their country of origin as well as in North America.

Churches do not need to work alone. The church could work with an International Mission Board (IMB) strategy coordinator to learn about their chosen people group and to develop strategies for reaching them at home and abroad. The church could also network with churches in other cities trying to reach their particular people group. The churches could learn from one another's experience. Joint mission projects could be developed for ministry at home or abroad.

The Forest Meadows Church in Dallas felt God leading them to reach the Sudanese in their city. They started with a Sudanese Christian who reached out to other Sudanese in his area. A group formed. A church quickly developed. Now they are also reaching out to Sudanese who live in other cities. As new believers travel back and forth from the U.S. to Sudan, they share their faith with family as friends.

Though a church planting movement has not yet developed, this suggestion for a strategy is one way it could begin. Will such a strategy work? We don't know, but this is the general approach being taken by Union Baptist Association.[298]

Endnotes

[278] As of this writing there are no identified church planting movements in North America. So this section will not describe what is happening but review some things that are being tried in other associations in the hope the reader will be encouraged to learn from these experiences and implement as local strategy aimed at facilitating church planting movements as God leads.

[279] This is where the book of Acts concludes, but it is not the end of the story. The author of Acts concludes "Boldly and without hindrance he preached the kingdom of God and taught about the Lord Jesus Christ." [Acts 18:31] The phrase "without hindrance" may suggest the movement of the gospel beyond Rome to other regions and other people throughout the earth, cf. Frank Stagg, *The Book of Acts: The Early Struggle for the Unhindered Gospel,* (Broadman Press, Nashville, TN) 1955.

[280] Rome is estimated to have had one million people during the first century. Compare that to New York City (21.2 million in the metro region) and Los Angeles (16.4 million in the CMSA) according to the 2000 Census.

[281] *World Urbanization Prospects: The 2001 Revision,* United Nations, 2002, p.1

[282] *Migration for the Population 5 Years and Over for the United States, Regions, States, Counties, New England Minor Civil Divisions, Metropolitan Areas, and Puerto Rico: 2000 (PHC-T-22),* U. S. Census Bureau (http://www.census.gov/population/www/cen2000/phc-t22.html)

[283] http://encarta.msn.com/encyclopedia_761576416/New_York_(city).html

[284] http://www.ncccusa.org/news/99news23.html

[285] Ibid., p. 136

[286] Ibid., 135.

[287] Wolfgang Simson, *Houses That Change the World*

[288] Jack Dennison, *City-Reaching*

[289] Ibid, 4.

[290] Nine of the ten most ethnically diverse Zip codes in the state of Texas are found in Houston.

[291] Stephen L. Klineberg, *Houston's Economic and Demographic Transformations: Findings from the Expanded 2002 Survey of Houston's Ethnic Communities*, Rice University: Klineberg, 2002, 11

[292] Info

[293] Info

[294] The number of churches more than doubled from 1960 to 2000. (What is the source of this information?)

[295] As of October, 2003, UBA has 520 congregations. Of these, 176 are Anglo, 158 African-American congregations, 101 Hispanic congregations, 38 Asian congregations and a host of others (African, Eritrean, Ethiopian, American Indian, Arabic, deaf, Haitian, Asian Indian, Romanian, Jewish and multi-ethnic).

[296] Cf. www.imb.org for annual reports and an overview of church planting movements

[297] A paradigm is sometimes called a mental model (cf. Peter Senge, *The Fifth Discipline*, get biblio data)

[298] If you would like to know more about the progress of our work, visit our web site at www.ubahouston.org.

CHAPTER 16

CHURCH PLANTING MOVEMENTS
IN MULTIHOUSING SETTINGS

Barbara Oden

The 100 million people who live in multihousing communities constitute the largest un-reached people group in this country. According to the National Multihousing Council, there are 51 million persons living in Private-apartment communities; 29 million living in Condominium/association communities; 14 million living in Manufactured-housing communities; 4 million living in Senior-housing communities; and 3 million living in Public-housing communities.[299] Of the 15 million apartment units, 8,543,000 are urban, 6,476,000 are suburban, and 918,000 are rural. Of the apartment dwellers, 51% are White, 19% are Black, 16% are Hispanic, and 14% fall into the category of "other." Of those who live in multihousing communities, 30% are "Down and Outers," with an annual income level of less than $20,000; 31% are "In and Outers," with annual income levels ranging from $20,000 to $49,999; and 28% are "Up and Outers," with an annual income level of $50,000 and up. Of the multihousing residents 32% are under 30 years of age; 21% are 31 – 44; 21% are 45-64; and 16% are 65 and over. [300] These statistics show that multihousing residents are found in every part of the country, represent the major population groups; cover the spectrum of socioeconomic levels, and represent a broad range of age groups.

Even though there is significant diversity among multihousing residents, most of them have one characteristic in common; they are *unchurched*. The national multihousing industry did a survey in the early 90s and discovered that 96% of all multihousing residents do not go to church anywhere.[301] This means that the Christian community reaches only 4 percent of all those living in multihousing settings in the United States. This is an amazing statistic in light of the fact that there are numerous churches in every metropolitan area. In an effort to inform and inspire people to reach out to this people group, we are going to point out the various types of multihousing communities, discuss perspectives related to multihousing communities, review existing strategies, and explore the need for a new paradigm to spark church planting movements in these settings.

Types of Multihousing Communities

The first issue in this subject to discuss is the types of multihousing communities. There are generally six different types of multihousing communities where people live.[302]

Low-Rise Contained Communities

Low-rise contained multihousing communities are buildings mostly of two or three stories, containing 50 or more units. Most control access to the property or residents since these communities are private property. Many have gated access to even get to the management office.

High-Rise Inaccessible Communities

High-rise inaccessible multihousing is accessible only by invitation. These multistory buildings usually have at least 200 units. They may consist of one or several buildings closely clustered.

Total Residential Multihousing Communities

Total residential multihousing is high density, highly inaccessible, mostly low-rise walkups, with community residents often unaware that it is classified as multihousing. These areas exist in many large cities.

Public Housing Communities

Public housing is either government owned or subsidized under government regulations. These might be low-rise or high-rise depending on the area. There are strict guidelines governing these properties.

Manufactured Housing Communities

Manufactured housing includes mobile home and prefabricated housing communities where people with limited economic resources reside. Some of the more affluent may reside in marinas. Another type of manufactured housing is found in the Recreational Vehicle Parks where "snow birds" (people who migrate from the northern to the southern part of the United States for the winter) reside.

Unperceived Multihousing Communities

Unseen (or unperceived) multihousing units are smaller units like duplexes or fourplexes dispersed among single family residences. They are accessible like single family dwellings.

Each type of multihousing community has unique characteristics with specific groupings representing a variety of socio-economic, ethnic, and lifestyle segments of the multihousing population. Due to their uniqueness, each multihousing community requires specialized methodologies

Perspectives Related to Multihousing

We must now take a look at the three different perspectives related to ministry and church planting in multihousing communities.

The local church perspective

Some local churches have been extremely effective in establishing multihousing ministries. Others, however, have not reached out to multihousing people. Some of the reasons why they have not done so is that they feel that: 1) getting into these communities is an impossible task; 2) they don't have the personnel to go and minister in these communities; 3) these people are not reachable; 4) people have problems with which the church does not want to get involved; 5) these people do not have anything to offer the church; 6) ministering to these people all week does not mean they will ever come to church; 7) multihousing residents do not want to be bothered.

Most of these ideas are unfounded and came from the media and from news articles discussing one situation in thousands. Church visitation nights became difficult when members had to try to get to someone in a multihousing setting. Finding the building and then the apartment took so much time that it was just easier to go visit someone who lived in a single family dwelling. Many Christians believed that you could not start a church with these people anyway. During the last few years, Southern Baptists have discovered how to get into these communities and build relationships. As believers have built relationships outside the walls of the church with the multihousing residents, they find that many of their fears about this ministry were just not true.

The Multihousing Resident Perspective

The second perspective we will examine is that of the multihousing resident. At the same time the church was discovering some of their ideas were erroneous, thousands of surveys were taken from multihousing residents. Out of all the answers to questions asked, there were six answers that kept surfacing from the residents to one particular question. The question was, "Why do you think most people don't go to church?" Here are the six answers: 1) All the church wants is our money; 2) We don't have the proper clothing needed to go to church; 3) The church is not friendly; 4) Church people really don't want us; 5) We are afraid we won't behave properly; 6) Church people are good at handing out tracts and Bibles and even praying with us, but they really don't care about getting involved with our problems.

These statements may seem erroneous, but that is what most residents believe. They also watch television and read newspaper articles. This is where much of their thinking comes from. Why try to go someplace where they feel they will not be welcomed and included? Why become a spectacle when they don't know the songs or where to find the Scripture passage? Why go someplace where people do not genuinely care whether they come back or not? As a church group comes to a property on a regular basis and begins to develop relationships with these residents, many of their preconceived notions are washed away.

The Management Team Perspective

If these two opposing groups do not present enough conflict to hinder proper ministry to multihousing people, a third opinion exists. The management team has an agenda also and it

411

normally does not include starting churches on their property. Their agenda is focused on resident retention and profit.

If management feels that anything happening on their property would keep the above two things from being reality— It will not continue. Although there is much more work for them on the property than is possible, the threat of people moving out keeps them from allowing most outside groups from intruding. Allowing a church group to have regular Bible studies or church onsite might make residents move out. It is just easier to say NO! If one religious group is allowed on property to hold religious events, than by law, all religious groups must be allowed to do the same thing. Again, it is just easier to say NO to all.

Current Strategy

For the last 17 years we have utilized a strategy that has yielded marvelous results. It is based on the presupposition that there are so many daily duties for a management staff to handle, that it would be a welcome idea for someone to provide the social and emotional assistance they need for the residents. If someone could come to the property as an Activities Committee or group, that would be a welcome addition as volunteer staff. If they would work with all the residents and not "Bible bang" (try to get all of them to go to church with them), this would be such a help for all. If a group would come to the property and hold classes, activities, and help with events such as Easter, Christmas and Halloween, the effort would not only be allowed, but welcomed. The management team only needs one Activities Group so the legal aspect is taken care of. The manager does not have to allow all groups to be another Activities Group.

A second advantage to this arrangement is that the manager gets to know this Group as they come to the property on a regular basis. As trust and confidence in this group is shown, a manager will usually be more than happy for Bible studies and worship to take place onsite.

After discussing the negatives and differences of the three parties involved in a multihousing ministry, how in the world can a church ever get onsite and stay onsite? How does one approach this situation? We have implemented the following guidelines to develop relationships with residents and management of multihousing communities.

Guidelines

Generally there are five principles to follow to get to the point of worship onsite.

Enter the "open the door"

One might approach this ministry in many ways, but the easiest is with the management team themselves, particularly with the manager. This person gets hit from all sides and not too many people respect the authority the ownership has given the manager. The residents are always complaining about something and the supervisor/owner only comes once in awhile to check up on progress. If progress is not consistent, the manager does not last long on that property. Approaching the manager is key to having a good relationship and to open the doors to the entire population on any given site.

The best approach is to pay a visit to the management office and ask to speak to the manager about coming to the property to start some **FREE** activities and classes. A good script would be to say, "My name is _____ and I am with the _____ Church. Our church has become concerned about our community and wants to be of service. We are no longer content to just sit in church on Sunday. We have decided to **CHOOSE** a multihousing community in which to begin some activities and classes on an ongoing basis. Would you like for your community to be that one? We will even do Sunday School and Church here if the residents want it. We just want to be of service to you and your community. We are not looking for money or lots of assistance from you. All we need is a **PLACE** to do the activities and we will get started. We would like to take an Interest Survey of the property to find out what kind of things the residents might be interested in doing." At this point it would be good to show a sample survey and a list of activities and classes other churches are doing on other sites. There may be varying answers to this dialogue from the manager, but generally they are interested when they see we will work with all the residents and not just a few who might come to our churches.

Let's assume that the door is now open and we can begin to work with the residents and for the management team.

Discover the interest of the residents

The second principle to follow is to **find out what the interest of the residents in the community might be**. A door-to-door survey is the best way, if the manager will allow it. If this is not a possibility then a mailing or telemarketing might work. You might also plan an Open House or Block Party on the property and have survey forms to fill out at this event. Finding out what the residents want and need saves much time and effort.[303]

Make appropriate preparations

The third principle relates to preparation. Once you have determined the needs or wants of the property, the church should decide what and how much it can do. Determine what you are going to do and find leaders for the activities and classes.

Some of the beginning activities may be for children, teens, singles, and senior adults. You may offer such things as a support group for single parents, tutoring, crafts, English-as-a-second language or investment classes. On more affluent properties you might even offer Opera Nights, Poetry Reading Class, Horticulture Seminars, and Travel Seminars. You may need some training for some of these activities before you begin. Your associational office would be a good place to start to find the training you might need.

Build relationships

You could start with the actual weekly/monthly cultivative activities and classes or you could begin with a property wide event such as a "block party" type event. The key is to do whatever it takes to build genuine relationships with the residents.

You don't provide these social programs and classes just to have something to do and to say you are ministering. These programs provide the vehicle to get to know the people and for them to get to know you. Out or these relationships come trust and friendship. You would be amazed at how naturally a witness could be and how easy it is to lead someone to the Lord once they know you care about them

Make disciples

Start a Bible study as soon as there is an interest. In almost all surveys taken someone indicates an interest in a Bible study. Get started! A Serendipity Bible is all you need. There are all kinds of lesson plans and topic already put together for you. People love to discuss what they think the Bible says. What a perfect time for a witness!

All of these suggestions naturally lead to a congregation meeting onsite. You ask, where does the pastor come from? How do we put together all of the things we know to make up a church. Just read the book of Acts and you will see how simple it is. There must be someone in your church who loves to teach and even to lead. He would make a perfect pastor. The people don't necessarily care how eloquent someone can be, but they do want to know that someone truly cares about them. Laypeople are the key to this work. Residents expect pastors and staff to provide these things. They get paid to do that. When laypeople, people just like themselves, begin to take the time to get to know them, they respond in a genuine way.

Actually, the easy part of this work is securing a place in which to minister. The difficult part is recruiting and sustaining the lay missionaries needed to build the relationships. We are so geared for mission trips that only last a few days or weeks. To think of an ongoing commitment is overwhelming. Most church members don't even know there is such a need. What is the best way to go about encouraging Christians in our church to move out of their comfort zones into this mission field?

Outline for Implementing this Strategy

Interest in ministry within multihousing alone does not meet the tremendous needs and opportunities for reaching and serving these people. We will outline some of the necessary activities for implementing multihousing strategy.

Awareness

It is difficult to ask anyone to commit to something they know nothing about. Someone needs to make the need known to the people before they can say yes or no. Realizing that 96% of all people who live in multihousing settings don't go to church anywhere makes one take notice. Recognizing that there are approaches and assistance in getting onsite to these people makes some more interested in going. Telling stories of real life situations and life changes also arouses interest. Letting them know about a boy who was never even going to even graduate from high school and is now an appointed missionary in Thailand is exciting. To think that something like this could happen over and over again encourages more to go.

Commitment

When they are aware of needs and opportunities, lay persons will commit to beginning some kind of Christian ministry. You cannot commit until you are aware. This can be done through Sunday School classes, worship services, scheduled Awareness Meetings, and one-on-ones. As soon as some commit to going, an orientation time needs to be quickly scheduled.

Orientation

The leaders will explain to the group how information will be gathered. This plan is determined by the locale. A long detailed explanation is not necessary—only how to go about the research. It is time to explain to the potential workers that nothing can be started without knowing what the people at the particular site would want to do. It is called "Cultivating Relationships." Discuss the Interest Survey and how to go about getting the best information.

Information

Research the area desired as completely as possible to find out what the interests, needs, desires, and thoughts of the people area. Put the information gathered together to determine a starting point. Don't start with too much too soon. A little goes a long way to being successful. Be patient.

Training

If any training is needed, now is the time to do it because now you know where you are going to start and what supplies and equipment will be needed.

Calendaring

Decide when, where, how often, and who will do what. If several do a little bit, it does not make it hard on one or two. One needs to begin at the time and frequency they are comfortable. If people onsite do not come, try another time. Be flexible.

Getting Started

Some sort of "Kick-Off Event" is good, if possible so you can meet as many of the people as possible. It does not have to be elaborate. Block parties are great at any time of the year.

Scheduling Events, Classes, Activities

Relationship building is crucial in building bridges to share the message of salvation. Begin with whatever you have decided to do and let things happen naturally as friendships are made. Remember – it is all about relationships!!!!

Starting Bible Studies/Congregations

Starting Bible Studies in the apartments is the next step in this strategy. As relationships are built, people begin to show an interest in spiritual matters and become open to studying the Bible with their family members and close friends. In some instances, congregations have been formed using local church lay missionaries as the leaders.

Analysis

An analysis of this strategy reveals that it has made a very positive contribution toward reaching multihousing residents. It has enabled churches that previously felt helpless to know how to establish a presence in these communities and work with the management to minister to the residents. The problem with this strategy, however, is that it reaches a comparatively small number.

Generally the management team offers an apartment or mobile home in which to provide ministry and church. These places can only hold 50 to 60 people at best. The lay missionaries from the church must continue ministering to these people for years and years, even indefinitely. It used to be said that they should continue until Jesus comes.

Many people have been reached, without a doubt. Some have moved on to enter full time ministry, while others have started a multihousing ministry some place else. God has blessed and hundreds of thousands have come to know Christ through this strategy. People have been won to Christ and the lay missionary disciples and leads in an ongoing manner. This has been all we have known to do since these are certainly baby Christians who should not be leading anything until they have sat under someone else's teaching for some time. As Southern Baptists we have sought to make these small churches function, as best we can, like the church model we have come from.

While some efforts such as Mission Arlington[304] have been very focused on starting congregations, others have been content to carry on ministries without every getting around to leading people to receive Christ and to gather in their apartments for worship, fellowship, and discipleship. In most cases there has not been a commitment to reproduction of disciples and of congregations utilizing the multihousing converts themselves in these efforts. The limitation of this strategy has been that it has focused on incremental growth and not on exponential growth. This means that there are literally millions of multihousing residents in North America who are not being reached with the Gospel and are as much an unreached people group as those in the most remote corners of the world. What can we do to be more effective?

A New Paradigm

In order to reach the millions of multihousing residents in North America for Christ, we need **a new paradigm**. While the strategy discussed above has yielded excellent results in some settings, we must acknowledge that there are areas where there are no large churches to provide financial support, where volunteers are not available to carry our the necessary ministries, and where multihousing management teams are not receptive to the idea of providing an apartment or activities room for religious activities. We need, therefore, a paradigm that can help existing multihousing strategies to experience unprecedented reproduction and that will guide in the development of new strategies to reach the millions who are a part of this unreached people group. This new paradigm is being used in some of the most strategic parts of the world (e.g., China, India, Muslim countries) to reach hundreds of thousands for Christ. This is the paradigm behind the Church Planting Movements that are sparking the greatest expansion of the Gospel in the history of Christianity.

Church Planting Movement
Paradigm Principles

The Church Planting Movement paradigm has already been described in this book. In this chapter, therefore, we are going to focus on the principles that have the greatest relevance to multihousing settings.[305]

Prayer

Multihousing efforts need to be bathed in fervent, persistent, informed, and focused prayer. Any time we seek to evangelize unreached people groups we can anticipate spiritual warfare. We, therefore, need to enlist intercessory prayer teams. These prayer warriors need to be kept informed so that they will pray specifically for every challenge that multihousing missionaries are facing. New converts need to be taught how to pray immediately after their conversion and enlisted to join the prayer efforts for a mighty demonstration of God's spirit in that community.

Abundant seed sowing

Those who have been involved in multihousing outreach efforts already have a wide variety of exciting, creative, and contextualized methods to cultivate relationships, share the message of salvation, and disciple new converts.[306] For existing strategies as well as for new strategies, however, there must be an uncompromising commitment to plant as many seeds as possible to lead as many people to Christ as possible. Church Planting Movement Missionaries in other parts of the world are asking themselves, "How many people in my people group heard the Gospel today because of my efforts?" Why can we not ask ourselves that same question regarding the unreached people group in the multihousing communities that God has placed in our hearts? He who sows abundantly will reap abundantly.

Intentional Church Planting

Missionaries and local leaders involved in church planting movements are irrevocably committed to starting churches. They have the deep and abiding conviction that this is the strategy that Jesus designed to evangelize the world. He said: "I will build my church and the gates of heaven will not prevail against it" (Matthew 16:18). Building on the biblical definition that has already been discussed in previous chapters, we must be committed to the arduous task of starting churches in every multihousing community.

A part of our paradigm shift needs to be that we must not be content to have just one church in a multihousing unit which often is limited by space available. We must commit to starting networks of churches in many units (apartments, mobile homes, etc.). We must also continually remind ourselves that ministry is not the end goal but that we must toil to see converted believers gathered as churches in every unit possible. What if we went to a property looking for people with whom we could share Christ? We could still build the relationships as are laid out in the outline above.

The difference would be that when one person would be led to the Lord, we would give them the tools for their first week assignment so they could lead someone else to the Lord. As this is done, our leaders would begin to disciple them and to encourage them to lead even more people to the Lord to start their own groups. We continue to lead others to the Lord and ask them to do the same thing. Pretty soon we could have 15 to 20 we are discipling to be leaders of their own groups. They in turn are encouraging their groups to lead others to the Lord and to start their own groups (and so on and so on). It is not necessary to known Genesis to Revelation in order to do this. Our Lay missionaries only need to be one step ahead of those they are discipling so they can give the same materials to them to disciple their groups. This concept could explode and cause a movement across the multihousing industry of America and beyond. If those we win are discipled to win others and taught how to teach them, the multiplication would spread so far so fast, we could not contain it. It is happening on the foreign field and there is no reason it could not happen here.

Authority of the Holy Scriptures

Missionaries involved in Church Planting Movements are committed to the principle that "the Bible is the source of authority for doctrine, church polity, and the personal life of each member." They explain that "the Holy Scriptures are the guide for the life of the church and its authority is not questioned." Some of the most crucial issues related to church planting movements have already been addressed effectively by those serving in multihousing efforts. Often we have faced the challenge of distinguishing between that which is biblical and that which is cultural in our strategies. We need to continue to be totally focused on the Word of God in every thing we do.

Local leaders

Leaders in church planting movements decide at the very start of their ministry that they are not going to be *church planters* but the *mentors of church planters*. They operate under the biblical conviction that the resources are in the harvest. The leaders will carry on the ministry that it takes for people to respond to the Gospel. Once converts are made, however, the leaders immediately begin to train them to share their faith and to lead participative Bible studies with their friends and family members. This procedure leads to reproduction. If the people who come from outside the multihousing communities are the church planters, then we will only have as many churches as they can plant, thus creating a bottleneck in the process. However, if every time that we initiate a ministry in a multihousing community we pray to the Lord of the harvest that He send forth laborers and that He give us discernment to discover them, model for them, train them and mentor them, we will be amazed at the way in which our ministry will multiply.

Lay leaders

Church planting movements are made possible by lay leaders. Typically lay bi-vocational leaders are from the same cultural and socioeconomic background of the people that are being reached. This ensures the methods that are used fit their setting. Also the fact they are bi-vocational means they can support themselves. This makes it possible for multihousing churches to multiply. If they don't need a church building and a paid staff, they can be started anywhere people respond to the gospel.

Churches in the homes

The principle of having churches meet in the homes is one that has been followed by many multihousing ministry leaders from the very beginning. We do not have to spend time convincing these leaders that churches can meet in apartments. Perhaps an area that we need to explore further, however, is that these are not cell groups of a central congregation but actually networks of house churches. As such they carry out the functions of a church in their apartments. Other chapters in this book will deal with the best way to address the issues of church polity, etc. It will suffice to say here, that house churches are being used of the Lord to reach millions of people who are not attending traditional churches.

Churches planting churches

The principle of churches planting churches is one that we need to adopt in multihousing ministries if we are going to see church planting movements among these people. In the past our mindset has been one of encouraging established traditional churches to allocate a number of volunteers from their membership to go into multihousing settings and begin a ministry among them, which may or may not result in the establishment of congregations in these settings.

The better approach calls for the house churches in multihousing settings to start other house churches. While it may take a traditional church to get the process started, the reproductive factor should be included in the DNA of the new house churches so that they are empowered to start other house churches. This can happen when people move from one multihousing community to another or when people in other communities are won to the Lord.

Churches starting churches is the only way that we will make an impact in many of our metropolitan areas with the Gospel. We just don't have enough established churches that are willing and able to reach every multihousing community in North America with effective church planting strategies. What if instead of starting one Bible study and congregation, we started one in *every building*? In some places it could be possible to start groups on *every floor in every building*. In a Mobile Home Community, what if one looked for leaders who already live there and started several groups in their homes? Could it be possible to reach even more people than we are reaching now? Certainly! The lay missionaries could train the leaders of these groups and then go on to a new sight and do it again. They could continue to train the leaders of several sites and let them lead the groups.

Rapid Reproduction

While it might appear to some that the emphasis on rapid multiplication might convey an exaggerated emphasis on quantity versus quality, the opposite can actually be true. Rapid reproduction conveys an urgency that lost people come to Christ. This emphasis also ensures that new house churches are not choked off by elements and practices that are not essential to the work of the kingdom. Training new converts to share their faith immediately after their conversion and encouraging and guiding new congregations to reproduce themselves maintains an excitement and a fervor that is contagious and keeps people focused on the Great Commission.

Healthy Churches

The principle of striving for biblically-centered, healthy, and well-balanced churches is based on the description of the manner in which the first century church in Jerusalem functioned. In this church there was evangelism, discipleship, worship, prayer, fellowship, and ministry. While each denomination needs to determine how these functions can best be carried out in multihousing settings, care needs to be given so that what is done has a biblical foundation and not simply a cultural one. To be healthy, churches, whether they meet in large sanctuaries or in homes, need to carry out these functions in a spirit of humility and dedication to the Lord.

Conclusion

If we are ever to make the necessary dent on this mission field for Christ that exists in multihousing areas, we are going to have to change our thinking and adjust our methods and goals in order to accomplish the task. What we have been doing has won a few. The masses, however, still do not know God exists for them. Most people in multihousing communities are unaware the Christians and churches are present and care about them. In the Multihousing Mission Work we have become traditional congregations. Even though many think we are coloring outside the box on these sites, we have not even gotten out of the box yet. Let's just throw that box away and seek the Lord for His way to reach these people.

Notes

[299] Statistics cited in Chris McNairy, "Multihousing Church Planting: We Call It Church," Alpharetta: North American Mission Board, 2003, 2.

[300] Statistics cited in "Private Apartment Communities as Church Planting Environments," Chris McNairy, National Missionary, Office of Multihousing Church Planting Ministries, North American Mission Board.

[301] See David Bunch, Harvey Kneisel,, Barbara Oden, *Multihousing Congregations*, Atlanta: Home Mission Board, 1993.

[302] For a more extensive discussion on this see, David Bunch, Harvey Kneisel,, Barbara Oden, *Multihousing Congregations*, Atlanta: Home Mission Board, 1993, and Daniel R. Sanchez, C. Ebbie Smith, Curt E. Watke, *Starting Reproducing Congregations*, Church Starting. Net, 2000.

[303] You can find all of these forms and more at www.DBAMultiHousing.com .

[304] Erma Holt Matthis, *The Mission Arlington Story*, Fort Worth: Scripta Publishing, Inc., 1996.

[305] David Garrison, *Church Planting Movements,* Richmond: International Mission Board, 2000.

[306] For a more extensive treatment of these approaches see www.DBAMultiHousing.com .

Chapter 17

Training Leaders for Church Planting Movements in North America

Jose Hernandez

Introduction

Planting the Gospel among unreached and under-reached people groups/segments in North America is a task that has involved a great variety of approaches. Whereas some methods have been effective, others have not and yet many groups still remain lost. An approach that has been experienced mostly overseas is the intentionality of facilitating church planting movements (CPM) which is the subject of this book.

The experience that the International Mission Board (IMB) has had with CPM has involved an equipping process for their missionary personnel. This process is composed of two main foci: 1) Training Strategy Coordinators, and 2) Training Trainers. As the church planting efforts in North America focus on the unreached and under-reached people groups/segments, similar approaches for CPM and the associated training processes need to be utilized.

Training Strategic Catalyzers

This section will focus on a *contextualized* equipping approach for North America based on the IMB Strategy Coordinator Training. In the application in North America, some liberty has been taken to make a change in terminology.

The phrase "Strategic Catalyzer" (SC) is used for the personnel's role of facilitating Church Planting Movements. Thus Strategic Catalyzer (SC) Training is designed to equip potential missionary personnel in the art and science of strategic thinking and master planning to facilitate Church Planting Movements in order to impact the LOSTNESS in North America. The emphasis is on evangelizing the lost and bringing them into new churches which reproduce. The hope of this approach is that we indeed can penetrate the lostness among unreached and under-reached people groups/segments in North America, that the Gospel will be planted and that a true church planting movement can be ushered in as the movement of God across our land in the lives of all peoples.

During the summer of 2002, it was my privilege to receive Strategy Coordinator Training in Singapore. This training was provided over a four-week period of time and covered a broad range of topics, activities and experiences. The contextualizing of this training for North American reflects modifications not only in terms of the content but also the process which includes the time periods. The content of the Singapore model has been evaluated in terms of the appropriateness of the topics to the North American situation. The selected topics have been adjusted to issues found in North American. Such issues as relationships to existing Southern Baptist structures (churches and associations) were considered and deemed as necessary. The next aspect considered has been the period of time relative to the training. Utilizing a four-week model was determined to be difficult due to pulling personnel from field work for that period of time along with the related expenses.

The suggested model of training for the pilot experiences attempts to retain the conceptual and most of the activities of the Singapore model but within a different delivery plan. The delivery is structured around three phases—a preparation phase (pre-workshop), a workshop phase and a master plan finalization phase (post-workshop). The following is an outline of this training model.[307]

Phase One—Pre-Workshop Preparation
(4 months prior to workshop)

This consists of the utilization of a pre-workshop (four-hour) meeting for personnel to be trained as Strategic Catalyzers in which the description and expectation of assignments are reviewed. In addition, a system of accountability to ensure a good handling of the assignments is determined.

The preparation of personnel prior to participating in training event through:

(1) Spiritual Preparation — This also includes spiritual preparation (Guided Study of the Book of Acts, Straight Street [this can be found at www.churchplantingvillage.net under the Learning Place]) of the participant. This allows the participant to connect with God in relationship to acquiring the right mind and spirit for the vision that God has in store for the participant in what Church Planting Movements will result. The spiritual preparation also includes the utilization of an intercessory prayer team in relationship to this equipping process.

(2) Conceptual Preparation—the provision of Church Planting Movements awareness materials (reading David Garrison's CPM book,[308] viewing the IMB video on CPM,[309] working

through the CPM workbook [a resource available from IMB], reading *To the Edge* by Jim Slack[310]).

(3) Demographic Preparation—Assignment of research and developmental projects that support the workshop process. Participant select one people group or affinity group for research. The research can be conducted through consultation with a variety of resources including the INTERNET. As a result of this research, the participant will develop People Group Profile. A description of the profile is provided. Templates for doing the demographic and worldview studies are provided.

(4) Assignments—The assignments will include:

a. Spiritual preparation and prayer strategy initial development with Intercessory Prayer Team determination
b. Directed research on people group profile (utilizing LASER, PROBE II[311]) and other research tools (instructions to be provided) and research to be shared in the workshop in document form
c. Directed research on Great Commission Christian partners (instructions to be provided), initial determination will be done
d. Guided readings and reflection with study of Acts to be used in workshop
e. Evangelism actions initial determination will be done (instructions to be provided)
f. Media resources initial determination will be done (instructions to be provided).

Phase Two—Workshop

Work with a training plan of 5 days, which relies on pre-workshop that MUST occur in order to be an effective workshop. This workshop works toward bringing synthesis through the dialogue associated with the presentations made. An effort is made to make a joint analysis of something remarkable that God is doing in the world through Church Planting Movements and a mutual exercise of applying these insights to our own unique individual situations.

A major outcome of this workshop is the development of the initial Master Plan for the Church Planting Movements. Foundational to this workshop is the spiritual aspect which precedes, continues during the workshop and follows the workshop experience. The workshop ends with a dedication of the participants and their work to the expansion of the Kingdom of God and making an impact on the Lostness in North America.

The workshop follows a progressive sequence which includes:

- Understanding of the concept of SC,
- Personal Holiness of the SC Team,
- A Biblical approach to the church planting,
- A profile on the focus group,
- Great Commission Christian partners,
- 100 Ministry/Evangelism Actions,
- Development of a Reproducible Equipping Concept,
- Master Plan for a Church Planting Movements,
- Evaluation Tools for the Master Plan.
- Identification and gaining support of Gatekeepers.

The workshop also follows a training process which includes:

- Daily readings provided the day before presentations,
- Focused prayer experiences,
- Presentations which cover the subject matters,
- Involve guests in elaborating specific areas of support to the SC work or exampling of SC type of work and Church Planting Movements,
- Written assignments which lead to the development of the Master Plan,
- Evaluations of each written resource piece by peers and leaders,
- Cross-fertilization learning from small group review of each other's materials and activities.

The training process will also include a modeling and practicing of actions such as personal evangelism, groups of three, follow-up, small group worship and leadership development. The workshop follows the development of the Master Plan by building on the PILLARS of Endvision, Church Planting Movements, Evangelism Actions, Media Usage, Scripture Distribution, Advocacy and Mobilization, Prayer.

Phase Three — Post-Workshop Follow up Assignments

The primary assignment will be the full development of the Master Plan for Church Planting Movements for the focus people group/area. Completion of the Master Plan may be preceded by the completion of any assignments not completed prior to the workshop. The Master Plan is submitted to the state SC Leader (State Director of Mission/Church Planting Director) one month after the end of the workshop. The State Leadership evaluates each Master Plan and after consultation with the field

SC will move toward implementation of the plan with periodic evaluations.

Participants

The selection of participants is done by the state partners. This level of participation is designed for personnel who will be the primary leaders in activities related to Church Planting Movements and will also be expected to participate in the full Strategic Catalyzer Training. It is suggested that participants be selected from the following categories of workers:

- Church Planting Missionaries
- Ministers of Missions
- Associational Missionaries
- Church and Community Workers
- Campus Ministry Workers
- Pastors or Church Leaders with an evangelistic church planting passion.
- Students (seminary/collegiate) seeking ministry in Church Planting Movements

The difficult step in selection is making a decision that this training may not be for all church planting personnel and missions personnel who are currently associated with our Southern Baptist missions system. For future recruitment of personnel an assessment of personnel according to Strategic Catalyzer profile criteria (to be developed) may need to be utilized. This same profile may be used for evaluation of current personnel. So the difficult step comes in relation to the determination of readiness of current personnel for a shift to an additional/new church planting strategy planning and implementation (for some, they are already there and need to be affirmed).

Another determination will be the expectations related to job descriptions and percentage of time to be spent in Church Planting Movements/Strategic Catalyzer activity. The IMB experience through the New Directions has been evidenced in a major reassignment of missionary assignments to the Strategy Coordinator role. Furthermore, the major of commitment of recruitment and appointment of new personnel were missionaries to work within the Church Multiplication Movements strategies. So the issue for the state partners will involve the determination of the assignments and/or time dedication to the Church Planting Movements strategies.

Perhaps the most important determinant in the selection is the worker's own openness to the possibility of experiencing Church Planting Movements in North America. For many, it would involve an understanding of what God is doing overseas in Church Planting Movements. Then a willingness or commitment to a strategy of house church/basic church planting for evangelizing and churching peoples in North America would be evidenced. These kinds of workers are ready to be involved in the equipping processes found in the Church Planting Movements/Strategic Catalyzer training.

Leaders

Determination of who should lead this workshop has been based on a person's participation in entire (CPM)/SC training process. They will have had a vision and understanding of the CPM paradigm and its possibilities for North America. I have used the phrase "catch and caught" to help communicate who should be involved as trainers for the full workshop. The "catch" is in terms of catching the understanding of the possibilities and processes related to church planting movements as conveyed through the preparation study and workshop *content*. The "caught" is in terms of realization of the content and the training processes which leads the participant to be caught by visioning or as said in SC training, the endvisioning, which sees Church Planting Movements occurring in North America.

In addition any field experience in lay church planting, basic/house church planting or pre-church planting movement type of expressions would prove valuable to the trainer as well as observing/studying the manifestations of church planting movements globally. In order to reproduce (note that reproduction is important as it is foundational to Church Planting Movements) the training processes with state partners, the process of identifying those that are catching and are being caught by the Church Planting Movements will be important. Resourcing these persons with the training materials will be essential so that they can take and further contextualize for equipping their team members and others who will join them in evangelizing, discipling and church planting efforts that result in Church Planting Movements.

Levels of Training

This material is addressed to the personnel that have a lead role at the state, regional or associational level. The roles at each of these levels will be determined locally as the leadership structures are developed. Some will have a director role and others will be team leaders. As the training is taken to the team member and the field implementation on the evangelism and church planting levels, the training plan and content will be adjusted. It may be that team members may be equipped through an abbreviated process, and those that will be the actual field workers, even a more abbreviated process.

Training Trainers

The training which the International Mission board (IMB) provides for the equipping of trainers focuses on eleven major areas: The foundation of the Bible; Understand God's Will; Preparing to be a Trainer; Understand the CPM church; Why does a new Christian not feel happy or feel special?; Individual testimonies on being saved; List the names of all your relatives who have not been saved; Materials used in sharing the gospel (the basic 6 lessons for the initial faith); The Simple and Lasting Guide to Bible Study; Set a end vision (Establish evangelism's generals); and Create your own Acts 29. The following is an outline of the format that is used for training trainers.[312]

Dr. Hernandez provides a detailed guide for training leaders who can contribute to church planting movements. This extremely helpful resource can be accessed and downloaded on the Church Starting Network website www.churchstarting.net. Search under Materials for Church Planting Movements for CPM—How to Build a Trainer.

CPM – How to Build a Trainer

Once we recognize the CPM's style and method, we should start our training work immediately, resulting in each person we encounter to be transformed into a "trainer." We are not doing leader training, nor are we training disciples, we are simply training others to be "trainers." This is like in 2 Tim. 2:2 where

Paul speaks to Timothy, saying "and the things you have heard me say in the presence of many witnesses entrust to reliable men who will also be qualified to teach others."

The Fast Pace of Spreading the Gospel

The day of the Lord's coming is near, how much time do we have to spread the Gospel to the world? Today, the populations of the world stands around 6 billion, but only one third are Christians. Particularly since the number of Christians is below 5% its population. Therefore, we need to rise up immediately to further our spreading of the Gospel. However, this should not be merely talk or hard-work but we should have God's calling, commandment, and the power and wisdom given by the Holy Spirit to employ the fastest way to spread the good news to the world, enabling all the new believers to be capable of training others to obey the commandments and share the Gospels to more people.

1. The foundation of the Bible

The Great Commission from Jesus (Matt 28: 18-20)

After Jesus arose from the dead, He spent 40 days teaching His disciples and encouraging them to spread the Word. In the book of Mathew, Jesus called the disciples to the mountain in Galilee. At this place, He gave them the most important and last commandment.

The most rightful commander

Jesus said, "All authority in heaven and on earth has been given to me." Here the risen Lord reminds us, right now - after the Lord revived - He already is the one with the highest authority in the whole universe. He stated clearly, "All authority in heaven and on earth has been given to me." This is pointing to everything that we imagined in this universe, all the heaven and the earth are included, and all the authority and power belongs to our heavenly Father; the King of Kings and Lord of Lords.

We can imagine someone with complete power and authority over us, would we not listen to him? If you really understand his status, then you will most definitely obey his commands. For example, a soldier should listen to his captains' commands moreover if it were the lieutenants and generals commands, now if the commander himself were to come and give the soldier the order, then the soldier's obedience will unquestionably be 100% . This soldier would not give the command another thought but would obey and accomplish the task right away. Today, our Lord Jesus Christ has clearly revealed to us His status in authority and power so how can we not completely submit ourselves to Him?

The greatest command

Jesus said unto them, "Therefore go and make disciples of all nations, baptizing them in the name of the Father and of the Son and of the Holy Spirit, and teaching them to obey everything I have commanded you. And surely I am with you always, to the very end of the age."

The beginning of the command is to "go." If we do not go, how are we able to lead others to the Lord? Today, everyone has his own road to go, so if we do not go, how are we to find them?

440

"Go" is a very important keyword for you can only do things if you "go." If you stay in place and not go anywhere, no one's going to come to you, therefore the first part of the command is to "go." Friends, let us set our hearts to go now! Once we go, we will see the route the Lord has set for us. Once we go, we will see the many people that need you. If you just stay in place, there will be no change nor will you be touched. At the same time, this will show that you do not have a heart obedient to the Lord.

The Lord wants "disciples of all nations," that is, everyone to be his disciples. This means that everyone is not just a believer, Christian, church member, fellowship member, etc…, but a disciple. If we are just what was stated above, then we do not satisfy Jesus' wishes. He wants us all to become "disciples." A "disciple" is a real learner, he follows the master's steps to learn everything the master knows until the day he is able to go out alone and become a master himself. Therefore we cannot just lead people to be believers, church members, etc…, but must train them to be a master that can train others.

Believing and being baptized will result in being saved as this is a very important witness that everyone sees. Baptism is not just being a witness for the Lord, it also a way to confirm your own faith. So we should teach others the way the Lord teaches us. Lord passes the gospel to us and likewise, we should pass it to others as well as teaching them to obey the Lords words. This is a very important principal, if we do this, then the Lord will surely be with us till the end of the age.

Our Heavenly Father's will

Once we recognize the CPM's style and method, we should start our training work immediately, resulting in each person we encounter to be transformed into a "trainer." We are not doing leader training, nor are we training disciples, we are simply training others to be "trainers." This is like in 2nd Timothy 2:2 where Paul speaks to Timothy, saying "and the things you have heard me say in the presence of many witnesses entrust to reliable men who will also be qualified to teach others."

At the same time we must understand the Lord's will which is to save everyone, starting within people's own family because God is concerned about you and wants to use you to save your whole family.

God calls us to share the gospel

Four different voices of sharing the gospel - In the universe, we can hear at least 4 different voices that tell us to go share the gospel.

The voice from above – this is Jesus' request.

- He said to them, 'Go into all the world and preach the good news to all creation. *Mark 16:15*
- Then I heard the voice of the Lord saying, 'Whom shall I send? And who will go for us? *Isaiah 6:8*
- Not only does the Lord want us to share the gospel, but according to Isaiah, the calling from above also tells us to share the gospel.

The voice from hell – the voice that comes from the spirits that are suffering in hell.

442

- *When both the rich man and Lazarus died, the rich man went to hell and Lazarus went to Abraham's side.*
- The rich man said to Abraham "I beg you, father, send Lazarus to my father's house, for I have five brothers. Let him warn them, so that they will not also come to this place of torment. ."Luke 16:27 - 28
- *Do we hear the voice of those that are suffering that is coming from below?*

The voice from inside – the voice that comes from within every individual

- Since Paul started to believe in Christ, he felt a calling from within himself that strongly urged him to go out and spread the gospel.
- He said, *"Yet when I preach the gospel, I cannot boast, for I am compelled to preach. Woe to me if I do not preach the gospel! If I preach voluntarily, I have a reward; if not voluntarily, I am simply discharging the trust committed to me."* 1 Corinthians 9:16-17
- Every one of us should be like Paul – we should all feel the call from within ourselves to go out and share the gospel once we come to know Christ.

The voice from outside – the calling from Macedonia

- *"During the night, Paul had a vision of a man of Macedonia standing and begging him, 'Come over to Macedonia and help us.'"* Acts 16:9
- Once Paul got his calling from the outside, he brought the gospel from Asia to Europe and later on, we see that the gospel is spread from Europe to North America, and finally throughout the world.

443

- Therefore, each and every one of us should be capable of hearing these 4 voices, requesting us to go and spread the gospel.

2. Understand God's Will – God loves you and want to save your family through you.

Noah
- o God loved Noah. Commanded build ark. Told people share good news, come in, be saved from flood. No one saw any danger: 300 yrs, not converts. Noah, wife, 3 sons: believed, entered.
- o At minimum: Noah saved own family. Very least: witness, win own family

Lot
- o Genesis 19 : Lot
- o God loved Lot.
- o God loved his family.
- o Messenger of God: anyone else related to you in this city? Get them. Be saved. Lot not as powerful testimony
- o Noah shared w all outside, none believed. Family believed.
- o Lot: even own daughter-in-law, laughed. Lot, wife, 2 sons, 2 daughters. Dragged them out. Lot's wife: looked back, salt. Only Lot & daughters.
- o Why? *Lot's testimony in family bad.*

Rehab
- o Joshua 2:17-20
- o Provided protection for Joshua & Caleb
- o God spared her whole family

Demon Possessed Man

- Mark 5:12-20
- Man of Gerasenes healed by Jesus and asked to follow Jesus
- Sent to share good news with his family
- Sent to the Decapolis (10 cities)
- Whole family saved

Cornelius

- A man of reputation and position
- Seeks after God
- Sends for Peter
- Influences his whole household

Lydia

- Business person
- Immediately led her family to Christ

Jailer At Philippi

- Adversary to the gospel
- Heard the gospel and immediately received
- Immediately brought Paul & Silas to share with his family and they believed.

You And Your Family
- God also cares about you and wants to save your entire family through you.

3. *Preparing to be a Trainer*

a) Build a **faithful life by:**

    1) **Offering your life** to God
    2) Being a **soldier of God**
    3) Having the **Spirit's protection and power**
    4) Having a **life of praise and worship**
    5) Living a **life full of prayer**

- Teach them to have a life full of prayer - Praying is one of the key essences to serving God. It is also the server's main source of power.
- Teach them to rely on the blood of Jesus - A trainer must search for the protection of Jesus' blood each day. He should pray for the blood to cover his path, head, and also act as a wall of protection around him.

b). Put on the **armor of God** - God's soldiers must put on their armor every single day. This armor is not to be put on only once but to be put on each day so that the Devil's every attack and schemes can be defeated.

c) Search for **anointing of Holy Spirit** - Teach them to search for the anointing oil of the Holy Spirit - Pray to have the spirit's power and to depend on it, so that the spirit can bestow the gifts of teaching, preaching, healing, joyfulness, praise, and evangelism.

d) Teach them to have a **life full of praise in all circumstances** - Every trainer should understand the importance of giving thankfulness in all situations. Regardless of problems encountered, whether good or bad, successful or not, praise ought to be given to God for giving praise is respecting God's authority.

e) Express gratitude and admiration - Every situation must be viewed positively at all times and encouragement should be given to his trainees, for one positive word can be the foundation of their faith and courage.

PROCESS (tips on process of sharing)

Assume the initiative.

▪ New convert: *share with disciple*

   o *"Welcome back to the family of God"....*
     Beginning point that assumes from Acts 17 that
     we are all men are created by God and therefore
     His children. We choose to sin and therefore cut
     off that relationship. Establishes common
     ground – not foreign
   o *Train. Practice. Confidence.*
   o *1ˢᵗ: novice. 2ⁿᵈ: expert. 3ʳᵈ: trainer.*
   o *Practice = comfort.*
   o *Tonight: do one thing*
     ▪ *Make phone call, personal,*
     ▪ *Must tell someone of the love of God.*

▪ New conversation

   o *Tell them. Don't ask them.*
   o *Lost sheep: may I save you? May I take you*
     home? Would you like to follow me home?
   o *Testimony: prayed for my father 11 years.*
     Prayed for someone to go to my father. List.
     Assignment. Wrote my father a letter—previously
     afraid of his anger. Told Christian. Father called

on phone: you Christian? How long? Why not tell me? What—you want to go to heaven but your father to go to hell? Told his father, led to Christ.

- New commercial event

  o *Leaflets on the street: not ask, offer. Not apologize—*
  o *If I pay salary to a person, I present salvation to that person.*
  o *Train for every person. Pray for all. Ask God to lead. Pray. Pray for lost. Like Peter: pre-Spirit, post-Spirit. Holy Spirit working with him. Tell the Story: 3,000, 5,000.*

4. Understand CPM Church

Time is running out as Jesus' coming is drawing near so we must use the most efficient and fastest way to share the gospel by preparing trainers. Usually *three different styles* of church:

Traditional church

- An Evangelistic Crusade is held at least once per year.
- They hope that every member is able to bring at least one person to Christ each year so the church can double in size every year, but at the end of the year, the number hasn't changed much.
- It is hard for Christians to invite others to church and even if those people come, they still might not believe in the Lord.

- Christians rarely share the gospel themselves; rather, they depend on their pastor or minister.

Cell Group church

- This is splitting a church into cell groups, each containing 10 people. Every week, there will be a fellowship at a church members' home in which other relative or friends are welcome to attend.
- Hope that within 6 months, they can double their size and split into two small groups. If this cannot be done, then it means that this small group has a problem. In this case, the small group must disband and formulate into other small groups containing different people and try the procedure again.
- Hope that every half a year the church is able to double its size.
- Usually inviting a friend or relative over to a home is much easier then inviting them to a church.
- There are times where small groups don't grow even after a year.

G-12 church

- Hope that every church member can lead 12 other people to Christ.
- These 12 people must be trained into a mature Christian before they begin training others.
- Hope that every year the church is able to 12 times its size.
- There are also many difficulties in the teaching methods.

CPM church

- Every member is trained into a trainer
- Every member is trained to find 5 non-Christian friends in a week. Invite them into their homes and share own testimony and bring the gospel into their lives.
- We teach every member to write down their individual testimonies and read it 10 times out loud or until they can memorize it.
- List all family members, relatives, friends, neighbors, classmates, and colleagues names that are non-Christians. Most of the time, everyone's list is around 100 people. Afterwards, they are to pick out the 5 people they want most to share the gospel with and group them as Group A. Then, they are to list the 2nd group of 5 as Group B and so on…
- Teach them the 1st of the 6 basic lessons of the initial faith – requesting them to write all the verses in this lesson down including examples – they will be split into groups of 3 to practice teaching each other until they become very familiar with this lesson. The first sentence of this lesson would be "Congratulations, you have returned into the Lord's family and have become a Child of God again." – this is a very important positive sentence because we were all once God's children, but we left Him and became lost but we are back again.
- When they return after this week, they are to find those 5 people in Group A and witness to them and teach them the 1st of the 6 basic lessons. If some of the people in Group A, then they are to replace those with people from Group B.
- Once the people that they testify to believe in the Lord, they are to do the same thing, i.e., list all

names of people who are non-Christians and teach them the 1st of the 6 basic lessons.
- After one week, the 1st group of people returns to learn the 2nd lesson and once they have learned it, they are to return and teach their next generation the lesson.

5. Why does a new Christian not feel happy or feel special?

- They have not shared the gospel leading them to have no joy from working and also no fruits of happiness.
- If the gospel is passed on to the next person, the Christian will be joyful.
- Satisfaction will be felt if a small group can be started.
- If the trainee can become a trainer then the trainer will start to enjoy the Christian life. (A metaphor can be given here using an average parent– they would want their children to marry and have kids of their own so they can enjoy the happiness of having grandchildren.)

6. Individual testimonies on being saved – Why Christians don't share?

- They do not know *who* to share the gospel with
  Help them list the names of all family members, relatives, neighbors, friends, colleagues, and classmates who have not come to know Christ.

- They do not know *how* to share the gospel

Help them write their testimony on being saved and request them to read testimony out loud 5 to 10 times.

Teach them the 1st of the 6 basic lessons of the initial faith – requesting them to write all the verses in this lesson down including examples – they will be split into groups of 3 to practice teaching each other until they become very familiar with this lesson.

7. List the names of all your relatives, coworkers, classmates, friends who have not been saved

- Have those you train list all of the people that they know who need the gospel
- Prioritize them in groups of 5 (preferably that are related or know each other already)
- Each person can easily list 100 people (begin with at least 20)

8. Materials used in sharing the gospel
(Use the basic 6 lessons for the initial faith – See Appendix 4)

9. The Simple and Lasting Guide to Bible Study

When a new believer fully understands and completes the basic truth, we should teach them instantly the most important factor in training a small group – "The Simple and Lasting Guide to Bible Study."

Whenever you preach or interpret the Bible for them, they can receive and learn. Yet most of these new believers will only rely on your output. They do not know how to receive the light, blessing and grace of

God by themselves. Therefore, we must teach them a Simple and Lasting Guide to Bible Study. This will not only enable them to start self Bible Study but also give them the capability to hold and lead a Bible Study group, allowing those in the Bible study group to do the same.

There are many spiritual growing and Bible study guide books, but most will not be able to help Christians understand how to study the Bible using their own ability therefore not allowing them to fully understand what truth God commends us to obey. In reality, there are no spiritual or Bible study guides that can replace God's word. A person can receive God's teaching and power directly from His word. In this way, he can trust and obey God's word. This is the most important learning. This is why we need to ask the light of the Holy Spirit to shine upon and guide us to spiritual growth.

Below are *three important questions* we must bear in mind when studying the Bible:

1.   What is the scripture about?
2.   What did the Holy Spirit speak to me today through the scripture, and how should I obey and approach this?
3.   How and what I should share with others of the truth I received from the scripture today?

10. Set a end vision (Establish generals for evangelism)

+ To train trainers setting a number of trainers to be trained within a year
+ To establish churches and again setting a number of churches to be established, including ones by you and by your trainers.
+ To set a number of non-believers you want to bring to Christ (A very important concept is to help all new believers become trainers. There will be many people who turn away and much failure and even things that are impossible; however, if 20%-30% of the new believers can become trainers, the result is amazing).

A. What is a Goal?

It is a very clear number or idea - it is a blueprint. Take running as an example. Why do you run? Is it to see how long you can run or how far you can run? No! Your real reason in running is to get in shape and to have a healthy body. This is what can be referred to as a goal. Your running distance and your running time is merely a step to reach your goal.

B. How big is the goal area?

You have to first find an area you will be working in and then within that area find a point where you will start your work.

C. Do not limit your vision

Your vision and faith must be big.

D. You must set many sub-goals

These sub-goals are goals within your main goal, which can be accomplished easily. These sub-goals should contribute to your main goal.

E. You should make sure that every step is possible to do

Every step must be effective and doable, including how to start the 1st step and in what way.

11. Create your own Acts 29

a) Once a goal is set, you must have a vision. At this time, you must pray and think about the road of ministry you are taking. This includes where you are going to start, the difficulties you might encounter, will you have co-workers come and help you, how the Holy Spirit open a route for you, and the strategy you will use to spread the gospel.

b) How your faith is will determine what your result will be like!

c) Create a continuation to the story of the book of Acts through your own ministry that might include the movement of the Holy Spirit, proclamation, acts of God, persecution and multiplied growth.

d) The number of days you do God's work will be the same amount of Jesus' grace and the Holy Spirits' great power that is on you. Remember, the amount of Jesus' grace and the Holy Spirit's power is sufficient throughout your days.

Conclusion

It becomes more and more apparent that hundreds or perhaps thousands of people groups/segments that live in North America do not have a personal relationship with Jesus Christ and are not members of a New Testament-type church. Many of these will only be reached through church planting movements that spread along the lines of their kinship and friendship networks. In order for this to occur, the training of Strategic Catalyzers who, in turn, will train trainers who will train other trainers is absolutely essential. This will ensure the exponential growth that is needed.

Endnotes

[307] We have contextualized the materials for this training model to the North American setting.

[308] David Garrison, *Church Planting Movements*, Richmond: International Mission Board, 2000.

[309] Like A Mighty Wave, Richmond: International Mission Board, 2000.

[310] Lewis Myers and Jim Slack, *To The Edge*, International Mission Board, 1998.

[311] Laser/Probe, North American Mission Board publications.

[312] For the implementation of the Training for Trainers strategy, the International Mission Board has developed a series of practical lessons (2 Kingdom Connections lessons; 6 Re-connecting with God lessons, and 8 Staying Connected with God mailboxes)

Chapter 18

Disciple-Making in Church Planting Movements

Billie Hanks

"As you start so you go" - this proverbial statement has proven to be reality in church planting!

The spiritual DNA of any church is deeply imbedded in the vision and attitudes of its founders. The way you think, pray, and plan will ultimately determine the ministry characteristics of each new church you plant. If disciple-making is truly at the heart of your vision, the churches you found will multiply naturally. Both your strengths and your weaknesses will be revealed through what you emphasize during the formative months and years of each new fellowship. The Lord's unmistakable mandate and spiritual objective for each new church remain timeless. His last earthly words clearly define the mission – He said,

"*...Therefore go and make disciples of all nations...*" (Matt. 28:19a)

The Great Commission

If the spiritual leaders of our day genuinely desire to see the Great Commission fulfilled, then positive grass root changes will need to be made. As new churches are planted, spiritual multiplication must take precedence over addition. This will occur naturally as a disciple-making mindset is established in each successive generation of new believers. This multi-generational approach to church planting requires a plan, which ensures that a trained Christian disciple will invest quality time in the life of each new believer.

Relational ministry was normal practice of the first century church; however, it was neglected in later centuries. Today, this highly effective pattern of new member assimilation and leadership development is once again being discovered and implemented by a growing number of cutting-edge churches, seminaries, and mission agencies. This New Testament methodology is being reinstated in both new and existing churches in many parts of the world. As Paul explained to Timothy, multiplication is the methodology of choice for those who are serious about the future expansion of the Christian faith.

"And the things you have heard me say in the presence of many witnesses, entrust to reliable men who will also be qualified to teach others." (2 Tim. 2:2)

Spiritual Multiplication

Perhaps you are reading and quietly thinking, "If spiritual multiplication were really that important, wouldn't we be hearing more about it in our churches today?" The reason why you don't is simple. Just pause to reflect. When the church planters of the last century were new believers, what percentage of them had the privilege of being personally discipled? Would you not agree that in many cases, the answer is predictable? Most new believers in the 20th and 21st centuries grew up listening to good preaching and attending one or more small group weekly Bible studies. Obviously, this was good, but sadly, only a few of those emerging Christian leaders received intentional personal instruction from anyone. Traditional spiritual education focused on *teaching*, but neglected *training*. Because of this oversight, many of today's pastors, missionaries, and lay leaders were never *shown* how to personally equip a new believer, and others never learned how to effectively share their faith.

As we plan toward global evangelization in the 21st century, it is abundantly clear that a return to Biblical methodology is imperative! It is also apparent that the needed breakthrough in multi-national missions is waiting on a new way of *thinking*. We need churches that focus on a Great Commission centered set of priorities. The New Testament pattern for equipping relationships must once again be established as our primary ministry model. Re-emphasizing this simple, life-changing practice will revolutionize any church's ministry. The secret lies in applying a basic principle that has never changed. Perhaps Solomon expressed it best when he said,

" He that walks with wise men will become wise...." Prov. 15:20

A successful equipping ministry comes from investing one's life in quality time with those who truly want to grow. This requires setting the pace so newer believers will have a pattern to follow. This early church approach to disciple-making is well established in both the gospels and the epistles; however, it escaped the attention of many outstanding pastors and seasoned Christian educators in the 20th century. The idea of *leading by example* is clearly Biblical, yet it remains the missing ingredient in many otherwise effective church-planting ministries.

Every new church needs to build a solid core of outstanding spiritual role models. This calls for equipping dedicated Christian disciple-makers who genuinely care about new believers. Fundamentally, this same spiritual need has existed throughout Christian history, so the challenge to "equip the saints" is not unique to our generation. Every new believer who accepts Jesus Christ deserves a Christian friend – one who can be enjoyed, trusted, and safely followed. Paul filled this role for many young believers including Titus and Timothy. He said,

"Follow my example as I follow the example of Christ." (1 Cor. 11:1)

The Biblical pattern for training disciples was revealed as a natural part of church life, so spiritual apprenticeship became the expected norm for leadership development. In effect, this observation-based training process functioned as Christianity's first seminary. The Lord modeled His *relational* approach – leading by example and the disciples simply followed. Today's churches cannot improve on this methodology because the Lord Himself passed it down to us!

"He appointed twelve designating them apostles, that they might be with Him..." (Mark 3:14a)

The Right Environment

A house church generally offers an accepting atmosphere where personal conversations flow freely. In this informal environment, people find it natural to discuss the Bible and pray about their many personal and family needs. This is one functional reason why home Bible studies so often grow into full-fledged house churches.

In some cultures, the high cost of purchasing land and constructing buildings make it totally impractical to think in terms of a western-style worship center. However, since house churches are both affordable and practical, they offer a worldwide alternative. Additionally, it is important to remember that the Lord did much of His teaching in this informal setting. It was typical for food and refreshments to be available in the homes where He ministered, so fellowship became closely associated with the Christian movement.

Leading God's Flock

In today's world, church leaders are constantly tempted to major on minors. This results in many poor decisions. Frequently, both time and money are invested on secondary pursuits, at the expense of the primary mission of the church. We all admire bricks and stone, because they are beautiful, but we must remember God is looking for disciples! No matter how many programs and new ministries a church may start; the Great Commission must always be its central driving purpose. Said another way, disciple-making must be the fervent passion of God's people!

The Right Priority

In New Testament imagery, Christians are the sheep of God's pasture. Their beliefs and closely held convictions are the clearest reflection of their shepherd's values. Their spiritual vitality and pattern of reproduction are the timeless reasons behind a shepherd's joy!

Paul's inner satisfaction came from observing the growth and faith of his own spiritual children. In that same spirit, our personal fulfillment will always be closely associated with the spiritual well being of those whom we are privileged to train.

"I have no greater joy than to hear that my children are walking in the truth." (3 John 4)

A shepherd never evaluates the condition of his flock based on the aesthetics of their surroundings. Nor does he focus his attention on the shape, size, and location of his barns. Like the Good Shepherd, he looks steadfastly to the safety and health of his lambs. They are the hope of the future, and he knows they deserve both his time and attention. In every way, they are dependent and defenseless, so his responsibility grows each time a newborn enters the fold. What the lambs *eat* and how they are *led* largely determines whether or not they will reproduce and multiply. Remember that all sheep were created and specifically designed to multiply, but poor spiritual health can override the great potential of that genetic disposition.

A magnificent barn is of little importance if a flock's size is slowly decreasing year after year! This observation should constantly remind us that sound doctrine and life-style evangelism are vitally important. How do we know this?

Because in various parts of the world, where multiplication ceased, Christianity is now regarded as dead, lifeless history! In those countries, traditional houses of worship are viewed as cold empty monuments representing the past and a form of religion based largely on ritual and legalism.

If barns were essential for spiritual growth to flourish, or for God's people to multiply, surely the Holy Spirit would have inspired the writers of the New Testament to say more about it. To be certain, barns are useful, but only when the size of a flock makes them practical. It is the enemy's *trick* to move a shepherd's heart away from the primary task of making disciples – to simply building, painting, and maintaining barns!

"...The good shepherd lays down his life for his sheep." (John 10:11)

Care Givers

Believers who are selected for the ministry of training new members must be spiritually alert and take their responsibility seriously. If disciple-making is their passion, they will want to ensure that all new members are properly equipped to grow, witness, and multiply. Through their ministry of disciple-making, lifestyle evangelism will quietly begin making a growing impact on the entire community. Surprisingly, this life-changing process of spiritual growth and multiplication is not difficult to initiate. It merely requires vision, a basic understanding of the need, and a wise investment of time. This puts the ministry of disciple-making well within the reach of every congregation. The application of this rewarding principle begins with a new mindset that focuses on people rather than programs or projects. Jesus said, "*if you love Me, feed My lambs...and tend My sheep...*" (John 21:15, 17)

How does disciple-making take place?

Reading the Bible, listening to uplifting spiritual conversations, and observing the lives of older believers is the most natural way for new believers to grow spiritually. By simply hearing the prayers and experiences of more mature Christians – They gradually develop a Biblically based value system. However, it is through the example of their discipler that they will experience their most rapid growth. Through observation they learn how to practically apply Biblical instruction. Each time they see a godly decision being made or hear wise advice being given – their faith grows a little bit more. Consciously or unconsciously they began wanting to make mature spiritual decisions. With this growth they begin desiring to understand and use their own spiritual gifts. At some point on this upward journey they become aware that God is practical and discover that He is also able to provide for all their needs!

"And my God will meet all your needs according to His glorious riches in Christ Jesus." (Phil. 4:19)

As new believers experience the presence of Christ in their lives, they become inspired to share their newfound happiness with others. This initial and spontaneous time of growth signals the opportunity for disciple-making to either begin or deepen their knowledge of Christ. Since young believers are not automatically equipped to understand what they read in the Bible, or appreciate sound Christian doctrine, they need special assistance. Typically, experiencing the reality of answered prayer will become a major spiritual milestone as they grow. This and a rewarding list of other new discoveries will develop slowly over time. The Bible says,

> "*Let us not become weary in doing good, for at the proper time we will reap a harvest...*" (Gal. 6:9)

The personal attention, which new Christians receive while being discipled, provides them with a wealth of practical instruction. They hear authentic expressions of faith and learn to trust in God's sovereignty by simply watching the lives of dedicated fellow believers. The more time they spend with the one being led to equip them, the faster they will grow.

Small prayer and Bible study groups are designed to provide new believers with fellowship and Biblical instruction, but discipleship training is uniquely different. This dynamic process takes place through personal friendship. It provides new believers with the opportunity to observe the "how to's" of witnessing, developing Christian character, living by faith, and discovering the functional aspects of their spiritual gifts. Paul said,

> "*Whatever you have learned or received or heard from me, or seen in me, put it into practice. And the God of peace will be with you.*"
> (Phil. 4:9)

Classical Spiritual Disciplines

Scripture memory, prayer, independent Bible study, sound hermeneutics, and simply enjoying the fruits of the Spirit are all basic components of personal spiritual growth. These important lessons are most effectively conveyed through the caring example of a more experienced Christian friend. During this inspirational process of transformation, new believers are guided to understand that obedience, faith, and love are the three best indicators of personal spiritual development.

"Therefore, if anyone is in Christ, he is a new creation; the old has gone, the new has come!" (2 Cor. 5:17)

With the Holy Spirit's assistance, new believers begin seeing life through eyes that recognize and value spiritual reality. Intuitively, this experience of transformation leads them to seek life's true purpose. They begin desiring to be more like their Master. Their role model on this spiritual pilgrimage is the life of the one discipling them. Their Christ-centered relationship provides the avenue for the Holy Spirit to produce this positive change!

"As iron sharpens iron, so one man sharpens another." (Prov. 27:17)

Over time, seasoned disciple-makers learn to differentiate between personality traits and the spiritual characteristics of a life that is being transformed by the Spirit of God. No one multiplies in the spiritual realm by simply having a winsome personality. Authentic ministry only takes place through the work of the Holy Spirit. Disciple-making is always His activity in and through us, and never something we can do for ourselves.

"I can do everything through Him who gives me strength." (Phil. 4:13)

A multiplying ministry vision is "caught" far more effectively than it will ever be "taught." Through observation, new believers discover that they are truly on mission with Christ (Matt. 28:18-20). They also learn that they are nothing less than His New Testament witnesses! Through regular fellowship, corporate worship, and discussions with dedicated Christian friends, they begin taking their place of service in the larger community of faith. Ever increasingly, they experience fellowship with God as they develop the desire to fulfill their high calling.

Daily Personal Witness

Beginning each new morning with specific prayer and asking for the opportunity to witness puts life's purpose squarely on track. James reminds us that we *"have not"* because we *"ask not,"* so petition is the first step in moving toward a life of spiritual reproduction. New believers advance several grades in the school of prayer when they learn how to offer this kind of request because it truly pleases God!

> *"This is the confidence we have in approaching God: that if we ask anything according to his will, he hears us. And if we know that he hears us – whatever we ask – we know that we have what we asked of him."*
> (1 John 5:14-15)

Evangelistic multiplication is typically waiting on one or more spiritual discoveries to be made during the disciple-making process. First, new believers need to be taught to *pray* for the privilege of being an empowered witness. Second, they need to be guided to exercise *faith* by carrying a small Bible or good gospel booklet. Third, they should be led to *dedicate* themselves to the purpose of encouraging and training those who respond to the gospel.

Dr. Hershel Hobbs once wisely said, "The work of evangelism is never complete until the one evangelized becomes an evangelizer." This describes spiritual multiplication as it takes place naturally in daily life. Remember the principle, "as you start, so you go!"

Peter's challenge to godly living (2 Pet. 1:5-8) defines the Biblical plan for all effective ministry. Above all else, each discipler's personal behavior will either enhance or diminish the impact of his or her verbal witness. Anger, crude language, immorality, greed, impurity, prejudice, jealously, and all other forms of sin will seek to undermine the power of the message we bear, so lets "pray without ceasing" asking for transparent integrity. The result of this request will be a life controlled by the Holy Spirit. All day, every day, He will empower us to be Christ's witnesses!

"But you will receive power when the Holy Spirit comes on you; and you will be My witnesses in Jerusalem, and in all Judea and Samaria, and to the ends of the earth." (Acts 1:8)

The Principle Applied

It is unrealistic to think in terms of multiplying healthy house churches without also multiplying the number of growing believers within each fellowship. The strength of every new church is revealed by the spiritual depth and vitality of its individual members. Without a disciple-making mindset, we run the risk of planting new churches that will someday resemble the very failures we have lamented in disciple-making in recent years. This is *why* the powerful resurgence of lay and personal ministry should be closely linked with today's emerging house church movement. Both of these ministries operate on the exact same principle and take us back to the most effective days of Christian global outreach!

Church programs that fail to produce personal spiritual growth result in shallow Christians. However, training that employs relational ministry produces spiritually healthy reproducing Christians. They, in turn, are ready to help start healthy reproducing churches. Why? Because we reproduce out of the overflow of what we really are.

Summary

Since leadership by example takes place through Christ-centered friendship, the warmth and relaxed atmosphere of a house church compliments the disciple-making process. Across the centuries, the felt needs expressed by new and growing believers have fundamentally remained the same. Recognizing and responding to those needs remains the timeless responsibility of the church in every generation. It is essential that we plan to meet this challenge in the 21st century!

Disciple-making is the work of God the Holy Spirit. He performs this ministry through His Word and the lives of dedicated Christians. It should be no surprise to us, that today's disciple-makers serving in house churches can impact our century just as powerfully as our forefathers impact was in the 1st century. Nothing that matters spiritually has actually changed. Relational ministry is just as effective today as when the Lord first modeled it.

Your next step is to *pray* for qualified workers, and faithfully disciple the new believers. The harvest is ready and the time has come to finish the work.

> *"The harvest is plentiful, but the workers are few. Ask the Lord of the harvest, therefore, to send out workers into His harvest field."* (Luke 10:2)

Chapter 19

The Role of the Laity in Church Planting Movements

Van R. Kicklighter

Many issues regarding a church planting movement in North America are unclear. While we long to see God move across our continent the way He has moved on virtually every other continent of the globe, we have to admit that we are not experiencing this kind of movement. Quite a number of us who are working to this end are asking the question "Why"? What is it about North America that makes it such a difficult place for the rapid spread of the Gospel?

There are many possible responses. Among them we could list growing secularization, emerging postmodernism, increasing consumerism, and disintegrating social structures among others. Perhaps none is more significant than the "professionalization" of ministry that occurred over the last several generations.

In modern Western culture, it has become the day of the professional. We have come to place great value on the professional. For example, all of us want a "professional" doctor when we are facing surgery. No one would choose an "amateur" to perform open heart surgery on us. The same is true when we look for lawyers, accountants, and other professional services. In fact, we even distinguish between professional occupations and other lines of work such as skilled trades to which we do not afford the same kind of professional status.

This same kind of sharp distinction between the professional and non-professional also developed in the church. In Christianity, this resulted in a division between the professional clergy and the people themselves known as the laity. While especially pronounced in Roman Catholicism, it has also come to mark virtually every form of Protestantism as well.[313] One of the influences of the Enlightenment was a desire for the religious leader to assume a position as a professional among other professionals, especially those in the empirical sciences. [314] This has resulted in a group of professional ministers that have specialized training, receive full financial support for what they do, have increasingly specialized areas of expertise, and believe that their training allows them to "do it better" than the untrained amateur.[315]

A simple look at dictionary definitions serves to illustrate how pervasive this has become in Western culture. The word clergy comes from an old French word meaning knowledge or learning. Webster defines clergy as "a group ordained to perform pastoral or sacerdotal functions in a Christian church." In contrast, laity is defined first as "the people of a religious faith as distinguished from its clergy" but more pointedly as "the mass of the people as distinguished from those of a particular profession or those specially trained." This distinction between a trained clergy and the untrained laity has enjoyed virtually unquestioned acceptance as the normal, even biblical, model of leadership.

What this has done is eclipse any understanding of the God given giftedness of the non-professional lay person for leadership. Leadership in the church, and by extension for mission, has come to "involve a series of clearly marked requirements that mean few can give leadership without some form of seminary education that prepares them for ordination to the professional ministry."[316] Our contemporary understanding of a person's "call to ministry" further illustrates this growing distance between professional clergy and laity. While God certainly "calls" certain people to unique roles of ministry, the fundamental call of the Bible is first to salvation in Jesus Christ which carries with it a call to be "a people on mission."[317] This call to be on mission is extended not just to a few, but to all of God's people. David Bosch observes that this transition is already underway, saying,

> The movement away from ministry as the monopoly of ordained men to ministry as the responsibility of the whole people of God, ordained as well as non-ordained, is one of the most dramatic shifts taking place in the church today.[318]

To the spiritually awakened person, the current state of the church's effectiveness in North America is causing increasing discontent and concern. Assuming we believe that it is God's desire that every people group, population segment and place have an intentional Gospel witness and resulting church fellowship, the day has come for us to reengage all of God's people in the mission activity called church planting. One characteristic of a church planting movement is the rapid, or exponential, multiplication of churches. In order to have the multiplication of churches, we must have the multiplication of leaders that are planting and leading these new churches. Our current approaches to training the professional, seminary educated pastor[319] simply can not equip enough leaders fast enough to fuel the rapid multiplication of churches. This is in no way a disparaging comment about the value of seminaries or what they do in training leaders. It simply is a recognition of the inherent limitations of this system of ministry preparation. Along side those that are coming out of our seminaries, we must re-invite the lay person to active involvement in Gospel sowing and church planting.

As we have been begun to talk about lay-led church planting around North America, it has been obvious that this raises deep, and sometimes troubling, questions for many people. Some leaders have been very vocal in voicing their concerns, even objections, to the use of lay people in church planting leadership. Many others, however, have real questions which are often not verbalized. The majority of the questions revolve around five key areas.

The Propriety of Lay Leaders in Church Planting

We get the English words lay and laity from the Greek word *laos*. In its most basic sense, it was used to describe the mass of people, or a crowd. Used in this way, *laos* describes the whole crowd or all of the people. In the New Testament, this is the word used to describe the whole people of God, or God's people. As such, it included all people that were followers of Jesus including church leaders such as pastors.[320] There is another Greek word, *laikos*, which was used to differentiate those that belong to the laity as opposed to the clergy. In this context, a lay person would be someone that was untrained or an amateur.[321] It is interesting to note that *laikos* is not used in the Bible, either in the Greek New Testament or the LXX translation of the Old Testament.

Certainly, in the day of Jesus, there was a clear distinction between the common people and those that were religious professionals. A strong clergy class had developed which was embodied by the scribes, chief priests, and the Pharisees. These men were the professional clergy of their day, giving their full attention to the Law of Moses and religious activity. Given a ready supply of trained and committed religious professionals, it is significant that Jesus did not choose these men for his early followers. In fact, Jesus seemed very intentional in selecting his disciples from among the most common people of his day, fishermen, tax collectors and other ordinary folk. Jesus seemed to feel no compulsion to select the best and the brightest from among the religious elite of his day. Instead, rather than going to the priestly class, he broke with a long legacy of Jewish tradition and chose future leaders from among the *laos*, those who were untrained, non-professionals in the religious matters of his day.

The development of a Christian clergy did not arise until the third and forth centuries. The term "priest" was not conferred on Christian clergy until around AD. 200. [322] Thereafter, the church adopted two clearly distinct categories of people; the clergy and the laity. The laity came to be viewed as "immature, not come of age, and utterly dependent on the clergy in matters" of religion. [323] With the adoption of this priestly functioning, an early form of church hierarchy developed in which the priestly leaders assumed specialized functions both in the church and in life that set them apart from everyone else. This developing dichotomy between those that served God full time and those that did not increasingly displaced the New Testament idea of *laos* representing all of God's people. [324] Under the rule of Constantine, Christianity became the official state religion. Now, the Kingdom of God and the kingdoms of this world had become one and the same and the hierarchy of the church became even more pronounced. Ordination and offices in the church were no longer based on giftedness, but were "state sanctioned and an institutionalized office [was] gained through rank and study" even to the point that when there was no clergy, there could be no church.[325]

While there is abundant biblical support for leadership roles in the church, it has virtually nothing to say about the distinction between laity and clergy. Charles Van Engen, in a stinging critique of this practice, sees the differentiation between the laity and the clergy since the time of Constantine as a primary cause of the church's ineffectiveness in mission.

> There is no biblical basis for such a distinction in the Church, and the unbiblical practice has only served to place "professional" clergy on a pedestal as being "close to God," removing the vast majority further from holiness and the activity of the Spirit in their lives. The rise of a clergy-laity distinction from the third century on continues in the Protestant denominations since the Reformation as one of the main sources of decline, secularization, and sinfulness of the Church.[326]

, from planting and leading churches? His assessment of the biblical foundations is accurate and his conclusion regarding the outcome of adopting this non-biblical distinction ought to give us pause to think. The fundamental question we ought to wrestle with asks: Is there anything biblically that prevents laity, the people of God

The Qualifications of Lay Leaders

We have already touched on this issue in the previous section. However, the question of biblical qualifications for leadership deserves further attention. I am not suggesting that all lay people should be planting churches. Not everyone will have the aptitude, giftedness, or calling for church planting. The same is true of ordained clergy. There is, however, a fundamental difference between a person's ability to perform certain ministry roles and biblical requirements that might exclude someone from a leadership role. What we want to explore in this section is whether there is anything in the biblical requirements for leadership that would preclude a lay person from church planting leadership.

The biblical requirements for leadership are found in 1 Timothy chapter 3 and Titus chapter 1. If we were to limit ourselves to just the biblical requirements without adding any extra-biblical expectations, what must someone be or know in order to qualify as a leader? Let's begin by looking at these two passages.

Here is a trustworthy saying: If anyone sets his heart on being an overseer, he desires a noble task. 2 Now the overseer must be above reproach, the husband of but one wife, temperate, self-controlled, respectable, hospitable, able to teach, 3 not given to drunkenness, not violent but gentle, not quarrelsome, not a lover of money. 4 He must manage his own family well and see that his children obey him with proper respect. 5(If anyone does not know how to manage his own family, how can he take care of God's church?) 6 He must not be a recent convert, or he may become conceited and fall under the same judgment as the devil. 7 He must also have a good reputation with outsiders, so that he will not fall into disgrace and into the devil's trap (1 Tim 3:1-7 NIV).

Since an overseer is entrusted with God's work, he must be blameless-not overbearing, not quick-tempered, not given to drunkenness, not violent, not pursuing dishonest gain. 8

Rather he must be hospitable, one who loves what is good, who is self-controlled, upright, holy and disciplined. 9 He must hold firmly to the trustworthy message as it has been taught, so that he can encourage others by sound doctrine and refute those who oppose it (Titus 1:7-9 NIV).

A careful reading of these passages reveals that much of what we typically look for in ministry leaders is not found here. For example, most ministry search committees will ask about ministry experience, educational attainment, ordination, and a track record of accomplishments. While no one would deny that these can be helpful, it is interesting to note that they are absent from the list of biblical requirements.

So, just what is it that God expects from those that would be "overseers" in ministry? The following table may help in clarifying the nature of God's requirements for spiritual leaders. Place a check mark in the appropriate column for each requirement identifying whether it is a skill needed, a character trait, or some other requirement.

Table 1.

Requirement	Skill	Character	Other
Above reproach			
Husband of but one wife			
Temperate			
Self-controlled			
Respectable			
Hospitable			
Able to teach			
Not given to drunkenness			
Not violent (gentle)			
Not quarrelsome			

Not a lover of money			
Must manage his own family well			
Not a recent convert			
Have a good reputation with outsiders			
Not self-willed			
Not quick tempered			
Loves what is good			
Upright			
Holy			
Able to encourage others			

As you think about leadership for a church planting movement, what kinds of people do you want to be looking for? Biblically, it seems that who you are is much more important than what you know. Certainly for the early disciples and apostles this was the case. We have already noted that Jesus selected his followers not from among the religiously educated but those that we would classify today as lay people. You will remember that when Peter and John were confronted by the priests, Sadducees, and religious leaders, they commented on their lack of training but noticed something important about their character:

> *When they saw the courage of Peter and John and realized that they were unschooled, ordinary men, they were astonished and they took note that these men had been with Jesus* (Acts 4:13, NIV).

This brief survey demonstrates that there is nothing biblically that prevents lay people from assuming leadership roles in church planting. Such was the case in the New

Testament era of church planting and, as we will see in an upcoming section, this is still true today.

The Appearance of Lay Led Churches

One of the hindrances to a church planting movement in North America is our understanding of church. Ask the person on the street to tell you what a church is and virtually everyone, even non-Christians, will have something to say. While I was planting churches, it was extremely common to make a contact with someone only to hear them say "I'll come once you get a church." I would often respond by telling them that we already had a church, we just didn't have a building yet. However, the impact of this distinction was usually lost on those I was attempting to reach. This serves to illustrate the functional definition of what constitutes church in our culture.

While the early Christian church did not have a building for the first 200 years, the thought of what constitutes church today has changed dramatically. The definition of church found in Webster's dictionary serves to remove any doubt about what people mean when they use the word "church." Webster's two top definitions: 1) "a building for public and especially Christian worship," and 2) "the clergy or officialdom of a religious body."

Certainly for Western Christianity and much for much of the rest of the world as well, church has come to mean a place where we go to partake in religious activities. Specifically, church is a building where people gather to participate in certain programs, led by a paid professional, and is something we engage in once a week. Church, when defined in this way, automatically excludes all but a select few from every being able to start or lead one. This understanding of church effectively eliminates lay people from participating.

The New Testament paints a much brighter picture for the involvement of the laity in church planting. Aside from the apostles themselves, the planting of new churches centered on the involvement of lay people. While Jewish worship was focused in the synagogue, which required a certain number of Jewish men to constitute, the New Testament portrays the church (*ekklesia*) simply as people "gathering" (see 1 Cor. 11 for a representative passage).[327] Typically, they gathered in private homes. Reinforcing this is the biblical pattern of the household or *oikos* functioning "as the basic unit in the establishment of Christianity in any city."[328]

One major difficulty with the contemporary expression of church lies in the fact that it is inherently difficult to reproduce with rapidity. If our goal is the planting of the Gospel among every identifiable group of people resulting in the rapid multiplication of churches, our current paradigm can only offer us the addition of churches, at best. We can not generate the kind of financial resources needed to provide seminary training, offer salaries and benefits to a church planting team, buy property and buildings, and provide the ministry and programming budgets required. Multiplication simply can not occur under the weight of these requirements.

It is encouraging to note that there are a number of lay-led church planting movements occurring around the world that mirror the simple, *oikos* pattern pictured in the New Testament. Bosch notes that striking examples of this came be found in small or "base" Christian communities spreading around the globe. They tend to take many different forms; "house church groups in the West, African independent churches, [and] clandestine gatherings in countries where Christianity is proscribed."[329] It is significant that not only do these tend to be small, simple, and highly reproducible expressions of church, they also demonstrate that the "laity have come of age and are missionally involved in an imaginative way." [330] David Garrison, in describing universal characteristics found in all church planting movements, identifies simple house churches as one of the ten. "Church buildings do appear in Church Planting Movements. However, the vast majority of the churches continue to be small, reproducible cell churches of 10-30 members meeting in homes or storefronts."[331]

It is clear that church planting movements can either be fueled or impeded by how the church is expressed. For church planting movements to thrive, there must be a ready supply of leaders and a form of church that is biblically faithful yet also readily reproducible. With relatively simple forms of church, the way is opened for large numbers of lay people to help plant and lead them.

The Evidence of Lay-Led Churches

While there isn't anything in North America that approaches a church planting movement right now, we are not left to merely speculate about some phenomenon that has never been experienced outside the hearts and imaginations of missionary dreamers. We have a number of historical as well as contemporary examples of lay-led church planting "movements." A look at a couple of the more notable ones will serve to illustrate the vital role lay people can, and must, have if we are to experience the rapid multiplication of churches.
.

In recent years, there has been a growing interest in Celtic Christianity and spirituality. While not covered in most Christian history treatments, something quite remarkable happened in Ireland and some of the surrounding countries beginning in the fifth century. The method of Patrick was quite revolutionary for his day, focusing on evangelism and church planting. After identifying responsive people, Patrick and his band would then encourage these people to take the gospel message to their family and friends. The approach of Patrick's missionary band would result in thoroughly indigenous churches being planted before moving to the next place. Each church, or churches, would be led by one of the recent converts and encouraged to form a missionary band of their own.[332] In a country where there was little or no Christian presence, Patrick and his missionary bands planted 700 churches and saw 30 or 40 of Ireland's 150 tribes become "substantially Christian" in just under three decades.[333]

What is so significant about this remarkable achievement is that it was largely a lay movement. Hunter comments that this was "more of a movement than an institution, with small provisional buildings of wood and mud, a movement featuring laity in ministry more than clergy."[334] Even in the famous Celtic monastic communities, a focus on the laity was evident. Celtic monasteries were populated by a wide range of people, teachers, families, craftsmen, and artists along with monks and nuns who all lived under the leadership of a lay abbot or abbess. Even in the monastery "they had little use for more than a handful of ordained priests, or for people seeking ordination; they were essentially lay movements."[335] What made Patrick's strategy so unique, especially for his day, was his missionary approach, use of indigenous methods, a focus on reproduction, and a theology that put the laity at the forefront.

A second illustration can be found in the protestant missions, or modern missions, movement. This movement was from the very beginning a lay movement.[336] The early foreign mission societies were fundamentally voluntary and often led by prominent laypersons. While there were certainly clergy involved, the hyper-Calvinism of that day was not conducive to missions. As a result, the real impetus for the missions call came from, and was sustained, by laypeople.

Concurrent with this was the pioneer movement in America. While most of the established denominations were hampered in their ability to address the opportunities of the westward expansion, the Methodists and especially the Baptists were free from these. For the Anglicans, Presbyterians and Congregationalists, every church required a seminary educated, ordained clergyman. The challenge of evangelizing and churching the west proved insurmountable under these requirements. Even where there was a desire to move into the "wild west" by these groups (which was not always the case), the system of educating and credentialing ministry leaders was unable to respond quickly and effectively enough to meet the growing opportunities.

Methodists and Baptists, on the other hand, were uniquely positioned to take advantage of the free and open market of the newly settled west. The itinerancy of the Methodist circuit riding preacher proved to an extremely effective missions strategy, gathering new "classes" over large distances with very few people. Wesley's use of laymen to lead the public services of these new societies has been described as "second only in its missionary significance to the adoption of field preaching."[337] Finke and Stark observe that the advance of

Methodism slowed, and eventually halted, with "the loss of the circuit riding preacher, a centralized church hierarchy, a diminished role for the laity, full time clergy becoming normative, increasing educational requirements, and rising affluence."[338] Baptist expansion was carried on by the farmer-preacher who took the gospel with him, often moving to find the next place in need of a church. He was also known to make regular preaching tours into the back country of his own accord.[339] These farmer-preachers were just like the people they were seeking to reach; common, uneducated, hard-working people. Baptist churches were typically started with as few as six to ten people and frequently met in the cabin of frontier settlers for several years before moving into simple church buildings. [340] The Methodists and Baptists were effective primarily because of their missionary spirit, extensive use of laypeople, and inexpensive, reproducible church strategies.

One final example of lay-led church multiplication is found in contemporary church planting movements occurring overseas. Although these are not North American, the characteristics of these movements are instructive for us. We have already looked at how simple forms of church are a distinctive of rapidly reproducing church movements. The fact that lay leaders assume primary leadership roles is a closely related attribute. David Garrison, who has tracked these church planting movements lists the use of lay leaders as one of the ten universal elements.

> Church Planting Movements are driven by lay leaders. These lay leaders are typically bivocational and come from the general profile of the people group being reached. In other words, if the people group is primarily non-literate, then the leadership shares this characteristic. If the people are primarily fishermen, so too are their lay leaders. As the movement unfolds, paid clergy often

emerge. However, the majority—and growth edge of the movement—continue to be led by lay or bi-vocational leaders.[341]

What is clear is that the leadership of lay leaders is an essential element of both historical and contemporary church planting movements.

There are three defining characteristics that can be distilled from this brief sketch. First, church planting movements emerge out of apostolic activity. In other words, the movement exists not for itself but for those on the outside, the lost non-Christian population. Laypeople are critical to this missionary activity since they have ready and deep relationships with non-Christians in ways that most professional clergy do not. Second, the nature of the movement is focused on community.[342] By this, I mean a Christian community that is a clear alternative to what exists in the surrounding culture. Laypeople may not have theological credentials but they are very effective in living out their faith in community with other believers and with those still outside the faith. Finally, the early forms and expressions of church are simple. Relatively simple expressions of church are readily reproducible and allow for, even require, leadership from those that are not formally trained.

The Role of Ordained Clergy

Many of you reading this are already ordained clergy or are preparing for service in that kind of role as a pastor, missionary or denominational worker. The question you are, no doubt, struggling with goes something like this; "If we go this route in North American church planting, what is my role? Is there a place for me"?

The answer is an unequivocal "Yes"! But it will be a different role from what most of us have seen or experienced. Fundamentally, it will involve becoming leaders that are skilled in understanding a changing North American culture and "gifted with the courage and endurance to lead God's people as missional communities."[343]

This is the command of Ephesians 4:11-13 where "ordained" leaders are given to the church to enable her to "carry out (her) fundamentally missiological purpose in the world: to announce and demonstrate the new creation in Jesus Christ."[344] The role of ordained leaders therefore transitions from being the one doing ministry to being one who equips others, specifically the laity, to do ministry. Even our understanding of ordination may be challenged by the scriptures. In this new kind of missionary church "all are ordained to ministry . . . all receive the same vocation to mission, and all are gifted in various ways for that mission."[345]

Ministry leaders will have to begin thinking and functioning like missionaries, not simply pastors. As Garrison notes, this shift in thinking may represent one of the greatest challenges those of us in paid, vocational ministry will face. "Missionaries involved in Church Planting Movements often speak of the self-discipline required to mentor church planters rather than do the job of church planting themselves."[346]

Alan Roxburgh has offered a very helpful diagram of this leadership transition. Figure 1 contrasts older ministry models with this emerging missionary leadership model.[347] Notice that this does not eliminate or minimize the importance of paid, vocational ministry leaders. What it does do is transition their role and the way they function. Rather than being at the top of the pyramid as in the traditional model, or at the bottom as in the renewalist, ministry leaders now move out to the point of the movement as it penetrates a lost culture with the message of Jesus. This, of course, assumes that it is the people of God, the *laos*, that are being mobilized as ministers

Figure 2.

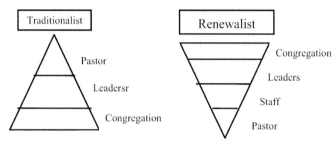

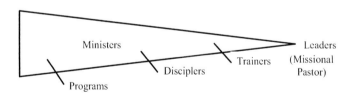

Conclusion

With North America becoming one of the great mission fields of the world, the need to see God unleash a church planting movement has never been greater. The days of approaching this continent as if it were Christian and churched are over. However, for those who are motivated by the challenge to function as missionaries, both clergy and laity alike, the greatest days of kingdom expansion still lie ahead. In order to address this enormous opportunity, we will need to mobilize the *laos*, the whole people of God. Anything short of this will impair or prevent the church planting movement we all long and pray to see in our generation. May God grant us the wisdom to do what we must do in order to be prepared when *He will do what only He is able to do.*

Endnotes

[313] Gordon D. Fee, "Laos and Leadership Under the New Covenant," *Crux* 25 (1989): 3.

[314] Darrell L. Guder, *Missional Church: A Vision for the Sending of the Church in North America* (Grand Rapids: Eerdmans, 1998), 194.

[315] R. Paul Stevens, *Liberating the Laity: Equipping All the Saints for Ministry* (Vancouver, BC: Regents College Publishing: 2000), 50.

[316] Guder, *Missional Church*, 195.

[317] Findley B. Edge, *The Doctrine of the Laity* (Nashville: Convention Press, 1985), 22.

[318] David Bosch, *Transforming Mission: Paradigm Shifts in Theology of Mission* (New York: Orbis, 1991), 467.

[320] Edge, *Doctrine of the Laity*, 9.

[321] Ibid.

[322] Bosch, *Transforming Mission*, 468 and Guder, *Missional Church*, 190.

[323] Bosch, *Transforming Mission*, 469.

[324] Guder, *Missional Church*, 191.

[325] Ibid.

[326] Charles Van Engen, *God's Missionary People: Rethinking the Purpose of the Local Church* (Grand Rapids: Baker Books, 1991), 151.

[327] Bosch, *Transforming Mission*, 468.

[328] Ibid.

[329] Ibid., 473.

[330] Ibid.

[331] David Garrison, "Church Planting Movements," on-line, Available from http://www.imb.org/CPM/Chapter3.htm.

[332] George G. Hunter III, *The Celtic Way of Evangelism: How Christianity can Reach the West Again* (Nashville: Abingdon, 2000), 22.

[333] Ibid., 23.

[334] Ibid., 26.

[335] Ibid., 28.

[336] Bosch, *Transforming Mission*, 470.

[337] Wade Crawford Barclay, *Early American Methodism 1769-1844* (New York: The Board of Missions and Church Extension of the Methodist Church, 1949), xxxviii.

[338] Roger Finke and Rodney Stark, *The Churching of America 1776-1990: Winners and Losers in Our Religious Economy*, (New Brunswick, New Jersey: Rutgers University Press, 1992), 150.

[339] William Warren Sweet, *Religion in the Development of American Culture: 1765-1840* (New York: Charles Scribner's Sons, 1952), 58.

[340] William Warren Sweet, *The Story of Religion in America*, 2nd ed. (New York: Harper and Brothers, 1950), 218.

[341] Garrison, "Church Planting Movements," on-line.

[342] Hunter, *Celtic Way of Evangelism*, 99.

[343] Guder, *Missional Church*, 183.

[344] Ibid., 185.

[345] Ibid., 200.

[346] Garrison, "Church Planting Movements," on-line.

[347] Alan J. Roxburgh, *The Missionary Congregation, Leadership, & Liminality* (Harrisburg, PA: Trinity Press, 1997), 65.

Chapter 20
Starting Organic Congregations in Church Planting Movements
Neil Cole

Have you ever heard a pastor repeat a sermon? Most have. He may have had a busy schedule and couldn't get around to a new sermon that week. This is not, however, always the case. Sometimes important thoughts are repeated for emphasis.

Jesus often repeated Himself. We have taken our cues for how to start churches from two almost identical sermons delivered by Jesus. At one time he taught the 12 Apostles how to reach the lost (Matt. 10) and in another occasion He instructed the 70 (Luke 10). When Jesus decides to repeat Himself in more than one of the gospel accounts, perhaps we should pay close attention to what He is saying. Nowhere else does Jesus get more specific in delineating outreach principles. In these two sermons on two separate occasions Jesus gives us the key principles for how to initiate a ministry that reaches lost communities.

Principles for Ministry to Lost Communities

We have uncovered five principles to help us in starting churches that reproduce in lost communities from Christ's messages.

Practice of Prayer

In both sermons Jesus begins with the same familiar words, "The harvest is plentiful but the laborers are few.

Therefore beseech the Lord of the harvest to send out workers into the harvest" (Matt 9:37-38). We believe that church is a spiritual entity before it is a physical reality. We have a saying that goes like this: *The church is conceived in heaven before it is born on earth. It must first be a glimmer in our Father's eyes.* So we begin churches by wooing the Father for new workers to come out of the harvest. The Father is easily wooed by the bride (as are most fathers) because He wants the church to reproduce more than we do.

We simply cannot skip this important step. Jesus began both sermons with the same appeal, "Beseech the Lord of the harvest for workers." We are to beg, beseech and plead with God for these workers. There is no substitute for going out among the lost people, looking deep into their eyes, and begging God for their souls. But of course, the Lord of the harvest longs to answer these prayers. He bled so that these souls could be saved.

It is in the prayer that the romantic part of church planting is introduced. This is very important to the church, to the Father and to the community we want to reach. This is the first step in starting churches that reproduce. *Pray first, pray last and in between pray hard!*

Pockets of People

Jesus instructs His disciples to not go the way of the Gentiles or the Samaritans but specifically to the lost sheep of the house of Israel (Matt 10:5). He sends the disciples out in pairs to various cities and villages looking for a pocket of people, a community of lost people that is receptive to the message of peace (Luke 10:1).

When looking for a pocket of people we have another saying: **Bad people make good soil. There's a lot of fertilizer in their lives.** Why is it that a majority of churches in America today are all trying to reach middle class suburbs? This has got to be one of the most difficult and hardest soils to reach yet all seem to try. We have come to see the poor as the heirs of the kingdom of God (James 2:5). We find that it isn't those who are well who need a physician but the sick. Jesus didn't come to call the righteous, but sinners to repentance (Luke 5:31-32).

After just a few months of hanging out at our first coffeehouse, my living room was full of new believers. The coffeehouse was transformed by the Gospel. Rather than follow traditional church planting theory and move into a larger location, we sent a small team to a new coffeehouse.

The second coffeehouse, called Portfolios, was a much darker and sinister place. A witch's coven would hang out there each night. There were warlocks, Satanists, and vampires there. I'd never even heard of vampires before (other than the fictitious ones like Dracula). But there is a subculture of people here who actually live a strange life based on the writings and mythological culture of vampires. Some file their teeth to become fangs. Some sleep in coffins, drink blood, drive hearses, and only come out at night. They also practice black magic and cast spells on people.

One night Rob Ferris, my co-worker in the start of Awakening Chapels, caught one vampire behind his back doing something suspicious with his hands casting some sort of spell. He later asked a friend who was in the occult and what he was doing. "The vampires have a spell they like to do to people they

495

don't like." His friend explained, "They walk up behind people and suck the spirit out of them." When Rob shared this with me my initial response was, "Suck away, you'll never thirst again!" But of course, that's not really the way to taste from the spring of living water, but I have no fear of such curses because I do have a spring of eternal life within me that is greater than any curse.

The first person to become a Christian at Portfolios was Emanuel. Rob, an excellent evangelist, was across the table from Emanuel and opened his Bible to Rom. 6:23 and gave it to Emanuel to read for himself. Just then Jody, a recruiter for the occult and part of the coven came and sat next to Emanuel. Jody likes to talk and has a foul mouth, so Rob prayed silently, "Lord, keep his ears open and his mouth closed." And Jody didn't say a word. Then Gene came and sat on the other side of Emanuel. Gene is an atheist philosopher who loves to talk but doesn't ever get very far. Rob prayed the same silent prayer and Gene didn't say a word. Finally, Psycho Seth came up behind Rob. Psycho Seth is the leader of the vampires. He is tall, thin, pale and dressed all in black with a long black trench coat and long frizzy hair down his back. Seth leans over and whispers to Rob, "I just want you to know that I have my sword with me." Rob, answers, "Oh, that's nice, I have mine to, Emanuel is reading it now." The Psycho Seth leaned over again and said, "No. I really do have my sword." And he opened his trench coat and there, hanging from his belt, was a real long sword. Rob prayed silently again, "Lord, keep his ears open and his mouth closed, and don't let him cut my head off."

Emanuel looked up from his reading at that moment with a confused look on his face. Rob, suddenly feeling a bit unarmed, asked to have his sword back to explain the verse to him. Emanuel wanted one more chance, so he read it again, and suddenly the lights went on in his eyes and a smile came across his face. He understood that the wages of his sin was death, "but the gift of God is eternal life in Christ Jesus, our Lord." At that moment, Jody got up to leave. Gene rose from the table and walked away, and Psycho Seth took his sword and left.

From that moment, Portfolios became holy ground. Emanuel was baptized the same day Scott was. Within a few weeks he was baptizing his first convert at the same beach. He baptized another convert a few weeks after that. Within a short time a second church was started from converts from Portfolios.

A couple years later, I was at the same coffeehouse discussing spiritual things with another occultist who was convinced that in the end of times he would be riding the white horse of the apocalypse. I politely disagreed. In the course of our conversation he casually mentioned that all the occultists had mutually decided that Portfolios was now neutral territory and that no one could cast anymore spells there.

He was surprised when I burst out in laughter. He didn't understand why I enlightened him so. I said, "You know perfectly well that Portfolios isn't neutral territory!" He countered, "Oh, yes it is, we all decided." "No," I answered, "You decided you can't cast any spells here anymore because this is now God's territory, this is sacred ground now and your spells don't work." He continued to object to my commentary until, we were interrupted by Scott, who brought a friend up to me and said, "This is Gorge, and he wants to accept Jesus right here, right now." And right in front of this occultist, while still claiming Portfolios as neutral territory, Gorge entered the kingdom of God.

In our experience, coffeehouses have proven to be fertile soil for the gospel. Now, however, we have expanded our vision to other arenas as well. We have churches that reach out to 12-step recovery groups, neighborhood gangs, homosexuals, occult groups, high school, college and university campuses, the homeless and local bars. Besides homes and apartments, we've had churches that meet in parks, beaches, storefronts, restaurants, faculty lounges, student unions, locker rooms and even church classrooms (aghast!). *The key is not in the building—whether it has a steeple or a chimney on the roof—but in bringing the kingdom of God to the people He is calling out.*

Our plan is to identify a pocket of people who do not have a vital kingdom witness and we enter into relationship with those people. We inject the kingdom virus right into the darkness and a church is born there from the changed lives. If they are not receptive, which happens frequently as well, we simply wipe the dust (bad soil) off our feet and move on to the next pocket of people.

Power of Presence

Jesus told the disciples as He sent them out that they had authority to do the works of God. They were to announce that the kingdom of God has come near—whether they were received or not (Matt 10:7-8). We have another saying in our churches: "Where we go, the King goes and where the King goes people bow." In the Great Commission, Jesus said these words, "All authority in heaven and earth has been given to me…I am with you." We must not forget this. The enemy is hoping that we will not realize this important truth, because he is vulnerable to us when we learn it.

Someone once asked Rob what the secret was to seeing so many people come to Christ. His answer was simple, "Two words: Show up." Non-Christians aren't fretting trying to figure out ways to get into church. Church is not something that they feel they need, want or are even curious about. Usually unbelievers see only two things churches are relevant for: marrying and burying—and many are trying desperately to avoid both! Jesus said to the church, "Go". When He addressed the lost (Matt. 28:18-20), He said, "Come to *me*," not "come to church". So often we erect a very difficult barrier to evangelism by expecting people to come to our churches to find Christ. Many non-Christians have more problems with church than with Christ, so we make their salvation that much more difficult.

We have another saying we often repeat in Awakening: ***There are two kinds of lost people in the world—the moths and the cockroaches. In the darkness it's impossible to tell the difference. The best way to discover the difference is to turn the light on. The moths will be drawn to the light and the cockroaches will flee.***

Jesus told us that we are a light that should not be hidden behind a peck measure with stain glass windows (Matt 5:14-16). Most of us don't turn all the lights on in our homes during the daytime. Why, because it isn't needed during the daylight. Light is made for the darkness. "You are the light of the world." We should be brought out into the darkness so that we can shine.

Jesus also noted that the disciples were not to import resources into the harvest but to find all the resources they needed in the harvest itself. His instructions were to not bring any extra clothes, food or money to sustain the ministry. This is crucial.

When Jesus said "the harvest is plentiful" He meant it as good news! We often read it as bad news, because it means that there are so many lost and dying people in the world. While that is true, if you were to tell a farmer that his harvest is plentiful he would rejoice at the good news, and so should we. The good news is not that so many are lost and dying, but that so many are going to be saved once we start taking the power of the kingdom into their world. All the resources needed for a great harvest are already found in the harvest itself, including finances, facilities and future leaders. All we need is to get out there and reap! There is much power in showing up. We neglect to remember the profound power found in just the story of Christ and Him crucified. We underestimate how powerful His resurrection is.

After Scott was first baptized he celebrated by getting high on speed. We were in a discipleship relationship and every week he would confess to surrendering to his addiction. He was already attending mandatory 12-step groups because of a court order. When discipleship and accountability didn't work we stepped it up and had him live with us for a short time. He stayed clean while he lived with my family but as soon as he moved back home, he fell again to the bondage. I didn't know what to do to end this, so I suggested a rehab center. He didn't like that idea and begged for another option. I said, "Well, there is one other radical option we could try." He said, "Great, what is it?" I said, "You and I get in the car right now and drive over and tell your drug dealer about Jesus," and with a smile I added, "maybe if your dealer gets saved, it will cut off your source."

Scott didn't know if he should take me serious…*but I was dead serious*. I said, "Listen bro, there is a darkness in your life. How are we to get rid of darkness? Can we vacuum it up? Can we just sweep it aside? No, there is only one way to overcome darkness—light. Paul says in Romans 12, 'Do not be overcome by evil but overcome evil with good.'" Scott could see now that I was serious.

He replied, "Well, alright, but it won't go well if you're with me, let me do it alone." I agreed, but added that if the next day he hadn't done it we would do it together.

He went to his dealer and shared the Gospel (you're probably imagining a sinister man as his dealer, aren't you? You sexist…it was a woman).

From that point on Scott never took any drugs. He was free. The power of Christ transformed his heart. We are often so quick to search for other ways to help people and overlook the most powerful—the simple message of Jesus internalized and shared with others.

Scott's dealer didn't become a Christian that day, but it was then that her son accepted Christ and Scott baptized him. Within a year or so, we heard that she did become a Christian after her son was taken from her and she was sent to jail. Eventually Scott led several of the boy's friends to Christ and baptized them. He started a new church in the "hood" made up of young kids looking for something better for their lives. He still shepherds them and is always introducing me to young people who have recently accepted Christ. He has even brought young people who struggle with addictions in to live with him for times of more intense discipling.

Person of Peace

This forth principle is one that I am indebted to my dear friend and mentor Thom Wolf for uncovering. This simple concept has led to many churches being born around the world. Jesus said to look for and even inquire about someone who would be receptive to our message of peace. When we find such a person we are to stay there and reach his/her entire household (*oikos*). We are to eat what he eats and stay where he stays (Luke 10:6-7). When a person of peace is discovered, the birth of a new church is assumed. If you saw a human hand sticking up out of the dirt the assumption would be that the rest of the body is yet to be uncovered. When someone comes to Christ in a new pocket of people we keep digging until we see the person of peace emerge and a new church born.

A person of peace is characterized by three things: He/she is person of (1) *Receptivity*. They are open to the message of the person and the peace of Christ; (2) *Relational connections*. They know lots of people and are an important part of the community, for better or worse; (3) *Reputation*. They are people of reputation, whether it is a good reputation (like Cornelius or the Ethiopian eunuch) or bad reputation (like the Samaritan woman or the Gerasene demoniac).

The Person of Peace becomes the conduit for the passing of the message of the kingdom to an entire community of lost people. His or her reputation gives credence to the message and becomes a magnet for a new church. A poor reputation can often be the catalyst for a dynamic church as the whole community sees the life transforming power of Jesus. We like to call the Person of Peace the first domino in a chain reaction for the gospel.

Here are some examples of persons of peace. I call them the first domino people.[348] When they become a Christian, others do likewise in the "oikos." Let me ask you to either give a thumbs up (if they are a person of good reputation) or a thumbs down (if they are a person of bad reputation) when I mention these first domino people:

(1) Matthew – a bad reputation. He was a tax collector. (2) Lydia - a good reputation. She was the seller of purple fabric, well respected business woman. (3) The Ethiopian Eunuch – a good reputation. He was in charge of the entire economy of the government. He was the first international missionary taking the Gospel to Ethiopia. All he had was the Bible and the Spirit of God and I ask you, is it enough? Or does he need our help? (4) Cornelius – a good reputation, he was well loved by everybody. (5) The Woman at the well – a bad reputation. (6) The Garesene Demoniac – two thumbs down. The man was a freak and yet God sent him to a place called Decapolis, (ten cities). A missionary to ten cities and he hadn't been baptized, he hadn't taken newcomers' classes, hasn't been to discipleship, and hadn't taken to my Green House Training, and yet he has gone to ten cities. Thirty minutes with Jesus was all it took. Amazing!

Find a person of peace in this *oikos* and when it is transformed, they become a people of purpose. Instead of drawing people out of community, and robbing what community already existed, he injects the Gospel, which is like a virus that transforms the community and so they become a church. The traditional approach is that we go to the neighborhood knock on the first door, if anyone is there, good, if no one is there we feel relieved. Then we knock on the next door. If some one is there we talk. Then go to the third door and find a lady who is interested. Her heart is open to Christ. Something has happened in her life and she wants to become a Christian.

Then what we do with her is the difference between a church planting movement and just church growth. Usually we would take her around the corner three blocks to where the church is and ask her to become a part of our community. Here is what Jesus said: "You go to the first door, and the people are there. When you talk with them you find that they are not interested in the Gospel. Jesus said, when you come into town inquire who is worthy. Even if they are not Christians, they will help you start a church by finding people who are worthy. You might ask, "Who is worthy?" Jesus said: "Whoever is not willing to leave mother or daughter for me is not worthy of me." It is someone desperate enough to leave everything for Christ. So you ask the people in the house, "is there anyone here who really needs to hear this message?' They might say, "yes, four blocks down, the guy is partying all night. Please go save that guy so I can go to sleep. So you go to that guy's house and knock on the door. He comes to the door, accepts Christ, his family sees a difference, the people in the neighborhood saw the parties he used to give, and it begins to spread. You have the church there in the neighborhood. But it doesn't stop there. The others who used to come to the parties from the other neighborhoods now help the Gospel to spread to the other neighborhoods and it is contagious. It goes from there, and there is a chain reaction that nobody can control, that nobody could have put on a ten-year plan. It's no one other than God.

People of Purpose

Jesus instructs us that when a pocket of people receive your message of peace it will rest upon them, they become the church in their own rich soil (Matt 10:11-13).

When the moths are drawn to the light and the person of peace brings several to Christ...a church is born. This is the formation of a people of purpose, born in the harvest, born for the harvest of the nations. Often, though not exclusively, the person of peace has the church meet in his/her home and may even be the new leader of the emerging church.

A church that starts this way is unique in that it is born out of the harvest and is found among the harvest and is bent on a mission to continue to reach the lost. This missional element will be the important drive to reach out and to reproduce spontaneously. Many house churches suffer from "*koinonitis*", where fellowship and community is the main and only thing. What is needed is a strong healthy dose of mission.

Churches that start this way are unhindered by cultural Christianity because they are born in the harvest. There is a simple purity to them that doesn't have the stain of the more placid and established Christendom. The people learn how to reach their friends from the start and don't know any better than to follow Jesus and expect Him to save their family, friends and ultimately, the nations. They become a people of purpose, a spiritual family called out by God on a mission.

The word on the street used to be that anytime, day or night, you could go to Milton's house and find available drugs and party 'till dawn. Milton is a painter in Long Beach, California. His house was a constant party. Everything seemed good for Milton, until his speed habit took over. Soon everything began to fall apart, his business headed for bankruptcy, his home fell into foreclosure, his truck (which is important for a painter) was repossessed and his wife left him. Milton fell on his knees in his living room and said, "Lord, I give up." and gave his life to Christ. God has graciously restored everything Milton lost…and more, much more.

Now, Milton's house is a church. This church started four years ago and they have given birth to twelve other churches. They have sent out church planters who have moved to Portland, Medford, San Francisco, North East Indiana, Paris, France, Spain, and North Africa and are on their way to San Diego. They have sent people on short-term mission trips to twelve different nations in 2002 alone. The church in Milton's house has only fifteen to twenty people coming regularly and yet it has missions that are more extensive than most mega churches.

This is my church, so let me tell you about some of the people at Milton's as I look around the room. Chris plays the guitar for us and is starting evangelistic Bible clubs on campus at Long Beach City College. Jared is starting a church in East Los Angeles. Milton is joining him and has also started an evangelistic Bible study with his employees every week. Elsa became a Christian just this past year and she's reaching out to neighborhood children. Kenya, Milton's wife, has started a weekly evangelistic outreach into a housing project in urban North Long Beach. Monica is on her way to Romania as a missionary. Last year she went to Cuba with a team of young people to train Cuban pastors to do Life Transformation Groups and theological education. The method is simple and reproducible and she trained 700 pastors while convincing the

Cuban government to sanction it. Lois is preparing to move overseas to Spain where she will be a part of a church plant reaching out to Muslims. Art, who is bound to a wheelchair because of a stroke, is reaching out at the care facility where he lives. Now we make room for two wheelchairs as his newest convert, Violet comes every week to praise the Lord. Scott now plays saxophone in our church and is writing new praise songs. He also has the church he started which meets in a coffeehouse just around the corner from the very coffeehouse where we first met.

This is the church, every one of them is reproducing and that will produce more and more churches. There are now two churches in Paris, four in San Francisco, one in Indiana, in the barrio of East LA and churches being started in Portland, Medford Oregon and San Diego. Rob and his family have moved to Salt Lake City to start churches there.

The word on the street is the same; if you want to join the party, go to Milton's house. The difference now is that you get the ultimate high; you have an active part of God's kingdom expansion. There is nothing greater.

Our aim is to do this, we want to lower the bar on how we do church and raise the bar on what it means to be a disciple and in so doing, the result will be that we will raise the standard of what church is. Make church simple. Make being a disciple the main thing and the kingdom will spread. That's our passion.

The challenge of 2 Timothy is the challenge of the Great Commission. We want to have influence that expands in both space and time. I want my influence to go a lot further than driving distance to my church. I want my influence to last longer than my eulogy. The only way that that can happen is for me to invest in people. I need to invest in people who will go farther than me and that will live longer than I. Jesus said these important words to his disciples "It is good for you that I go away, because if I didn't go away, the helper couldn't come." This is the important key to church planting. If Jesus is there physically, then the Kingdom of God is bound by whatever location he is in. But once the Holy Spirit comes, wherever we go, he is there. And now we can spread the Gospel all over China and at the same time in India and South America, Africa, and even North America.

Questions About Church Planting Strategy

In conclusion, I want to deal with some of the questions that are often asked regarding our church planting strategy.

What's a Life Transformation Group?

It is a group of two or three that meet together once a week for accountability, to read the Scriptures throughout the week, pray for their lost friends in their "*oikos*" , and also confess their sins one to another It's that simple. They give attention to the DNA. The Word, the Relationship, and the Apostolic mission.

What Constitutes a Church Planting Movement?

We are seeing a lot of good numbers and transformation of life and I praise the Lord for it, but I don't think we are seeing a church planting movement yet because most of what's happening is Christians are getting turned on. Kingdom can mean so much more than it has been in the past. They want to be used by God and they are being used by God. We reproduce disciples, leaders, churches and movements. Movements, for us, have been networks.

Now we have about thirty networks around the country and overseas. Each network has between five and, probably the biggest is, twenty churches that meet in homes or places. Most of these churches are growing through transformation of Christians rather than conversion. There are some networks, like Awakening Chapels that are mainly conversion from the harvest. These are the ones that grow the fastest and we need to see more of those. It appears to be so much easier to find Christians who want to get on board. It is actually harder. It's a lot easier to get out there in the fields and just win some people to Christ and let the chain reaction happen, but they have not done that.

We look for church planters that are apostolically oriented. You send a pastor or a teacher to do a church planting job and they will stick with that. You have to send an apostle or a prophet if you want to start a movement. When we send them, we don't start a regional church; we want to church a region. So their goal is to start lots of churches. They can't start them all themselves so they eventually have to start raising leaders and sending them off.

How Much Cultural Diversity Resides in These Groups?

What about the cultural and ethnic composition of these Life Transformation Groups. Some are multicultural and some are not. Characteristically, I can speak to my own, Awakening Chapel is very ethnically diverse, all English speaking but sometimes it is their second language and they birth churches that are not English speaking.

Why Some Groups
Do Not Reproduce

In some settings, we are experiencing church saturation efforts in which many churches are being started. New people are being won to the Lord and leaders are being trained, but we have not seen these churches start other churches.

What I find to be roadblocks to the multiplication are these three things: buildings; budgets; and big shots. Buildings are a problem because they are not organic so they don't multiply. Budgets are a challenge because a church planting strategy that is based on financial subsidy in not going to lead to reproduction. By big shots I just don't mean big personalities but the idea that you must have formally trained leaders in order to have a church. Requiring academic degrees as prerequisites for leadership hampers a church planting movement.

---

[348] For a more extensive discussion on this see, Neil Cole, *Cultivating a Life for God*, Carol Stream: ILL: Church Smart Resources, 1999, 39-53.

Chapter 21

The Use of Media in Church Planting Movements
W. Mark Snowden

"Are my media productions making any difference?" The thought emerged through a dangerous phase of chemotherapy in 1986. I had been diagnosed with testicular cancer the previous year right at the time of my daughter's birth. My doctors watched me closely for 15 months, but the cancer came back in my lungs. Faced a second time with the thought that I could die, the Lord began moving in my heart to search for answers. God healed me and I am healthy today. The chemo even destroyed malaria parasites I had picked up on a photo shoot in West Africa. However, the questioning remained, so I began to research media and its effects in church planting.

What I learned was that communications media tools are best used in the context of a comprehensive church planting strategy. However, there is no magic bullet or single approach to recommend. Yet here I am some 20 years later serving as a media strategist and trainer to church planters for the International Mission Board, SBC. Here are the big three that every church planter should know about media:

1) Media are catalysts that are used of the Lord to move people from one stage to another; 2) Media work best within a well-planned media mix otherwise they're like fireworks; 3). Audience and reader response requires follow-up for churches to be planted.

Catalytic Communications Media

Ask a group of U.S. church planters to name different types of communications and they'll astound you with their extensive listings. The media—press, TV, newspapers, radio. Then they'll include the videos, CDs or cassettes, telephones, magazines, books, billboards, and the Internet. With a little more reflection, they'll throw in drama, puppets, multimedia slide shows, and even storytelling. When prompted, church planters will include public relations, marketing, advertising, and communications research as vital in their communications efforts.

The inherent assumption in church planting communications media is that following Jesus is the minority opinion. But it doesn't have to stay that way. Research dating back to the 1970s shows that public opinion can change through three factors: the introduction of novel ideas (new), standing by once-popular (old) beliefs, and the influence of media. Today's church planter must master several communications media basics to successfully influence a community for Christ.[349]

Think quick! What media have most influenced you? Did you read the newspaper every day? Listen to the radio on the way to work? Couldn't wait for the latest sports magazine to hit the stands? C'mon and name at least one type of media that have been important to you. Write it in the margin of this book.
Now, write "Caution!" in bold letters by it. Now, why would I want you to do that? It's because whatever worked in your life is what you will want to try and use in some place where it might not have the same effects. Understanding media effects on a certain group of people is the key to understanding

how they work as a catalyst. Knowing your bias, the use of media by Christians where you hope to plant churches, and even knowing how authorities like political figures and the government use media is important.

On the northern side of Lake Titicaca, I closed my hotel door and was stunned to see an AIDS poster! Two couples and a single man explained why abstinence was the only way to be totally sure to prevent AIDS. The next day I began noticing several ways that Peruvian health ministry was seeking to disseminate AIDS prevention information. It provided a great insight into one medium of communication that was strategically placed. In Ecuador, IMB missionary Guy Muse ran two spots during the national soccer finals. The TV ads offered enrollment in a free Bible study. Some 1,200 people called to enroll within minutes of seeing the advertisement. Their response was attributed to the strategically-placed spots.

Attribution Theory says that behavioral changes are *attributed* to some external stimulus such as an advertisement. *Example: Step 1. See pizza ad. / Step 2. Go get pizza.* Translation: Throw stone. Kill giants. Or…Read tract. Accept Christ as Savior. In the Bible, the death of Goliath was attributed to the stone thrown by David. Your attribution strategy works somewhat the same way. You give someone a tract, they read it, and decide to become a Christian. The new believer is Goliath, you are David, and the tract's message is attributed to leading to salvation. God is praised!

Cognitive Processes

Your attribution strategy serves to help people think through various stages of a spiritual decision process. Specifically, it can do one or all of these things:

Assigns a cause to an event; people know what triggered their response to an invitation, offer, or next level of personal involvement

- ⇒ Interpreting from realm of personal experiences; each person may interact with the message in a different way depending upon their circumstances
- ⇒ Understanding gives "control"; eliminating guesswork is important for good stewardship of resources, and leading people to deeper levels of commitment
- ⇒ Memories remain **filtered;** filtering their experiences causes a variety of responses which can be sometimes good and bad
- ⇒ Predicts future behaviors; over time you can anticipate what kind of response you'll have to efforts. I was kidded and even warned once for running a full-page ad in the state Baptist paper promoting my services in leading conferences in churches. However, my experience was that few, if any pastors, would respond and only through relatively bold promotion like this could I elicit response from across the state. The result was that out of the month-long advertising campaign, I was able to assemble a network of trainers. I personally led 55 of these events in 20 months.[2]

There are pros and cons of attribution strategies. Sometimes, media efforts can appear as "fireworks." The people say oh and ah, but quickly say, "What else do you have?" Their hearts are not always turned just by showing up and releasing something to a potential audience. Sometimes media can serve like fireworks. Church planters shoot off a JESUS film or run a program without great influence being made. However, many times the individual efforts work to great effects.

Church planters can count on catalytic media to work in many aspects simultaneously. Evangelism is only the beginning. As people come to faith in Christ, accelerated discipleship, maturing believers, and leader training is possible by using the appropriate media. Many LifeWay products and other Christian publishers provide workbooks and other resources for the new believer and continues right on through every phase of church life. What tends to be lacking are media that lead all believers (including new believers) to participate in perpetually new church starting efforts.

This is why a radical product such as "Following Jesus" was developed. Avery Willis put together a team of cross-cultural church planting, communications, and Bible storytelling experts. The FJ series is really a movement aimed especially at the 70% of the world's 1.5 billion lost that has a non-reading (oral) learning preference. The FJ series begins with a biblical foundation for non-Christians, and then after making a decision takes into account the new believers, maturing believers, those engaging in ministry, leader training, and missionary basics. The group made sure that a complete church planting workshop lasting several weeks was incorporated in discipleship training for new believers![350]

Media Products

Products abound that disciple Christians, but few serve as catalysts. Many offer biblical information, are worship-oriented, or provide assistance for problems Christians face on a daily basis. However, few are catalytic for involving believers in church planting efforts. Church planters should evaluate all their resources with an eye toward status quo or catalytic involvement as Jesus commanded in the Great Commission. Yes, biblical foundations are essential, but how much training was necessary before Jesus sent His disciples on their first mission in Matthew 10? Jesus used his disciples as an advance team to "climatize" Israel for His messages of the Kingdom of God. Much of the dramatic response (catalysts) to Jesus' message was attributed to these disciples' efforts to the point that Jesus saw "Satan falling like lightning from heaven." (Luke 10:18 NIV)

Finally, don't forget that involving others in your church planting efforts is a privilege. One media that has proved successful in involving scores of Christians around the world in missions in the Internet Web missions service, PeopleTeams.org. The site hosts or links to teams of missionaries who publish their own Web sites. PeopleTeams presently has more than 600 teams online. Whether you are planting churches in the United States or the United Emirates, PeopleTeams.org has a place for your team's efforts.

The Media Mix

Media work best within a well-planned media mix otherwise they're like fireworks

516

The best way to help catalytic media accelerate response to the gospel is by integrating communications efforts. After King David united Israel, he desired Jerusalem for his seat of rule. Jerusalem was tightly held by the Jebusites. David used his knowledge of the water shafts and grappling hooks to command his men. Further, he gave an incentive to his men that whoever took Jerusalem would command his army. That is how Joab got his job. David did not walk up to the door with a slingshot! Jerusalem was certainly a giant adversary, but nothing like Goliath. His strategy was different and much more sophisticated.

The story of taking Jerusalem is profound because it required a united army, research, and incentives. David's army took the city, but only with an integrated approach. Church planters need to use an integrated communications strategy. Integrated marketing communications holds some, but not all the clues that a church planter needs for creating a marketing mix.

Integrated Marketing Communications

^   **Advocates** - Action-oriented>Leading>Reproducing
^   **Desired Behaviors** - Evaluate>Model>Advocate>Consistency
^   **Partial Commitments** - Receptive>Options>Trials>Change
^   **Attitudes** - Open>Understand Implications>Positive
^   **General Networks** - Unaware>Introductions>Distinctions>Know [3]

The strength of Integrated Marketing Communications (IMC) lies in its media mix. A church planter does well to build on the strengths of "combined media effects over time." Secular marketers get wrapped up in product, place, price, and promotion. Those are useful categories, but can relate to only a single medium (the weakness of attribution theory). "A 'one best' strategy is typically used in approaching the market and generic competition is typically ignored in the process."[4]

Careful church planters research neighborhoods and seek sub-sets of the larger groupings of people. The goal is to build databases using five research methods to adequately understand the people you intend to reach:

Communications Research in Church Planting Strategies
1. Existing research – scouring libraries, webs, and printed research
2. Observational research – visiting locales and experiencing the environment
3. Questionnaires – quantifiable responses from a representative sampling
4. Focus groups – qualitative input from representative groups of about a dozen
5. Interviews – especially important to conduct among leaders for buy-in and perspectives for implementation [5]

Research reveals to church planters what media work best at which stage of a Christian decision-making process. The key is knowing the "best" media. Often, in a media-saturated area, all media seem to have the same importance. Yet, in a Turkish city, I simply walked up to a school playground and through an interpreter asked a group of older children the call letters of their favorite radio station. They shouted one FM radio station's letters and frequency number with laughter and joy! The radio dial was full, but in thirty seconds, I had a pretty good idea where to start to air spots or programs to reach families with children in a certain area of that urban center.

Great attention is given to evangelism because so much work goes into the front-end strategies, but seeds of leader training are often built right into the overall approach. An IMB missionary had trained a mature church to start new churches while he went statesiding for awhile. When the missionary returned, the church leaders apologized for not starting a new church as planned, but observed that they couldn't do it because the missionary took the evangelistic video to the States with him. If your church was started by a media blitz, then will this be the methodology employed by that church's leaders one day? Defining the media mix is not impossible, but should take into account thoughtful stewardship of time and financial resources.

Consider this media mix from a church-planting strategy in Mexico. When I was a summer missionary in Chihuahua, Mexico, I was teamed with a missionary "kid" in her early 20s to help a group of local Baptist youth prepare puppet scripts to air live on television every Saturday afternoon. I wrote a Christian comic book using our puppets and promoted it on the show. It was only available at the Baptist bookstore. The Baptist bookstore promoted attendance at evangelistic revival meetings conducted throughout the city and into the poverty-stricken canyons on the outskirts of town. During the week the puppets performed at events; a public swimming pool, home Bible studies, Backyard Bible Clubs, and at local churches. A number of Bible studies as mission points were established in ten weeks. The Bible studies were satellites of a mother church whose members provided the backbone of the outreach.

The funny thing was that no one considered what we were doing was "media ministry." Yet, our media efforts were intentional and that is why I was invited to spend the summer working with them.

Over and over again I hear our regional media strategists tell me that their best "media" strategies are those that are church planting strategies. They use words like "seamless," "non-interfering," and "just part of the work" to describe a media mix. I know my work is cut out for me when missionaries say they don't want to consider media in their church planting strategy because they don't have time for a media strategy. The best media mix should not stand out, but be appropriate for the people.

The bottom line is that the integrated communications strategies achieve synergy by working together in a comprehensive plan. Account for every phase of church planting – evangelism, discipleship, leader training, missionaries, and partner-building advocacy – and use a multiple media approach.

Applying Integrated Communications Strategies

- Describe how principles from Integrated Communications Strategies.
- How can the best media mix be linked together lead people toward a desired goal?
- What media work best for evangelism, discipleship, training leaders, missions, and partner-building advocacy where you serve?

Anticipating response

Audience and reader response requires follow-up for churches to be planted. King David drew the ire of Shimei right in the middle of Absalom's revolt. However Shimei was not in favor of David's rebellious son. Rather, he still angry that King Saul was dead! Church planters might desire that everyone respond to an invitation to follow Christ, experience transformational discipleship, become a reproducing church leader, etc., but they often have difficulty knowing how to follow-up with those with whom they are communicating. Response strategies provide church planters with the skills for judging and evaluating what they are experiencing. Diffusion of Innovations is a helpful model to develop response strategies.

Diffusion of Innovations
Innovators (2.5%)
Venturesome, educated, multiple information sources
Early Adopters (13.5%)
Leaders in social setting, slightly above avg. education
Early Majority (34%)
Deliberate, many informal social contacts

Late Majority (34%)
    Skeptical, below average social status
Laggards (16%)
    Fear of debt, neighbors and friends are info sources [6]

Not included in the graphic is the sociological phenomenon that Everett M. Rogers found when the innovation achieves critical mass. When 24% to 28% of the target group has adopted the innovation, then a sustainable movement will ensue. This is helpful not only as a numerical goal, but is important when planning your departure from the church planting effort. This "exit strategy" is often overlooked in church planting.

Anticipating response helps the church planter understand the dry periods when people are reluctant to show outward response to his communications efforts. The big brass bands have all gone home and the "dark night of the innovator" lends a certain gloom. Others tend to keep watching the change to see if it works and when it does make a distinct difference, then delighted participants will share their interest with others. [7]

Response to communications is affected by trial commitments and evaluations prior to the eventual identification with Christ, other Christians, or the church planting process. The weakness of Integrated Marketing Communication tends to be the linear process expectations. Another weakness is the inherent product marketing approach. Social change comes at significant costs. The "cost of discipleship" and other significant distinctions need to be clearly communicated over time. The church planting strategist quickly learns that unless the participant understands clearly what is expected of them, then they cannot make the emotive jump to deeper loyalties.

Church planters must be proactive to avoid creating the wrong response when using media:
1. ***Contextualization***: Strategies should address the content that is most relevant to a local believer. "Often times, the subtle shift from proclamation to real communication triggers a response that was previously absent. Effective communication requires understanding the language and worldview of the people you are trying to reach."[8] The ideal is to keep media locally-relevant and avoid generic media products.
2. ***Reproducibility and subsidy***: Avoid introducing inappropriate technology or resources that cannot be easily obtained, duplicated, or used without outside assistance. Creating dependence upon something that is not inherently indigenous or common to the group creates problems in the long term. Future churches being planted will always have a rear-view mirror approach where their default is the method that was used with them.

Response to communications efforts will likely vary. Church planters might be stunned to hear that Muslims showed the JESUS film in a local mosque. Perhaps they'll respond like those who heard about it North Africa back in the early 1990s and send in waves of videotapes in response to a spiral of interest. Radio programs augmented the showings so that discipleship was immediately available over the airwaves when there was no visible Christian church group able to handle it locally.

Interviews with Baptist pastors in Middle America lamented that their Baptist newspapers closed for financial reasons. It turned out that news of church planting efforts often served as informal case studies that encouraged them to initiate new church starts. Meanwhile, in Brazil, the Woman's Missionary Union was lauded by convention leaders for using their curriculum to encourage women to start Bible studies, later to invite their husbands to attend, and then suggest ways that the Bible study group could call a seminary graduate to be their local group's pastor and constitute a church. In one interview, Baptist convention leaders credited about half of the Brazilian churches as being initially planted by the Brazilian WMU's missions magazine.

In each case, a media strategy – intentional or informally carried out – served as specific catalysts for church planting.
Apply this to your own work:
- How would you plan for and respond to those with whom you communicate?
- Who do you anticipate to respond first, a few months later, and those much later? Who are downright defiant of your presence in their midst?
- Over the next two years, would your communications media mix change any, adapt constantly, or stay the same?

Putting a Media Strategy to Work

Church planting depends upon gathering people together. Communications media serve as catalysts to cluster people around a common interest. These interests can lead to a Bible study group and even a church. The point is to ignore costs during the strategy planning phase, but eventually balance the reality prior to implementation. When the vision is shared for elements of a change strategy, then other partners that specialize in communications media may walk beside you. Radio and television ads, puppets, cassette distribution, chronological Bible storying dramas, media packets, press releases, music, and even advertised offers contribute to communications effectiveness. Your peoples' preferences should be noted without regard to existing general media.

STEPS TO A MEDIA STRATEGY

1. Develop messages to communicate based on needs, values, outcomes, and opportunities.
2. Audience(s) that need your messages and why (includes situation analysis of various environments)
3. List the best communication channels that punch through the clutter for each audience (research aids in decision-making accuracy)
4. Establish budget and controls such as reporting, accountability to the mother church(es), feedback, etc.
5. Identify a realistic timeline for execution (usually 18 months to 2 years).
6. Solicit feedback periodically to evaluate response, public opinion, levels of participation, and overall effectiveness.
7. Adapt and re-deploy communications media.

The ideas presented in this chapter seek to use media to exceed making contacts and bring people together for church-planting. It is easy to point out the evangelism phases, but media within a mature and growing body of believers also deserves the same attention. The idea is not to have the media tail wagging the church-planting dog, but use media to complement and accelerate the work to allow the God to be glorified.[351]

Recommended free resources online:

http://newwway.org/articles/articles_index.htm
   Media in church planting
http://www.communication-strategy.net
   Communications in missions
http://www.mediastrategy.org/
   Evangelistic media
http://www.missionresources.com/
   Media sources
http://www.mislinks.org/practical/mobilization.htm
   Mobilization of resources

Endnotes

[1] Elisabeth Noelle-Neumann, "The theory of public opinion: The concept of the Spiral of Silence" in J. A. Anderson (Ed.), *Communication Yearbook* 14, Sage, 1991, p. 256-287

[2] Joel Davis, "Good Ethics is Good for Business," *Journal of Business Ethics,* 13:873-885, 1994

[3] Adapted from Don Schultz & others, *Integrated Marketing Communications*, McGraw-Hill, 1993

[4] Philip Kotler and Alan Andreasen, *Strategic Marketing for Nonprofit Organizations*, 3rd Ed., Prentice-Hall, Inc., 1987, p. 64

[5] The Media Research Toolbox by this author is located online at http://newWway.org/research that provides instruction how to carry communications research for existing data, observation, questionnaires, focus groups, and interviews.

[6] Based on the work of Everett M. Rogers who hoped to "enhance the prediction of innovative behavior." *Diffusion of Innovations*, 4th edition, Free Press, 1995

[7] Ginger Trumfio, "The Selling Never Stops," graphic based on the work of Anthony Palermo of Brock Control Systems, *Sales & Marketing Management,* July 1994, p. 38

[8] David Garrison, *Church Planting Movements: How God is Redeeming a Lost World*, WIGtake Resources, 2004, p. 179

[350] More information is available online at http://FJseries.org .

[351] For more information contact Mark Snowden at msnowden@namb.net

Chapter 22

What Will It Really Take?

Daniel R. Sanchez

What will it really take for us to see church planting movements in North America with the same magnitude they have impacted other parts of the world? Can we realistically expect such miracles here? The authors in this book convincingly address these questions.

In summary, some major factors that will contribute to the initiation and development of church planting movements in North America are:

- Realistic Assessment;
- Cultural and Life-stage Sensitivity;
- Focused Prayer;
- Passionate Spirituality;
- Doctrinal Orthodoxy;
- Biblical Definition of Church;
- Functional Definition of House Church;
- Persistence;
- Reaching the Lost,
- Training of Trainers,
- Commitment to Multiplication;
- Indigenous Strategy;
- Commitment to Simplicity;
- Appropriate Church Planting Models;
- Strategic Partnerships;
- Strong Core Values;
- A Compelling Vision.

We discuss these factors.

Realistic Assessment

To experience church planting movements, we must face a basic reality, North America is becoming more unchurched every year.

Loss of Churches

Mike Steele, points out that in the decade of the 90's saw a loss of more than 50,000 churches (5000 a year) in the major denominations alone.[352] The number of evangelical churches dropped from 383,000 in 1993 to around 325,000 churches by the year 2000.[353] American churches lose an estimated 2,765,000 people a year to nominialism and secularism.[354] The American Church loses 72.11 churches per week or 10.27 per day.[355] "During the last ten years, the combined communicant membership of all Protestant denominations has declined by 9.5% (4,498,242), while the national population increased by 11% (24,153,000)."[356]

Not one county in the U.S. has a higher percentage of churched people than it did 10 years ago."[357] In 1900, there were 27 churches for every 10,000 persons. Today, there are 11 churches for every 10,000 persons.[358] Half of all the churches last year did not add one new member through conversion growth. Evangelical churches have failed to gain an additional two percent of the American population in the past fifty years.[359] In other words, we are not even reaching our own children. With an unchurched population of between 180 million and 190 million, the U.S. ranks third behind China and India in the number of unsaved people.[360]

While a few denominations are to be commended for the time, resources, and personnel they are committing to church planting efforts, the fact remains that many denominations are losing ground rapidly. Even those that are utilizing incremental church planting strategies are not growing fast enough to offset the overall decline.[361]

Unchurched Population

A realistic analysis of the spiritual condition of North America reveals that despite occasional surges of religious interest due to personal and national calamities, we basically have a population that is becoming more unchurched every day. This realistic analysis also leads us to seek to understand the society that surrounds us. What are the conditions in society that make people groups and population segments responsive to the gospel? Often it is political crisis and persecution, a leadership crisis and an ideological vacuum, a spiritual vacuum, an economic crisis, or some other type of crisis in the society. An understanding of the signs of the times will enable us to be sensitive to the segments of society that are being most responsive to the gospel message.

Cultural and Life-Stage Sensitivity

A second necessary factor for experiencing church planting movements in North America relates to coming to cultural and life-stage sensitivity. If full-scale church planting movements are going to occur in North America, significant numbers of church members will need to wake up and face the reality that the modern generation as a whole is not responding to the traditional church approach. Research done by Michael Foust, entitled: *Southern Baptist Convention*, "Nine Habits of Effective Evangelistic Churches," reveals that of the generation born between 1977 and 1994, only 4 percent are Christian,[362] making this group, Generation X, the most unchurched generation. By comparison 65 percent of the generation born before 1946, are Christian.

Speaking of the characteristics of Generation X, Bob Granholm explains that the 18-35 year old group is less concerned about structure and hierarchy, is disconnected from traditional churches, and is starting small informal fellowships. They gather for worship in homes, coffee shops, warehouses, fast-food restaurants, industrial complexes, parks and other unconventional places. [363] Krieder points out the sobering global implications of reaching Generation X with the gospel as he teaches that Generation X is the largest generation in the history of mankind, numbering in the region of a couple of billion. The global media message constantly addresses this group. Today's Generation X, says Krieder, is tomorrow's mainstream society and whatever Generation X has done to the church will be lasting and normative.[364]

Generation X is the largest generation in history, is the most unchurched generation in North America, and has the greatest potential to influence history worldwide. Given these facts, the urgency of utilizing methodologies that will reach the largest possible number of them is self-evident. *To what extent are we willing to be innovative in order to accomplish this?*

Passionate Spirituality

Those who have studied church planting movements abroad have observed that in nearly every case, they have occurred in the presence of political and/or religious persecution. This fact has prompted some to state that church planting movements cannot take place on a wide scale unless there is persecution on the part of the government or some segment of the society in which Christians live. In some countries, persecution has served to weed out casual Christians and has ensured that those who follow Christ are willing to pay the price, even with their own lives. It is undeniable that there is a depth of commitment and a boldness that is evident in areas where Christians experience persecution in their daily lives.

At the same time the question that needs to be asked is *whether it has been the persecution per se or the quality and depth of commitment* that has contributed to the rapid expansion or the gospel and exponential growth of churches. It is fair to say that in some areas where persecution exists but there is little or no commitment on the part of Christians (often nominal), church planting movements have not taken place. A church leader in a Western European country, utilizing a play on words related to the Greek word "*marturia*," said "during times of persecution we learned to be *martyrs* but not *witnesses*." Those who are beginning to see the spark of church planting movements in North America are calling for a radical commitment on the part of Christian workers and new converts to Christ and to a lifestyle that honors Him in every way.[365]

This necessary factor is what Christian Schwarz has called "passionate spirituality."[366] He uses this term to describe Christians who have a genuine relationship with Christ and are on fire for the Lord. They live committed lives and practice their faith with joy and enthusiasm.

Neil Cole affirms the significance of a vital, vibrant relationship with Jesus Christ as a prerequisite for a church multiplication movement. He explains that a spontaneous church multiplication movement must begin with the question, "Who is Jesus to me?" Spontaneous multiplication, like a spreading virus, is contagious. Until Jesus changes one's life, that person will not be able to change anyone else. The question is not the strategy or method but the depth of the spiritual life of the group. Church planting movements, says Cole, start with, "who is Jesus to you?"[367]

This spirit resonates with Albert von Ostertag's observation regarding first century Christians. After asserting that it was not the methods but the spirit by which early Christians communicated the message, he explains:

> The church received from Christ not merely the command but also the mighty, irresistible drive of life and love to transmit to her environment the life she had received,[368]

Whether this passionate spirituality is brought about by persecution, a sense of brokenness, or some other factor, it is clear that utter dependence on God and unwavering commitment to share the message of salvation is a prerequisite for church planting

movements to occur. It is also clear that passionate spirituality will not result from a "health and wealth" approach to the gospel. It is only when costly discipleship is taught and expected that people are willing to make the depth of commitment that produces passionate spirituality.

Doctrinal Orthodoxy

The issue of doctrinal orthodoxy is a crucial one for church planting movements. In discussing the various types of house churches and their motivation, Rad Zdero believes that many streams exist in the house church movement. Whatever the approach, Zdero is convinced that a commitment to orthodox theology is absolute indispensable in church planting movements.[369] The meaning of orthodox theology is belief based on and faithful to biblical teachings.

The apostle Paul did not take doctrinal purity for granted. After having started the church at Ephesus, he sent Timothy there to "stop the men who are teaching wrong doctrine" (1Tim. 1:3). In order for basic churches to have sound doctrine and correct motivation, they need a solid biblical foundation, which is imbedded in their DNA from their inception. The most effective antidote for heresy is a clear understanding and strong commitment to the basic doctrines of the Bible. Emotion and enthusiasm are not enough to keep a group from straying.

Christian A. Schwarz explores a sobering issue that relates to the discussion of the tie between doctrinal purity and church growth. He points out that the sects are characterized by great enthusiasm. "Their doctrine remains theologically false, despite their enthusiasm and 'successful' numerical growth."[370]

Schwarz cautions saying that "pure doctrine" alone does not induce growth. Regardless of how orthodox the dogma and view of Scripture is, a church can hardly expect to experience growth, as long as its members do not learn to live their faith with contagious enthusiasm and to share it with others. The quality characteristic "passionate spirituality" demonstrates empirically the theological core of the matter in church growth: the life of faith as a genuine *relationship* with Jesus Christ.[371]

If, however, we are to experience wide-spread church planting movements in North America we need a passionate spirituality coupled with a passionate orthodoxy. It is extremely important to have a solid understanding of the doctrines of the Bible and at the same time a passion for winning the lost and discipling them in the context of New Testament centered churches.

Definition of Church

One of the most crucial factors pertaining to church planting movements has to do with the manner in which the church is defined. A biblically sound, functionally focused, and structurally flexible definition of church is imperative if church planting movements are going to have the freedom to proliferate in North America.

Biblically Sound

The Bible describes the church in a number of ways. It is the Body of Christ (Eph 1:15-23, Rom 12: 3-8, 1 Cor 12: 12-31); bride of Christ (Eph 5:22-32); household of God (1 Tim 3:14-15); pillar and foundation of the truth (1 Tim 3:14-15); temple of Holy Spirit (1 Cor 3: 9-17, 1 Pet 2: 4-10); and priesthood of God on earth (1 Pet 2:4-10).

In the Bible we also find a description of the nature of the Church. It: belongs to Christ (Matt 16:18); is built on foundation of Christ, the apostles, and prophets (Matt 16:18, Eph 2:19-22), is Holy (Matt 18:15-18, Acts 5:11, 1 Cor 1:2, Eph 5:22-32); Universal (Gal 3:26-28, Eph 2:11-22, Rev 5:9, 7:9); is United (Jn 17:20-23, 1 Cor 1:10, Eph 4:1-6); and is led, empowered, and gifted by Holy Spirit (Acts 13:1-3, 1 Cor 12:1-30).

536

Functionally Focused

In Acts 2:40-47, as well as in other New Testament passages, we find a description of the functions of the early church. It functions as a body of followers of Jesus Christ who are called out to: communicate the Gospel (Acts 2: 40); baptize new believers (Acts 2:41; 8:12, 36-38, 10:44-48, Rom 6:1-4); follow Christ's teachings (Acts 2: 42; Matt 28:18-20, 1 Cor 14:26, 2 Tim 2:2, 4:2); fellowship and encourage one another (Acts 2: 42, 1 Thess 5:11, Heb 10:24-25); observe the Lord's Supper (Acts 2: 42; 1 Cor 10: 14-22, 11:17-34); pray (Acts 2:42); experience God's power, reverence and awe (Acts 2:43; 1 Cor 11:17-34, Heb 12:28-29); minister to each other (Acts 2:44, 1 Cor 16:1-4, 2 Cor 8:1-5, Gal 6:9-10); minister to others (Acts 2:45); experience joy (Acts 2: 46); have a common purpose (Acts 2:46); have a positive witness (Acts 2:46); worship (Acts 2:47; 13:1-3, 1 Pet 2:1-10); add new converts (Acts 2:47); sing (1 Cor 14:26, Eph 5:19-20, Col 3:12-17); fast (Matt 6:16-18, 9:14-15, Acts 13:1-3, 14:23); read the Word (1 Tim 4:13); and practice discipline (Matt 18:15-18, 1 Cor 5:1-13, 2 Cor 2:5-11).

Structurally flexible

Several biblical passages give us an idea of the flexible structure of the early church. It had: a recognizable membership (Matt 18:15-18); baptized believers (Matt 28:18-20, Acts 2:41); faithful believers (Matt 18:15-18, 1 Cor 5:1-13); carefully selected leadership 1 Tim 3:1-13, Titus 1:5-9); plurality of elders (Acts 14:21-23, 20:17-31, Phil 1:1); and interdependence of congregations (Acts 11:22-26, 15:1-35).

Some tend to define the church in *organizational terms*. They perceive it in terms of professional staffs, membership size, elected officers, formal organizational structures, ownership of buildings, and established financial procedures. Even though these are important factors in many churches today, the question must be asked, are they absolutely essential for all churches?

Others perceive the church in *organic (or functional) terms.* They cite Acts 2 as an example: "all the believers met together constantly and shared everything they had… They worshiped together at the Temple each day, met in homes for the Lord's Supper, and shared their meals with great joy and generosity – all the while praising God and enjoying the goodwill of all people" (40-47). Those who perceive the church in organic terms see the church as a community of believers relating to one another as they live out the Christian life. If we define the church in organic or functional terms, we enable the establishment of thousands of congregations that otherwise would not be able to exist due to the organizational requirements that some people have for the church. We need to ask ourselves, what are the essential requirements for the church as described in the Bible?

The Baptist Faith and Message of the Southern Baptist Convention gives the following definition of a church:

> A New Testament church of the Lord Jesus Christ is an autonomous local congregation of baptized believers, associated by covenant in the faith and fellowship of the gospel; observing the two ordinances of Christ, governed by His laws, exercising the gifts, rights, and privileges invested in them by His Word; and seeking to extend the gospel to the ends of the earth."[372]

In his discussion on the classic marks of a true church, Stan Norman asserts a true church demonstrates four marks:

- A true church is united in fellowship and the bounds of the Holy Spirit with a congregation set apart from the world in pursuit of holiness in worship and service.
- A true church is the unity of all the redeemed of all the ages as will ultimately be revealed and enjoyed in the final state.

538

- A true church is committed and submitted absolutely to the revelation of Jesus Christ as given by the apostles.
- A true church manifests its authenticity in the right preaching of the Word, the right administration of the ordinances, and the right administration of church discipline.[373]

The Greek word for church is *ekklesia* which is composed of two words: ek, meaning "out of" or "out from" and *kalleo*, meaning "I call." This word also conveys the meaning of being assembled together.[374] *A church therefore, is a group of believers in Jesus Christ who have been called out of the world to experience the Christian life in community with fellow believers , to function under the authority of Christ and to carry out His mission (Eph 1:22,23).* This group of believers can meet any time and anywhere it can congregate to carry out the basic functions of a church. Others will define the church in different ways. The important thing is for the definition to be biblical and for it to provide guidance in the selection of models that are needed in the various socio-cultural, socio-economic, and socio-political settings.

Definition of House Church

Another factor necessary for church planting movements in North America relates to a proper understanding of house churches. People who hear about church planting movements taking place especially through the instrumentality of house churches often ask, "are these really churches?" Some have even called them "phantom churches." Before we dismiss house churches as a second class expression of the "real church," we need to remind ourselves of the fact that the apostle Paul did not hesitate to call them churches. The expression "the church that is in your house" appears repeatedly in his letters (e.g., Rom 16:5).

The fact that the Lord is blessing the use of homes for the conversion and discipleship of millions of people throughout the world should motivate us to understand this instrument more fully. Wolfgang

Simson sheds much needed light on this subject of house churches using his term, "Housechurch." He declares that such 'churches' are supernatural and communal ways of expressing the Christian life hat is based in homes. These congregations are the way redeemed people live locally and the organic way disciples follow Jesus together in everyday life. Since, Simson says, the redeemed do not any more belong to themselves, they adopt a mainly communal lifestyle. Housechurches emerge when truly converted people stop living their own life for their own ends, start living a community life according to the values of the Kingdom of God, and start to share their life and resources with those Christians and Not-Yet Christians around themselves. It is the result of the conviction that we do not only experience Jesus Christ and His Spirit in sacred rooms dedicated for that express purpose, but in the midst of life. In that sense, the organic housechurch is the deathbed of egoism, and therefore the birthplace of the Church. True community starts, where individualism ends.[375]

Tony Dale contends that House churches are no new phenomena. He points out that from the book of Acts, to the growth of the church in China over the past 50 years, house churches have been at the center of church growth in each succeeding generation. Dale continues showing that whether to escape the persecution of communism, the close scrutiny of a Moslem dictatorship, or just the simplicity of church life that seems to be so lacking in most western churches, house churches are again making a comeback. Dale says we need to ask why the Holy Spirit is allowing this resurgence of an old idea in a new generation.[376]

In his review of the various expressions of the church in the New Testament, Stan Norman indicates that in the New Testament the word "church" is used to refer to believers at any level, ranging from a very small group meeting in a private home to the group of all true believers in the universal church. Norman observes that a "house church" is called a "church" in Rom. 16:5 ("also greet the church in their house") and 1 Cor. 16:19 ("Aquila and Priscilla greet you warmly in the Lord, and so does the church that meets at their house").

Norman continues showing that the church in an entire city is also called a "church" (1 Cor. 1:2; 2 Cor. 1:1; and 1 Thess. 1:1). The church in a region is referred to as a "church" in Acts 9:31: "So the church throughout all Judea and Galilee and Samaria had peace and was built up." The church throughout the entire world can be referred to as "the church." Paul says, "Christ loved the church and gave himself up for her" (Eph. 5:25) and says "God has appointed in the church first apostles, second prophets, third teachers…" (1 Cor. 12:28). In this latter verse the mention of "apostles" who were not given to any individual church, is a clear reference to the church universal.[377]

A biblically-based definition for house churches is a prerequisite for effective church planting movements.

Persistence

Church planting movements do not take place overnight. As we read Garrison's book, we are awed by the large numbers of churches that have been planted in many regions. A careful study of the details however reveals that in a number of instances there were several "false starts" and that *the church planting movement actually started with a few churches* in its initial stage. For example, Garrison describes the experience in the *Yanyin* province. The church planter partnered with ethnic Chinese church planters and a small team of local believers. The group of believers planted six churches in 1994 and 17 more the next year. The third year 50 more churches started and by 1997. Just three years after the starting, the number of churches had expanded to 195. The movement had spread throughout the region taking root in each of five people groups. At this point the movement was spreading so rapidly that the strategy coordinator felt he could safely exit the work without diminishing its momentum. In his absence, the movement nearly tripled as the total number of churches grew to 550 with more than 55,000 believers.[378]

Again, while the final numbers are impressive, we must not lose sight of the fact that *this movement started with the planting of six churches*. Because the planters learned from their mistakes, persisted, and used methods that ensured reproduction, the movement took off, exceeding everyone's expectations.

Another reason why persistence is needed is that the response rate of people to the gospel message varies from one group to another and one region to another. In some areas people are responding after only the first or second presentation of the gospel while in other areas it is taking much longer for people to respond. Don Dent, for instance, is regional leader for an area that is not yet responding at the same rate as those who live in China and some parts of India. His approach is:

> We continue to use the Church Planting Movement principles because these maximize the harvest no matter where a person is working. As we continue to work faithfully, we come closer to seeing the start of a church planting movement. If you are multiplying instead of adding, there is a much greater likelihood that this will lead to a church planting movement.[379]

Yet another factor that fosters persistence is an understanding of the obstacles that are present in any given setting. Don Dent explains:

> Different types of persecution affect the response to the gospel differently. When there is *top-down persecution* in which the official government persecutes Christians, generally the gospel spreads rapidly. It is the government and not family members who persecute Christians. In this type of setting family members and close friends can get together, share the good news of salvation and see many conversions. When persecution is *from the bottom up*, in which family members and close friends persecute new believers among them, it is more difficult for the gospel to spread rapidly. In some areas, new believers are killed by their own families. Typically in these settings people take much longer to make a decision for Christ and having done so, take much longer to share a gospel message with others. This, therefore, affects the rate of response to the gospel.[380]

An understanding of the obstacles faced in each setting is helpful in that church planters will not expect the same results in every setting. While in North America there is no official government

542

persecution of Christians, church planters need to be aware of the obstacles that are present and must seek to overcome them. This understanding will help church planters continue to be persistent even if the response rate is not at the same level as is found in other parts of the world.

Persistence is an indispensable quality in North America. Society in general is accustomed to quick fixes. If an approach doesn't work immediately, it is cast off like an old garment and the search begins for a new approach. This attitude regrettably can be found in those who are responsible for church planting efforts. We must be willing to stay the course in the initial stages of church planting movements in North America if we are to see the results that are being seen elsewhere in the world.

Reaching the Lost

One of the most crucial factors in starting a church planting movement is that of reaching people who are lost and have had no previous long-term connection with a church. When these come to a saving experience with Christ, they are truly excited about sharing their faith with others and have no preconceptions of what a church ought to be like. They are willing to meet in their homes, place of employment, or wherever they can to study the Bible, fellowship with one another, and to grow in their Christian faith. Conversely, those who "tend to be very reactionary and rabidly against the institutional church" [381] very likely come from the ranks of churched or previously churched people. Neil Cole stresses the importance of reaching the lost in order to have church planting movements:

> We are seeing a lot of good numbers and transformation of life and I praise the Lord for it, but I don't think we are seeing a church planting movement yet because most of what's happening is Christians that are getting turned on. .. There are some networks, like Awakening Chapels that are almost 80 to 90 percent conversion from the harvest. These are the ones that grow the fastest and we need to see more of those, but we haven't yet. Part of it is the fact that it

appears to be so much easier to find Christians who want to get on board. It is actually not easier, it is harder. It's a lot easier to get out there in the fields and just win some people to Christ and let the chain reaction happen, but we have not done that.[382]

One of our greatest challenges in starting church planting movements is to design strategies to reach the lost and to have the discipline to keep from getting distracted by methodologies that focus principally on reclaiming Christians for the church. *While this is an important ministry for existing churches and others, it must be kept in mind that attracting Christians to basic church networks is not going to result in church planting movements.*[383]

Training Trainers

In order for church planting movements to take place, there must be an enablement of new believers from their moment of conversion on. In his chapter on *Organic Churches and Church Planting Movements*, Neil Cole points out that this pattern was established by Christ himself. He cites the deliverance and conversion of the Gerasene demoniac as an example. The transformed Gerasene wanted to follow Jesus, but Jesus told him: "Go home to your people and report to them what great things the Lord has done for you, and how He had mercy on you: (Mark 5:19). The Gerasene did just that "And he went away and began to proclaim in Decapolis what great things Jesus had done for him; and everyone marveled" (v.20) Enabling new believers to share their faith immediately after their conversion contributes to the rapid expansion of the gospel.[384]

Dr. Bill Fudge takes this a step further when he emphasizes the need to train new converts to become trainers of trainers. He states:

One of the keys to this Church Planting Movement is that leadership training focuses not on "training of leaders" but upon *'training of trainers.'* The leader associated with this movement states that "trained leaders expect to care for their congregation and lead it, whereas *trainers are expected to start and lead a congregation, AND train those in that congregation to also BE TRAINERS, thus start and lead a group of new believers while training those in turn to do the same.* The word description of that simple change in concept from "leaders" to "trainers" is a bit convoluted, and the outworking of it appears at first glance to be "chaotic," but the end result is often VERY fruitful as those saved realize their part in sharing the gospel of Jesus. The *"training of trainers"* approach is actually a fulfillment of the Great Commission words of Jesus to "teach them to obey all that I have commanded you."[385]

Commitment to Multiplication

In order for full-blown church planting movements to take place in North America, there must be an understanding of the factors that contribute to them and an unbending commitment to multiplication. Neil Cole explains that church multiplication is church planting with multi-generational reproduction. He declares that in church multiplication movements, daughter churches have granddaughters who have great, great granddaughters and so on. He explains that if all you do is spin off daughter churches, and those daughter churches don't have daughters, no matter how many times you do it, it's not multiplication.[386]

A commitment to church multiplication requires that all of the methodologies employed must contribute in a direct way to the exponential growth of basic churches within their networks. This requirement has implications for evangelism. Every person that we lead to the Lord must be trained to start to witness to others immediately and to enable these new converts in turn to win others. This same principle of reproduction needs to be imbedded in the DNA of each new church so that it too will start others that in turn will reproduce. In other words, we need to plant church planting churches. Bill Easum and Dave Travis point this out that the sooner a congregation plants a new church, the easier it is for the new church to become a planting center. Congregations that plant their first church within three to five years of their birth, say these authors, find that it is much easier to plant subsequent churches.[387]

Some church multiplication efforts are indeed reaching many people for Christ. In order for these to become movements, they need to develop the type of methodology that will enable them to experience rapid reproduction by utilizing the meeting places that are available to them, training the basic church leaders as they minister (just in time training), keeping their methodologies simple (e.g., participative Bible studies) so that they can be easily reproduced, and utilizing self-supporting basic church leaders so that the rapid reproduction of the movement will not be hampered by practices that require long-term training, the need to build expensive buildings and large infusions of financial resources. *In order for church planting movements to really take off here in North America, we need to have an unbending commitment to utilize only the methodologies that contribute to multiplication.*

Indigenous Strategy

One of the biggest challenges facing the proponents of church planting movements is that of developing a financial support strategy that enables reproduction instead of obstructing it. The biggest obstacles to the development of such a strategy are existing patterns of funding and concurrent expectations. For over a century, mission agencies in North America have provided financial support (salary, housing, insurance, etc.) for church planters.

Even though, many of these agencies utilize a phase-down plan whereby the newly established churches gradually assume financial support for church planters, the fact remains that in many areas new churches are not started because mission agencies have not provided financial support. Time and space do not permit an in-depth evaluation of this strategy and a realistic assessment would lead us to conclude that this strategy will continue to be used in the years to come.[38] Perhaps the best that we can hope for is for a parallel track for basic church strategies to be developed.

After analyzing numerous church planting movements around the world, Dr. Jim Slack has developed valuable suggestions on the use of financial resources. He states that every situation is different so universal rules are not viable. He continues showing that basic issue is that of knowing how to initiate, develop, and grow locally, indigenous workers without creating dependence. As a third matter, Slack states that the basic problem is that financial subsidy of church planters generally slows down the work, makes people dependent, changes the strategy to one of un-reproducibility, and takes away the initiative of church planters.

Overcoming these problems demands, according to Slack, that missionary education recognize that missionaries who have money naturally want to give subsidy and that the heart will always win over the head, if not educated. Slack continues showing that money and missionary presence are both subsidy. Money is dangerous; money subsidy close to the initiating of the work is even more dangerous. Missionary presence, however, is less dangerous when it is focused on training ministry and materials.

Slack correctly observes that subsidy (money and personnel) to jump start the work must be handled carefully. Further, the location and the economic situation of people must be considered. The poorer, the less educated, and the less mobile the people are, the greater the likelihood will be of creating dependency.

Slack concludes that training and materials are better subsidy if language specific. Training should avoid the extraction of workers from their home environment. The church starter should limit) we work with o as to avoid the danger of creating dependency. Missionaries serving as pastors has seldom proven to be good. [389]

Slack also offers specific guidelines for funding basic church leadership training: (1) You can pay for expenses for trainers you bring in. (2) You can pay for "rental" of a venue for the duration of the event. Usually the House Church folks will take care of this so don't mention this or offer it. If they bring it up you can discuss it. Don't do long-term leases or purchase training sites. (3) You should try not to pay for expenses of participants except in extreme situations. (4) You can expect to sell materials to cover the cost.

Remember issues of Reproducibility if you are expecting them to pass on what they have learned. Length of training sessions can vary based on the type of training from two days to two months or more. Your first priority should be training trainers on whatever topic(s) you are providing training. Your second priority is training church planters and missionaries. The areas in which you have a lot to offer are: Church Planting Movement approaches, urban strategies, unreached people group-specific topics, or cross-cultural issues.

While these guidelines were designed to address situations abroad, they have application for basic church strategies in North America. As the International Mission Board appoints and supports Strategy Coordinators to initiate church planting movements, National State, and local mission agencies can appoint and support Strategic Catalyzers to serve as catalysts for church planting movements.[390] *These workers, however, must adhere to a policy of not providing salaries for the leaders of house churches. It is absolutely impossible for the rapid multiplication of basic churches to take place if financial resources are used for this purpose.* There are simply not enough funds to support simple house church leaders. *A policy of providing salaries for basic church leaders can result in "ecclesiastical birth control."* You only have so many resources. In addition to this, a spirit of dependency will stifle a church planting movement quicker than almost anything else.

Some mission organizations may need to go through a period of transition into this type of funding strategy while others may need to develop a parallel track for basic churches. Unless this issue is dealt with adequately, the likelihood of on-going church planting movement is very small.

Commitment to Simplicity

Church planting movements are occurring today in areas where simple, easily reproducible methods are being employed. Neil Cole explains that if disciple-making and multiplying is to reach all, we must find a way to make it available to all. We must employ means so that the Faith can be passed on from generation to generation. Most methods, he says, have been too complex and leader dependent to move to others in ways that they can pass it on to succeeding generations. Cole concludes that not all Christians are meant to be leaders, but all are meant to be reproducing disciple-makers![391]

Dr. Bill Fudge describes the simple methodology that he has seen employed in church planting movements abroad: (1) Every member is trained to be a trainer; (2) Every member is trained to find 5 non-Christian friends in a week, invite them to his home, share his testimony, and bring the gospel into their lives; (3) Every member is taught to write down his individual testimony and read it 10 times out loud until he can memorize it; (4) Every member is instructed to list all family members, relatives, classmates, and colleagues that are non-Christians. Most of the time, everyone's list is around 100 people. Afterwards, they are to pick out the 5 people they want most to share the gospel with and group them as group A. Then they are to list the 2nd group of 5 as Group B and so on.

Fudge continues saying that leaders should (5) Teach them the 1st of the 6 basic lessons of the initial faith – requesting them to write all the verses in this lesson down, including examples. They will be split into groups of 3 to practice teaching each other until they become very familiar with this lesson. The first sentence of this lesson would be: "Congratulations, you have returned to the Lord's family and have become a Child of God again." This is a very important positive sentence to underscore the truth that we were all once all God's children, but we left Him and became lost but we are back again.

Then, says Fudge, (6) When they return after this week, they are to find those 5 people in Group A and witness to them and teach them the 1st of the basic lessons.; (7) Once the people who receive the testimony and believe in the Lord, they are to follow the same process, i.e., list all the names of the people who are non-Christian and teach them the 1st of the 6 basic lessons; (8) After one week, the 1st group of people returns to learn the 2nd lesson and once they have learned it, they are to go back to their homes and teach their next generation the lesson.[392]

If we are to see church planting movements in North America, we need to be ruthless in the employment of only the materials, methods, and tools that are simple enough that they can be easily reproduced within the intellectual, financial, social, and material resources of new converts

Appropriate Church Planting Models

Another factor important for church planting movements in North America relates to appropriate Church planting models. Frequently asked questions are, "Isn't the basic church model the same as the cell-based church model?"and "Since many of the existing churches in North America started in homes, what is the difference between these and the basic church approach?"

The fact is that similarities exist between some of the elements of these models and have caused confusion. A comparison of these three models of church (Traditional, Cell, and Simple) invariably involves some generalization. For example, not all traditional churches are alike in every respect. There will be some exceptions. It is with an apology to all of the churches that are atypical that we will attempt to point out the *distinctive characteristics of each model*.[393]

Traditional Church

The typical traditional church can be any size. Its activities are carried out in congregational meetings. Except for churches that have bi-vocational pastors, the leadership (pastor and staff) is supported fully through a church budget. Traditional churches have weekly worship services (Sunday and Wednesday) in a designated facility owned by the church.

Generally, a strong central figure serves in the leadership of the church. Most of the pastors have had formal theological training. This type church has lay leadership in Sunday School and in occasional leadership training events. Much of the focus in Sunday School is geared toward increasing the knowledge of its members.

Unless extraordinary efforts are taken, growth in the traditional church stops when the building is full. Typically there are few if any accountability groups. Oversight of most of the ministry is exercised by the pastor. *The most appropriate analogy for reproduction in this model is that of a mother-daughter relationship. When church planting occurs, the church creates a daughter congregation which has the status of a preaching point, a mission, and then a constituted church.*

Typically the top leadership for the church comes from the outside. In terms of structure, a constituted church is considered autonomous even though it can affiliate with other churches (e.g., Associations) and conventions (state and national). Often traditional churches have a big "back door" challenge. The offerings are typically used for staff salaries, facilities, programs and mission offerings and projects.

The Cell Church

Cell churches typically have between 5 and 20 members. They utilize lay-led cells with highly trained top leadership. The ordinances are not carried out in the cells but in the central congregation. Leadership support is carried out in two levels with the lay-leaders supporting themselves and the upper-level leadership being paid by the church. Celebration typically takes place in the central congregation on Sundays.

The cell church usually requires a pastor who is a strong leader and a visionary who can communicate his vision. Training for all levels of leadership takes place weekly. Discipleship also takes place in the cells during the week. Usually, cell churches do not have a Sunday School program. Their goal is to multiply to the limit of their structural support. Evangelism, *koinonia*, and accountability take place in small groups. The control of these cells is from the top down. ***The most appropriate analogy for reproduction in this model is that of an Octopus – if you cut an arm off, it will grow it back.***

Leadership rises from within and is rarely brought in from the outside. The Cell Church model utilizes a highly organized structure The Cell-based approach helps in seeking to narrow the back door of the church. The offerings are typically used for staff salaries, facilities programs and mission offerings and projects.[394]

The Basic Church Model

The basic church model is usually made up of 5 to 20 members (sometimes up to 50 or 100). The leadership comes from laypersons There are no highly trained leaders in the basic churches themselve although the trainers of the leaders (e.g., Strategy Coordinators Strategic Catalyzers) are generally highly trained. The ordinances are carried out in the local group. The leaders of basic churches are self supported. Celebration may be intermittent in some cases. In others however, there are no joint celebrations and no paid facilities.

The local basic churches do not have strong central leaders. Training is required and may occur weekly, monthly, or quarterly. Usually basic churches do not have typical, graded Sunday Schools. Evangelism, *koinonia*, and accountability occur in small groups. Control of basic churches is typically diffused although most of them are a part of local, regional, and national networks. *The most appropriate analogy for the reproduction in this model of basic churches is that of a Starfish: You can cut off any part of the fish and it will grow a whole new starfish.* In basic churches leadership rises from within. The structure consists of independent units, yet in network with one another. This approach is very effective in helping to close the "back door" of the church. The offerings are used for local ministry and outreach.

It is our hope that this brief comparative analysis of these three church models will help the readers to understand that while there are some characteristics that all of these have in common, they have significant differences in philosophy, structure, leadership, and reproductive patterns. It also needs to be pointed out that some church planting efforts employ a combination of these models. Additional study of the similarities and differences will help church planters in the selection of the appropriate model.

Strategic Partnerships

North America cannot be evangelized and discipled by any single denomination. The task demands the cooperation of many Great Commission Christians to impact the entire regions with the gospel. This joint participation, however, does not necessarily result in interdenominational or non-denominational churches that often end up forming their own denominations. There can be ways, however, to participate together in evangelistic projects (e.g., Scripture distribution, Jesus Film, media efforts, evangelistic events), and sharing training, and materials, and resources for the establishment of churches. These churches will benefit from association with their respective denominations.

The International Mission Board of the Southern Baptist Convention has developed guidelines for relation levels:

1. In level one, the goal is entry to the target population (e.g., tourism, business, education, etc). The guiding principle is acceptability to the target population,
2. In level two, the goal is prayer for the population, ministry to felt needs for the purpose of pre-evangelism. The guiding principle is response to spiritual and physical needs.
3. In level three the goal is Evangelism and Scripture distribution. The guiding principle is commitment to biblical evangelism.
4. In level four, the goal is the establishment of New Testament churches The guiding principle is commitment to New Testament Church planting.
5. In level five, the goal is ministerial training, theological education, ordination, deploying missionaries, etc. The guiding principle is doctrinal purity.[395]

At levels one through three, International Mission Board personnel are encouraged to work with other Great Commission Christians. For example, there can be many cooperative efforts related to evangelism events and Scripture distribution. It is at levels four and five that IMB missionaries focus on planting churches and establishing theological educational centers that focus more closely on polity and doctrine that is reflective of their denominational sending agency Similar guidelines can be developed to promote cooperation with other Great Commission Christians in North America to impact an entire region with the gospel while at the same time making allowance for the churches that are started to establish their own denominational identity.

Strong Core Values

Church planting movements must have strong core values that provide motivation and guidance. In his book, *Going to the Root: Proposals for Radical Church Renewal*, Christian Smith posits cor values that have application for church planting movements. He teaches:

- Build intentional Christian community: make it a priority to build community with discipleship, accountability, commitment and perseverance. Do church without full-time paid, professional clergy. Decentralize leadership and decision-making.
- Open up worship services: have worship that is God-centered, collective, participatory, physically active, Spirit-led and narrative (telling the story of God's redemptive work).
- Overcome the edifice complex: gather in homes or "secular" venues.
- Cultivate a grace-full spirituality of everyday life.
- Focus on spirituality for everyday living: family relations, work, shopping, commuting, etc.
- Practice lifestyle evangelism: avoid techniques that trivialize and over-simplify the Gospel, tell people the full truth (that the saved life is not always roses), don't just tell people, but show them through your life, while avoiding works-righteousness (i.e., focusing on your good works rather than on Jesus), be a contrast culture rather than a counter culture, live simply and avoid mass-consumer materialism (that big, popular idol).
- Work for social justice: champion the cause of the vulnerable, the marginalized, work for change in institutions that oppress people and mock the Gospel and its values (e.g., as William Carey successfully opposed Sati in India, or 19th century Christians helped abolish slavery), get educated on the root causes of issues before plunging into activism. Seek unity but not uniformity nor relativism: talk to and seek to understand Christians from all traditions;
- Use the Five-fold ministries to equip the saints: build up and develop a network of churches by a team of apostles, prophets, evangelists, pastors and teachers (Eph. 4:11), each of them train up-and-coming people in the same and other ministries, equip all house church members to do the work of the ministry, building up the Body of Christ, aiming at unity of faith and knowing Jesus, growing in maturity to be more Christ-like, avoiding winds of doctrine and the trickery of false teachers, seeing that every member does his or her share in causing growth of the Body (Eph. 4:7-16).[396]

Prayerfully articulating biblically based core values will ensure that leaders as well as participants will be able to stay focused and avoid strategies and methodologies that divert attention or undermine church planting movements.

Compelling Vision

Jesus commanded us to "make disciples of all nations." Whether we interpret *ta ethne* to mean people groups or political nations with fixed geographical boundaries, the fact remains that we are to lead all of the people in these entities to become committed followers of Christ. This goes far beyond leading isolated individuals to a saving knowledge of Christ. We must have the vision to reach entire nations for Christ. This includes the nations and people groups of North America. In other words, we need to have a Great Commission vision for North America. A compelling vision will lead us to develop the methodologies that will help us to attain it. It is not enough for us to compare our current results with previous results or to compare ourselves with what other groups are doing in the area of church planting. *The bottom line is what are we doing to fulfill the Great Commission?*

Focused Prayer

Church planting movements do not take place in random unpredictable ways. They are always accompanied by fervent persevering prayer. Curtis Sergeant describes the role of prayer in the church planting movement that he was instrumental in starting. He affirms that a tremendous amount of specific prayer focused on the people group and its evangelization. God moved, says Sergeant, because His people asked. Specific prayer for the people group or population segment is absolutely essential if we are to see unprecedented numbers of congregations started among them.

Conclusion

If church planting movements are going to win significant numbers of unchurched people in North America, the factors that we have discussed above need to be addressed prayerfully and passionately. To repeat these factors: Realistic Assessment; Cultural and Life-stage Sensitivity; Focused Prayer; Passionate Spirituality; Passionate Orthodoxy; Biblical Definition of Church; Functional Definition of House Church; Persistence; Training of Trainers, Commitment to Multiplication; Indigenous Strategy; Commitment to Simplicity; Appropriate Church Planting Models; Strategic Partnerships; Strong Core Values; and A Compelling Vision.

The church planting strategists that contributed chapters to this book have offered insights that are valuable in the initiation and development of church planting movements in North America. As we look at the social and religious scene in North America today, several realizations are abundantly clear:

1. The number of Christian churches in North America is declining every year.
2. Incremental growth in church planting, by itself, is not getting the job done.
3. Church planting movements have the potential for the type of exponential growth that will impact entire nations.
4. Basic church strategies can be instrumental in reaching people groups and population segments that traditional approaches are either missing or finding limited effectiveness among.

5. A paradigm shift is needed in many of our churches, associations, state conventions, mission agencies, leaders, and seminaries.
6. A biblically sound definition of "church" can ensure we have a solid theological foundation and free us to utilize culturally relevant church planting models to reach large segments of the population in North America today.
7. We are not starting from scratch in North America. There are philosophies, programs and structures already in place. We must work lovingly and cooperatively with those who employ traditional methods while simultaneously developing approaches that will foster church planting movements. We may need to have some parallel structures within our organizations to enable the fostering of church planting movements.
8. While there is much we can learn from church planting movements abroad, we need to continue to develop strategies that are contextualized for North America.
9. In order to experience sustained church planting movements, we need to address adequately legitimate concerns regarding such issues as doctrinal integrity interrelationship of churches, training, and utilizing the laity, discipleship and incorporation of converts and the use of financial resources.
10. In the final analysis, church planting movements are the work of God.

If we are to see a surge of church planting movements in North America, we need to be desperate enough to pray passionately to be willing to re-examine God's Word, and to be led by His Spirit to utilize whatever biblically sound approaches are needed to reach the massive unchurched people groups and population segments in North America that need the Gospel of Jesus Christ.

J.D. Payne presents a challenge that we must take to heart:

Unless the Spirit of our Sovereign Lord moves across North America, we will never experience Church Planting Movements on the scale that we are seeing in other parts of the world. But I will conclude with a question to ponder: "If the Spirit so moved, would we be ready to receive His blessings or would our ecclesiologies, and missiologies hinder or even prevent Church Planting Movements?" Remember, the Children wandered for forty years because they were not ready to receive God's blessings. It is my desire that the North American Church be a participant, rather than an observer (or worse, a hindrance), if God so desires to move.[397]

May all evangelical church starters heed this imperative message!

Endnotes

[352] Patrick Johnstone, *Operation World*, 1993.

[353] Dudley, *Faith Communities Today*, March 2001,(www.hirr.hartsem.edu)

[354] American Society for Church Growth (ASCG), "Enlarging Our Borders," Report presented to the Executive Presbytery, January 1999, cited in Larry Kreider, *House Church Networks: A church for a new generation*, Epharata, PA: House To House Publications, 67.

[355] Ibid.

[356] Charles Arn, Institute for American Church Growth, "Enlarging Our Borders," Report presented to the Executive Presbytery, January, 1999.

[357] Ibid.

[58] Glenn Smith, "A New Kind of Church: Glocal," unpublished paper, 2002, 1.

[59] Arden Adamson, secretary-treasurer, Wisconsin-Northern Michigan District, "Enlarging Our Borders," Report presented to the Executive Presbytery, January, 1999,cited in Larry Kreider, *House Church Networks: A church for a new generation*, Epharata, PA: House To House Publications, 67.

[60] Arden Adamson, secretary-treasurer, Wisconsin-Northern Michigan District, "Enlarging Our Borders," Report presented to the Executive Presbytery, January, 999,

[61] See Mike Steele's chapter in this book.

[62] Michael Foust, *Southern Baptist Convention*, "Nine Habits of Effective Evangelistic Churches," June 2001.

[63] Bob Granholm, "Proposal for a House Church Network in the Lower Mainland British Columbia, Canada), October 1999, www.dawn.ch

[364] Larry Kreider, *House Church Networks: A church for a new generation*, Epharata, PA: House To House Publications, 14.

[365] Neil Cole, Cultivating a *Life for God*, Carol Stream, IL: Church Smart Resources, 1999, 28.

[366] Christian A. Schwarz, *Natural Church Development*, Carol Stream, IL: ChurchSmart Resources, 1996, 26-27.

[367] Neil Cole, "Oh, so that's what a church multiplication movement looks like!" *House2House*: Special Dawn Report, Austin: H2H Magazine, 5.

[368] Albert von Ostertag, *Ubersichtlche Geshiehte der protesttiche Missioinem von der Reformation bis aur Gegenwart* (Stuttgart, 1858), 4.

[369] Rad Zdero, "Initiating a House Church Movement in North America," www.rad@housechurch.ca

[370] Christian A. Schwarz, *Natural Church Development*, Carol Stream, IL: ChurchSmart Resources, 1996, 26-27

[371] Ibid.

[372] Article 6 of the 1963 and 2000 SBC "Baptist Faith and Message."

[373] Stan Norman, "Ecclesiological Guidelines to Inform Southern Baptist Church Planters," un-published paper, New Orleans Baptist Theological Seminary, September, 28, 4004.

[374] For an excellent discussion of this, see Robert Fitts, op. cit., 29.

[375] Wolfgang Simson, *Houses That Change The World*, 79.

[376] Tony Dale, "Watch Out! A Tidal Wave Is Coming," House 2 House, Special Issue, 8-10, Austin: www house2house.tv.

[377] Stan Norman, "Ecclesiological Guidelines to Inform Southern Baptist Church Planters," un-published paper, New Orleans Baptist Theological Seminary, September, 28, 4004.

[378] David Garrison, *Church Planting Movements*, Richmond: International Mission Board, 1999, 11.

[379] Daniel R. Sanchez' Interview of Don Dent at Southwestern Baptist Theological Seminary, April 21, 2004.

[380] Ibid.

[381] Rad Zdero, "Initiating a House Church Movement in North America," www.rad@housechurch.ca

[382] See Neil Cole's chapter in this book entitled, "Starting Organic Churches."

[383] While there are several definitions for the term "basic church," in this chapter I will use it as synonymous with "basic church." I define a "basic church," as one that carries out the functions of a New Testament church as described in Acts 2:40-47. This coincides with Stan Norman's statement that "In most New Testament passages, the church is depicted as a local assembly of Christians who meet, worship and in the name of Jesus Christ." Stan Norman, "Ecclesiological Guidelines to Inform Southern Baptist Church Planters," un-published paper, New Orleans Baptist Theological Seminary, September, 28, 4004.

[384] For additional information on training for trainers, see David Garrison, *Church Planting Movements: How God is Redeeming a Lost World*, Midlothian, VA: WIG Take Resources, 2004, 307-312.

[385] Bill Fudge, "The Fastest Growing Church Planting Movement," chapter 6 in this book.

[386] Neil Cole, "Oh, so that's what a church multiplication movement looks like!" House2House: Special Dawn Report, Austin: H2H Magazine, 6.

[387] Bill Easum and Dave Travis, *Beyond the Box: Innovative Churches that Work*, Loveland, Co. Group Publishing Inc., 2003, 125.

[388] For additional discussion on this, review Dr. J.D. Payne's chapter, "Suggested Shifts in Preparation for Church Planting Movements."

[389] Jim Slack, "Observations about Subsidy," unpublished article.

[390] For additional information on this, review Dr. Joe Hernandez' chapter, "Rapid Church Multiplication/Strategic Catalyzer Training: A Contextualized North American Model."

[391] Neil Cole, *Cultivating a Life for God*, Carol Stream, IL: Church Smart Resources, 1999, 33.

[392] Bill Fudge, "Comparison of Styles and Types of Churches," [bfudge@lwconline.com].

[393] I am indebted to Bill and Susan Smith for sharing with me a chart with these comparisons.

[394] For additional information on Cell-Based churches, review Harold Bullock's chapter, "From Cell-Based Churches to Church Planting Movements."

[395] Lewis Myers and Jim Slack, *To The Edge*, Richmond: International Mission Board, 1999, Section 4, page 29.

[396] Christian Smith, *Going to the Root: 9 Proposals for Radical Church Renewal*, Waterloo, Ont.: Herald Press, 1992

[397] J.D. Payne, "David Garrison's Church Planting Movements and North America: A North American Perspective?" Unpublished paper.

THE TRILOGY
COMPANION

A Reader's Guide to the Trilogy of Henryk Sienkiewicz

Edited by
Jerzy R. Krzyżanowski

COPERNICUS SOCIETY OF AMERICA
and
HIPPOCRENE BOOKS
New York

First Edition

Copyright © 1991 by CSA Literary Projects and Jerzy R. Krzyżanowski

All Rights Reserved

Published by the Copernicus Society of America,
Edward J. Piszek, president,
in its program of modern translations of Polish literary classics which
began with "The Trilogy" by Henryk Sienkiewicz,
to which these studies are a special supplement
compiled and edited by Jerzy R. Krzyżanowski, PhD.

"The Trilogy Companion," November, 1991 ISBN 0-87052-221-3

"With Fire and Sword," May, 1991 ISBN 0-87052-974-9

"The Deluge," October, 1991 ISBN 0-87052-004-0

"Fire in the Steppe," May 1992 ISBN 0-87052-005-9

Distributed in the U.S.A. by
Hippocrene Books, Inc.
171 Madison Avenue
New York, N.Y. 10016
Tel. (212) 685-4371

Cover Illustration: Jozef Brandt, *Ein Gefecht*, Museum Purchase, 1889,
in the collection of The Telfair Academy of Arts and Sciences, Inc.,
Savannah, Georgia

Map by Lizbeth Nauta

Printed in the United States of America

Contents

From the Editor

The modern translation of the Trilogy by W. S. Kuniczak represents not only a new and original approach to the problems of translating fiction but it also reintroduces Sienkiewicz to English-speaking readers after an absence of nearly a century. If one is to judge by public acceptance, and by the mixture of surprise and awe displayed by book reviewers all across the country, this reintroduction is an astonishing success, all the more remarkable because the Trilogy has never fared well in the hands of translators here and in other countries. While Sienkiewicz's *Quo Vadis?* deals with a theme and history which are more or less familiar to the Western reader, being set in ancient Rome during the time of Christian persecutions, the Trilogy transports us into 17th century Poland, into a history and geography which are almost totally unknown in the United States, including three terrible invasions by rebellious Cossacks, the mighty Swedes and the scourge of Europe—the Turkish armies of the Ottoman Empire. Neither the time frame nor the territory are familiar to most modern readers, which is why we thought it necessary to provide this companion piece that may explain or clarify some of the problems they may encounter in their reading of the Trilogy.

First, we introduce the briefest possible outline of Poland's 1,000 years of recorded history, with emphasis on the setting for the Trilogy's three interrelated novels: *With Fire and Sword*, *The Deluge*, and *Fire in the Steppe*. A special map may also help the reader to follow the flow of historical events as depicted there. Next we deal with the issue of translations in general, and the translations of Sienkiewicz's works in particular, although space limitations allow for only the most abbreviated comment. Volumes have been written on this subject and we supply a short bibliography of critical literature on Sienkiewicz for readers who may wish to know more about him. Bearing in mind that not all our readers may have read the Trilogy we include the three introductions written for the 1991-92 Copernicus Society edition. W. S. Kuniczak explains the problems he encountered in his modern, adapted translation of this 19th century classic, and the route he took to find his solutions. And finally, in order to help the readers find their way through the awesome maze of difficult and unfamiliar Polish, Ruthenian and Lithuanian names used throughout the novels, we have created three short glossaries for an easy reference. Kuniczak chose to transliterate these names phonetically along the lines suggested by the Modern Language Association, and while transliteration is an established literary process used in previous translations of the Trilogy, it may be useful for students and other interested readers to have the original Polish spellings at their fingertips.

The Trilogy is not a history text. It is a set of novels to be read as an entertainment as well as for its soaring message of human hopes and values. We hope that this modest *Trilogy Companion* will add to your pleasure.

—J. R. K.

The Setting: History at a Glance

Poland, the second largest Slavic country, lies in the exact geographic center of the continent of Europe, between united Germany in the West and the Soviet Union in the East. Its population today numbers almost 40 million. Another 15 million Poles live abroad, with some 10 million persons who identify with Polish origins or descent in the United States, Canada and the other countries of the Western Hemisphere. In its present borders it is an almost homogeneous nation, largely Roman Catholic in religion, and speaking only its one Polish language, but in the more than 1,000 years of its recorded history this is a rather recent political development. Traditionally Poland had been the home of many peoples, languages, religions and cultures which were occasionally in conflict with each other, and which gave the multi-ethnic Poles an extraordinarily rich and vital cultural identity that kept the nation alive through a uniquely dangerous and unsettling history.

The first official recognition of Poland as a state came in 966 A.D. when the nation converted to Christianity under its original dynasty of Piast dukes and kings, and then went on to become one of the largest and most prosperous European countries, not so much by conquest as by its cultural influence and political alliances. Under its next ruling dynasty, the Jagiellonians, Poland united with neighboring Lithuania (which at that time included all the territories and peoples of Byelorussia and the Ukraine) and formed a commonwealth known as "The Republic of the Two Nations" that lasted until the closing years of the 18th century. Always culturally oriented towards the West and deeply influenced by the European Renaissance throughout the 16th and 17th centuries, Poland and its partners in the Commonwealth flourished in politics, economics, the sciences and the arts and as Europe's largest territorial and military power, developing a unique political system in which the king shared his power with a parliament of elected gentry. This gentry, known as *szlachta*, was

6

by no means an exclusive small minority of all-powerful feudal aristocracy as in the Western nations of the era, but rather a broad stratum of lords and country squires who farmed their own lands and who were obliged to serve in the armed forces in times of national danger. In time, these numbered almost a million persons out of a population of almost eight million within the two nations, and this included all the Lithuanian and Ruthenian nobility, both major and minor, who were admitted to the privileges of the Polish gentry in the act of union. Peasants and other classes were not represented in these parliaments—as they were nowhere in the Europe of their time—but could be admitted to the ranks of gentry by some act of merit, especially by heroism in war.

In theory all the members of the *szlachta* enjoyed equality under law. In practice, the wealth and influence of some families raised them above others so that in time the magnates among them enjoyed immense power, running their vast territories as if they were independent princes, and commanding greater wealth and armies than the treasuries and forces of the Commonwealth itself. In contrast with the Western aristocracies, however, none of their Polish titles were hereditary; all of these marshals, palatines, castellans, lord constables and other territorial officials held their positions only in their lifetime by appointment from the king and senate, and passing to their heirs only the properties they owned; and only the old Lithuanian and Ruthenian nobles passed on their title of Prince to their descendants. It may be worth noting that such titles as Baron or Count were unknown in Poland and denote the favor of some foreign ruler.

The influence of the *szlachta* was both beneficial to the country and eventually destructive, since any form of popular democracy without a careful system of checks and balances must lead to some abuse of public trust, opportunism, corruption or outright anarchy which makes government impossible. After the Jagiellonian dynasty died out in 1572, the nobility won the privilege of electing their monarchs by popular vote, thus gaining absolute control over the fate of the entire nation, and bitterly resisting all later attempts to strengthen the central government and the king. Add to this extraordinary concession the two constitutional privileges of *Liberum Veto* and Confederation—by which any deputy at any local dietine or the national assembly could overturn any measure simply by shouting *"Veto*, I protest!"—and by which the gentry (which also meant the army) could legally rebel against all acts of government it judged as dangerous to the country, and you have a system doomed by its own idealism to eventual destruction. All this, it should be noted, evolved and prospered in a time when elsewhere in Europe kings ruled by "divine right," answerable to no one and responsible only to themselves.

As a result, the internal and international position of Poland continued to weaken while the strength of its autocratic neighbors grew everywhere around it, and the Commonwealth found itself less and less able to resist invasions by Sweden in the North, Brandenburg Prussia (or Germany) in the West, Russia and rebel Cossacks in the East, Hungarians in the South and the awesome might of the Ottoman Empire in the South and the Southeast. Conflicts with the Ruthenian populations of the Commonwealth in the Ukraine and the eastern borderlands could not be resolved, and a series of bloodily suppressed rebellions by Ruthenian serfs and the warlike Cossacks led finally to the massive 1647-49 revolt of the Cossackry under the charismatic Bohdan Hmyelnitzki. It was a merciless, fratricidal struggle that cost almost a quarter of a million lives (with 100,000 Jews slaughtered by the rebels), which challenged the Polish hegemony in the East and eventually aided in the rise of a powerful new Russia.

It is this desperate and bloody era that Sienkiewicz chose as the setting of his Trilogy, not only to "uplift the hearts" of his Polish countrymen (who, in his time, no longer had a country of their own) but also as a powerful plea for unity, brotherhood, human understanding, tolerance of the rights of others and a return to those ancient moral and spiritual values that gave the Poles the unparalleled freedoms they enjoyed for 500 years.

No sooner had Hmyelnitzki's holocaust abated when the Russians and their Cossack allies launched themselves against Lithuania, and a terrible new war erupted in the North and Northwest with the

1655-58 invasion by Sweden under King Charles Gustav who aimed to turn the Baltic Sea into a Swedish lake and almost succeeded. No sooner were the Swedes and their Prussian allies driven out of Poland and northern Lithuania, when the Hungarians broke in from the South, and no sooner were they thrown back across the Carpathian mountains, when the Turks, the Tartars and all the might of the Moslem world hurled itself into the southern reaches of the Commonwealth in a Holy War designed to overwhelm Christianity itself. Only a brilliant victory by King Jan III Sobieski over the Turks in 1683 at Vienna ended the Turkish threat to Europe and secured a brief period of respite for the Polish people, but as Sienkiewicz himself describes it in one prophetic internal commentary within the Trilogy, this was the respite of a stricken giant "who was no longer able to rise to defend himself."

Poland entered the 18th century drained of almost all its strength by foreign wars and internal turmoil. Its social and political problems seemed insurmountable. The *szlachta*, convinced of its supremacy in every field, quarreled and fought each other over every issue, electing foreign kings one after another, and clinging blindly to all its outdated privileges and prerogatives. Only the dire dangers from Russian, Prussian and Austrian imperialisms that loomed over the country in the second half of the 18th century managed to bring the gentry to its senses but it was too late. A valiant effort to reshape the political structure of the Polish-Lithuanian state, end the *Liberum Veto* and Right of Confederation, free the oppressed serfs, reorganize the armies, and open up the government to all classes of the population, resulted in the Constitution of May 3, 1791, but Poland's alarmed authoritarian neighbors—principally the ruthless Empress Catherine II of Russia—moved at once to thwart it. Bribery, corruption and finally invasion, brought about a series of partitions between Russia, Prussia and Austria, and in 1795 Poland disappeared from the maps of Europe. It did not reappear until the end of the First World War in 1918.

It is in that dark century of political non-existence, broken only by intermittent flashes of bloody and heroic uprisings against Tsarist Russia in 1830 and 1863, that only the immense riches of Polish literature and culture kept alive the spirit of the nation. Working in exile in Paris, the great Romantic poets Adam Mickiewicz and Juliusz Słowacki tugged at the conscience of the nation and created a messianic vision of a resurrected Poland, while their fellow exile, the world-renowned pianist and composer Frederic Chopin, tried to muster Western interest in the Polish cause. Meanwhile tens of thousands of other exiles were marched in chains into Siberia where they were to perish almost without a trace, or scattered through the world to fight "for your freedom and ours" in a variety of wars of independence, including both the American War of Independence and the Civil War.

Only in the late 1860s, two decades after Sienkiewicz was born in a small country manor in northeastern Poland, did a semblance of normal life return to the Poles. It opened a period in which some of the most important works of Polish literature sprung into being, largely as a means of resistance to foreign domination, especially in the areas controlled by Tsarist Russia where even the Polish language was forbidden in offices and schools. That literature kept alive the unquenchable sense of Polish national identity, reminding of the past in order to prepare the nation for a future won not by force of arms but through education, the arts and sciences, industry and economic progress.

It was, however, by force of arms and political organization that Poland, aided by help from Poles abroad, achieved its independence after the collapse of Russia, Prussia and Austria-Hungary in 1918. No longer part of a Polish-Lithuanian Commonwealth (since Lithuania also acquired its political independence with the fall of the Russian Tsars) the Poles reorganized their state in their original territories, without those ancient and historic lands in which the heroines and heroes of Sienkiewicz's Trilogy lived and fought.

The 20 years of peace between the two World Wars were barely enough to heal the social, economic and political wounds inflicted by more than a century of partition and foreign exploitation, when Nazi Germany and Soviet Russia conspired to erase Poland once again from the maps of Europe and the Second World War erupted across Polish lands in 1939. Six million Poles died in that world-wide slaughter. Hundreds of thousands were deported once more to Siberia or died in combat within Poland, in Russia, in Africa and the West, fighting heroically in every allied campaign on land, sea and air, but when the war ended in 1945 the nation fell once again into the hands of Moscow. Perhaps the finest tribute to the work of Henryk Sienkiewicz lies in the fact that once again his Trilogy offered sustenance and hope to a desperate people, teaching that no national calamity is ever absolute, that "there is always hope wherever children continue to be born," and that a nation which has endured as much as the Poles in their extraordinary history cannot be erased.

It is in that spirit and with that conviction that the Solidarity movement was born, a Polish-born Pope preached freedom throughout the world, and the dark night of Soviet Communism receded from Europe. The disintegration of the Soviet empire which started on its irreversible course in the 1990s promises a new life to the Poles as well. Free again, working to rebuild their democracy within their own borders, the Polish people pay homage to Sienkiewicz as they have done consistently for more than a century.

But his message is for all the world, not merely for Poland, which is why it must be carried to the world in ever new translations, adapted to the times and languages of the cultures in which they are read. Without such translations neither the author nor his work would exist outside the narrow limits of a single people, as our following essays show.

The Art of Translation

by Jerzy R. Krzyżanowski

"Of all the literary arts," wrote E. V. Rieu, the distinguished English translator of Homer, "translation has been the most neglected in the long history of criticism. Yet it has been widely practiced ever since the catastrophe at Babel produced a market for its products, and with so many good and bad examples at our disposal it should not prove impossible to establish it on a sound theoretical basis."

Great literary works belong to world literature. But to be appreciated throughout the world they must be understood by everyone, no matter where they come from or into which culture they are being transferred. Thus the problem of individual translation becomes paramount in the dissemination of cultural values because it is impossible for any reader to master all the languages representing each and every culture. To use modern terminology, "a text has to be sent to the end-user through the medium of the recipient's own language," undergoing on its way all the necessary changes inherent to that medium. The three basic components of the translation process are thus the original text, the medium, and the receiver in the broadest sense, be it an individual reader, a group or class of readers in a foreign culture or an entire foreign society. Each of these components should be properly understood in order to comprehend how the process works, or how a Polish novel can be read and appreciated by an American readership which may know nothing of Poland or the Polish language.

Let us begin with the original text, something that has existed in Polish literature for 100 years (to use the Trilogy of Henryk Sienkiewicz as our best example) and is as familiar to the Polish reader as any other vital part of his or her heritage and history. Such a literary work possesses its own structure—the plot, the story line, a set of characters, a spatial and temporal environment—and all of these are related to the reader's own experience by hundreds of references, associations, reminiscences, images and feelings. It also has its own form: the language, consisting of vocabulary, sentence structure, idioms, metaphors and a near infinity of structural and stylistic devices created by the writer. In poetry it also has a rigid versification pattern made of a regularity of stresses that result in a certain rhythm, rhymes that bind one verse to another, stanzas and external poetic forms that make it poetry rather than a work of literary prose. These sentence rhythms, by the way, are also present in truly fine prose fiction, although it may take a well-trained eye and many readings to note them. In short, each work of literature has its own unique, original form intrinsically anchored in its original language.

But what happens when we encounter more than one "original" text, be it an author's own handwritten manuscript, his final typescript, or a printed text corrected with his own hand? And what about "a second revised and rewritten edition?" Or an original text discovered long after the text went into print, whether in book-form or in some other publication? In other words, we must first establish what editors and publishers call "the canonical text"—a problem familiar to students of the Bible with its *apocrypha*, defined in dictionaries as "works of doubtful authorship or authenticity." The same applies to any literary text and its different versions that may coexist quite happily in a variety of forms with no one the wiser. Only when we have such a canonical text for a work of literature, usually edited by a scholar of some authority, can we proceed to apply the new medium to it, giving it the language into which we want the text translated.

But this is only the start of the headache because the new language, like the original language of the text, is more than a vocabulary, phonetics and grammar. Everything said above in reference to the original text and its native language applies to the new one, as well as a great deal of additional information needed for the reader, not only to help him or her appreciate the literary quality of the work but simply to make it understandable. And while in religious, scientific and expository prose there are many ways to explain the subject matter to the readers (such as footnotes, appendices etc.) a literary text would be impoverished by such manipulations and, in most cases, ruined. Prose fiction has to speak to the reader directly, its even flow uninterrupted even for a moment, and it must do so by its own power within the new language, striving for the effect desired by the author with its own imagery, its rhythms and its beauty in another medium. In some cases certain major changes must be introduced, as when translating verse with the two languages completely incompatible linguistically. But even in a work of literary prose—the novel, the short story or the essay—the internal structure of the original has to be adjusted to the esthetic requirements of the language of translation. "I call it," continued E. V. Rieu in his discussion on translation, "the principle of equivalent effect, and regard it as signifying that that translation is the best which comes nearest to creating in its audience the same impression as was made by the original on its contemporaries. Higher than this, I hold that no translator can aim."

And finally we come to the target or recipient of the new translation: the foreign reader, either an individual or an entire society or culture. How can he (or they) grasp a situation that occurred in a foreign country, in some cases hundreds of years ago, unless that direct form of appeal speaks directly to them? How much would they be able to retain after putting down the novel whose setting, context, characters and their motivations are totally foreign to them, and whose action is bewildering because it has no bearing on their personal or cultural experience? Reading, after all, is more than just a pastime. We read for knowledge, information and enrichment as well as for beauty. But how can anyone appreciate something that he or she doesn't entirely understand?

It is at this point that a truly skilled translator, who knows exactly what the foreign reader might miss unless he or she is helped towards better understanding and appreciation, weaves in a certain amount of information and adjusts the language to the readers' needs. And here we come to the crucial juncture of the entire process: how different from the canonical text can a translation be?

The case in point—that of the Sienkiewicz Trilogy translation—is one of almost unbelievable complexity. Nothing was ever simple for or about that man and the creation of a canonical text of his Trilogy defied even him. The normal basis for a new edition is the first edition, usually supervised, corrected and approved by the author, but Sienkiewicz was a man in almost constant motion. He wrote many of his novels while traveling, sending them piecemeal to the editors of newspapers where they were instantly printed in daily installments, which may have done wonders for the circulation but damaged the novels. The newspaper serials abounded in misprints, mistakes and omissions which could be corrected only later in the book editions, but even then Sienkiewicz complained bitterly about them.

"The first printing is loaded with nonsense," he wrote in one instance, but he was often helpless to do anything about it. Sometimes he introduced fresh changes of his own. "I am sending you the beginning of the novel's ending," he wrote in August 1884 to the publisher of the second edition of *With Fire and Sword*. "Nothing remains from the earlier printing, beginning with the enclosed page 729. The epilogue will also be slightly changed." A few days later he followed with another letter: "*With Fire and Sword* is indeed slightly larger now but not so much that this should be noted on the title page. Perhaps the best solution would be to write in the second edition: *revised by the author....*" Only after the 1896 edition of his collected works started to appear was he able to remedy the problem, although subsequent contracts with various other publishers made it impossible to correct all errors. As late as 1907 Sienkiewicz was reminding his publisher that he should correct the latest edition by himself. "I am very much concerned by this," he wrote, "for in all previous editions there are unforgivable mistakes, and yet each *editio princeps*" (or basic edition) "should be as careful as is possible." Many of those misprints, false tries and uncorrected errors were automatically reprinted in subsequent editions, and found their way quite naturally into the translations.

After World War II when all previous contracts expired, and there was an acute need to salvage and preserve whatever part of the Polish cultural heritage escaped the wholesale destruction decreed by the invaders, the first carefully prepared, 60-volume Collected Edition of Sienkiewicz's work was published in the years 1948 through 1952. Based upon all available manuscripts and the surviving *editio princeps*, or approved editions which had been either supervised or corrected by Sienkiewicz himself, this has become the standard text for Sienkiewicz's works published ever since, and served as the basis for W. S. Kuniczak's new Trilogy translation. It may be added that this is the first translation into any language, made directly from the Polish texts of this universally accepted and approved edition which is the best that we shall ever have as a canonical text.

American readers do not need an introduction to W. S. Kuniczak who serves as the medium of their new translation. His own trilogy consisting of three major, widely reviewed and acclaimed novels which were translated into more than 10 foreign languages in numerous editions, makes him a master of modern story-telling who has a complete and absolute command of the English language and of his own native Polish tongue as well. His demonstrated skills as an American writer give him the grasp of literary techniques essential for a first-rate, accurate translation, and both the talents and professional perceptions that assure the highest literary quality in his work. His solid academic background and years of special study allowed him to supplement Sienkiewicz's text with the necessary historical information needed by the reader as he explains later on in this *Trilogy Companion*.

The following pages also offer a sample of how Sienkiewicz's texts were manipulated by other translators, sometimes with ludicrous results; there are examples of how the same fragment of the Trilogy was handled by two different translations; and finally W. S. Kuniczak presents some of the problems he encountered and how he went about finding the solutions, making his own important contribution to the art of translating literary prose.

Sienkiewicz and His Translators

by Jerzy R. Krzyżanowski

Long before he received the Nobel Prize in Literature in 1905, Henryk Sienkiewicz had been among the most widely read and translated authors in America and Europe. A 1953 bibliography of his works in foreign translations lists more than 1,800 items in 42 languages without claiming to be in any way complete. No new bibliography has been compiled since then although the list of references has grown significantly; it goes far beyond the translations of his most popular novel, *Quo Vadis?*, which is available in virtually every civilized language, and includes his other major novels, short stories, essays, journalism and correspondence which were often translated more than once. All these writings evoked some response from scholars and reviewers, both critical and enthusiastic, in and since their time. None have passed unnoticed but a complete, updated new bibliography has not yet appeared. A 1966 study, *Henryk Sienkiewicz's American Resonance* by Mieczysław Giergielewicz, lists 194 American articles and reviews; it is a list which will be certainly expanded with the appearance of the 1991 translation of *With Fire and Sword* and *The Deluge*, and the forthcoming May, 1992 edition of *Fire in the Steppe* (Pan Wołodyjowski) by W. S. Kuniczak. Almost all these articles and reviews deal with Sienkiewicz's works in translation, often without referring to the Polish originals. This makes it possible for us to compare the opinions of the foreign critics, based in most cases solely on the literary value of the translations they had read, with the author's own reaction to these voices, since he knew several foreign languages and was able to make some valid observations.

Sienkiewicz had an ambivalent attitude towards the translations. On the one hand, like every author, he wanted to be known and read by foreign readers, particularly since he spent many years in almost constant travel all over Europe, Africa and the United States and had a deep appreciation of foreign cultures. But his personal situation as a subject of the Russian Empire, which included the better part of Poland at the break of the century, made him a victim of unscrupulous foreign publishers who took advantage of the fact that Russia had not signed the Bern Convention of 1886 protecting authors' rights, and often published multiple editions of his work without paying him any royalties whatever. The principal American publisher of his novels (Little, Brown and Company) made an exception to that rule in 1897 by paying him a royalty of 2,500 French francs for a package that included the entire Trilogy, *Quo Vadis?* and several volumes of short stories published up to that time in the United States, but his dealings with many other foreign publishers meant little more than costly and upsetting law suits, often to no avail. As early as in 1887 he commented on the permission he granted a Paris publisher to translate *With Fire and Sword* and *The Deluge* into French: "It was just a meaningless formality because there is no convention between France and Russia and no permission is needed." And 13 years later in 1900 he wrote to his French translator, Antoni Wodziński: "They've stolen my *Teutonic Knights* in America, I'm suing for my Trilogy in Italy, and all that bears directly upon me, upsets me, and makes concentration quite impossible. I would like to escape to some distant place but first I must finish some (ongoing) work which isn't helped by my gout."

He continued in another letter: "The very sight of my book translated into any other language makes me sick. I don't ask for it, I don't want it, I can't stand it, I don't profit by it, and all I get from it are problems, as if I weren't the man who gives those things away for nothing." And a few months later he wrote in the same mood: "Each of my translated novels makes me feel as if it were some young Polish girl from a noble family who was displaying herself before a French crowd, hoping to impress them. I can't even begin to explain how little I care (for that kind of thing.) It all looks ugly to me. And since I can't prevent it, the least I demand in the strongest fashion possible is that they don't trim me or my work to suit the French taste. If it's too long for them, then let them not read it."

At long last in 1899 Sienkiewicz got a chance to air his grievances in public in the very country that caused all his financial woes. Invited that year to take part in the centennial celebrations of Russia's greatest poet, Aleksandr Pushkin, he wrote an open letter to the organizer, Prince Esper Uktomskiy, in which he said among other things: "For years various Russian periodicals have been printing translations of my works and booksellers published them in separate editions. Of course they wouldn't do it if it didn't bring them profits rather than a loss. Their profits may have been even higher since I never demanded any royalties nor collected any. But now an opportunity arises and I intend to use it. Let every publisher who ever printed any of my works give something to a fund for starving children on the occasion of your poet's anniversary." And in a gesture of total contempt he enclosed a 50 ruble note out of his own pocket. The prince reacted with some bitter comments but from that time on some royalties started to arrive from Russia.

On the other hand, Sienkiewicz tried to be very complimentary towards his translators. Writing to Wodziński on the French translation of his *Bez dogmatu* (Without Dogma), Sienkiewicz commented: "I read it with great interest, as if it weren't mine. Your charming and delicate language does not take anything away from the original, and often surpasses it with the finesse of expression to such an extent that I began to ask myself if this weren't due to the superiority of the French novel over the Polish one."

As far as his American translator, Jeremiah Curtin, was concerned, Sienkiewicz showed him every hospitality and public support, although he expressed doubts about his character in private correspondence, diplomatically avoiding any critical comments about the quality of his work. In a letter to his friend Karol Potkański, written from Ragaz, Switzerland, in 1896, he explains how and why he tried to avoid a meeting with Curtin.

"Curtin sent a wire to Abakanowicz too," he wrote. "I asked (Abakanowicz) to reply: 'Sienkiewicz left for Switzerland' without saying where. I'm just afraid that you might disclose my location and console myself with the hope that you merely told him I left for Parc St. Maur..."

Explaining his obvious contempt and detestation of the persistent Curtin, Sienkiewicz continued: "Four years ago Curtin promised me (a share of royalties) but didn't send a penny, because what I received came from the publishers, Little Brown and Company. All right, so he won't pay, but why should he harass me at the same time, talking my head off about his successes with *Quo Vadis?*, and so on? Enough is enough."

When they did finally meet a year later, Sienkiewicz proved to be a polite host to a "business partner," and with good reason as the future would show, since by 1915 *Quo Vadis?* would sell 1.5 million copies in Curtin's translation in America alone, which was an astronomical number for the time. But once again his private thoughts about Curtin, expressed in yet another letter to Potkański, were quite at odds with his official attitude and deserve to be quoted at some length.

"What have you done, Cain, to your brother?" he wrote to Potkański who had apparently told Curtin where to find Sienkiewicz. "Jeremiah Curtin arrived, naturally. He is the most awful and colossal bore that the imagination of nine poets could conceive. He clutches at your sleeve while talking, and he repeats one and the same thing ten, twenty or twenty-five times. He talks about nothing except *With Fire and Sword, The Deluge, Pan Michael* and *Quo Vadis*. He has no other topic. It seems as if the world were only partially created until the advent of his mission as translator, and all that exists today are only two crucial subjects and two major questions: my novels and his translations. I can't even begin to suggest to you the horror of all his compliments. He sits at my table and goes on and on without interruption from breakfast to dinner. He even talks while eating and drinking and then grabs me by the knees for 40 minutes or more. And when I escape to write a letter I can still hear his voice at my back: 'You must go to America.' The monster doesn't want to tell me how long he is staying. His wife is neither ugly enough nor pretty enough to make up for it all, and they are driving me to utter desperation because, I'm telling you, even if I could contain one thousandth part of the incense he blows in my ear I'd burst like a bomb filled with dynamite. I'm wondering now if I ought to throw him off a cliff tomorrow, and if I do it—and if they cut off my head for it in Zurich—it'll be your fault."

Could Pan Zagloba express that any better? "There is no talk of business," Sienkiewicz complains. "He makes out he came only to see me but he started asking at once about a future American novel with Kościuszko and Pułaski. He probably heard about it from Little and Brown. Maybe he is afraid that I'll get it copyrighted and he won't be able to do a translation on his own, because it seems that he makes more money on translating than I do on my originals. Such is this Curtin with whom Providence and fate torment me with your help. This has all gone so far beyond any limits that it has acquired the character of a comedy, but it goes on and on..."

And a week later, on June 12, 1897, Sienkiewicz again escaped Curtin's clutches long enough to write another desperate letter to Potkański. "He has not, and will not leave here. On the contrary, last night at supper he related scenes out of *Quo Vadis?* for an hour and a half, holding me by the string of my eyeglasses just to make sure (I wouldn't get away.) 'And Petronius!'—naturally, the animal pronounces it Pee-tronius—'how splendid he is! Is he not? And Eunice, oh my God!' Pronounced You-nice, of course. 'And Hilo!...' and so on and on from nine to ten-thirty..."

Hindsight provides a superb note of irony here. On the same day Mrs. Curtin noted in her diary, which was translated in excerpts together with a selection of her letters and published in Poland only in 1986: "We don't know how long we are going to be here, a lot will depend on Sienkiewicz. He works intensely but he is a very nice man." But a week later she informed her mother: "We have to endure all that until we get from Sienkiewicz everything we want." And then she explained: "Sienkiewicz is very nice, he'll do anything Jeremiah proposes. He wrote a letter to Brown saying that he wants Brown to publish his books, and if anybody else brings them out it would be against his wish and best interest."

But a month later, on July 12, she let slip a most revealing item: "We've heard from Brown. He has got Sienkiewicz's letter and he is pleased. Jeremiah prepared that letter in such a clever way that all Sienkiewicz had to do was copy it (and sign it.)" This is, of course, the story behind the first of a whole series of letters which Curtin forced out of the harassed writer and later used to give himself exclusive rights to the American translations of Sienkiewicz's works.

But Mrs. Curtin had more than just business on her mind. Playing a major role in the translation process, although she didn't know a word of Polish while Curtin had merely a smattering of it, she noted in her diary on July 19-24, 1897: "J. sent away a package with the following stories: *Charcoal Sketches*, *Be Blessed* and *The Organist of Ponikla*. He is very pleased with them, and rightly so, because they are much better than their originals." Eventually the Curtins learned to treat Sienkiewicz as some sort of factory that manufactured money. They watched over his work schedule, prodded him about new contracts and deadlines, hovered over him and seldom left him out of sight, all to make sure that he would grant them exclusive translation rights to everything he wrote for little or no money. But when after many years of cooperation the aging writer apparently permitted someone else to translate his new novel, Mrs. Curtin flew into a rage.

"A falsified edition of *On the Field of Glory* has appeared," she noted on April 1, 1906, "and we have got a copy of it from Brown this week. It's too bad Sienkiewicz isn't a man of honor; but that he is not, and that nobody can depend either on his spoken or his written word, or (even) a contract, we learned to our humiliation and cost. He stands very low in his relationship with Jeremiah to whom he owes his foreign reputation, since if his books had been translated by somebody else they would not create any sensation at all. Jeremiah improved on them in English when compared with the originals, and at the same time he did a faithful translation and worked hard to enliven and beautify every thought. In an ordinary translation, *With Fire and Sword*, *The Deluge* and *Pan Michael* would never have been known outside of Poland. And if that happened, most probably *Quo Vadis?* would have remained totally Polish, like many excellent Polish books whose authors still remain unknown outside their own country for the lack of a competent translator." And this was written a year and a half after Sienkiewicz became a Nobel laureate as a clear sign of his truly world-wide recognition!

Looking at that strange relationship between Curtin, the translator who could speak only English to his Polish author, Sienkiewicz who understood English well enough to communicate but not enough to appreciate its finer literary and stylistic points, and Mrs. Curtin who played an active role in all the translations without a word of Polish to her credit, one can wonder how sincere that relationship could have been, and what control over the translations Sienkiewicz was equipped to exercise even if he wished to. We know that Sienkiewicz loathed Russia and the Russians, that Curtin was an avid Russophile who could applaud even while his wife was being body-searched on the Russian border ("the same thing that would make him furious in another country," as Mrs. Curtin noted), and that he wrote such a pro-Russian and anti-Polish introduction to his version of *With Fire and Sword* that it appalls an objective reader to this day. And yet Sienkiewicz objected to it in only the mildest manner possible. "One should have, perhaps, underscored the difference between the Ruthenians and the Russians," he wrote to Curtin in 1892 about that introduction, pointing out that Russians "were called Muscovites in those days and had their own country, while the Ruthenians were a part of the Polish Commonwealth."

For reasons not quite clear to anyone today he completely disregarded passages which challenge his own vision of that time and space, lauding the Russians (rather than Ruthenians), condemning the Poles, and suggesting that the best thing that ever happened to them was to become the subjects of the Russian Tsars. "The Poles... have always been deficient in collective wisdom," Curtin wrote, to give just one example of his attitude, "and there is probably no more astonishing antithesis in Europe than the Poles as individuals and the Poles as people." Knowing how patriotic Sienkiewicz always was, even to the point of refusing to speak in Russian on official occasions, we may wonder how two such contrasting attitudes could have been reconciled.

The only explanation seems to be the business character of their relationship. Curtin was making $1,000 a month on his Sienkiewicz translations—a very handsome sum at the break of the century, equivalent in today's high-priced costs of living to at least $20,000.

Sienkiewicz, who was always burdened with financial problems, and who was almost obsessed with money when dealing with the foreign publishers who exploited him so shamelessly in so many cases, must have been pleased to be getting at least some royalties from his American publisher, if not from his translator.

We should also put to rest the myth of Curtin's "instant fascination and love for Sienkiewicz's fiction" so often attributed to him as proof of his expertise and genuine interest in the Polish language. We now know that this entire story is a fabrication, as are Curtin's own *Memoirs* from which this "proof" is quoted, and that both are the creation of Mrs. Curtin who wrote those *Memoirs* long after Curtin's death, as Professor Michael J. Mikoś proves beyond a doubt in his forthcoming study on the Curtins. It's true that Curtin eventually learned enough Polish to be able to work from original texts, but as late as 1897 he used the Russian version of *Teutonic Knights* as his basis for comparison with Sienkiewicz's original manuscript and his own translation. His translation of *With Fire and Sword* was made entirely from a Russian text, which was not only inferior to the original but also heavily censored by Russian authorities. It's hard to believe today that this was the only English-language text of that novel for more than 100 years, and that it served as the basis for innumerable translations into other European languages as well.

We should add that Sienkiewicz's sarcastic references to the Curtins are not without foundation. Their "discovery" of Sienkiewicz also meant the discovery of a potential gold-mine which they exploited to the fullest, making a fair fortune on the translations alone, and acquiring everything they needed to live comfortably and securely to the end of their days. On the envelope of Sienkiewicz's last letter to Curtin written on November 6, 1906, there is a note penciled probably by Mrs. Curtin which reads: "This came about three weeks before Jeremiah died. He called for it several times when sitting up and looked it over."

The publishers' cuts to which Sienkiewicz alluded in his earlier-quoted letter to his French translator, Antoni Wodziński, were sometimes so cruel that kinder publishers advertised their products as

traduction nouvelle et absolument complete, while others (especially
the Italian publishers who so enraged Sienkiewicz that he tried to sue
them, and a German editor) bragged about their revised and
expurgated "family" editions for children and the young. One can
only imagine the Japanese version of *Quo Vadis?* (quaintly titled as
Kuo vadisu) compiled in 1928 by Takeshi Kimura from Curtin's
English and Reclam's German renderings, along with assorted French
and other translations! And if that isn't bad enough, there are the
recollections of Yang De Yoo, Sienkiewicz's Chinese translator, who
explains how the Chinese version of *Quo Vadis?* came into being: by
way of two pirated Japanese renditions and Curtin's English translation as the basic reference! Recalling the almost inconceivable
harassments under which Mei Rukai, Sienkiewicz's most recent
Chinese translator, had to work between 1957 and 1979 (including
the grim years of China's "Cultural Revolution"), we may be
unsurprised to discover that in his understanding of the Trilogy,
Curtin's English version "described the state of a nation living in
humiliation for more than a century." Perhaps that is why the
Chinese translations sold more than 50,000 copies each when they
were published in the early 1980s.

There is no question that Sienkiewicz appreciated the literary
qualities of translations above any commercial considerations which,
in his case, gave him little profit. Talking in an 1887 interview
about one German translator of *With Fire and Sword*, he complained
that "his German language does not measure up to the beauty, vigor
and stylistic coloration of the original.

"How will he translate *Quo Vadis?*" he wrote to Wodziński about
another French translator. "Because it's not just the problem of
knowing the language, but also the ability to find the correct
equivalents, the problem of artistic sensibilities, the command of
expressions, of talent, etc." Commenting on yet another potential
translator of that novel he expressed some doubts because "a lot
depends on a translator's classical education, over and above the
question of style, otherwise he would make thousands of mistakes."

As future adaptation into different media, the theater and the
movies would quite quickly prove, he was right to worry, although

he made no complaints about it in his lifetime, other than voicing his usual protests about the violations of his author's rights. "Things go about as usual in Warsaw," he reported to his young friend, Wanda Ulanowska, in 1913. "The current sensation here is *Quo Vadis?* which is playing in five cinemas at the same time. Everybody is going out to see it. A French (film) company with whom I signed a contract five years ago is suing the Italian Cines company. They also offer me 10,000 crowns, but I don't think that is good enough since they'll make millions on it." And a few months later he added, as skeptically as always: "The court proceedings between the Film d'Art company and the Cines company are under way. They promise me some 300,000 crowns out of it, but I'll believe that when I've the money in my pocket. Not before!"

Trying to sum up the problems of translations, and of Sienkiewicz's works in particular, we can conclude that in many cases such work has been abused and exploited for commercial reasons with little regard for its artistic values. And yet as bad as they might have been, the various translations made the Polish author famous throughout the world, bringing his works to millions of foreign readers, and making his novels and short stories a permanent part of world literature, which is mankind's most precious and enduring heritage and the custodian of its most sacred values. For better or worse, they served their purpose for more than 100 years, and now, at this end of the 20th century—when we are taking stock of some basic problems and a great reevaluation of human life and values is taking place everywhere around us—the voice of Sienkiewicz will speak to the world again in beautiful, correct and powerful English, as clearly and convincingly as it has always done in his native Polish.

Two English Translations of the Trilogy

by Albert Juszczak

The Jeremiah Curtin translation of the Trilogy, published by Little, Brown and Company between 1890 and 1893, had been the principal available English text of Sienkiewicz's three-part masterpiece for 100 years, although there was another version of *With Fire and Sword* at roughly the same time. Samuel Binion, whose handsomely rendered version was published by Crowell in 1905, tried to compete briefly with Curtin but could not hold his own against the pressures that the Curtins brought to bear on the harassed Sienkiewicz. When Curtin finally supplied his publishers with a letter, claiming to have translated the Trilogy directly from Polish, and bearing Sienkiewicz's signed authorization as his preferred translator, Binion retired from the contest, and Curtin's version became the sole representative of the Trilogy in English until W. S. Kuniczak's current work appeared in 1991-1992.

Binion's defeat may have been both a pity and a blessing in disguise. On the one hand, he left the field wide open to Curtin whose work became the reference for many other translations into lesser languages, and this rendered a distinct disservice both to Sienkiewicz and the reputation of Polish literature at large. On the other hand, had Binion prevailed, W. S. Kuniczak may not have felt compelled to do his own translation. He told me once that Binion's use of language would have pleased almost any author. But he could not stand the thought "that Curtin's barely animated puppets, so stiff and wooden that they creak whenever a mouth flies open," were the only heroes of the Trilogy that our fellow Americans would ever read about.

It is interesting therefore to make a comparison between the original Polish text (for those readers who might be able to read it), a word-by-word literal translation into English followed by a sample of the Curtin text, and the present translation by W. S. Kuniczak, to see how and why this latest English version is superior to its predecessor. Even an untrained eye can see how much more accurately Kuniczak's skilled professionalism renders the original text, dealing not merely with the words but with the thoughts and feelings behind them, and how much more real and believable Sienkiewicz's characters appear in his hands.

Time and space limitations permit only a brief selection. We chose a random fragment from *With Fire and Sword* although almost any paragraph could serve the same purpose. It is a desperate yet heroic scene after a battle with the Cossack forces in which Prince Yeremi Vishnovyetzki (Jeremi Wiśniowiecki in its Polish spelling) had won a major victory after months of almost superhuman struggles. Yet moments later he learns that the Polish authorities in Warsaw have decided to negotiate with the rebels, that they are ready to appease their leader Hmyelnitzki, and that the patriotic Prince and his weary band are to give up any further fighting. Feeling that all his sacrifices were in vain, he bursts into a speech of angry disappointment. He says:

> "Nie chcę ja żyć w tej Rzeczypospolitej, bo dziś wstydzić się za nią przychodzi. Oto czerń kozacka i chłopska zalała krwią ojczyznę, z pogaństwem się przeciw własnej matce połączyła. Pobici hetmani, zniesione wojska, zdeptana sława narodu, zgwałcony majestat, popalone kościoły, wyrżnięci księża, szlachta, pohańbione niewiasty, a na te klęski i na tę hańbę, na której wspomnienie samo pomarliby nasi przodkowie—czymże odpowiada ta Rzeczpospolita? Oto ze zdrajcą i hańbicielem swym, ze sprzymierzeńcem pogan układy rozpoczyna i kontentacje mu obiecuje! O Boże! daj śmierć, powtarzam, bo nie żyć nam na świecie, którzy dyshonor ojczyzny czujemy i głowy dla niej niesiemy w ofierze."
>
> (*Ogniem i mieczem*, vol. II, pp. 168-169)

A word-by-word translation would read as follows:

"I do not want to live in this Republic, for today one comes to be ashamed for her. Here the Cossack and peasant mob has flooded with blood the fatherland, has joined with the pagandom against its own mother. Defeated are the hetmans, the armies mowed-down, the nation's glory tramped down, the majesty violated, churches burned out, slaughtered are the priests, the gentry, the women disgraced, and to these disasters and this disgrace at the very memory of which our ancestors would have died, with what is this Republic responding? Here, with the traitor and its disgracer, with the ally of the pagans it begins negotiations and promises him satisfactions! O God! give me death, I repeat, for it is not for us to live in the world, those who feel the fatherland's dishonor and bring our heads as a sacrifice for her."

Jeremiah Curtin translated this excerpt as follows:

"I do not wish to live in this Commonwealth, for today I must be ashamed of it. The Cossack and the peasant mob have poured blood on the country, and joined pagandom against their own mother. The hetmans are beaten, the armies swept away. The fame of the nation is trampled upon, its majesty insulted, churches are burned, priests and nobles cut down, women dishonored, and what answer does the Commonwealth give to all these defeats and this shame, at the very remembrance of which our ancestors would have died? Here it is! She begins negotiations with the traitor, the disgracer, the ally of the Pagan, and offers him satisfaction. Oh, God grant me death! I repeat it, since there is no life in the world for us who feel the dishonor of our country and bring our heads as a sacrifice for it."

(*With Fire and Sword*, p. 331)

We selected this particular excerpt for its special quality of a fine, Baroque oratorical style predominant in the 17th century, which Sienkiewicz rendered so faithfully in Polish in his novels, as a good example of a complex syntax, ornamental structure of the sentences and high rhetorical impact which are so different from our modern speech forms. Jeremiah Curtin's translation of this particular excerpt keeps very close to the original in a word-for-word translation, and is quite faithful in that regard to its content and its intended style, but

29

it conveys no idea of the real meaning of the speech that only its emotional content can provide. He carries none of the impassioned fire, the rage and the soaring bitterness and despair in Prince Yeremi's voice which the original text hurls upon the reader, and so it misses the impact of Vishnovyetzki's magnificent eloquence. In short, being able to read and understand only the words he sees on the printed page, but linguistically quite unable to grasp the feelings behind them, he robs the reader of a powerful emotional experience and impoverishes the novel.

W. S. Kuniczak, a Polish-born American novelist and writer whose mastery of both languages is beyond reproach, and who understands exactly what is being said in our chosen excerpt and how it is spoken, has rendered the same speech in quite a different manner. His translation reads:

> "What sort of people are we?" he demanded. "Is there no end to the shame we have to endure? Here a foul rebel mob swamps the land with blood, brings in the Tartars against its own people, destroys the King's army and enslaves its Hetmans! It tramples the nation's glory in the mud and spits on its laws, burns churches, murders priests and slaughters the gentry! It sells its own women and children into slavery, and how does the Commonwealth reply to these horrors that all our ancestors would have died rather than endure? It comes hat-in-hand to negotiate with traitors. It promises to reward her tormentor and to offer him whatever he might want if he'd just stop butchering his own countrymen! Give us death, dear God! Relieve us of this burden of dishonor because this is no world for men like us to live in!"
>
> (*With Fire and Sword*, p. 421)

It is easy to see how Kuniczak captures and conveys Prince Yeremi's highly-charged rhetorical style, and how he grasps and renders the meanings and emotions contained in those impassioned speech lines. But he also updates and translates the allusions implied by the Prince, clarifies the context and solidifies the references, thus adding to the modern reader's understanding of the text.

Two examples from the above translation should suffice to show this. When Prince Yeremi says in the original: "Here the Cossack and the peasant mob has flooded with blood the fatherland, has joined with the pagandom against its own mother,"—and it is heartbreaking to have to use such stilted, convoluted English in place of the soaring Polish that Vishnovyetzki uses in his speech—this translation replaces "pagandom" with "Tartars" and "mother" with "people."

It does so because it isn't possible to expect the modern American reader, or for that matter any other reader who isn't a Pole by birth or heritage, to be intimately acquainted with Poland's long history, or the grim Polish ethnic memory connected with the Tartars, or to grasp at once that it is these dreaded and hated Tartars the Prince has in mind rather than some disembodied notion of pagans in general.

Furthermore, unless the reader knows that the 17th century Cossacks were recruited, at least in part, from runaway Polish and Ruthenian serfs and outlawed fugitive nobles, that they were of the same Slavic stock as the Poles, that Hmyelnitzki himself was a Polish noble, and that the Ukraine in which they lived was an integral part of the Commonwealth at that time, the reference to "its own mother" makes very little sense, whereas the image of turning against "its own people" makes the point quite clearly.

In the same context, when the Prince makes a non-specific reference to "women dishonored" the American reader can't grasp the full meaning of that dishonor to 17th century Poles of the eastern borderlands such as Vishnovyetzki. Rape is the obvious notion, but there is also the image of the degradation the women endured in slavery when they were driven by the Tartars to the auction blocks in Turkey, sold in their tens of thousands for harem or domestic use all over Asia Minor, or used as trade goods by their Tartar captors. The reference to "selling its own women and children into slavery" is a reminder of that Tartar practice, as is the implication that it was the Cossacks who brought them as their allies into the Commonwealth, which is something that Vishnovyetzki and his men could never forgive.

The key word here is the Polish *hańba*, the root of *pohańbienie*. It isn't merely shame, disgrace, or even dishonor. It denotes such utter degradation and such total and complete humiliation that no self-respecting human being could ever accept it. Indeed, *pohań-bienie* has a ring of such abysmal finality about it, and it suggests such brutality in its application, that death itself would be preferable to it. A man or woman who is *shańbiony* or *shańbiona* is hardly able to live with his or her own image, far less among others.

Then as now to the Polish mind, freedom is such a basic quality of human existence, while slavery is such an unforgivable insult to humanity, that it is this powerful image as much as any other that appalls the proud and patriotic Vishnovyetzki. Thus making one deft change in the Prince's statement, Kuniczak not only clarifies his viewpoint but provides the reader with a wealth of additional information.

There are more such examples elsewhere in this remarkable translation. Historical information of all kinds is so skillfully inserted, and its presence is so minimal in the total context of the novel, that it is quite impossible for the general reader to tell where the original ends and the subtle fabric of new information begins. It will be up to scholars, if they are so inclined, to dot their own texts with asterisks and footnotes which a literary artist could never accept. "A novel," Kuniczak wrote in a recent paper prepared for his 1992 college lecture series, "must be a seamless work, moving without a break and consisting of a single homogeneous texture. But mystification of the reader is never an author's intention and a good translator is duty-bound to weave into that tight-knit, uniform linguistic entity all the information needed by the reader that the author, for one reason or another, left out of the novel." Doctoral dissertations will be written on this work before very long and perhaps it's best to leave dissection to the scholars.

It is worth noting that despite these clarifications, stylistic rearrangements and information implants, Kuniczak's text not only doesn't lose any of the artistic qualities of the original masterpiece in Polish, but makes it more dramatic, expressive and dynamic, thus speaking to the modern reader as powerfully and directly as only a masterful work of literary fiction can.

Introduction to *Fire and Sword*

by Jerzy R. Krzyżanowski

More than 100 years ago, on May 2, 1883, a Warsaw newspaper started a serialization of a new novel, *Ogniem i Mieczem* or *With Fire and Sword*, and a great new literary reputation was made overnight. The author was Henryk Sienkiewicz, the 36-year-old editor of *Słowo*, the newspaper that published his novel. He was known to the reading public mostly through short stories and some interesting reportage from his journey across America in 1876-78, but the young writer was by no means Poland's leading author.

Then came *With Fire and Sword* and Sienkiewicz became an on-the-spot celebrity while his novel and the two sequels that combine to form his famous Trilogy became instant classics. Such was the readers' interest and enthusiasm for the work, and such was its immediate literary reputation, that both the work and the author acquired almost mythological dimensions. In a phenomenon that approached the Bible, Sienkiewicz's Trilogy became a national bestseller which would stay at the top of the charts in Poland for 100 years, maintaining its status despite changing times, styles and literary fashions. Even in the most ruthless era of communist domination in the late 1940's and the 1950's, when Poland existed in an atmosphere of censorship and strict cultural controls, every new edition of the Trilogy was sold out the day it appeared.

Since then it has seen print in more than 30 languages and a variety of forms that included children's comic-strips. Generations of Polish readers think of it as among the greatest novels in their literary history while Polish film directors use its scope and setting for successful historical adventure dramas of unusual color. In short, the continuous success of these three interrelated novels testifies to their vitality and importance which ignore national and cultural

33

boundaries, spans the gaps in time between literary eras, and demands that these works be known in any time and language no matter how far removed from Sienkiewicz's Poland they might be.

They appeared on the Polish literary scene in an era much like our own today, marked by a sober and pragmatic approach to reality, and requiring authors to present a candid and clear-sighted view of the social and political problems of their times. Readers, as critics insisted, demanded novels that depicted their own time and age, reflecting on their own lives in society, and helping them to understand the world around them in a clear and uncomplicated manner. The name of the game was Realism, proclaimed in *fin-de-siecle* 19th century Europe by such famous novelists as Flaubert in France, Turgenev in Russia, and an expatriate American, Henry James, in England. The time of Tolstoy and Joseph Conrad was still some years distant.

But once aroused, the readers' appetite for "real" people in their novels' pages—vibrant and exciting men and women who were believable in their attitudes and motives—could be projected into times past as well. Sir Walter Scott had already signaled historical realism in his chivalric novels, making his medieval settings seem as tangible as the contemporary images of Paris and London. The great historical adventures of Alexandre Dumas' *The Three Musketeers* and *Count of Monte Cristo* had enthralled vast international audiences since the 1840's with their fast-paced, colorful action-drama set against a rich and accurately rendered historical background. The precedent for bringing history to life through the techniques of the contemporary novel already existed, but in Poland, despite many attempts in that field, the historical novel before Sienkiewicz had never been a spectacular success. He changed that once and for all.

Sienkiewicz had spent two happy and exciting years in the United States, traveling down the great rivers and across the continent in the time of wagon trains, stage coaches and Indian campaigns, hunting, fishing and camping in the Sierras, and absorbing both the beauty and the dangers of the vast open spaces at their unspoiled best. His *Letters from America*, which established his reputation as a perceptive and incisive reporter, ring with authenticity and that love of nature that permeates the early chapters of *With Fire and Sword* where the narrative descriptions of the Ukrainian Steppe glow with remembered American imagery. There is something both moving and appealing in the image of this young Polish writer wandering through the prairies, breathing the vastness of America and the variety of its many peoples, while George Armstrong Custer made his last stand at the Little Big Horn and the great Indian nations of the plains receded into history.

It's easy to see these American impressions in the early pages of *With Fire and Sword* where Sienkiewicz, who had never set foot in the legendary Wildlands which bordered the 17th century Polish-Lithuanian Commonwealth that he writes about, transposes his vision of the prairies, the endless landscapes, and the sea of grass "where a man might ride unseen, for days, like a diver drifting through an ocean" onto the rich and turbulent canvas of his imagined Ukrainian Steppe. Even a bateau journey down the Mississippi finds its counterpart in a voyage down the Dnieper River by Sienkiewicz's young hero, Yan Skshetuski, whose awe-struck sense of wonder is heightened by the sight of "huge reptiles"—clearly remembered from America—slipping into the vast stream out of the muddy sandbars. Not much imagination is required a few moments later, when Skshetuski and his small detachment are overwhelmed by Tartars on an island where they stop to rest, to hear the volleys of Custer's doomed troopers in the desperate musketry of Skshetuski's dragoons.

In a few short stories that Sienkiewicz wrote after his return to Poland in 1879, including *The Lighthouse Keeper*, he drew on his American experience to explore the Polish ethos of patriotism and remembrance, looking into the past for clues about the future, and celebrating a fierce love of freedom. That issue of personal liberty, in both its worthy and unworthy aspects, became the main theme of *With Fire and Sword*. It must be remembered that the savage era in which the work is set represents the sunset years of the Polish-Lithuanian Commonwealth, the rise of Russia and Prussia as modern empires, and the loss of national existence for the Poles who wouldn't have a country of their own for more than a century.

The Polish-Ukrainian borderlands, or *kresy* as they were known in Poland, have had a long and often fabulous history marked with love and hatred, passionate unity and violent disagreements, and moments of near-idyllic coexistence that were invariably ruptured by treachery, selfishness and greed. Deeply steeped in folklore, age-old legends of departed glories and traditions of unbridled freedom, the *kresy* had created whole populations of colorful and turbulent heroes whose lives abounded in conflicts and emotions that simply begged for the pen of a skilled literary artist. And while the Ukrainian Cossacks found their spokesman in Nicolai Gogol, whose *Taras Bulba* romanticized their history, Polish readers had to wait 30 years longer for Sienkiewicz and his epic of their Golden Age. It should be noted here that the strangely glowing and poetic spirit of those vast, open and untrammeled lands, combing lyric beauty with the fierceness of a prairie fire, found its ultimate expression in the English masterpieces of Joseph Conrad who had been born in a *kresy* manor house as Józef Korzeniowski in the 1850s.

All the ingredients needed for a literary masterpiece—realism and an underlying romantic tradition, the author's sensitivity to nature and his love of freedom along with a deep-seated longing for human understanding, brotherhood and justice—came together in Sienkie-wicz's novel thanks largely to his remarkable talents as a storyteller.

In his case, however, these elements were to serve a deeper social and historic purpose, coinciding with a popular need for literature that would help a nation in distress retain its identity. Ruthlessly divided in 1795 between the neighboring empires of Russia, Prussia and Austria, the Polish nation fought back in bloody uprisings that left their fields and forests littered with their dead and dotted their landscapes with ruins and gibbets. Arrests, mass deportations to Siberia, curtailment of civil rights to such a drastic point that the Polish language was banned in schools and offices, and tragic persecution on all social levels, had left the Poles with no means of national existence other than the dimly recalled memories of disaster. The realistic novels of Polish writers were so heavily censored by the Tsarist Russian authorities in Warsaw that the best of them, *The Doll* by Bolesław Prus, couldn't even mention Poland's Russian masters, although this brutish and malevolent presence was felt in all its pages. Sienkiewicz himself, writing a horrifying expose of the Russification of Polish schoolchildren in 1879, found it expedient to relocate his story to the Prussian-held territories of Poznan in order to maintain his uneasy standing with the Russian censors in his part of Poland. Thus only by stepping deeper into history could he recall and resurrect the waning spirit of his prostrate nation and give his people a badly needed reassurance that "Poland Is Not Yet Lost," as the Napoleonic-era song, soon to become their national anthem, continued to remind.

Setting out to "uplift the hearts of my countrymen," as he put it, and in the process creating a work of such profound universal values that William Faulkner found in it a beacon for his own literary career, Sienkiewicz chose one of the bloodiest and most dramatic periods of Poland's long history: a local uprising of disgruntled Cossacks against Polish landlords that changed into a full-scale civil war in the 1640's. Against this violent background, full of swords and fire, which shook the foundations of the Polish-Lithuanian Commonwealth that had ruled those regions for 100 years, he projected an adventure story full of love and murder, friendship and betrayal, cold-blooded treason and passionate devotion, sacrifice and cynicism and cowardice and courage; painting, in short, a portrait of humanity at its best and most absurd, with all its pathos and humor and frailties and follies. *With Fire and Sword* is a novel that invades the reader and takes command of all his emotions so that the only question he or she can ask as they turn the pages is a breathless and impatient: "What's next?"

And then, just as the headlong rush of images and events proves almost overwhelming, giving the reader little time to stop and ponder the deeper meanings that flow beneath the story, there come those moments of profound reflection that mean as much to today's English-speaking readers as they did to the troubled Poles of Sienkiewicz's era. The reader stops to ask whether there might be more to life than pure enjoyment and the spirit of adventure. He begins to grasp and understand the power of a cause that can be more important to private men and women than to their own personal welfare and unrestrained individual liberties.

"How can he do this?" the reader asks, in wonder, watching Yan Skshetuski as he suppresses his most fervent longings so that he might devote himself wholly to his country. "What kind of man could be that selfless in a public cause or that oblivious of his own wellbeing?"

And the age-old Polish answer comes at once from Skshetuski's own comrades and companions—the heroes as well as the rollicking buffoons—that life is only worth living and enjoying if each of us has something for which he would be willing to give up his life no matter how much he loves the idea of living. It seems that just as individuals have to interrupt their materialistic concerns now and then, and take time-out to ponder their lives' real meaning, so do great nations and organized societies. But these are matters that readers discover for themselves while exploring the rich environment that Sienkiewicz created for our fascination.

The first readers of *With Fire and Sword* were quick to spot all these themes and currents even as they devoured the pages in pure enjoyment of an action story. Stanisław Tarnowski, the leading Polish critic and literary historian of his time, speculated in 1897 that "Sometime in the future, our memoirs and perhaps even literary histories will recall the when *With Fire and Sword* made its first appearance, there was hardly a conversation that didn't start and end with that topic . . . That the protagonists of the novel were thought and talked about as if they were real . . . that young children, writing home from school, would first report on their own health and that of their siblings, and then relate the latest thing said by Zagloba or Skshetuski . . . and that while young ladies either wrote or wanted to write to the author, begging him—for God's sake!—to save Skshetuski in the next installment, their mothers and grandmothers offered tearful prayers that their own sons might rise to the greatness of Skshetuski's soul."

A typically unsatisfactory aspect of Jeremiah Curtin's first translation into English, made more than 100 years ago, lies in his strange decision to provide his version of *With Fire and Sword* with a labored and lengthy Russian apologia in which he argues against Sienkiewicz's vision of *kresy* borderlands and the relationships between various nationalities who lived there. That kind of editorial intervention forms a wholly unwarranted intrusion into a work as universally oriented as this one, with heroes and villains richly apportioned to each side, and no one, in either the literature or the history, presented without some redeeming features.

Today it's safe to view this work as a timeless historical novel of equal meaning to anyone who reads it. The novel's unmistakably Polish character is all the more appealing for Americans who have always cherished traditions of freedom, independence, courage and adventure. We hope that in this first modern translation from Polish, made from my father's revised 1948 edition and adapted for today's English-speaking readers, this treasured Polish author will speak to everyone as clearly and as beautifully as he has for 100 years to countless millions of his countrymen all over the world.

BALTIC
SEA

GULF OF
RIGA

• Wo
LI
• Kie

• Pitten
• Goldinga
• Riga
• Lenwa
C O U R L A N D
• Mitawa
SEM
• Birze
• Poniewież
• Wornie • Szawle
SAMOGITIA   ZMUDYA
• Rosienie   • Oniks
• Królewiec
N I E M E N
• Kiejdany • Wilkomież
• Labiawa • Tilsit
WAR   • Kowno
• Brunsberga   • Troki
Bartoszyce   DUCAL PRUSSIA   • Wilno
Lidzbark • Lec   (Vilnius)
• Olsztyn   • Oszmiana

PITTEN LAND

• Dyjament

• Lebark
• Słupsk   • Puck
P O M E R A N I A   • Gdańsk
GREAT
• Walcz   • Starogard   • Malbork
NOTEC
• Tucholа
• Bydgoszcz • Chełmno
• Ostroróg • Nakło
Międzyrzecz Kruszwica • Inowrocław   • Torun
• Poznań   P O L A N D • Gniezno
• Grodzisk   W A R T A
• Leszno

• Lida

• Grodno
• Nowo

DUCHY OF
MAZOVIA   N A R E W   • Tykocin
• Płock   • Wołkowysk
• Pułtusk   • Słonim   M

• Łęczyca
• Pjątek   P O D L A S I E   B L A C K
• Kalisz   • Uniejów Sochaczew • Warszawa   • Kobryn
• Sieradz   • Łowicz   (Warsaw)   • Pin
• Piotrków   • Rawa   • Węgrów
• Wieluń   • Bodzentyn   • Biała • Brest
• Radomsko • Radom   • Łuków Litovsk
• Częstochowa Kielce Opatów
V I S T U L A   • Kazimierz
• Olsztyn   • Chęciny   C H E Ł M L A N D
• Jędrzejów   B U G
• Siewierz   • Zamość
• Olkusz   • Sandomierz
LITTLE POLAND
• Baranów   • Bełż   • Sokal
• Kraków   Kamionka Strumiłowa
• Zator   • Wieliczka • Tarnów • Łańcut
• Kęty   • Bochnia   Przeworsk • Jarosław   • Gliniany
Żywiec Nowy Sącz   Przemyśl Sadowa • Lwów (Lvov)
• Stary Sącz • Krosno Krasiczyn R U D N I E S T R
• Sanok   • Drohobycz Sambor   • Rohatyń
• Stryj   • Żydaczów
DNIESTR   • Halicz   Buczac
• Obertyn   • Czerw
• Gwoździec
• Kołomyja

DETAIL OF ACTION IN
Fire in the Steppe

━━━━━ Turkish Invasion Route
1672

• • • • • • • • Basia's Journey to Raszkow

▰▰▰▰▰▰▰ Basia's Escape Route

KAMIENIEC
PODOLSKI   CHREPTIÓW
USZYCA
MOHYLÓW
JAMPOL
WAŁADYNKA
RASZKÓW

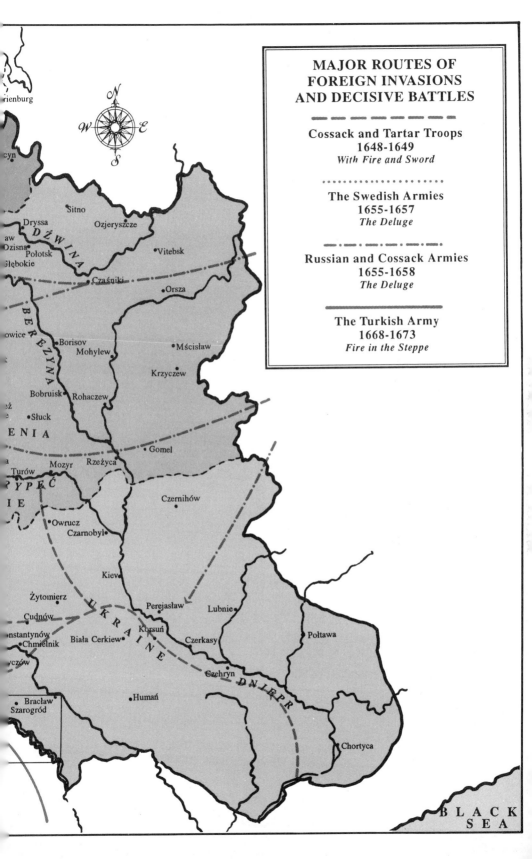

MAJOR ROUTES OF FOREIGN INVASIONS AND DECISIVE BATTLES

Cossack and Tartar Troops
1648-1649
With Fire and Sword

The Swedish Armies
1655-1657
The Deluge

Russian and Cossack Armies
1655-1658
The Deluge

The Turkish Army
1668-1673
Fire in the Steppe

rienburg

cyn

Sitno

Dryssa
DŹWINA
Ozjeryszcze

aw
Dzisna   Połotsk
Głębokie

•Vitebsk

Czaśniki

•Orsza

BEREZYNA

owice

•Borisov
Mohylew

•Mścisław

Krzyczew

Bobruisk•   Rohaczew

eż

•Słuck

ENIA

•Gomel

a   Mozyr   Rzeżyca

Turów

PYPEĆ

IE

•Owrucz
Czarnobyl•

Czernihów

Kiev•

Żytomierz

Cudnów

Perejasław   Lubnie•

nstantynów

Korsuń

•Chmielnik   Biała Cerkiew•   Czerkasy

Połtawa

yczów

Czehryn   DNIEPR

UKRAINE

•Bracław
Szarogród

•Humań

•Chortyca

BLACK
SEA

Introduction to *The Deluge*

by Thomas Napierkowski

In 1905, partly on the basis of his Trilogy, (*With Fire and Sword*, 1883-84; *The Deluge*, 1884-86; and *Pan Wołodyjowski*, 1887-88), Henryk Sienkiewicz was awarded the Nobel Prize for Literature. The citation of award focused on the Polish author's "outstanding merits as an epic writer." Elaborating on the decision of the Swedish Academy, C.D. af. Wirsen describes Sienkiewicz as "one of those rare geniuses who concentrate in themselves the spirit of a nation" and who portray the character of their people in the eyes of the world. "If one surveys Sienkiewicz's achievement," he continues in his presentation address, "it appears gigantic and vast and at every point noble and controlled. As for his epic style, it is of absolute artistic perfection."

Having withstood all the tests of time, as James A. Michener notes in his foreword to W. S. Kuniczak's translation of *With Fire and Sword*, Sienkiewicz's great, multi-volume masterwork "remains the soaring prototype of the national epic." Furthermore, *The Deluge* here presented, is arguably the best of the Trilogy's three interrelated novels.

For people who have the eyes to see into the true human meaning of historical events, the Trilogy is not only "a mirror of a nation's soul" as so many critics recognize today, but a compendium of all those racial memories and feelings that make history a living entity rather than just a listing of facts, dates and figures. Indeed, it is a great deal more than even that. In the profundity of its analysis and its depth of vision it borders upon the prophetic, and that is nowhere clearer than in *The Deluge* which is the Trilogy's structural and thematic heart.

Here for all to see is a definition of the Polish national character and historical experience, in both their worthy and unworthy aspects, that offers and almost point-by-point foreshadowing of all those spiritual and political forces which came together so dramatically in Poland within this decade, shattered the grip of communism throughout Central Europe, helped to restore political and economic freedom to half a dozen nations, and rewrote the dark pages of Soviet domination which cast such a gigantic shadow on the world since 1945. Unthinkable for more than two generations, this astounding bloodless revolution which began with Solidarity in Poland appears almost obvious in Sienkiewicz's brilliant Trilogy, written 100 years earlier. This monumental epic clearly documents that indomitable national will to live which makes the Poles so committed to their independence that they've been described as "an authoritarian's despair." There is no doubt that this great work, written to uplift the hearts in 1883, inspired that nation in its modern struggle to reestablish political pluralism, rebuild their democratic institutions and return to a free economy. Now it is here in English, to teach and inspire others.

On this prophetic or philosophic level the Trilogy is a leap across the centuries into our own time, specifically into the agony that gripped the Polish people since 1939. "The more things change," the reader says in wonder, "the more they are the same." Invaders come and go. Victories become disasters. One ruthless enemy replaces another. But the nation lives, the people survive deep within themselves and eventually triumph, and the road to these immemorial Polish resurrections is always the same. We read *The Deluge* as if it were a 17th century allegory of our times, recounting all that happened to the Poles and Poland since the Second World War in 1939 and the forced imposition of a Soviet-style system which began in 1944. We experience similar defeats, disasters, treasons and betrayals, the ruthless foreign domination, the resistance focused around charismatic leaders and spiritual forces, Solidarity, martial law and everything that followed, all told in human, personal terms in a work of literary fiction whose author never knew an independent Poland. Indeed, for him as for all his countrymen for more than a century, that Poland lived merely in their hearts.

On its most accessible level, *The Deluge* sweeps even the most jaded reader into an adventure filled with relentless action, centered around the two universal themes of love and war, and involving an unforgettable cast of fictional and historical characters who are developed and portrayed with far more depth than is usual in works of epic fiction. The end result is gripping suspense and reader fascination. *The Deluge* is, in fact, the impassioned tale of two simultaneous struggles: the doomed yet triumphant love of Andrzej Kmicic for his beloved Olenka (or Andrei Kmita, as simplified in this translation for the English reader), and a patriotic struggle against an onslaught by Sweden, Russia, resurgent Cossacks, and a stirring Prussia which savaged the Polish-Lithuanian Commonwealth in the second half of the 17th century. Both these motifs are marked with rivalry, alienation, separation, courage and treachery, dangers and escapes, disguises and assumed names, betrayal and redemption, plots, battles, tactics, tragic failures and eventual reunion in love and in victory; and both acquire brilliant clarity in one powerful intuitive moment when the confused and misled Andrei Kmita, lost in despair on a personal cross-roads of his own, identifies Olenka with his country, finds his way again, and plunges into his patriotic duty with a devotion that only love can give.

On another level, *The Deluge* excels as a historical novel in which Sienkiewicz brings to life the people, movements, events and the spirit of a turbulent past age where not just individuals but entire cultures stand in open conflict. Like a true master of the epic genre, he fills this vast historical arena with fully-fleshed fictional characters who take active part in the sweep of the history around them, interact with actual historical figures, and fulfill their destinies in the context of the universal whole. So powerfully drawn that it is impossible to think of them as merely invented, these characters give expression to the impact which history has upon the living, and produce a picture of the age in real and human terms.

Two men—Sir Walter Scott and Alexandre Dumas—are generally recognized in Western European literatures as the masters of this genre; the first producing powerful "costume pieces," while the second concentrates on adventure "recounted with gusto and careless responsibility." Sienkiewicz strives for both effects at once and achieves immeasurably more. In the words of one American critic, Sienkiewicz "seizes the outer aspect of an age with all the broad grasp of Scott, and peoples it with characters as vivid, virile, keen-witted and heroic as those of Dumas;" but where those two great predecessors halt, content to stay within the limits of historical adventure, that's where Sienkiewicz's true artistry begins. Going beyond both of them, Sienkiewicz "strikes below the surface events which concern his heroines and heroes to the deeper issues." He throws his imagination upon an epic canvas, and brings to life the mind, soul and character of the Polish nation; and nowhere is that spirit better shown than here in *The Deluge*.

It is well established that Sienkiewicz paid his debt of serious scholarship to the facts of the age being recreated. Despite this, he was occasionally accused of romanticizing some aspects of his work; and even though historians have long viewed the successful defense of Częstochowa in the winter of 1655 as the turning point in the last great Swedish invasion of Poland, his portrayal of that miracle has disturbed some critics.

Polish chronicles of the period wax eloquent on this point; and Sienkiewicz gives a scrupulous, almost word-for-word reflection of those contemporary accounts. Moreover, if we look at that great, heroic act of faith and courage through or own modern eyes, and use it as a palimpsest for the behavior of the Polish people within the last ten years, Sienkiewicz's vision is wholly justified. In this century as in the 17th, Poland lay devastated by war, abandoned by allies, and betrayed into the hands of a ruthless enemy who turned the country into an exploited colony. Then unexpectedly, as during the Swedish deluge that overwhelmed the country, the nation was lifted to new life by a "miracle:" the election of the first Slavic Pope in history. Directed by the exhortations of that Polish priest and spurred by an unquenched love of liberty to yet another monumental effort, an exhausted people "lifted up their hearts," found new resources of courage and endurance, and brought about an astounding bloodless revolution. That is the theme and substance of *The Deluge*, although of course *that* story is full of blood and fire spilled across an enormous stage.

On a purely literary level, the Trilogy is the paramount example
of the literary epic, fulfilling all requirements of that difficult and
demanding genre which so few writers are even able to attempt. This
may not be the moment to examine examples of the epic, so let this
much suffice: in theme and structure the Trilogy deals with episodes
crucial to the history of the nation and the people it describes. It
does so in strict compliance to a literary tradition that goes back all
the way to Homer. Indeed, one commentator goes out of his way to
point out that these warriors of the Polish-Lithuanian Commonwealth
"fight, love, hate, embrace each other, laugh, weep in each other's
arms, and give each other wise advice with a truly Homeric simplicity. They are deeply versed in stratagems of love and war. . .They
have their Nestor, Agamemnon and Achilles sulking in his tent." And
just like Homer, this 19th century Polish storyteller offers carefully
crafted hyperbolic descriptions and focuses on personal duels within
battle scenes.

The setting in ample, embracing a vast geographic area. The
heroes, both historical and invented, play roles of national importance. The actions sometimes border on the superhuman; and
although the gods take no part in the story, the Christian faith, the
Black Madonna, and other spiritual forces are essential to the people
who live in these novels. It is even possible to detect conventions
such as epic catalogs and epic similes.

Other criteria of the epic require that the author "use words in a
very distinguished way" and that he treat "many sides and a wide
range of life;" and among Sienkiewicz's greatest achievements in the
Trilogy are his descriptions of nature and events, his amazing
richness of vocabulary, his wonderful command of dialogue, and his
excellent reproduction of the era's everyday speech as used by the
full spectrum of the population. Moreover, few writers of any era
deal so successfully with such a vast mosaic of different kinds of
people within a single work, or speak on behalf of an entire nation,
which is the final classical condition for an epic. In that regard,
Sienkiewicz himself is our foremost witness. "Nations are represented by their poets and their writers," he said in response to the Nobel
Prize. "Consequently, the award of this prize glorifies not only the

author but the people whose son he is. It has been said that Poland is dead, exhausted and enslaved. But here is proof of her life and triumph."

However it was the Polish people themselves who best confirmed this point at a delayed 50th birthday celebration for their beloved spokesman when they presented him with a small estate, bought through a nation-wide subscription fund, and who continue to buy out every edition of the Trilogy as soon as it appears.

Here then is one of the great epics of the modern age which has been lost for more than three quarters of a century for those of us who read and think in English. Scholars have long recognized the virtual impossibility of transplanting the epic. In the case of the Trilogy, the problem was deepened by vast cultural differences between West and East, and an astounding Western ignorance of (and indifference to) the histories, cultures and civilizations of many nations at the "wrong" end of Europe.

All that, however, was changed on May 3 this year with the appearance of W.S. Kuniczak's modern translation of *With Fire and Sword*, and now with this truly splendid edition of *The Deluge*. Kuniczak is superbly suited to this task. Indeed, he may well be the only modern writer capable of carrying it out to a successful end. Himself an author of a modern epic—an honored trilogy of the Polish national experience in the Second World War—he is a bilingual, Polish-born, British-trained American novelist whose passion for the Trilogy of Henryk Sienkiewicz led him to suspend his own literary career, abandon his own writing, and sacrifice more than eight years to this gigantic task.

The task has been well worth the enormous effort.

Kuniczak mirrors Sienkiewicz's imagery, recreates his language within another culture, and bridges the gaps in readers' understanding of those distant and unknown historical events. *The Deluge* comes to life as never before in English, and English-speaking readers throughout the world can now appreciate the impassioned power which Henryk Sienkiewicz exerted over his own countrymen for a hundred years. As Dr. Jerzy Maciuszko notes in his review of this great achievement in *World Literature Today*: "We are dealing here

47

with two masterpieces. The original is the greatest prose epic of Polish literature, the other a masterpiece of translation."

Introduction to *Fire in the Steppe*

by Jerzy J. Maciuszko

When Henryk Sienkiewicz finished writing *Fire in the Steppe* (Pan Wołodyjowski) in the spring of 1887, the final line of his epilogue read: *'Here comes the end of the books written in sweat and toil over the last few years to uplift the hearts.'* That epilogue, which is like a paean of reassurance in its projection into a distant future, and at the same time an answer to the author's contemporary critics, does not appear in this translation for reasons noted later. But it sums up a monumental effort by a selfless man who single-handedly set out to revive the national consciousness of a captive people and succeeded beyond his wildest dreams. It may be fair to say that what Sienkiewicz did for the Poles in Polish, his new American translator W. S. Kuniczak continues in brilliant modern English for a far larger audience and succeeds beyond anyone's expectations.

Writing his own foreword to this new translation, James A. Michener called the Trilogy a sacred book. In most Polish homes it stands beside the Bible. It has rallied the Polish people in their most tragic moments for more than a century, giving them faith and hope when neither appeared to be realistic, and it continues to inspire each new generation. Yet it is not merely an apotheosis of grandeur and lost glories but also a grim lesson in humanity, decency, loyalty and determination, which warns not only Poles but every other people that even the greatest civilizations fall if they lose sight of their moral and spiritual values. Written with love and that controlled, disciplined passion that makes for great writing, it has withstood every test of time, and although it has often been compared with a variety of famous English and American novels there is really nothing quite like it in any other literature beyond the works of Homer.

Like its two epic predecessors (*With Fire and Sword*, 1883-1884,

49

and *The Deluge*, 1884-1886), *Fire in the Steppe* enthralls and captivates as a grand, love and adventure story while bringing alive a vital fragment of European history. It began appearing serially on June 2, 1887 in three Polish newspapers simultaneously—*Słowo* (The Word) in Warsaw, *Czas* (Time) in Krakow, and *Dziennik Poznański* (The Poznan Daily) in Poznan—which, at that time, lay within the three empires of Russia, Prussia and Austria-Hungary that had partitioned Poland 92 years before, and continued running without an interruption until the middle of May, 1888. Only a part of the text was ready when the printing started and there was always the fear that Sienkiewicz, writing at great speed under difficult personal conditions and almost always traveling, might run out of material. Both the continuity of action and the cohesion of the plot had to depend upon the author's memory in those almost unimaginable days before computers, telephones, express mail delivery (or even typewriters) and it was only the prodigious mental discipline of this self-motivated literary genius that saved his novels time and time again. Even so, false tries and repetitions appeared in the printed texts of all the three books and later found their way into earlier word-for-word translations, much to the author's embarrassment and distress. It is only now that W. S. Kuniczak, working from the final definitive texts of Professor Julian Krzyżanowski's 1948-52 Collected Works edition, has been able to restore Sienkiewicz's original vision in another language. The author who turned to the 17th century to comfort his countrymen, shows us a nation rising back to greatness through courage, faith, endurance and devotion after successive devastations by rebellious Cossacks, invading Swedes and the avalanche of the Moslem world which tried to overwhelm Christianity itself in an attack on Poland. He does so honestly and fairly, showing his fictional and historical characters with all their vices as well as their virtues, and holding nothing back, no matter how painful. He speaks in the language of the century he describes which defies any orthodox systems of translation, often inventing words and phrases in a purposely antiquated Polish that only a devoted Polish-born translator could attempt to render into another language, and he creates an epos of the first magnitude which defies analysis in another culture. The fact that this translation succeeds so brilliantly in that transposition seems almost miraculous in itself.

It was the fashion for a time among the minor Polish literary critics, particularly in the years of Communist domination, and aped to this day by foreign book reviewers who cannot read Polish and must depend on second-hand opinion in their criticism, to denigrate Sienkiewicz and his work, charging him with idealizing the past, taking liberties with history, and relegating him to the role of a children's author, but even they admit that he succeeded in his self-appointed mission. His voice rang loud and clear when a desperate people needed to hear it the most. He did uplift the hearts of his grateful countrymen in his own time when there was no Poland on the maps of Europe, then through all the horrors of Nazi occupation during World War II and the dehumanizing aftermath of Soviet Communism which tried to rewrite history and subvert the character and traditions of the Polish people to suit its own purpose. He also suffered from attacks by his contemporary critics in a period ruled by social realism in literature and the arts, for whom his giant step into a more heroic age, presented in a language that could stir even ordinary people, seemed like a dangerous return to the populist romanticism of an earlier era.

Fire in the Steppe is at least in part Sienkiewicz's reply to these charges of idealizing bygone times. No other piece of 19th century literary prose possesses such graphically shocking images of human cruelty, although few match it in the simplicity of its gentleness and love, and the modern reader may well ask why Sienkiewicz does not spare us those dreadful scenes of unremitting horror. The answer goes to the very heart of this monumental work. Writing the final book of his Trilogy, Sienkiewicz took note of those critical voices among his literary peers. He was particularly aware of the admonitions of Bolesław Prus, a literary giant in his own right, whose *The Doll* was the paramount example of socially-conscious Polish realism. Gone in *Fire in the Steppe* are some of the hyperbolic metaphors for military glory. The Homeric quality is tempered and subdued until the last moment. The obligatory final victory, essential to romantic literature, gives way to a disaster; and a single scene of horrifying cruelty, preceded by a carefully paced progressive series of accounts that document Man's inhumanity to Man, and followed by the tragedy of a young man's madness, comes as a realistic balance for Sienkiewicz's earlier glorification of the era.

Discussing *Fire in the Steppe*, a distinguished Polish literary critic, Zygmunt Szweykowski, sums up his argument in this respect as follows: "The reality of life in the Commonwealth in that time (i.e. the 17th century) shows its ugly face in all of its horror . . . The illusion of the fable is gone. However even now Sienkiewicz does not think of leaving the reader in a state of hopelessness. Over and above the illusory suggestions which served him well in the first two parts of the cycle, he wants to leave the sense of (the nation's and the era's) greatness, which in his judgment, reflects a reality that does not require irrealistic myths and can stand on its own."

This role of greatness in *Fire in the Steppe* is supplied by a historical figure rather than any character of the fiction, in the person of Jan Sobieski, Grand Hetman of Poland and later King Jan III Sobieski, who saved the Christian world from the Turks at Vienna in 1683. In his study of Henryk Sienkiewicz, published by Twayne's World Author series, Mieczysław Giergielewicz stresses the fact that Sobieski is shown here "not merely as a defender of his own country but also of Christendom." Sobieski's triumph over the Turks at the earlier battle of Khotim (Chocim) in 1674 appears as a detailed historical essay in the author's epilogue, set two years after the action of the book, the doomed heroic climax of the novel and the end of the story, and so it was quite properly left out of this modern translation which is designed for 20th century readers. Much as he wished to use it for its triumphant, upbeat note of a delayed victory, Kuniczak had to bow to the conventions of the modern novel which restrict material only to that which helps in character development and advances the story. Sienkiewicz's epilogue is sometimes seen as something of an afterthought, as if he were abandoning the art of the novelist for the safer province of academic history. It plucks again at those uplifting strings so dear to his Polish readers but it plays no structural role in the novel, ties no loose ends relating to the characters, and detracts somewhat from the novel's climax for the sake of an external historical effect. It is no accident, however, that in contrast to the two preceding novels of the Trilogy, the unforgettable protagonists of *Fire in the Steppe*—the Little Knight (Pan Volodyovski in his transliterated spelling) and his beloved Basia—are based upon real persons and not entirely on Sienkiewicz's art and imagination. Basia, indeed, is the apotheosis of his lost young wife.

Writing their own excellent scholarly introductions to *With Fire and Sword* and *The Deluge*, Professors Jerzy R. Krzyżanowski and Thomas Napierkowski more than adequately cover the colossal impact that this epic work had on its contemporaries, the message that it has for readers everywhere today, and its position as a prime example of the national novel which has no counterpart in any other literature of the world, so that no more needs to be said on that subject here. What may be added, however, is a brief discussion of the creative sources which allowed Sienkiewicz to raise the epic novel so far above the other 19th century masters of the genre. The roots of this Homeric quality may be found in the *Iliad* and the *Odyssey* which were Sienkiewicz's own favorite reading matter, as well as in the period Polish writings in which he steeped himself both in his diligent study of the times and for his private pleasure. Principal among these were the 17th century *Memoirs* (Pamiętniki) of Jan Chryzostom Pasek, a fighting squire of the Polish-Lithuanian Commonwealth who lived through many of the events recounted in the Trilogy, knew many of the historical figures pictured there, and was an active witness to the times and its various peoples. Of great help to him were the *Annales*, also known as *The Climacterics* (Klimaktery) by the Baroque chronicler Wespazjan Kochowski, the *Historical Sketches* (Szkice historyczne) by Ludwik Kubala and the seminal work of another contemporary historian, K. Szajnocha, especially his *Two Years of Our Times* (Dwa lata dziejów naszych.) According to Samuel Sandler (viz. *Bibliography*), Sienkiewicz depended on both Kubala and Szajnocha for anecdotal material and the customs of the age. It should be noted that in preparing for the eight-year labor of his new translation, W. S. Kuniczak went back to these and many other sources of Sienkiewicz's fabled creativity so that he could reaffirm his grasp on the master's novelistic vision, and project an accurate rendering of the times for the modern reader.

More will be said later about this devoted American disciple of the Polish master. But what of the great novelist himself? How did he work? How did he manage to control, propel and maintain the massive flow of his creativity? Contemporaries have left us a picture of a man writing at a near-frantic pace, among a litter of broken pens and cascading papers, who had to be literally torn away from his writing table in order to eat. In reality, he antedated the systematic disciplined professionalism preached and displayed by every modern writer from Hemingway to Mailer, contemptuous of the Victorian amateurs of his time, and substituting hard work on a sustained basis for so-called 'inspiration.' He wrote at fixed times every day wherever he happened to be, setting himself a daily quota he never failed to meet, and seemingly oblivious of the enormous pressures required to keep control of his immense material. Considering the length, scope and breadth of his Trilogy (almost two million words in this translation), the number of characters, plots, sub-plots and story lines in the three interrelated novels, and the speed at which Sienkiewicz was obliged to work, the result can be nothing but astounding.

Sienkiewicz's method was to devise a kind of blueprint of each of his novels with as many details of time, place, action and character appearances as he was able to anticipate. Then he would put the plan on paper, fully aware that truly rendered fictional characters always took on their own lives and went their own way, and then he memorized it and let it settle in his mind. When ready to write, he would divide his material into blocks of time by weeks rather than days and let his editors decide on the daily installments they printed in their papers. Ironically enough, his systematic approach to creating his magnificent fiction earned him some scorn from his Polish literary peers who couldn't reconcile his rigidly scheduled, day-by-day production with their own 19th century notions of art by inspiration. Yet it is hard to imagine how he could have managed to produce such a vast work as the Trilogy in any other way.

It is even harder to imagine that Sienkiewicz knew what he would say in *Fire in the Steppe* before he started writing *With Fire and Sword*, and yet that conclusion is inescapable once the entire triptych is displayed for leisurely critical study and analysis. Everything that may have gone before in the Trilogy that puzzled the reader is suddenly logical and clear; everything makes sense; and even the prophetic message of triumph within disaster comes as no surprise, so that the ringing victory of the epilogue isn't really necessary after the story ends. In the long process of heroic struggle that begins with the rebellion of the Cossacks in 1648, told in such thrilling terms in *With Fire and Sword*, and then runs on through the astonishing twists and turns during the Swedish onslaught (1655-58) recounted in *The Deluge*, a single multi-level theme threads the various skeins of plot and characters together and brings them to the only logical conclusion: human beings must retain their humanity, no matter what happens to them or around them, and the salvation of mankind lies within each man.

With Fire and Sword, *The Deluge* and *Fire in the Steppe* are separate parts of a single, carefully designed structure and can be read as independent novels but there are marked differences between them. One of these is the harshness of reality and the cruelty of history already noted here. The other is a marvelous evolution in the role that women play in these thousands of tumultuous pages, so that what starts with the idealized figure of Helen in *With Fire and Sword*—the quintessential romantic heroine of Victorian fiction whose main role is to be the object of heroic rescue—and passes far beyond traditional limitations into the strength, courage, clear-sightedness and wisdom of *The Deluge's* Olenka, becomes at last the brave, undaunted, feminine but indomitable Basia of *Fire in the Steppe*, the most beloved heroine of Polish 19th century writing who would be quite at home almost anywhere in the 20th century. She would certainly be at home in today's America and would probably cope with it very well.

Indeed, America plays a surprising role throughout the Trilogy which may have a special meaning for Sienkiewicz's new American readership today. Critics have speculated that *Fire in the Steppe* may have been the first of the three novels that Sienkiewicz planned, because he researched the life of Jerzy Michał Wołodyjowski, a gallant little contemporary of Jan Chryzostom Pasek, several years before he started writing *With Fire and Sword*, but his travels through America in 1876-78 suddenly changed his schedule. It was in San Francisco that he met the two prototypes of his most famous characters, the roistering Pan Zagloba and gentle Pan Longinus, and decided that one novel wouldn't be enough. In all probability Sienkiewicz's Zagloba was based upon Captain Korwin-Piotrowski, a San Francisco immigration inspector who had fought the Russians in the Polish 1830 insurrection, emigrated to America, wandered across the plains and claimed to have been both an army scout and an Indian fighter. A prodigious drinker, good-natured braggart and teller of tall tales, he was the perfect prototype of Sienkiewicz's inimitable Zagloba, as was another Californian exile, a gentle Lithuanian of gigantic stature who turned into Pan Longinus in the young Polish writer's swift imagination.

These two providential meetings completed the main cast of the Trilogy since Sienkiewicz, barely an inch or two above five feet in height, always identified with the Little Knight, Pan Volodyovski, and the entire glorious epic of love, war, intrigue, heroism and adventure took root in the future author's mind under the western skies. Bringing the Trilogy even closer to America is the fact that the magnificent descriptions of the wild 17th century borderlands of southeastern Poland are closely patterned on the American West, as Sienkiewicz's published *Letters from America* so clearly attest. The writer had never visited those long-lost Wild Lands and Ukrainian Steppes that he recreates so brilliantly in both *With Fire and Sword* and *Fire in the Steppe*. But he saw the American plains and the western prairies, heard all the tales told around the campfires, admired the Indians, and literally fell in love with the untrammeled land and its vibrant people. Moreover, several of the early ambushes and battles in *With Fire and Sword* clearly derive from American newspaper accounts of clashes with the Indians and the stories of raids and massacres popular in America during Sienkiewicz's enthusiastic visit.

American readers can be grateful to W. S. Kuniczak for an exalted reading experience. His artistry has given us a masterpiece of translation which brings continuing applause from the best American critics and resurrects Sienkiewicz in America for new generations. The superb literary skills of this Polish-born American novelist create a bridge between the Polish and Anglo-Saxon cultures and open a new chapter in the history of literary translation equal to, and at times surpassing, the original.

Translating the "Untranslatable" Trilogy of Henryk Sienkiewicz

by W. S. Kuniczak

Ever since Jeremiah Curtin's translation of Henryk Sienkiewicz's Trilogy dismayed English-speaking Poles, it's been a point of dogma that their national prose epic was untranslatable into English, since his hasty word-for-word rendition, done in one lightning draft from a Russian text to beat out competition, creates such images as Polish nobles who butt their heads in greeting.

In reality, the butting nobles are saying '*Czołem!*' which can be anything from "Hullo!" to a formal "Greetings!" and using an expression that refers to the forehead, either dipped in a friendly nod or lowered in a bow. My most unnerving moment in plowing through Curtin's peculiar imagery was a scene where two old friends leap into each other's arms while shouting: "*With the forehead!*" Faced with such absurdities, most Poles concluded that the special language that Sienkiewicz used in his deliberately antiqued 19th century telling of 17th century events, could be truly rendered only in the Polish, and any attempt to put it into English was doomed before it started.

The essential difference between the two languages is indeed a gulf to confound Columbus. The multilayered maze of Polish meanings in which so many words depend on context and allusion, is compounded here by a Victorian passion for interior clauses, still present in the Polish, that make even a normal declarative sentence seem like a brightly painted "Baba" doll, the kind that contains a dozen smaller dolls inside it. Where the essentially witty flow of cultivated Polish seems like a minuet in quick-time, the straightforward snap and crackle of 20th century English sometimes sounds like a communications shorthand.

The fact is that the Trilogy is impossible to render with a rigid, word-for-word translation into fluid, idiomatic and coherent English which may be grasped in the 1990s with the same emotional effect that the author wanted in the 1880s. The technical problems of transposing both the meaning and effect desired by the author into another culture are beyond the reach of those who do not actually create literary prose on a daily basis. One can be very well equipped for critical analysis without knowing how to solve the problems that a working novelist confronts and tackles every day.

The need to preserve the antique flavor of the work, to retain all of Sienkiewicz's wonderful sense of time and place which he deliberately sprinkles with antiqued allusions, to grasp and translate exactly what he wished to say, to adhere to his vast panoramic vision and his sense of mission, and then to paint his people as he wanted them perceived, rather than turning them into ludicrous caricatures reproduced on a foreign canvass, isn't for the amateur or the faint of heart. And finally there is the basic evolutionary truth about the constant shift in human perceptions, and the ongoing change, growth, flowering and decay of every living language. Philosophic concepts, values and ideals don't travel well across the years between languages and cultures, and what Sienkiewicz wanted seen as noble or heroic— or even as contemptible, deplorable or absurd—acquires quite the opposite meanings and effects at this end of the 20th century, especially in English.

I watched a screening of a Polish-filmed version of *The Deluge* a few years ago, and while the clearly Polish segments of the audience wept at the beauty and grandeur of it all, the American spectators laughed at what they saw as antique posturings, full of sound and fury, in which unreal people did incomprehensible things for unexplained reasons. Add to this catalog of a translator's horrors the vast historical arena in which this monumental Trilogy is set, and which Sienkiewicz didn't have to explain to his Polish audience, and you'll create a bewildering mystery on this side of the Atlantic. Bear in mind an American culture oriented almost exclusively towards England, an educational curriculum that ensures utter ignorance of anything to do with the "wrong" side of Europe, a minimal literary interest in an unknown corner of the Slavic world which leaves no glimmer in any reader's mind of those ancient turmoils recounted in the Trilogy, and it seems certain that an accurate transposition of the author's vision into modern English by way of the orthodox word-for-word translation must confuse the reader. The established academic word for the word-for-word theory of translation, is that it is "faithful." But in the case of the Sienkiewicz Trilogy it's always been the fidelity of a straying spouse before he or she is caught *in flagrante*, and found sadly lacking in grace, taste, style, virtue and good sense.

The problems were obvious. Yet knowing all the pitfalls is almost as good as having a ready-made solution. Moreover, I had an immense natural advantage over previous Trilogy translators, being a Polish-born American novelist who has been producing English-language fiction for 32 years, but whose basic training in European history, cultures and traditions was acquired in Europe. Furthermore, although I was blessed with a sound classical education, I didn't have to face the unrewarding task of changing a novelist's Polish into an academic's English. This plus the fact that I knew the Trilogy inside-out, having read it lovingly more than forty times, gave me the hope that I might succeed where amateurs failed.

It's fair, however, to ask, why anyone should bother. What is this fabled Trilogy that it deserves any amount of effort? Graduates of creative writing courses who are incapable of any literary criterion except "what's it like," compare it to *War and Peace* and *Gone with the Wind*. So do book-reviewers who do not read Polish and must rely on what they're told by local academics. A better way is to think of it as an unending feast. Throw in Cervantes for Quixotic flavor, add a dose of Homer, season with broad, gut-wrenching humor (much funnier than Falstaff's!) and some sharp, sly digs at human frailty and follies, pour in all the blood and gore spilled by Stephen King, toss in the best of the Ludlum thrillers as well as all the nobler teachings of the Christian church, bring it to boil in an imagination as vast and wild as the American West, and you'll have something that might approximate the many-layered texture and the awesome taste of a set of books that have been called "a portrait of a nation" and "both the mirror and the cradle of a people's soul."

This is literature in the grand manner, written with a purpose when novelists viewed themselves as the brokers of their nation's conscience. It asserts the efficacy of hope in times when men have little in which to believe and even less to hope for. It celebrates courage and endurance as the only qualities that can stand up to those continuing betrayals of our humanity which turn ideals into ideologies. It shows that even the most powerful civilizations fall when private greed takes precedence over the public good. It urges a return to decency and good faith in our human dealings with each other. Above all it challenges that narrow and self-centered lack of a worthy purpose which destroyed the ancient Poland of Sienkiewicz's novelistic vision and which continues to corrupt many of the social and political fabrics of our times.

In bringing this work forward into the final years of the 20th century I make some definite stylistic adjustments to modernize the way in which Sienkiewicz addresses his English-speaking readers but I take care to preserve his 17th century heroines and heroes in their original dimensions so that they may continue to advance the author's vision, purpose and ideas, and that means an occasional dipping into history to flesh-out characterization and explain their motives and behavior. In this respect rather than merely trading languages we are bridging cultures.

This task, however, faced other structural, cultural and linguistic problems that do not normally plague those who supply a new language for an author's work. One of them was the urgent need to provide a historical background for today's English-speaking reader for whom 17th century Poland is a puzzling and confusing mystery. The Polish text presupposes a thorough knowledge of the times and their various peoples that Sienkiewicz, writing for an audience that absorbed that knowledge at the mother's breast, left out of the novel. An even greater problem lay within the language, style and construction. Sienkiewicz used a purposely antiquated Polish, including words and phrases that he had invented, to underline the long-lost quality of the departed glories and the antiquity of the values he wished to recall. Furthermore, he wrote for a 19th century audience in that century's terms which create entirely different meanings in our modern eyes. Some good friends, fine scholars all, suggested several lines of compromise—including marginal notations, appendices and footnotes—which I refused in favor of a novelist's solution as I believed Sienkiewicz would have done, because a novel lives or dies by its own momentum, and one moment of distraction that shatters the spell often loses the reader. I fixed upon Sienkiewicz's intentions rather than strict allegiance to each written word, feeling that my first duty was to render the heart and spirit of the work, with all due regard for its stylistic letter.

I was careful to antique my own modern English so as to preserve the flavor of the era, and to render an exact sense of the time and place by translating the sounds and the sights trapped within the language and the feeling hidden in the speech lines. I paid strict attention to Sienkiewicz's own style and his sentence rhythms, especially in the translation of folkish aphorisms and rollicking little ditties, to the dialects used by a rich variety of people, to both the Polish and American metaphor, simile and idiom which can be ludicrous in their innocent collisions, and I searched out the necessary English equivalents for the rough-hewn speech of the Cossacks, the peasantry and the soldiers, and to the grandiloquence of some of the gentry which, by the way, has excellent counterparts in the historicals and the comedies of Shakespeare.

I clung to the master's form and structure wherever I could, although I had to bow occasionally to the needs of our contemporary readers. I standardized chapter length, which meant increasing the number of chapters. Transitional lines and paragraphs had to be inserted now and then to lead the modern reader from one rephrased notion or idea to the next. Most of these came from elsewhere in the text and very few were totally invented, although it often took a dozen lines to convey the meaning that the Polish language can convey in three. Speech lines which in Polish carry their own stage directions and visual effects, had to be reconstructed to show what was happening, otherwise the reader would miss some critical imagery and draw the wrong conclusions. Since Polish meanings depend quite heavily on accent and allusion, the way in which a given line of dialogue is spoken had to be often illustrated with adverbial clauses, which also helped to deepen characterization. Purists may hate me for it but that can't be helped; the language of the reader is always more important in translations, just as the home-grown culture of an immigrant must always bow before the new reality in which he finds himself. Some of the compound sentences suffered rearrangement, and here and there an overlong expository paragraph became a half dozen lines of dialogue that conveyed the same information at a quicker pace. But I inserted nothing which did not explain or advance the author's story, characterizations, imagery or purpose, and in no way did I touch his viewpoint or historical perceptions. I deleted only repetitions which Sienkiewicz, writing his huge work at great speed to make newspaper deadlines, left within his pages, or cumbersome genealogical dissertations that could be rephrased through a few lines of simple dialogue, or one-time appearances by unimportant persons who play no structural role in any of the novels, and this I did largely to diminish the number of those difficult personal names that only Poles are able to pronounce and which bloom in the pages of the Trilogy like thistles in a field. I sought to internationalize this Polish literary and historical experience by bringing it in line with the conventions of the contemporary novel, and finally—knowing that mystification of the readers was not the author's purpose—I worked new clarifying historical material into the novel's texture.

The Trilogy moves at torrential pace in which detail blurs for the unaccustomed eye, and yet it was exactly that sense of hurtling mass in an accumulation of unexplained and puzzling historical detail, which took the life out of the early orthodox translations. Lost in its journey to another culture, and trapped within Curtin's barely animated puppets, the spirit of the Trilogy had to be wholly recreated for the Western reader so that he or she could be free to move, without confusion and distraction, through that colossal historical arena which Sienkiewicz created for another audience. Writing for 19th century minds and hearts in their own rich and decorative language—so much more fluid and accommodating than the hard-edged precision of 20th century English—he concentrated on his story lines, eschewing the necessary interiors which add dimension to characters in 20th century fiction, and thus unwittingly contributing to the colossal comprehension gap between his time and culture and our own. This too had to be addressed in a modern manner.

The basis for all this seems clear but perhaps it ought to be explained. Sienkiewicz was a novelist. Despite appearances, the novelist does not communicate with words but with the sounds, images and environments he creates to captivate and enthrall his readers. Words are mere tools, no more important than a painter's paint-box, and slavish adherence to them doesn't make much sense, particularly in a hundred-year leap across two vastly different cultures whose languages and usage have nothing in common. It seems to me that people who judge the merits of translated literature by counting words, comparing lines, and demanding asterisks and footnotes as the *'sine qua non'* of fidelity, can't know very much about either writing or reading a work of literary fiction. That might work for technical manuals and textbooks but not in a novel which depends for its life on an even flow of imagery and language. I may be wrong but I do believe that novels are written (and translated) for readers, not for analysts or critics. If I am wrong—if it is more important to create material for scholarly dissertations than to introduce a vast, new general American readership to an important and exciting European classic which has been lost to them for several generations—then I confess that I see myself less as a translator than a collaborator with the author's spirit.

And finally there is the matter of my transliteration of the immensely difficult Polish and Ruthenian names which, as we all knew from the beginning, may dismay Polish readers who are deeply and emotionally attached to this classic. For many the Trilogy is a return to childhood. Logic, however, rather than emotions, demands accommodation because an untrained eye simply doesn't register an unpronounceable stream of consonants to which readers are not accustomed within their own language. Character identification must be instantaneous in a work of fiction and names which can't be pronounced in some reasonable fashion cannot be remembered. We had to ask ourselves in opting for transliteration whether the fortification of individual egos was more important than the introduction of an important Polish writer to a new American readership. The answer seemed clear.

There is nothing new about transliteration. Every English version of Sienkiewicz's work (and many others in Asia, America and Europe) used it in some fashion without a word of protest from the author, because every culture strives to be understood in another language and he knew this better than almost anyone. Oddly enough, British Historian Norman Davies, writing in the New York Times Book Review on June 30, 1991, takes me to task for not carrying transliteration far enough! Either way, it seems clear that the phonetic spelling recommended by the Modern Language Association causes no concern among knowledgeable people who understand the rules of literary fiction and the needs of the readership for which the translation was made.

GLOSSARY I:

Principal Characters in the Trilogy

Original Polish spelling is given in parentheses. For historical personages dates are provided. The initials WFS, TD, FITS indicate the books of the Trilogy where the character appears in a major role: *With Fire and Sword*, *The Deluge* and *Fire in the Steppe* respectively. Polish forms of address Pan (Lord, Sir, Mr.), Pani (Lady, Mrs.), and Panna (Lady, Miss) are often used with either first or last names of characters, as well as with their respective titles, and are shown here in quotation marks if used extensively in the novels.

Babinitch, Andrei (Babinicz, Andrzej); TD—see Kmita, Andrei

Billevitch, Tomasz, "Pan Tomasz" (Billewicz, Tomasz); TD—Polish nobleman, Constable of Rosyen (Rosienie), uncle of Olenka

Billevitch or Billevitchovna, Aleksandra or Olenka, "Panna Aleksandra" (Billewiczówna, Aleksandra or Oleńka); TD—young Polish noblewoman, the heroine of *The Deluge*, in FITS wife of Kmita

Bohun, Yuri (Bohun, Juri); WFS—Cossack hero in Hmyelnitzki's army

Bojhobohata-Krasienska, Anusia (Borzobohata-Krasieńska, Anusia); WFS, TD—lady-in-waiting to Princess Grizelda Vishnovyetzka

Burlaj (Burłaj); WFS—Cossack military leader

Butrym, Yozva (Butrym, Józwa); TD—Polish soldier from the Lauda country

Charles Gustav (Karol X. Gustaw, Carolus Gustavus, 1622-1660); TD—King of Sweden 1654-1660

de la Gardie, Pontus (Magnus Gabriel de la Gardie, 1622-1686); TD—Swedish general

Dontzovna, Horpyna (Dońcówna, Horpyna); WFS—young Ruthenian witch

Drohoyovska, Krystyna, Krysia, "Panna Krysia" (Drohojowska, Krystyna); FITS—young Polish noblewoman, wife of Ketling

Hassling-Ketling of Elgin, Ketling; TD, FITS—Scottish officer in the Polish service

Hmyelnitzki, Bohdan (Chmielnicki, Bogdan, 1593-1657); WFS—Cossack political and military leader

Devlet Girey (Islam III Girey, d. 1654); WFS—Khan of Crimean Tartars 1644-1654

Kemlitch (Kiemlicz); TD—Polish soldier in service to Kmita

Kharlamp, "Pan Kharlamp" (Charlamp); WFS, TD—Polish officer in Lithuanian army

Kmita, Andrei, "Pan Andrei" (Kmicic, Andrzej); TD, FITS—Polish officer in Lithuanian army, Seneschal of Orsha, protagonist of *The Deluge*

Kordetzki, Augustin (Kordecki, Augustyn, 1603-1673); TD—Polish priest, Prior of Yasna Gora monastery

Kowalski, Roche (Kowalski, Roch); TD—Polish officer in Lithuanian army, "nephew" of Zagloba

Kshetchovski (Krzeczowski or Krzyczewski, Stanislaw Michal, d. 1649); WFS—Cossack military leader

Krivoinos, Maxim (Krzywonos, Maksym, d.1648); WFS—Cossack military leader

Kuklinovski (Kuklinowski); TD—Polish officer in Swedish service

Kurtzevitch, Kurtzevichovna, Helen (Bulychów-Kurcewicz, Kurcewiczówna, Helena); WFS, TD—Polish-Ruthenian princess, the heroine of *With Fire and Sword*, bride of Skshetuski

Lubomirski, George (Lubomirski, Jerzy, 1616-1667); TD—Lord High Constable of Poland

Luśnia, Zydor (Lusnia, Zydor); FITS—Polish sergeant in Volodyovski's service

Mellehovitch, Azia (Mellechowicz, Azja); FITS—Tartar officer in Polish service

Michael Korybut, Prince Michael (Michał Korybut Wiśniowiecki, 1638-1673); TD, FITS—son of Prince Yeremi and Princess Grizelda, King of Poland 1669-1673

Mueller von der Luehne, Burchard (Miller); TD—German general in Swedish service

Mushalski, "Pan Mushalski" (Muszalski); FITS Polish officer

Novovyeyska, Eva, Evka (Nowowiejska, Ewa, Ewka); FITS—young Polish noblewoman

Novovyeyski, Adam (Nowowiejski, Adam); FITS—Polish officer, Eva's brother

Opalinski, Kristof (Opaliński, Krzysztof, 1609-1655); TD—Voyevode of Poznan, Polish politician, ally of the Swedes

Podbipyenta, Longinus, "Pan Longinus" (Podbipięta, Longinus); WFS—Lithuanian officer in Prince Yeremi's service, hero of Zbarajh

Pototzki, Mikolai (Potocki, Mikołaj, d. 1651); WFS—Polish Grand Hetman, defeated by Hmyelnitzki

Radeyovski, Hyeronimus (Radziejowski, Hieronim, 1622-1666); WFS, TD—Polish politician, ally of the Swedes

Radzivill, Boguslav, "Prince Boguslav" (Radziwiłł, Bogusław, 1620-1669); TD—Lithuanian magnate, ally of the Swedes, antagonist of Kmita

Radzivill, Yanush, "Prince Yanush" (Radziwiłł, Janusz, 1612-1655); TD—Grand Hetman of the Lithuanians, Voyevode of Vilna, ally of the Swedes, cousin of Prince Boguslav

Sakovitch (Sakowicz); TD—Polish nobleman in Prince Boguslav's service

Sapyeha, Pavel (Sapieha, Paweł Jan, ca. 1600-1665); TD—Grand Hetman of the Lithuanians (after Radzivill), Voyevode of Vitebsk

Skshetuski, Yan, "Pan Yan" (Skrzetuski, Jan); WFS, TD—Polish officer in Prince Yeremi's service, protagonist of *With Fire and Sword*, one of the principal characters of the Trilogy

Sobieski, Jan, 1624-1696; FITS—Grand Hetman of Poland, elected King of Poland 1674 (Jan III Sobieski)

Soroka (Soroka); TD—Polish sergeant in Kmita's service

Tcharnyetzki, Stefan (Czarniecki, Stefan 1599-1665); WFS, TD—Polish military leader, Castellan of Kiev, later Grand Hetman of Poland

Tuhay-bey (Tuhaj-bej, d. 1651); WFS—Tartar general, ally of Hmyelnitzki

Vyershul (Wierszull); WFS, TD—Polish officer in Prince Yeremi's service

Vishnovyetzka, Grizelda, "Princess Grizelda" (Wiśniowiecka, Gryzelda); WFS, TD—wife of Prince Yeremi, mother of Prince Michael (King Michał Korybut Wiśniowiecki)

Vishnovyetzki, Yeremi, "Prince Yeremi," Yarema (Wiśniowiecki, Jeremi Michał Korybut, 1612-1651); WFS—Polish military leader, Prince of the Transdnieper, father of Michał Korybut, King of Poland

Vladyslav IV (Władysław IV Waza, 1595-1648); WFS—King of Poland 1632-1648

Volodyovski, Michal, "Pan Michal" (Wołodyjowski, Jerzy Michał); WFS, TD, FITS—Polish officer, the protagonist of *Fire in the Steppe*, one of the principal characters of the Trilogy.

Wittemberg, Arvid (Wittemberg, Arwid); TD—Swedish field marshal

Yan Casimir (Jan Kazimierz, Johannes Casimirus, 1609-1672); WFS, TD—King of Poland 1648-1668

Yezorkovska, Barbara, Basia, Baska (Jeziorkowska, Barbara, Basia); FITS—young Polish noblewoman, heroine of *Fire in the Steppe*, wife of Volodyovski

Zachvilihovski (Zaćwilichowski); WFS—Polish nobleman

Zagloba, Onufry, "Pan Zagloba" (Zagłoba, Onufry); WFS, TD, FITS—Polish nobleman, one of the principal characters of the Trilogy

Zamoyski, Sobiepan (Zamoyski, Jan "Sobiepan");TD—Polish magnate

Zjendjan (Rzędzian); WFS, TD—servant of Skshetuski.

GLOSSARY II:

Names of Principal Geographical Locations

Many geographical names in the Trilogy refer to small regional or local towns (some no longer in existence) or to rivers and their tributaries. We list here only those that either play a significant role in the novels or had a historical character in the 17th century events. English spelling or transliteration is listed first, followed by the Polish spelling used in the original text of the novels, no matter whether these locations are Polish, Ruthenian, Ukrainian, Russian or Lithuanian. The symbol (R) indicates a river.

Bar — Bar
Belgorod — Biełgorod
Berestetchko — Beresteczko
Birjhe — Birże
Bokh (R) — Boh
Bratzlav — Bracław
Brest Litovsk — Brześć Litewski
Brovarki — Browarki
Byelotzerkiev — Białacerkiew
Demyanovka — Demianówka
Dnieper (R) — Dniepr
Dniester (R) — Dniestr
Felshtyn — Felsztyn
Futory — Futory
Horordishtche — Horodyszcze
Hreptyov — Chreptiów
Hvastov — Chwastów
Kahamlik (R) — Kahamlik
Kamentchug (R) — Kamienczug
Kamyenetz — Kamieniec Podolski

Khortytza — Chortyca
Khotim — Chocim
Kiev — Kijów
Keydany — Kiejdany
Konotop — Konotop
Konskovola — Końskowola
Konstantinov — Konstantynów
Korsun — Korsuń
Krakow (Cracow) — Kraków
Kudak — Kudak
Lipkov — Lipków
Lubetch — Lubicz
Lubnie — Łubnie
Lvov — Lwów
Mahnovka — Machnówka
Matchin — Matczyn
Mohilev — Mochylów
Myshikishke — Myszykiszki
Nijh — Niż
Novosyel — Nowosiólki

Nyemirov — Niemirów
Old Zbarajh — Stary Zbaraż
Omelnitchek (R) — Omelniczek
Orcl — Orzeł
Orsha — Orsza
Partchev — Parczew
Pereyaslav — Perejesław
Pilavtse — Piławce
Pilvishkye — Pilwiszki
Ploskirev — Płoskirów
Plotzk — Płock
Podlasye — Podlasie
Podolia — Podole
Pohrebyshtchye — Pohrebyszcze
Polonne — Połonne
Ponevyesh — Poniewież
Prohorovka — Prochorówka
Rashkov — Raszków
Rosyen — Rosienie
Rozloghi — Rozłogi
Sandomir — Sandomierz
Saulas — Szawle
Sietch — Sicz
Silesia — Śląsk
Sloboda — Słoboda
Spitchin — Śpiczyn
Tasmina (R) — Taśmina
Taurogen — Taurogi
Tchabanovka — Czabanówka
Tcharny Las — Czarny Las
Tchehryn — Czehryn
Tchenstohova — Częstochowa
Tcherkassy — Czerkasy
Tchernihov — Czernihów
Tchertomelik — Czertomelik
Tchornoi Ostrov — Czarny Ostrów
Toporov — Toporów

Turov — Turów
Tykotzin — Tykocin
Upita — Upita
Uystye — Ujście
Valadynka — Waładynka
Vasilovka — Wasiłówka
Vilno/Vilna — Wilno
Vinnitza — Winnica
Vishnovyetz — Wiśniowiec
Vishovaty Stav — Wiszowaty Staw
Vistula (R) — Wisła
Vlodava — Włodawa
Vodokty — Wodokty
Volhynia — Wołyń
Volotchysko — Wołoczysko
Vrajhe Urotchysko — Wraże Uro-czysko
Vyelkopolska — Wielkopolska
Warsaw — Warszawa
Wild Lands — Dzikie Pola
Yahorlik — Jahorlik
Yampol — Jampol
Yarmolinsk — Jarmolińsk
Yasna Gora — Jasna Góra (at Częstochowa)
Yavorov — Jaworów
Yellow Waters — Żołte Wody
Zaborov — Zaborów
Zamost — Zamość
Zaporohje — Zaporoże
Zaslav — Zasław
Zbarajh — Zbaraż
Zborov — Zborów
Zbrutch (R) — Zbrucz
Zmudya — Żmudź
Zjendjany — Rzędziany
Zolotonosha — Zołotonosza

GLOSSARY III:

Special Terms and Foreign Words

Special terms and foreign words used in the W. S. Kuniczak translation of the Trilogy are always translated on their first occurrence, in the next English sentence. They are, however, listed here alphabetically for readers' convenience, followed by a brief explanation and the language in which they are used: Germ.—German; Lat.—Latin; Pol.—Polish; Tart.—Tartar; Turk.—Turkish; Ukr.— Ukrainian or Ruthenian; Russ.—Russian.

ataman — Cossack military leader (Ukr.)
baba — old woman, derogatory for woman (Pol., Ukr.)
baghadir — hero (Ukr., Tart.)
bat'ko — informal: sir, or uncle (Ukr.)
bey — title of respect (Turk.)
boyar — Russian noble (Russ.)
effendi — lord (Turk.)
esaul — Cossack non-commissioned officer (Ukr.)
gojhalka — home-brewed vodka (Ukr.)
Gott mit uns — God is with us (Ger.)
hetman — military commander-in-chief (Pol.)
hohols — contemptuous: Ukrainian peasants (Ukr.)
hospodar — king, ruler (Ukr.)
hospody pomuluy — God have mercy (Ukr.)
hulay horodyna — siege tower (Ukr.)
husaria — Polish elite armored cavalry (Pol.)
hutor — farm (Ukr.)
knahina — princess (Ukr.)

knaz — prince (Ukr.)
kolaska — small carriage (Pol.)
kosh — encampment (Tart.)
kujhen — Cossack military settlement (Ukr.)
lakh, (pl. Lahiv) — contemptuous for: Poles (Ukr.)
lauda — rural gentry from Lauda area (Pol.)
lytzari — knights (Ukr.)
matushka — diminutive for: mother (Ukr.)
maty — mother (Ukr.)
maydan — open space, field (Tart.)
Mirhorodtsy — Cossacks from Mirhorod (Ukr.)
moloytzy — young Cossacks (Ukr.)
murjah (or *mirza*) — title of respect (Tart., Turk.)
na pohybel — damn you, death to you (Ukr.)
na slavu — for glory (Ukr.)
na sh'chastye — for good luck (Ukr.)
nepravda — not true, lie (Ukr.)
Nijhovsty — Cossacks from the lower Dnieper (Ukr.)
pancerni — armored cavalry (Pol.)
pa'neh — sir, lord, master (Ukr.)
pomyluyte pa'neh — have mercy masters (Ukr.)
shtcho s'toboyu — what's wrong with you (Ukr.)
Sietch — main Cossack camp on the lower Dnieper (Ukr.)
Sitchovtsy — Cossacks from the Sietch (Ukr.)
slava bohu — thanks be to God (Ukr.)
spasaytes — save yourselves (Ukr.)
spasi — have mercy, save us (Ukr.)
starosta — county official, sheriff (Pol., Ukr.)
starostvo — county (Pol., Ukr.)
sukmana — long peasant coat (Pol.)
szlachta — nobility, landed gentry (Pol.)
tabor — wagon train, wagon camp (Ukr.)
tchaban — horseherder, shepherd (Ukr.)
tchambul — Tartar cohort (Tart.)
vataha — Cossack cohort (Ukr.)
vatashka — unruly military leader (Ukr.)

voyevode — palatine, state governor (Pol., Ukr.)
yassyr — Tartar slave caravan, slavery (Tart.)
yataghan — short Turkish sword (Turk.)
Zaporohjans — Cossacks from Zaporohje (Ukr.)
Zaporohje — country along the lower Dnieper (Ukr.)

Bibliography

Selected bibliographical and critical sources on Sienkiewicz and his works

Books:

(Anonymous Author), *Henryk Sienkiewicz: The Author of Quo Vadis?*, Little, Brown and Co., 1984.

Coleman, Arthur Prudden and Coleman, Marion Moore, *Wanderers Twain. Modjeska and Sienkiewicz: a View from California*, Cherry Hill Books, 1964.

Coleman, Marion Moore, *Fair Rosalind: The American Career of Helena Modjeska*, Cherry Hill Books, 1969.

Curtin, Jeremiah, *Memoirs*, State Historical Society of Wisconsin, 1964.

Czapliński, Władysław, *Glosa do Trylogii* (A Note to the Trilogy), Ossolineum, 1974.

Falkowski, Zygmunt, *Pzede wszystkim Sienkiewicz* (Before All Else, Sienkiewicz), Pax, 1959.

Gardner, Monica, *The Patriot Novelist of Poland, Henryk Sienkiewicz*, J. M. Dent, 1926.

Giergielewicz, Mieczysław, *Henryk Sienkiewicz*, Twayne, 1968.

Giergielewicz, Mieczysław, *Henryk Sienkiewicz's American Resonance* (includes a bibliography of American reviews), Antemurale, 1966.

Górka, Olgierd, *Ogniem i mieczem a rzeczywistość historyczna* (With Fire and Sword and Historical Reality), Drukarnia Nowoświecka, 1934.

Jodełka, Tomasz, ed. *Trylogia Henryka Sienkiewicza: szkice i polemiki* (Henryk Sienkiewicz's Trilogy: Studies and Polemics), PIW, 1962.

Korniłowiczowa, Maria, *Onegdaj: Opowieść o Henryku Sienkiewiczu i ludziach mu bliskich*, (Day Before Yesterday: A Tale About Henryk Sienkiewicz and People Close to Him), PIW, 1968.

Kosko, Maria, *La Fortune de 'Quo Vadis?' de Sienkiewicz en France* (The Fortunes of Sienkiewicz's 'Quo Vadis?' in France), L. Rodstein, 1935.

Kosko, Maria, *Un 'best-seller' 1900: 'Quo Vadis?,'* J. Corti, 1960.

Kridl, Manfred, *A Survey of Polish Literature and Culture*, Mouton and Co., 1956.

Krzyżanowski, Jerzy R., ed., *The Trilogy Companion*, Copernicus Society of America, 1991.

Krzyżanowski, Julian, *Henryka Sienkiewicza żywot i sprawy* (The Life and Problems of Henryk Sienkiewicz), PIW, 1966.

Krzyżanowski, Julian, *Kalendarz życia i twórczości Henryka Sienkiewicza* (A Chronology of Henryk Sienkiewicz's Life and Works), PIW, 1954.

Krzyżanowski, Julian, *Pokłosie Sienkiewiczowskie: Szkice literackie* (The Sienkiewicz Harvest: Literary Sketches), PIW, 1973.

Krzyżanowski, Julian, *Twórczość Sienkiewicza* (Sienkiewicz's Literary Output), PIW, 1970.

Kuczyński, Stefan, *Rzeczywistość historyczna w 'Krzyżakach'* (Historical reality in the 'Teutonic Knights'), PIW, 1963.

Lednicki, Wacław, *Bits of Table Talk on Pushkin, Mickiewicz, Goethe, Turgenev and Sienkiewicz*, M. Nijhof, 1956.

Lednicki, Wacław, *Henryk Sienkiewicz: A Retrospective Synthesis*, Mouton and Co., 1960.

Maciuszko, Jerzy J., *The Polish Short Story in English. A Guide and Critical Bibliography*, Wayne State University Press, 1968.

Miłosz, Czesław, *The History of Polish Literature*, Macmillan, 1969.

Modjeska (Modrzejewska), Helena, *Memoirs and Impressions: An Autobiography*, Macmillan, 1910.

Nofer, Alina, *Henryk Sienkiewicz*, Wiedza Powszechna, 1959.

Piorunowa, Aniela and Wyka, Kazimierz, eds., *Henryk Sienkiewicz. Twórczość i recepcja światowa* (Henryk Sienkiewicz. Creative Work and Its Worldwide Reception), WL, 1968.

Sandler, Samuel, *Wokół Trylogii* (Around the Trilogy), Ossolineum, 1952.

Stawar, Andrzej, *Pisarstwo Henryka Sienkiewicza*. Szkice (The Writings of Henryk Sienkiewicz. Sketches), PIW, 1960.

Szweykowski, Zygmunt, *Trylogia Henryka Sienkiewicza*. Szkice (The Trilogy of Henryk Sienkiewicz. Sketches), Wydawnictwo Poznańskie, 1961.

Selected Periodicals: Articles in English

American Statesman, July, 1891.
Bellman, December, 1916.
Bibliographical Quarterly, January, 1902.
Blackwood Edinburgh Magazine, April, 1889.

Book News, May, 1897.

Books (Ottawa), July, 1991

Booklist, May, 1991.

Bookman, February, 1900; February, 1901; March, 1901.

Buffalo News, July, 1991.

Bulletin of the Polish Institute of Arts and Sciences in America, Winter, 1945-1946.

Catholic World, February, 1898; May, 1898; April, 1918.

Century, July 1898; December, 1909; May, 1910.

Christian Science Monitor, July, 1991.

Contemporary Authors, vol. 134, December, 1991.

Cosmopolitan Magazine, May-October, 1906.

Critic, February, 1894; April, 1906.

Current Literature, February, 1898; March, 1901; April, 1901; August, 1901.

Current Opinion, January, 1917.

Dial, November, 1916.

Elmira Star-Gazette, July, 1991.

Education, June, 1899.

Independent, July, 1898.

Library Journal, March, 1991.

Literary Digest, December, 1897; February, 1901; March, 1901; January, 1902; December, 1916; January, 1926.

Literary Era, January, 1901; April, 1901; February, 1902.

Literary News, November, 1893; January, 1902.

Living Age, August, 1901.

Milwaukee Journal, June, 1991.

Munsey's Magazine, March, 1898.

Nation, October, 1896.

National Magazine, March, 1898.

New York Newsday, June, 1991.

New York Times Book Review, June, 1991.

North American Review, August, 1902.

Orlando Sentinel, July 1991.

Outlook, March, 1898; August 1901; March, 1908; November, 1916.

Plain Dealer, April, 1991.

Poland, January, 1926.

Polish-American News, August, 1991.

Polish Review (London), January, 1917.

Polish Review (New York), Summer, 1964; Autumn, 1964; Summer, 1965; Summer, 1970.

Publishers Weekly, March 1991; August, 1991.

Review of Reviews, January, 1906; June, 1906; January, 1917.

Sawanee Review, July, 1919.

Slavic Review, June 1965.

Thought, December, 1939.

World Literature Today, October, 1991.

Zgoda, July 1991; August, 1991.

Contributors:

Todd Armstrong, MA
Graduate student, Ohio State University, Columbus Ohio.

Albert Juszczak, PhD
Assistant Professor, Hunter College, New York, N.Y., and
president of the Kosciuszko Foundation (1979-86). Author of
various literary criticisms, studies and translations.

Jerzy R. Krzyżanowski, PhD
Professor Emeritus, Ohio State University, Columbus, Ohio.
Translator, literary critic, author of numerous studies on Polish
literature and Professor of Slavic Languages and Literatures.

W. S. Kuniczak, MS
Writer-in-Residence and Associate Professor, Mercyhurst College,
Erie, Pennsylvania; Visiting Professor, Alliance College,
Cambridge Springs, Pa. Novelist and translator.

Jerzy J. Maciuszko, PhD
Professor Emeritus, Baldwin Wallace College, Cleveland, Ohio.
Author, translator, literary critic, former chairman of the
Slavic Department, Alliance College, Cambridge Springs, Pa.

Thomas Napierkowski, PhD
Professor of English, University of Colorado in Colorado Springs.
Medieval scholar, writer, lecturer, literary critic,
president-elect of the Polish American Historical Association.

Karen Teeple-Krzyżanowski, MA
Teacher, Huber Ridge School, Westerville, Ohio.